CONTENT

CW01498723

v

PARKIN ◆ POWELL ◆ MATTHEWS
ECONOMICS
STUDY GUIDE
FOURTH EDITION

We work with leading authors to develop the
strongest educational materials in economics,
bringing cutting-edge thinking and best learning
practice to a global market.

Under a range of well-known imprints, including
Addison-Wesley, we craft high quality print and
electronic publications which help readers to
understand and apply their content,
whether studying or at work.

To find out more about the complete range of our
publishing please visit us on the World Wide Web at:
www.pearsoneduc.com

PARKIN ◆ POWELL ◆ MATTHEWS

ECONOMICS

STUDY GUIDE

FOURTH EDITION

Brian Atkinson *formerly of University of Central Lancashire*

Addison-Wesley

An imprint of **Pearson Education**

Harlow, England · London · New York · Reading, Massachusetts · San Francisco
Toronto · Don Mills, Ontario · Sydney · Tokyo · Singapore · Hong Kong · Seoul
Taipei · Cape Town · Madrid · Mexico City · Amsterdam · Munich · Paris · Milan

Pearson Education Limited
Edinburgh Gate
Harlow
Essex CM20 2JE
England

and Associated Companies throughout the World.

Visit us on the World Wide Web at:
www.pearsoneduc.com

Third edition published 1997
Fourth edition 2000

ISBN 0201-64854-7

British Library Cataloguing-in-Publication Data
A catalogue record for this book can be obtained from the British Library.

10 9 8 7 6 5 4 3 2 1
04 03 02 01 00

Typeset in 10/12pt ITC Century Book by 42
Printed and bound in Great Britain by Henry Ling Ltd,
at the Dorset Press, Dorchester, Dorset.

INTRODUCTION

Before You Begin . . .

Our experience has taught us that what first-year economics students want most from a study guide is help in mastering course material in order to do well in examinations. We have developed this *Study Guide* to respond specifically to that demand. Using this *Study Guide* alone, however, is not enough to guarantee that you will do well in your course. In order to help you overcome the problems and difficulties that most first-year students encounter, we have some general advice on how to study, as well as some specific advice on how best to use this *Study Guide*.

Some Friendly Advice

The study of economics requires a different style of thinking from what you may encounter in other courses. Economists make extensive use of assumptions to break down complex problems into simple, analytically manageable, parts. This analytical style, while not ultimately more demanding than the styles of thinking in other disciplines, feels unfamiliar to most students and requires practice. In order to do well we suggest:

Don't rely solely on your previous knowledge of economics. If you have taken economics before you will have seen the material on supply and demand on which your tutor will lecture in the first few weeks. Don't be lulled into feeling that the course will be easy. Your previous knowledge of economic concepts will be very useful, but it will not be enough to guarantee high marks in exams. Your tutors will demand much more detailed knowledge of concepts and ask you to apply them in new circumstances.

Keep up with the course material on a weekly basis. Read the appropriate chapter in the textbook *before* your tutor lectures on it. In this initial reading, don't worry about details or arguments you can't quite follow – just try and get a general understanding of the basic concepts and issues. You may be amazed at how your tutor's ability to teach improves when you come to class prepared. As soon as your tutor has finished covering a chapter, complete the corresponding *Study Guide* chapter. Avoid cramming the day before or even just the week before an exam. Because economics requires practice, cramming is an almost certain recipe for failure.

Keep a good set of lecture notes. Good lecture notes are vital for focusing your studying. Your tutor will only lecture on a subset of topics from the textbook. The topics your tutor covers in a lecture should usually be given priority when studying. You should also give priority to studying the figures and graphs covered in lectures.

Use your tutor for help. When you have questions or problems with course material, ask for help. Remember, tutors are there to help you learn. We are often amazed at how few students come to see us to ask for help. Don't be shy. The personal contact that comes from one-to-one tutoring is professionally gratifying for us as well as (hopefully) beneficial for you.

Form a study group. A very useful way to motivate your studying and to learn economics is to discuss the course material and problems with other students. Explaining the answer to a question *out loud* is a very effective way of discovering how well you understand the question. When you answer a question in your head only, you often skip steps in the chain of reasoning without realizing it. When you are forced to explain your reasoning aloud, gaps and mistakes quickly appear, and you (and your fellow group members) can quickly correct your reasoning. The Short Answer questions and the Discussion questions in the *Study Guide* and the Review questions at the end of each textbook chapter are good study group material. You also might get together *after* having worked the problems in the *Study Guide* chapter, but *before* looking at the answers, and help each other solve unsolved problems.

Work old exams. One of the most effective ways of studying is to work through exams your tutor has given in previous years. Old exams give you a feel for the style of question your lecturer may ask, and give you the opportunity to get used to time pressure if you force yourself to do the exam in the allotted time. Some institutions keep old exams in the library, others in the department. Students who have previously taken the course are usually a good source as well. Remember, though, that old exams are a useful study aid only if you use them to *understand* the reasoning behind each question. If you simply memorize answers in the hopes that your instructor will repeat the identical question, you are likely to fail. From year to year, examiners routinely change the questions or change the numerical values for similar questions.

Use the other study aids. In addition to the *Study Guide* you will benefit from using *Economics in Action* software. This is truly interactive tutorial software available for IBM-compatible computers. It is an integrated tutorial, graphing, demonstration and testing program that covers all the main themes in the textbook using three modes. The tutorial mode places you in an economics-related job situation and leads you through assignments that reveal and explore economic concepts and principles. The free mode allows you to interact with economic models by changing parameters and observing the effects on graphs. The quiz mode gives you graphical or data-related multiple-choice questions. When you select an answer, you are given a detailed explanation (and graphical illustration) of why your answer is right or wrong. All software modes are closely integrated with the textbook. You can find a rich feast of economics ideas and study materials on the Parkin, Powell, Mathews Web site. You can access this on www.econ100.com

Another very useful site is at www.bized.ac.uk. This has many resources for students of economics and business. To give just a sample, it includes materials on study skills, revision notes, lists articles and contains material from the Office for National Statistics. Its particularly useful for finding information about particular companies.

Using the Study Guide

You should only attempt to complete a chapter in the *Study Guide* after you have read the corresponding textbook chapter once and listened to your lecturer lecture on the material. Each *Study Guide* chapter contains the following sections.

Chapter in Perspective. The purpose of this first section is to briefly situate the material of a particular textbook chapter in the context of what has come before and what will follow. Since you will see so much detailed information throughout the course, we try to paint the bigger picture for you in broad strokes so that you don't feel lost. This is the 'look at the forest instead of the trees' section.

Helpful Hints. Where you encounter difficulty in mastering concepts or techniques, you will not be alone. Many students find certain concepts difficult and often make the same kinds of mistakes. We have seen these common mistakes often enough to have learned how to help students avoid them. These hints point out these mistakes and offer tips for avoiding them. The hints focus on the most important concepts, equations and techniques for problem solving.

Self-Test. Besides the Helpful Hints, this will be the most useful section of the *Study Guide*. The questions are designed to give you practice and to test the skills and techniques you must master to do well in exams. There are plenty of the types of questions you are most likely to encounter in your course exams – True/False and Multiple-Choice questions.

There are other types of questions, described below, each with a specific pedagogical purpose. Before we describe the seven parts of the Self-Test section, here are some general tips that apply to all of the parts.

Use a pencil to write your answers in the *Study Guide*. This will allow you to erase your mistakes and have neat, completed pages from which to study.

Draw graphs wherever they are applicable. Some questions will ask explicitly for graphs; many others will not but require a chain of reasoning that involves shifts of curves on a graph. *Always draw the graph.* Don't try and work through the reasoning in your head – you are much more likely to make mistakes that way. Whenever you draw a graph, even in the margins of the *Study*

Guide, label the axes. You may think that you can keep the labels in your head, but you will be confronting many different graphs with many different variables on the axes. Avoid confusion and label. As an added incentive, remember that on exams where graphs are required, examiners will deduct marks for unlabelled axes.

Do the Self-Test questions as if they were real exam questions, which means do them *without looking at the answers*. This is the single most important tip we can give you about effectively using the *Study Guide* to improve your exam performance. Struggling for the answers to questions that you find difficult is one of the most effective ways to learn. The athletic adage – no pain, no gain – applies equally well to studying. You will learn the most from right answers you had to struggle for and from your wrong answers and mistakes. Only after you have attempted all of the questions should you look at the answers. When you finally do check the answers, be sure to understand where you went wrong and why the right answer is correct.

If you want to impose time pressure on yourself to simulate the conditions of a real exam, allow two minutes for each Multiple-Choice question and one minute for each True/False question. The other types of question vary considerably in their time require-ments, so it is difficult to give generally applicable time estimates for them. However, we believe that such time pressure is probably not a good idea for *Study Guide* questions. A state of mind of relaxed concentra-tion is best for work in the *Study Guide*. Use old exams if you want practice with time pressure.

The seven parts of the Self-Test section are:

Concept Review. This part contains simple 'recall' questions, designed to check your memory of basic terms and concepts. These questions should build your confidence. If you have understood the terms and con-cepts in the chapter, you should get very few of these questions wrong. This part is not a test of deep under-standing or of mastery of analytical skills.

True or False. These questions test your basic knowl-edge of chapter concepts as well as your ability to apply the concepts. These are the first questions to challenge your understanding to see if you can identify mistakes in statements using basic concepts.

Multiple Choice. These more difficult questions test your analytical abilities by asking you to apply con-cepts to new situations, to manipulate information and to solve numerical and graphical problems.

Read each question and all five choices carefully before you answer. Many of the choices will be plausible and will differ only slightly. You must choose the one *best* answer. A useful strategy in working these questions is first to eliminate any obviously wrong choices and then to focus on the remaining alterna-tives. Be aware that sometimes the correct answer will be 'none of the above choices is correct'. Don't get frustrated or think that you are dim if you can't im-mediately see the correct answer. These questions are designed to make you work to find the correct choice.

Short Answer. Each chapter contains several Short Answer questions. These are straightforward, confidence-building questions about basic concepts. They can generally be answered in a few sentences or, at most, in one paragraph. These questions are useful to answer out loud in a study group.

Problems. The best way to learn to do economics is to do problems. Each Self-Test includes numerical or graphical problems. In many chapters, this will be the most challenging part of the Self-Test. It is also likely to be particularly helpful for deepening your under-standing of the chapter material. We have, however, designed the questions to teach as much as to test. We have purposefully arranged the parts of each question to lead you through the problem-solving analysis in a gradual and sequential fashion, from easier to more difficult parts.

Discussion Questions. These are questions that are suitable for you to talk about in seminars or with your friends in order to clarify your thinking.

Data Questions. Each chapter includes a data ques-tion. These have been chosen to test your ability to apply economic concepts to 'real life situations'. Since real life does not come in well-defined chapters, the questions often require you to use ideas from earlier chapters. For reasons of space, the answers are not always set out in full but instead refer you to parts of the main text.

Answers. The Self-Test is followed by answers to all of the questions. Be sure not to look at the answers until you have attempted to answer all of the questions. When you do finally look at the answers, use them to understand where you went wrong and why the right answer is correct. The detailed answers to the Problems should be especially useful in clarifying and illustrating typical chains of reasoning involved in economics analysis. If the answers alone do not clear up your confusion, go back to the appropriate sections of the textbook. If that still does not suffice, ask your tutor for help or go to your study group members, and get help and clarification.

If you effectively combine the use of the textbook and the *Study Guide*, you will be well prepared for exams. Equally importantly, you will also have developed analytical skills and powers of reasoning that will benefit you throughout your life and in whatever career you choose.

Do You Have Any Friendly Advice For Us?

We have attempted to make this *Study Guide* as clear as possible, and to avoid errors. No doubt, we have not succeeded entirely, and you are the only judges who count in evaluating our attempt. If you discover errors, or if you have other suggestions for improving the *Study Guide*, please write to us. In future editions, we will try and acknowledge the names of all students whose suggestions help us improve the *Study Guide*. Send your correspondence to:

Business and Economics Publishing
Higher Education Division
Pearson Education
Edinburgh Gate
Harlow
Essex
CM20 2JE

Acknowledgements

This *Study Guide* has benefited from help and advice from many sources. In particular it has drawn on the American and Canadian Study Guides, and I would like to thank all those who helped in preparing these editions.

Publishers Acknowledgements

The publishers would like to thank the following for permission to reproduce material: Office for Official Publications of the European Communities, *The Economist*, The Bank of England, Office for National Statistics, Economics and Business Education Association, The *Guardian*, Macmillan Press and Causeway Press.

The publishers would also like to thank Avi Cohen and Harvey King for their past contributions to this publication and Mark Rush for his kind permission to reuse material and questions from the US Study Guide.

Brian Atkinson

Chapter 1

What is Economics?

The fundamental economic problem is scarcity. Because wants exceed the resources available to satisfy them, we cannot have everything we want and must make choices. This problem leads to economizing behaviour – choosing the best or optimal use of the resources available. Economics, as a subject, is the study of how we use limited resources to try to satisfy unlimited wants. What economists do is also discussed.

This chapter summarizes eight big ideas of economics – such as that every choice involves a trade-off. It also introduces some of the methods used by economists and shows that, contrary to popular opinion, economists do agree on many issues.

Helpful Hints

1 The definition of economics (the study of how people use limited resources to try to satisfy unlimited wants) leads us directly to important economic concepts – choice and opportunity cost. If wants exceed resources, we cannot have everything we want and therefore must make *choices* among alternatives. In making a choice, we forego other alternatives, and the *opportunity cost* of any choice is the value of the best foregone alternative. Also, if wants exceed resources, then wants and individuals must *compete* against each other for the scarce resources.

2 The basic assumption made by economists about human behaviour is that people try to make themselves as well off as possible. As a result, people respond to changed incentives by changing their decisions. The key idea is that an individual compares the additional (or 'marginal') benefits from taking an action to the additional (or 'marginal') costs of the action. If the marginal benefits from the action exceed the marginal costs, taking the action makes the person better off, so economists assume that the person takes the action. Conversely, if the marginal benefits fall short of the marginal costs, economists assume that the action is not taken.

The key aspect of this analysis is that only the *additional* benefits and costs – not the *total* benefits and costs of the action – are considered. Only the additional benefits and additional costs are relevant because they are the ones that the person will enjoy and pay if the action is undertaken. Keeping straight the distinction between additional benefits and costs versus total benefits and costs is a vital part of economics, particularly of microeconomics.

3 Scientists use theory to abstract from the complex descriptive facts of the real world and focus only on those elements essential for understanding. Those essential elements are fashioned into models – highly simplified representations of the real world.

Economic models attempt to focus on the essential forces (competition, self-interest) operating in the economy while abstracting from less important forces (whims, advertising, altruism). Unlike physicists, economists cannot perform controlled experiments to test their models. As a result, it is difficult to conclusively prove or disprove a theory and its models.

4 Remember that economic models are not claims that the real world is as simple as the model. Models claim to capture the simplified effect of some real force operating in the economy. Before drawing conclusions about the real economy from a model, we must be careful to consider whether, when we reinsert all the real-world complexities we have omitted from the model, the conclusions will be the same as in the model.

5 The most important purpose of studying economics is not to learn lots of economic facts, but rather *how* to think about economics. The value of an economics education is the ability to think critically about economic problems and *to understand how* an economy works. This understanding of the essential forces governing how an economy works comes through the mastery of economic theory and model-building.

6 This chapter is designed to give you a broad introduction to economics. It therefore covers a lot of ground. Don't worry if you find it a bit overwhelming; all the ideas in this chapter will be explored in greater detail later in the book.

SELF-TEST

CONCEPT REVIEW

1 The fundamental and pervasive fact that gives rise to economic problems is _____ . This simply means that human wants _____ the resources available to satisfy them. The inescapable consequence is that people must make _____ .

2 When we choose an action, the value of the best forgone alternative is the _____ cost of that action.

3 The process of evaluating the costs and benefits of our choices in order to do the best we can with limited resources is called _____ or _____ .

4 An economy is a mechanism that determines _____ is produced, _____ it is produced, and _____ _____ it is produced.

5 Economists develop economic theories by building and testing economic _____ .

6 Every choice is a _____ off.

7 While all economies must have some way of coordinating choices, there are two fundamental mechanisms. The _____ mechanism relies on the authority of some kind of central planning, while the _____ mechanism relies on the adjustment of _____ in economic markets. A _____ economy has elements of both of these fundamental mechanisms.

8 The highest value alternative forgone is the _____ cost of what is chosen.

9 Statements about what *is* are called _____ statements, while those about what *ought* to be are called _____ statements.

10 The branch of economics that studies the choices of individual households and firms is called _____ , while the branch that studies the behaviour of the economy as a whole is called _____ .

11 The cost of a small increase in an activity is called a _____ cost. The benefit that arises from a small increase in benefit is called a _____ benefit.

TRUE OR FALSE

___ **1** Scarcity is a problem only for capitalist (market) economies.

___ **2** Economics is the study of how to use unlimited resources to satisfy limited wants.

___ **3** The notion of opportunity cost is illustrated by the fact that because Fred studied for his economics examination last night he was unable to see a film with his friends.

___ **4** The opportunity cost of any action is the cost of all foregone alternatives.

___ **5** The UK is a pure market economy.

___ **6** Careful and systematic observation and measurement are basic components of any science.

___ **7** Economics is not a science since it deals with the study of wilful human beings and not inanimate objects in nature.

___ **8** An increase in the income tax rate will cause total tax revenue to fall. This is an example of a positive statement.

___ **9** A positive statement is about what *is*, while a normative statement is about what *will* be.

___ **10** Economic models are of very limited value in helping us understand the real world because they abstract from the complexity of the real world.

___ **11** Macroeconomics includes the study of the causes of inflation.

___ **12** Testing an economic model requires comparing its predictions against real-world events.

___ **13** When the predictions of a model conflict with the relevant facts, a theory must be discarded or modified.

MULTIPLE CHOICE

1 The fact that human wants cannot be fully satisfied with available resources is called the problem of
  a opportunity cost.
  b scarcity.
  c normative economics.
  d what to produce.
  e for whom to produce.

2 The problem of scarcity exists
  a only in economies which rely on the market mechanism.
  b only in economies which rely on the command mechanism.
  c in all economies.
  d only when people have not optimized.
  e now but will be eliminated with economic growth.

3 When the government chooses to use resources to build a dam, those resources are no longer available to build a road. This illustrates the concept of
  a a market mechanism.
  b macroeconomics.
  c opportunity cost.
  d a closed economy.
  e cooperation.

4 Renata has the chance either to attend an economics lecture or to play tennis. If she chooses to attend the lecture, the value of playing tennis is
  a greater than the value of the lecture.
  b not comparable to the value of the lecture.
  c equal to the value of the lecture.
  d the opportunity cost of attending the lecture.
  e zero.

5 The question, 'Should personal computers or mainframe computers be produced?' is an example of the
  a 'what' question.
  b 'how' question.
  c 'where' question.
  d 'who' question.

6 The Latin term *ceteris paribus* means
  a 'false unless proven true'.
  b 'other things remaining the same'.
  c 'after this, then because of this'.
  d 'not correct, even though it is logical'.

7 One student from a class of 30 can walk easily through a door. Assuming that all 30 students simultaneously can therefore walk easily through the same door is an example of the
  a opportunity cost fallacy.
  b fallacy of composition.
  c fallacy of substitution.
  d *post hoc* fallacy.
  e no economic links with other economies.

8 A normative statement is a statement regarding
  a what is usually the case.
  b the assumptions of an economic model.
  c what ought to be.
  d the predictions of an economic model.
  e what is.

9 'The rich face higher income tax rates than the poor' is an example of
  a a normative statement.
  b a positive statement.
  c a descriptive statement.
  d a theoretical statement.
  e b and c.

10 An economic model is tested by
  a examining the realism of its assumptions.
  b comparing its predictions with the facts.
  c comparing its descriptions with the facts.
  d the Testing Committee of the Royal Economic Society.
  e all of the above.

11 When economists say that people are rational, it means they
  a do not make errors of judgement.
  b make the best decision from their perspective.
  c act on complete information.
  d will not later regret any decision made now.
  e do not let emotion influence decisions.

12 The branch of economics that studies the decisions of individual households and firms is called
  a macroeconomics.
  b microeconomics.
  c positive economics.
  d normative economics.
  e home economics.

13 All of the following are microeconomic questions *except*
  a technological change.
  b wages and earnings.
  c distribution of wealth.
  d production.
  e consumption.

SHORT ANSWER

1 What is meant by scarcity and why does the existence of scarcity mean that we must make choices?

2 If all people would only economize, that would solve the problem of scarcity. Agree or disagree and explain why.

3 What is 'market failure'? How can it arise?

4 Explain why some unemployment can be efficient.

PROBLEMS

1 Assume that it takes one hour to travel from London to Glasgow by airplane and five hours by train. Further, suppose that the air fare is £100 and the train fare is £60. Which mode of transportation has the lower opportunity cost for the following people?
  a a person who can earn £5 an hour
  b a person who can earn £10 an hour
  c a person who can earn £12 an hour

2 Suppose the government builds and staffs a hospital in order to provide 'free' medical care.
  a What is the opportunity cost of the free medical care?
  b Is it free from the perspective of society as a whole?

3 Indicate whether each of the following statements is positive or normative. If it is normative (positive), rewrite it so that it becomes positive (normative).
  a The government ought to reduce the size of the deficit in order to lower interest rates.
  b Government imposition of a tax on tobacco products will reduce their consumption.

4 Suppose we examine a model of plant growth which predicts that, given the amount of water and sunlight, the application of fertilizer stimulates plant growth.
  a How might you test the model?
  b How is the test different from what an economist could do to test an economic model?

5 In sciences such as chemistry, controlled experiments play a key role. How does that relate to economists' use of *ceteris paribus*?

DISCUSSION QUESTIONS

1 'Economic theories are useless because the models on which they are based are unrealistic.' Is this a good argument?

2 Does everything have an opportunity cost?

DATA QUESTIONS

1 Two thirds of Holland lies below sea level. In 1953 a huge storm flooded large parts of the country, killing more than 2,000 people. This caused the Dutch to devote huge resources to the 'Delta Project' – a massive sea barrage which prevents the sea encroaching onto the land.

But the problem remains. If global warming becomes a reality, then the sea will rise and Holland will again become vulnerable to storms. Hence it is not surprising that the Dutch are world leaders in the search for sources of energy that do not pollute the atmosphere and for measures to reduce the effects of pollution. Thus the Dutch propose to plant large numbers of trees across the world to absorb carbon dioxide.

a What is meant by 'opportunity cost'? How can this concept be related to the above passage?

b Distinguish between command and market economies. Which decision-making mechanism do you think was used by the Dutch in making the decisions outlined above? Why did they choose this mechanism?

2 Saving lives costs money. More important, it needs resources. There are lots of examples of this. Every year children are killed when they run on to the road. It would be quite possible to reduce this number by improving road safety education and by building safety barriers along the road side. This is often done outside schools, but it could be done on a much wider scale. Similarly 'sleeping policemen' would reduce the speed of cars on housing estates.

Another example of how more resources could save lives is in medicine. If everyone had regular medical check-ups then diseases would be caught early and treatment would be more successful.

a Why don't governments take such measures and so save lives?

b How do you think market mechanisms would approach the problem of allocating resources to medicine?

ANSWERS

CONCEPT REVIEW

1 scarcity; exceed; choices

2 opportunity

3 optimizing or economizing

4 what; how; for whom

5 models

6 trade

7 command; market; prices; mixed

8 opportunity

9 positive; normative

10 microeconomics; macroeconomics

11 marginal; marginal

TRUE OR FALSE

1 F Scarcity is a universal fact.

2 F It is the study of limited resources and unlimited wants.

3 T The opportunity cost is the alternative forgone.

4 F It is the best alternative forgone.

5 F It is a mixed economy.

6 T All sciences have these characteristics.

7 F Science is not defined by subject but by method.

8 T Positive because it can be tested.

9 F Normative statements are about what *ought* to be.

10 F The abstraction is what makes them useful.

11 T Inflation affects the whole society.

12 T Test predictions, not assumptions.

13 T A model's predictions must be consistent with the facts to become part of accepted theory.

MULTIPLE CHOICE

1 b Definition.

2 c With infinite wants and limited resources, scarcity will never be eliminated.

3 c Road is a forgone alternative.

4 d Choosing the lecture means its value is greater than tennis. Tennis is the best alternative forgone.

5 a The 'what' question asks in part, 'What goods and services are produced?'

6 b *Ceteris paribus* is the economic equivalent of a controlled experiment: its use allows us to determine the effect from each factor alone even though many factors may play a role in affecting a variable.

7 b In this case, the fallacy of composition is arguing that what is true for a part must necessarily be true for the whole.

8 c Key word for normative statements is *ought*.

9 e Positive statements describe facts about what is.

10 b If its predictions do not match the facts, it is discarded.

11 b Rational choice is an individual's best choice based on available information.

12 b Definition.

13 c is a macroeconomic topic.

SHORT ANSWER

1 Scarcity is the universal condition that human wants always exceed the resources available to satisfy them. The fact that goods and services are scarce means that individuals cannot have all of everything they want. It is therefore necessary to choose among alternatives.

2 Disagree. If everyone economized, then we would be making the best possible use of our resources and would be achieving the greatest benefits or satisfaction possible, given the limited quantity of resources. But this does not mean that we would be satisfying all of our limitless needs. The problem of scarcity can never be 'solved' as long as people have infinite needs and finite resources for satisfying those needs.

3 Market failure arises when the market does not use resources efficiently. It can occur for several reasons. One is that when a single producer controls an entire market it can raise the price. It can also arise when producers do not take account of the costs they impose on other people, for example when they cause pollution and when goods have to be consumed by everyone equally. Air traffic control is an example.

4 Unemployment can lead to greater efficiency when it helps people get their most productive job, even though this means they are unemployed for a while.

PROBLEMS

1 The point here is to recognize that the opportunity cost of travel includes the best alternative value of travel time as well as the train or air fare.

   a Thus, if the opportunity cost of the time spent travelling is the £5 an hour that could have been earned (but wasn't), the opportunity cost of train travel (in pounds) is the £60 train fare plus the £25 (£5 an hour times 5 hours) in forgone income for a total of £85.

   b In this case, the opportunity cost of air travel is the £100 air fare plus £10 in forgone income, for a total of £110. Therefore, for a person whose best alternative use of time is to earn £10 an hour, the opportunity cost of travelling by train is the same as the opportunity cost of travelling by air.

   c For a person who could have earned £12 an hour the opportunity cost of train travel (£120) exceeds the opportunity cost of air travel (£112).

2 **a** Even though medical care may be offered without charge ('free'), there are still opportunity costs. The opportunity cost of providing such health care is the best alternative use of the resources used in the construction of the hospital and the best alternative use of the resources (including human resources) used in the operation of the hospital.

   b These resources are no longer available for other activities and therefore represent a cost to society.

3 **a** The given statement is normative. The following is positive: If the government reduces the size of the deficit, interest rates will fall.

   b The given statement is positive. The following is normative: The government ought to impose a tax on tobacco products.

4 **a** The prediction of the model can be tested by conducting the following controlled experiment and carefully observing the outcome. Select a number of similar plots of ground which will be subject to the same amount of water and sunlight. Plant equal quantities of seeds in all the plots. In some of the plots apply no fertilizer and in some of the plots apply (perhaps varying amounts of) fertilizer. When the plants have grown, measure their size and compare growth in the fertilized plots and the unfertilized plots. If plant growth is greater in fertilized plots, we provisionally accept the model and the theory on which it is based. If plant growth is *not* greater in fertilized plots, we discard the theory (model), or modify its assumptions. Perhaps the effective use of fertilizer requires more water. Then construct a new model which predicts that given more water (and the same amount of sunlight), fertilized plants will grow larger than equivalently watered unfertilized plants. Test that model and continue modifying assumptions until predictions are consistent with the facts.

b Economists cannot perform such controlled experiments and must instead change one assumption at a time in alternative models and compare the resulting outcomes. Such differences in outcomes can then only be tested against variations in data that occur naturally in the economy. This is a more difficult and less precise model building and testing procedure than exists for the controlled fertilizer experiment.

5 Chemists can check the predictions of a model by conduction controlled experiments and observing the outcomes. For instance, when deterring the effect of temperature on a particular reaction, chemists can ensure that, between different experiments, *only* the temperature changes. Everything else is held constant. Economists usually cannot perform such controlled experiments and instead must change one variable at a time in a model and compare the results. This approach involved the use of *ceteris paribus*, wherein only one factor is allowed to change. Additionally, economists' models can be tested only against variations in data that occur naturally in the economy. Thus, economists face more difficult and less precise model building and testing than is possible for the controlled experiments of chemists and other scientists.

DISCUSSION QUESTIONS

1 Economic theories are like maps which are useful precisely because they abstract from the real world. They yield predictions which can be tested in the real world. Any attempt to include all the complexities of the real world would make a theory unmanageable.

2 Virtually everything has an opportunity cost. For example, looking at a beautiful view has an opportunity cost in that time is spent watching it. So, from a very wide perspective, every human activity has an opportunity cost.

DATA QUESTIONS

1 **a** The opportunity cost of any action is the best alternative foregone. In this case the resources used to build the Delta Project and to plant trees could have been used for other purposes.

b When command mechanisms are used, decisions are made by the government while market mechanisms allocate resources through markets. In this example it was the Dutch government that made the decisions. Hence it is an example of the command mechanism. They did this because they decided that the market mechanism would not work in this case.

2 **a** Governments don't take such measures because resources are scarce. The land, labour and capital used to implement life-saving measures would have to be paid for by giving up something else.

b Markets would allocate resources to medicine just as they would to any other good or service – if people wanted some medical service, it would be provided if they could pay. Command economies would involve the government deciding which services should be provided, perhaps as a result of political pressure. Neither system would be able to provide all the medical services that everyone would like because the opportunity cost would be too high.

Chapter 2 — Making and Using Graphs

Chapter in Perspective, Text Pages 22–39

As a science, economics is characterized by systematic observation and measurement as well as by the development of economic theory. In both of these components of economic science, the use of graphs plays an important role.

Economic theory describes relationships among economic variables and graphs offer a convenient way to represent such relationships. Moreover, representing data graphically can be extremely useful for quickly conveying information about general characteristics of economic behaviour. As we will see in the next few chapters, graphical analysis of economic relationships is especially helpful when we are interested in discovering the theoretical consequences of a change in economic circumstances.

This chapter reviews all the concepts and techniques you will need to construct and use graphs in this course.

Helpful Hints

1 The chapters of the text discuss numerous relationships among economic variables. Many of these relationships will be represented and analysed graphically. Thus an understanding of graphs will greatly facilitate mastery of the economic analysis of later chapters.

2 If your experience with graphical analysis is limited, this chapter is crucial to your ability to understand readily later economic analysis. If you are experienced in the construction and use of graphs this chapter may be very easy. Even in this case, the chapter should be skimmed and the Self-Test in this *Study Guide* completed. The main point is that you should be thoroughly familiar with the basic concepts and techniques of this chapter.

3 One way to remember the formula for slope is to think of it as 'the rise over the run'. The *rise* is the change in the vertical axis, or Δy. The *run* is the change in the variable measured on the horizontal axis, or Δx.

4 Slope is a *linear* concept since it is a property of a straight line. For this reason, the slope is constant along a straight line but is different at different points on a curved (non-linear) line. When we are interested in the slope of a curved line, we actually calculate the slope of a straight line. The text presents two ways of choosing such a straight line and thus two alternative ways of calculating the slope of a curved line: (1) slope across an arc, and (2) slope at a point. The first of these calculates the slope of the *straight line* formed by the arc between two points on the curved line. The second calculates the slope of the *straight line* that just touches (is tangent to) the curve at a point.

5 A straight line on a graph can also be described by a simple equation. The general form for the equation of a straight line is:

$$y = a + bx$$

If you are given such an equation, you can graph the line by finding the y-intercept (where the line intersects the vertical y-axis), finding the x-intercept (where the line intersects the horizontal x-axis), and then connecting these two points with a straight line:

To find the y-intercept, set $x = 0$.

$$y = a + b(0)$$
$$y = a$$

To find the x-intercept, set $y = 0$.

$$0 = a + bx$$
$$x = -a/b$$

Connecting these two points $((x = 0, y = a)$ and $(x = -a/b, y = 0)$ or $(0, a)$ and $(-a/b, 0))$ yields the line in Fig. 2.1.

Figure 2.1

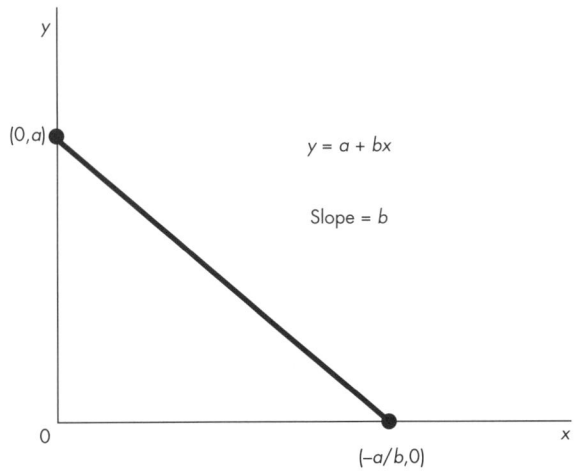

For any straight line with the equation of the form $y = a + bx$, the slope of the line is b.

To see how to apply this general equation, consider this example:

$$y = 4 - 2x$$

To find the y-intercept, set $x = 0$.

$$y = 4 - 2(0)$$
$$y = 4$$

To find the x-intercept, set $y = 0$.

$$0 = 4 - 2x$$
$$x = 2$$

Connecting these two points, $(0,4)$ and $(2,0)$, yields the line in Fig. 2.2.

Figure 2.2

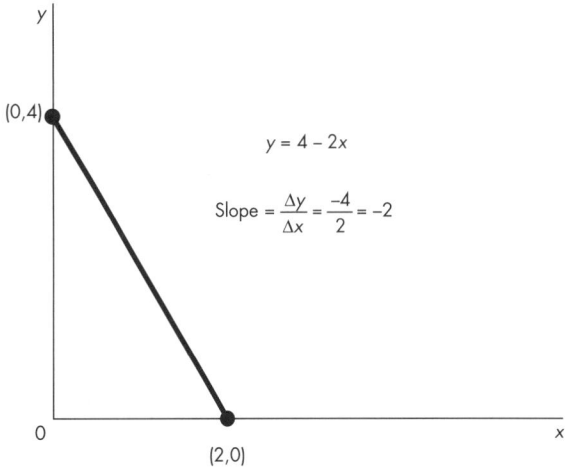

The slope of this line is –2. Since the slope is negative, there is a negative relationship between the variables x and y.

SELF-TEST

CONCEPT REVIEW

1 A graph that measures an economic variable on the vertical axis and time on the horizontal axis is called a(n)_____ -_____ graph.

2 The tendency for a variable to rise or fall over time is called the _____ of the variable.

3 Suppose the value of one economic variable is measured on the x-axis and the value of a second is measured on the y-axis. A diagram that plots the value of one variable corresponding to the value of the other is called a(n)_____ diagram.

4 If two variables tend to move up or down together they exhibit a(n) _____ relationship. Such a relationship is represented graphically by a line that slopes _____ (to the right).

5 Two variables that move in opposite directions exhibit a(n) _____ relationship. Such a relationship is represented graphically by a line that slopes _____ (to the right).

6 Suppose variables *A* and *B* are unrelated. If we measure *A* on the *y*-axis and *B* on the *x*-axis, the graph of *A* as we increase *B* will be a(n) _____ line.

7 The slope of a line is calculated as the change in the value of the variable measured on the _____ axis divided by the change in the value of the variable measured on the _____ axis.

8 A straight line exhibits _____ slope at all points.

9 To graph a relationship among more than two variables, we simply graph the relationship between _____ variables, holding all other variables constant.

TRUE OR FALSE

___ 1 A time-series graph measures time on the horizontal axis.

___ 2 A time-series graph gives information about the level of the relevant economic variable, as well as information about changes and the speed of those changes.

___ 3 A two-variable time-series graph can help us see if the two variables tend to move together over time.

___ 4 A one-dimensional graph that represents measured rainfall along a horizontal line is an example of a scatter diagram.

___ 5 If the graph of the relationship between two variables slopes upward (to the right), the variables move up and down together.

___ 6 If variable *a* rises when variable *b* falls and falls when *b* rises, then the relationship between *a* and *b* is negative.

___ 7 The graph of the 'relationship' between two variables that are in fact unrelated will be either horizontal or vertical.

___ 8 The slope of a straight line is calculated by dividing the change in the value of the variable measured on the horizontal axis by the change in the value of the variable measured on the vertical axis.

___ 9 The slope of a curved line is not constant.

___ 10 If we want to graph the relationship among three variables, we must hold two of them constant as we represent the third.

___ 11 In Fig. 2.3, the relationship between *y* and *x* is first negative, reaches a minimum, and then becomes positive as *x* increases.

Figure 2.3

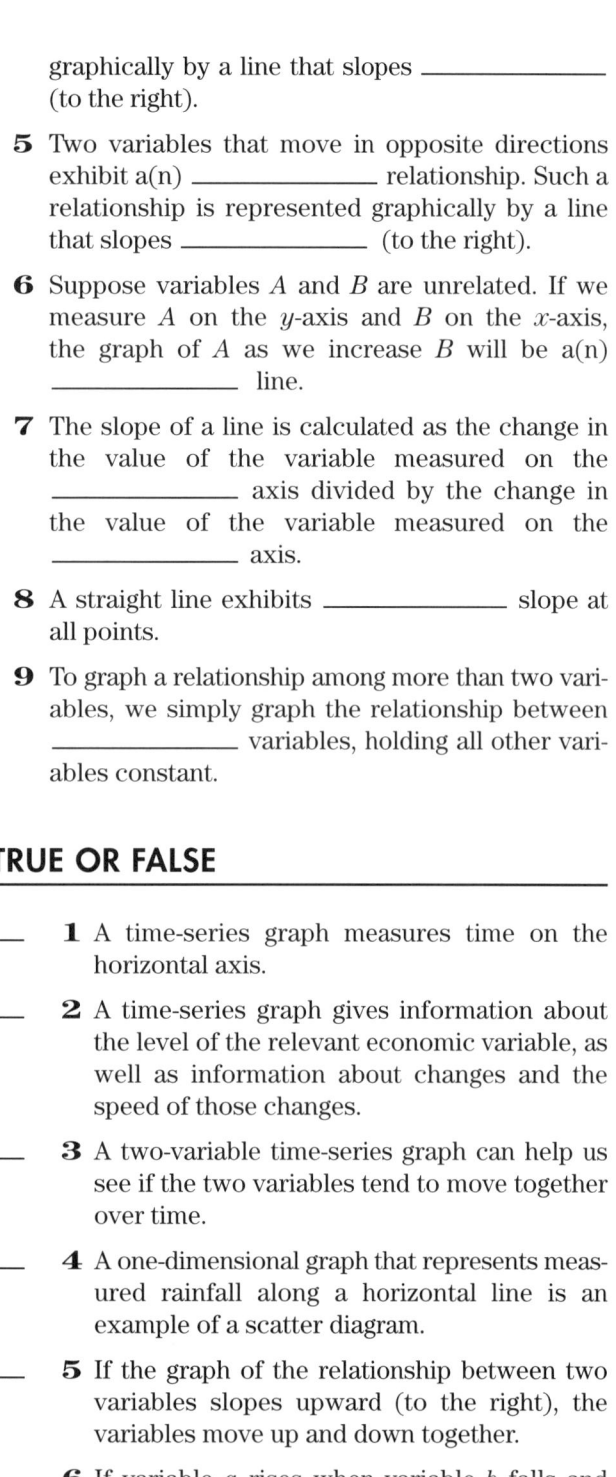

MULTIPLE CHOICE

Table 2.1

Year	x	y
1998	6.2	143
1999	5.7	156
2000	5.3	162

1 From the information in Table 2.1, it appears that
  a x and y tend to exhibit a negative relationship.
  b x and y tend to exhibit a positive relationship.
  c there is no relationship between x and y.
  d there is first a negative and then a positive relationship between x and y.
  e there is first a positive and then a negative relationship between x and y.

2 If variables x and y move up and down together, they are said to be
  a positively related.
  b negatively related.
  c conversely related.
  d unrelated.
  e trendy.

3 The relationship between two variables that move in opposite directions is shown graphically by a line that is
  a positively sloped.
  b relatively steep.
  c relatively flat.
  d negatively sloped.
  e curved.

4 What is the slope of the line in Fig. 2.4?
  a 2
  b 1/2
  c 3
  d 1/3
  e −3

5 If the line in Fig. 2.4 were to continue down to the x-axis, what would the value of x be when y is zero?
  a 0
  b 2
  c 2/3
  d −2/3
  e −3/2

6 If the price of an umbrella is low and the number of rainy days per month is large, more umbrellas will be sold each month. On the other hand, if the price of an umbrella is high and there are few rainy days per month, fewer umbrellas will be sold each month. On the basis of this information, which of the following statements is true?
  a The number of umbrellas sold and the price of an umbrella are positively related, holding the number of rainy days constant.
  b The number of umbrellas sold and the price of an umbrella are negatively related, holding the number of rainy days constant.
  c The number of rainy days and the number of umbrellas sold are negatively related, holding the price of an umbrella constant.
  d The number of rainy days and the price of an umbrella are negatively related, holding the number of umbrellas sold constant.
  e None of the above statements is true.

7 Given the data in Table 2.2, holding income constant, the graph relating the price of strawberries (vertical axis) to the purchases of strawberries (horizontal axis)
  a is a vertical line.
  b is a horizontal line.
  c is a positively sloped line.
  d is a negatively sloped line.
  e reaches a minimum.

Figure 2.4

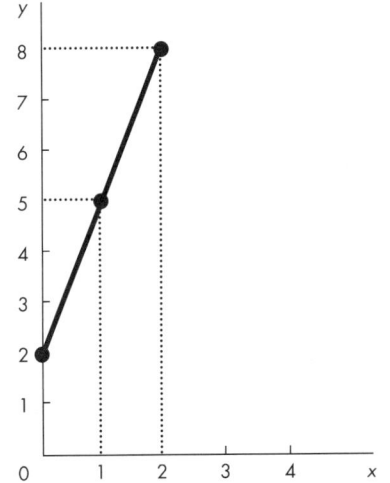

Table 2.2

Weekly family income (pounds)	Price per box of strawberries (pounds)	Number of boxes purchased per week
300	1.00	5
300	1.25	3
300	1.50	2
400	1.00	7
400	1.25	5
400	1.50	4

8 Consider the data in Table 2.2. Suppose family income decreases from $400 to $300 per week. Then the graph relating the price of strawberries (vertical axis) to the purchases of strawberries (horizontal axis) will
  a become negatively sloped.
  b become positively sloped.
  c shift to the right.
  d shift to the left.
  e no longer exist.

9 Given the data in Table 2.2, holding price constant, the graph relating family income (vertical axis) to the purchases of strawberries (horizontal axis) is
  a a vertical line.
  b a horizontal line.
  c a positively sloped line.
  d a negatively sloped line.
  e a positively or negatively sloped line, depending on the price that is held constant.

10 If the equation of a straight line is $y = 6 + 3x$, then the slope is
  a -3 and the y-intercept is 6.
  b -3 and the y-intercept is -2.
  c 3 and the y-intercept is 6.
  d 3 and the y-intercept is -2.
  e 3 and the y-intercept is -6.

Figure 2.5

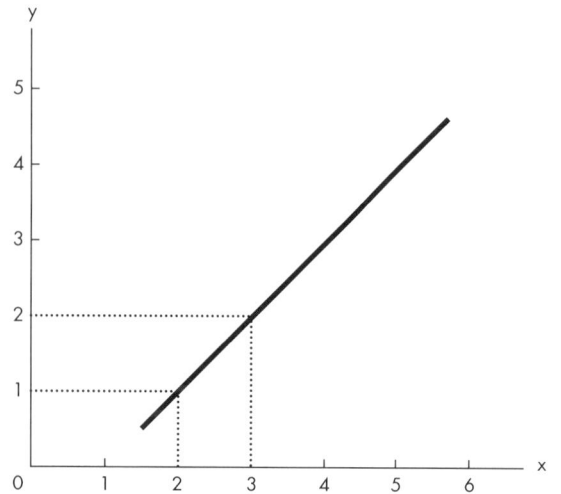

11 In Fig. 2.5, between $x = 2$ and $x = 3$ what is the slope of the line?

  a 1.
  b -1.
  c 2.
  d **3**.

12 In Fig. 2.6, how does the slope of the line between $x = 4$ and $x = 5$ compare with the slope between $x = 2$ and x = 3?
  a The slope is greater between $x = 4$ and $x = 5$.
  b The slope is greater between $x = 2$ and $x = 3$.
  c The slope is the same.
  d The slope is not comparable.

Figure 2.6

(a)

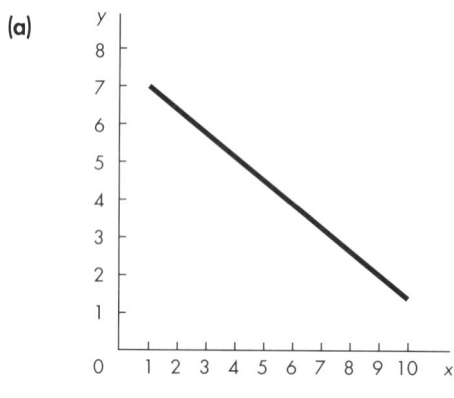

(a)

(b)

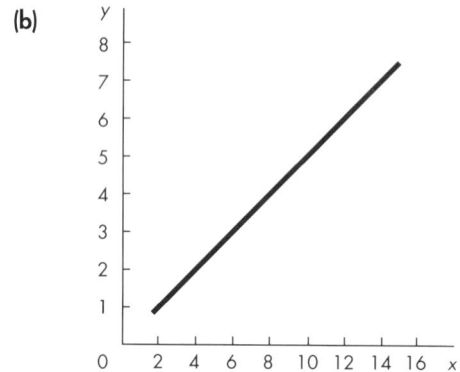

SHORT ANSWERS

1 Draw a two-variable time-series graph that illustrates two variables that have a tendency to move up and down together. What would the scatter diagram for these two variables look like?

2 Draw a graph of variables x and y that illustrates each of the following relationships:
a x and y move up and down together.
b x and y move in opposite directions.
c as x increases y reaches a maximum.
d as x increases y reaches a minimum.
e x and y move in opposite directions, but as x increases y decreases by larger and larger increments for each unit increase in x.
f y is independent of the value of x.
g x is independent of the value of y.

3 What does it mean to say that the slope of a line is –2/3?

4 Explain how we measure the slope of a curved line
a at a point.
b across an arc.

5 How do we graph a relationship among more than two variables using a two-dimensional graph?

PROBLEMS

1 Consider the data in Table 2.3.
a Draw a time-series graph for the interest rate.
b Draw a two-variable time-series graph for both the inflation rate and the interest rate.
c Draw a scatter diagram for the inflation rate (horizontal axis) and the interest rate (vertical axis).
d Would you describe the general relationship between the inflation rate and the interest rate as positive, negative or unrelated?

2 Compute the slope of the lines in Fig. 2.6(a) and (b).

Table 2.3

Year	Inflation rate (per cent)	Interest rate (per cent)
1991	5.4	6.4
1992	3.2	4.3
1993	3.4	4.1
1994	8.3	7.0
1995	11.8	7.9
1996	6.7	5.8
1997	4.9	5.0
1998	6.5	5.3
1999	8.6	7.2
2000	12.3	10.0

3 Draw each of the following:
a a straight line with slope –10 and passing through the point (2,80).
b a straight line with slope 2 and passing through the point (6,10).

4 The equation for a straight line is $y = 6 - 2x$.
a Calculate:
i the y-intercept
ii the x-intercept
iii the slope
b Draw the graph of the line.

5 Use the graph in Fig. 2.7 to compute the slope
a across the arc between points a and b.
b at point b.
c at point c, and explain your answer.

Figure 2.7

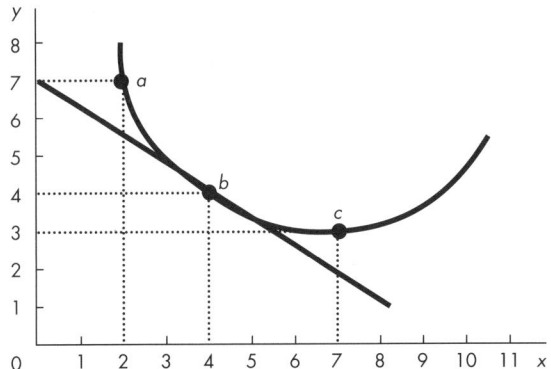

DISCUSSION QUESTION

1 Why do economists often use graphs instead of numbers?

DATA QUESTIONS

Table 2.4 shows the percentage unemployment rate in the United Kingdom and in the European Union as a whole.

Table 2.4

	1990	1991	1992	1993	1994	1995	1996	1997	1998	1999
UK	7.0	9.8	10.1	10.4	9.6	8.8	8.2	7.0	6.3	6.3
EU	–	8.2	9.3	10.7	11.1	10.7	10.8	10.6	10.0	9.6

Source: *Regions: Statistical Yearbook 1999,* Tab 0601, Statistical Office of the European Community (Eurostat), July 1999.

Graph the data in Table 2.4 and answer the following questions:

1 In what year was unemployment lowest in the United Kingdom? In the European Union as a whole?

2 In what year was unemployment highest in the United Kingdom? In the European Union?

3 Would these data support the hypothesis that unemployment was caused by international factors or by influences in one country?

4 Was the unemployment record better in the United Kingdom or in the European Union as a whole?

ANSWERS

CONCEPT REVIEW

1 time-series

2 trend

3 scatter

4 positive; upward

5 negative; downward

6 horizontal

7 vertical (y); horizontal (x)

8 constant

9 two

TRUE OR FALSE

1 T Other variables are plotted on the vertical axis.

2 T The graph enables us to see the changes.

3 T A visual representation allows comparison.

4 F A scatter diagram shows the relationship between variables.

5 T This illustrates a positive relationship.

6 T A rise in one variable and a fall in another represents a negative relationship.

7 T Such a relationship can take any pattern.

8 F Slope is the change in the variable on the vertical axis divided by the change in the variable on the horizontal axis.

9 T Slope of a straight line is constant.

10 F Changes in more than one variable can be shown.

11 T Arc ab would have a negative slope, arc bc a positive slope.

MULTIPLE CHOICE

1 a Higher values of x are associated with lower values of y.

2 a Definition.

3 d Graph may be steep, flat or curved, but must have a negative slope.

4 c Change in vertical axis is 3 for each change in horizontal.

5 d Minus, because to the left of the y-axis.

6 b c would be true if we change 'negatively' to 'positively'. Can't judge **d** without additional information.

7 d Higher price is associated with lower purchases.

8 d At each price fewer boxes will be purchased.

9 c Sales increase as income increases.

10 c Use formula $y = a + bx$. Slope = b, y-intercept = a.

11 a The slope equals the change in the variable along the vertical axis divided by the change in the variable along the horizontal axis i.e. $(2 - 1)/(3 - 2) = 1$.

12 c The figure is a straight line, and the slope of a straight line is constant.

SHORT ANSWER

1 Figure 2.8(a) illustrates a two-variable time-series graph of two variables with a tendency to move up and down together. Figure 2.8(b) illustrates a scatter diagram for such variables.

Figure 2.8

(a)

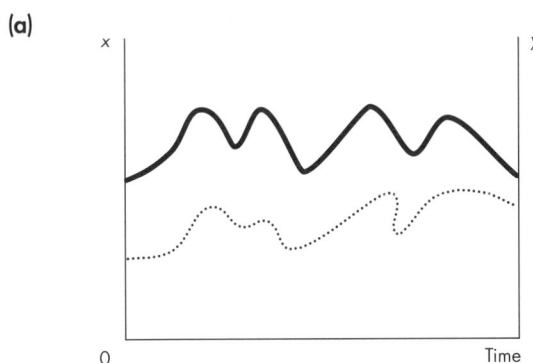

(b)

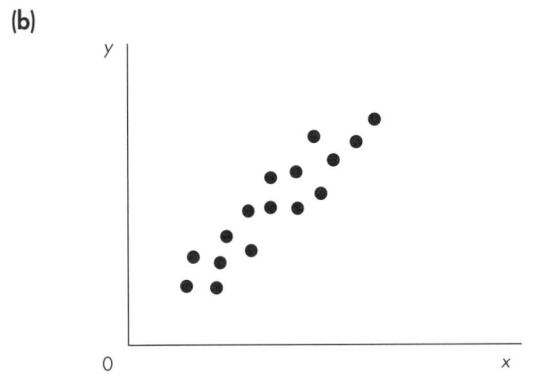

2 Figures 2.9 (a) to (g) illustrate the desired graphs.

3 The negative sign in the slope of –2/3 means that there is a negative relationship between the two variables. The value of 2/3 means that when the variable measured on the vertical axis decreases by 2 units (the 'rise' or Δy), the variable measured on the horizontal axis increases by 3 units (the 'run' or Δx).

4 In both cases we actually measure the slope of a straight line.
  a The slope at a point is measured by calculating the slope of the straight line that is tangent to (just touches) the curved line at the point.
  b The slope across an arc is measured by calculating the slope of the straight line that forms the arc.

5 To graph a relationship among more than two variables, we hold all of the variables but two constant, and graph the relationship between the remaining two. Thus we can graph the relationship between any pair of variables, given the constant values of the other variables.

PROBLEMS

1 a A time-series graph for the interest rate is given in Fig. 2.10(a).
  b Figure 2.10(b) is a two-variable time-series graph for both the inflation rate and the interest rate.
  c The scatter diagram for the inflation rate and the interest rate is given in Fig. 2.10(c).
  d From the graphs in Fig 2.10(b) and (c), we see that the relationship between the inflation rate and the interest rate is generally positive.

Figure 2.9

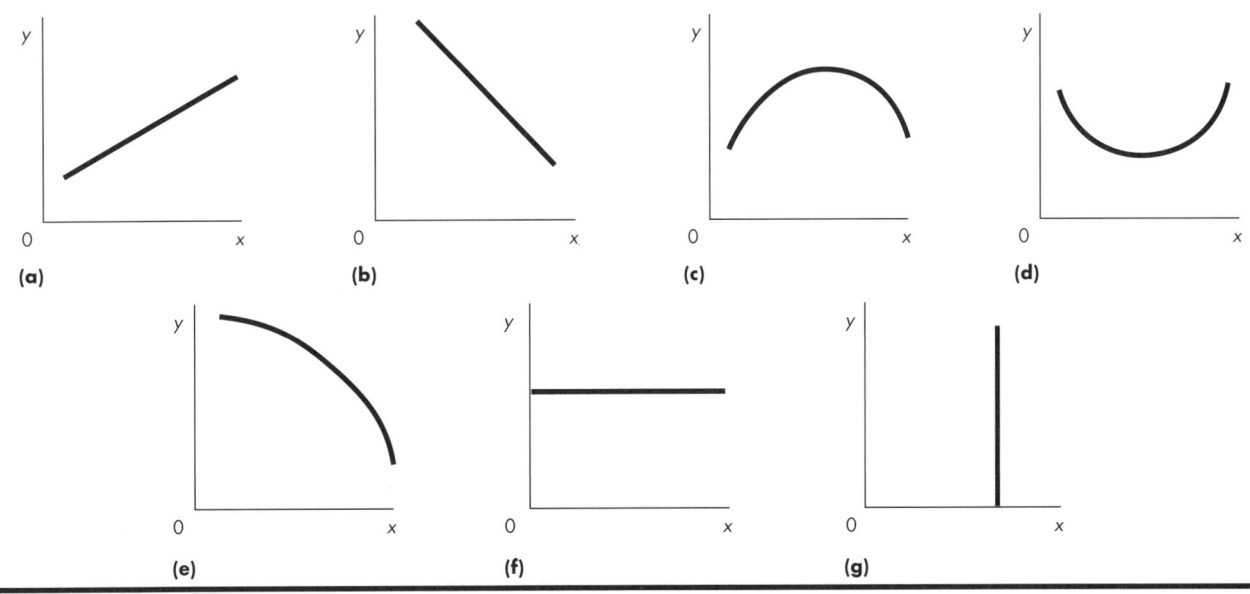

Figure 2.10

(a)

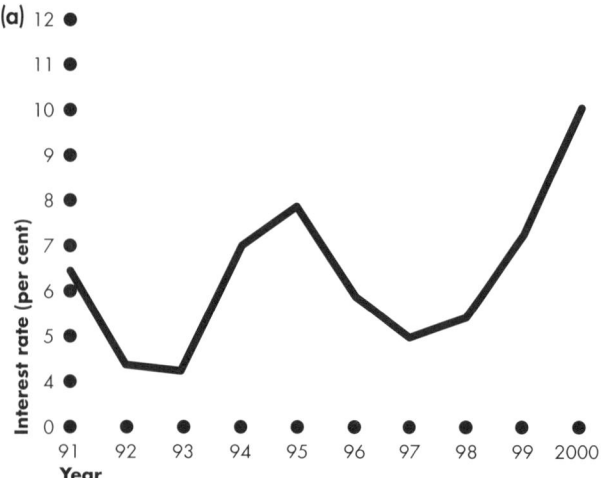

(b)

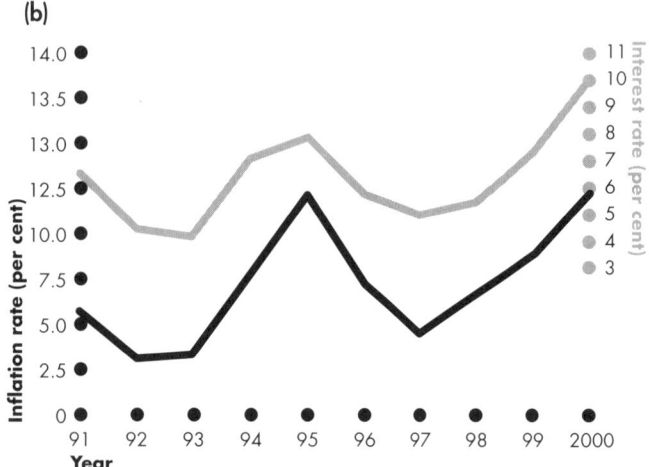

(c)

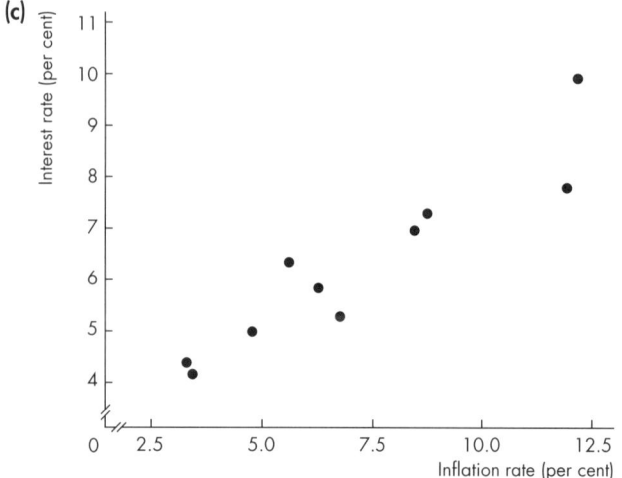

2 The slope of the line in Fig. 2.6(a) is –2/3 and the slope of the line in Fig. 2.6(b) is ¹/₂.

3 a The requested straight line is graphed in Fig. 2.11(a).
   b The requested straight line is graphed in Fig. 2.11(b).

4 a   i To find the y-intercept, set $x = 0$.
$$y = 6 - 2(0)$$
$$y = 6$$

   ii To find the x-intercept, set $y = 0$.
$$0 = 6 - 2x$$
$$x = 3$$

   iii The slope of the line is –2, the value of the b coefficient on x.
   b The graph of the line is shown in Fig. 2.12.

Figure 2.11

(a)

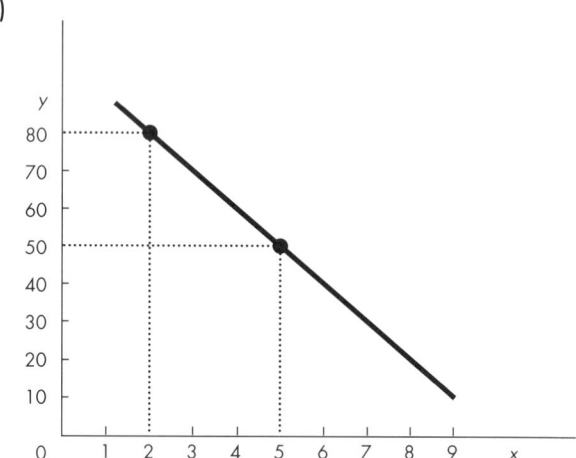

(b)

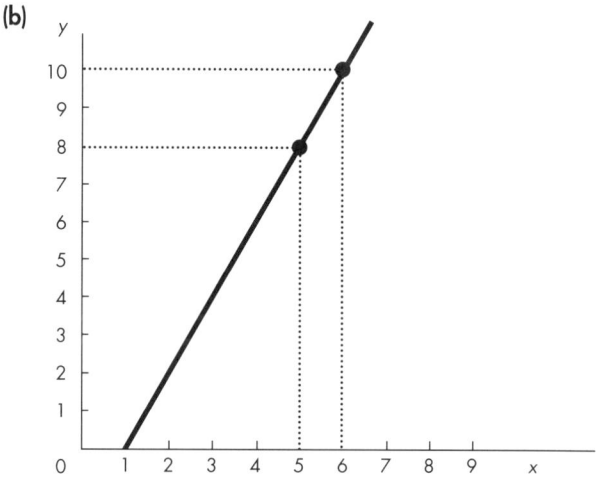

Figure 2.12

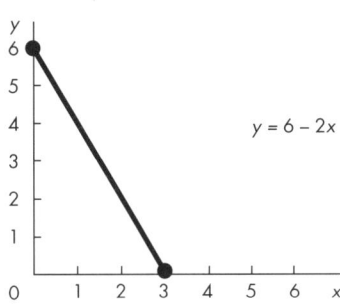

5 a The slope across the arc between points a and b is $-3/2$.

b The slope at point b is $-3/4$.

c The slope at point c is zero because it is a minimum point. Near a minimum point the slope changes from negative to positive and must pass through zero, or no slope, to do so.

DISCUSSION QUESTION

1 Graphs make understanding economics easier because they make it possible to picture relationships which may be hidden in a mass of figures. They can also make it easier to understand theory by showing how two variables are related. However, economists also make considerable use of numbers, particularly in economic research where statistical analysis can help make the relationship between variables more precise than is possible with graphs.

DATA QUESTIONS

1 The graph is shown in Fig. 2.13. The lowest unemployment rate in the United Kingdom was in 1999; in the European Union as a whole it was 1991.

Figure 2.13

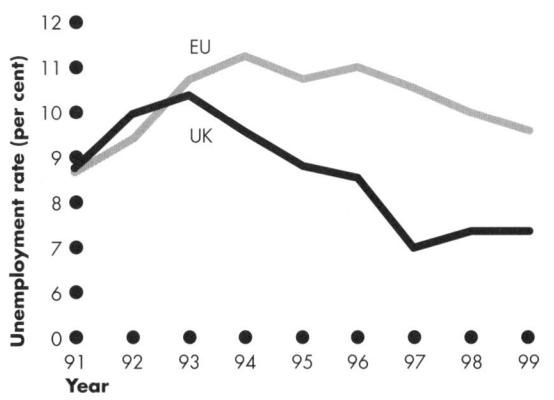

2 The rate was highest in the United Kingdom in 1993; in the European Union as a whole it was highest in 1994.

3 The graph shows that unemployment rates were similar and followed similar patterns. This suggests that they were determined by common international factors. However, there are differences, and this suggests that factors within countries (such as government policy) can have an effect.

4 Unemployment was lower in the United Kingdom for most of the period.

Chapter 3 Production, Growth and Trade

Chapter in Perspective, Text Pages 40–65

In the first chapter we learned that the existence of scarcity is the fundamental and pervasive social problem giving rise to economic activity. Because all individuals and all economies are faced with scarce resources choices must be made, each of which has an opportunity cost. Specialization in production is the key to obtaining maximum output from scarce resources, and leads to lowest opportunity costs. Since workers specialize as producers but consume a variety of goods and services, exchange is a necessary complement to specialization.

This chapter explains why specialization and exchange are the natural consequences of attempts to get the most from scarce resources (that is, to optimize). It also discusses the critical role of opportunity cost in explaining both why individuals and countries specialize in the production of goods and services and why tremendous gains occur from specialization and exchange.

Helpful Hints

1 This chapter reviews the absolutely critical concept of *opportunity cost* – the best alternative forgone. A formula for opportunity cost, which works well in solving problems that involve moving up or down a production possibility frontier is:

$$\text{Opportunity cost} = \frac{\text{Give up}}{\text{Get}}$$

Opportunity cost equals the quantity of goods you must give up divided by the quantity of goods you will get.

2 The production possibility frontier (*PPF*) provides a good example of how economists make use of simplifying assumptions. Although no country produces only two goods, by making their assumption we can understand various aspects of the real world.

3 Opportunity cost can be related to the slope of the production possibility frontier (*PPF*). As we move down between any two points on the *PPF*, the opportunity cost of an additional unit of the good on the *horizontal* axis is:

$$|\text{ slope of } PPF|$$

The slope of the *PPF* is negative, but economists like to describe opportunity cost in terms of a positive quantity of forgone goods. Therefore, we must use the *absolute value* of the slope to calculate the desired positive number.

As we move up between any two points on the *PPF*, the opportunity cost of an additional unit of the good on the *vertical* axis is:

$$\left| \frac{1}{\text{slope of } PPF} \right|$$

4 A production possibility frontier represents the boundary between attainable and unattainable levels of production for a fixed quantity of resources and a given state of technology. It indicates the best that can be done with existing resources and technology. Thus the production possibility frontier will shift out if the quantity of resources increases (for example, an increase in the stock of capital goods) or if there is an increase in the ability to produce (that is, a technological improvement).

5 The text defines absolute advantage as a situation where one person has greater productivity than another in the production of all goods. We can also define absolute advantage in the production of one good. In comparing the productivity of two persons, this narrower concept of absolute advantage can be defined in terms of either greater output of the good per unit of inputs, or fewer inputs per unit of output. The text shows that the gains from trade depend on differing comparative advantages. People have a comparative advantage in producing a good if they can produce it at lower opportunity cost than others.

SELF-TEST

CONCEPT REVIEW

1 The fundamental _____ _____ is how to use limited resources to produce and consume the goods we value.

2 The four factors of production are _____ _____ _____ and _____ .

3 Resources such as iron ore and running rivers are examples of _____ resources; the skill of a computer programmer and the physical strength of a bricklayer are examples of _____ resources; and a shoe factory and an olive-pitting machine are examples of _____ resources.

4 The graphical representation of the boundary between attainable and unattainable production levels is called the _____ _____ _____ .

5 The _____ _____ of a choice is the value of the best forgone alternative choice.

6 Two key activities that can shift the production possibility frontier out are _____ progress and _____ accumulation.

7 The opportunity cost of producing capital goods now in order to expand future production is forgone current _____ goods.

8 If Marta can produce salad forks at a lower opportunity cost than Jill, we say that Marta has a(n) _____ advantage in the production of salad forks.

9 The economic system that permits private individuals to own the capital resources used in production is called _____ .

10 _____ _____ is the opportunity cost of producing one more unit of a good or service.

11 _____ _____ is the benefit people receive from consuming one more good or service.

12 A system in which goods are traded directly for goods is known as _____ .

13 In order for exchange to take place in such a system there must be a double _____ of wants.

TRUE OR FALSE

___ **1** Increasing opportunity cost results from the equal usefulness of scarce resources in all activities.

Figure 3.1

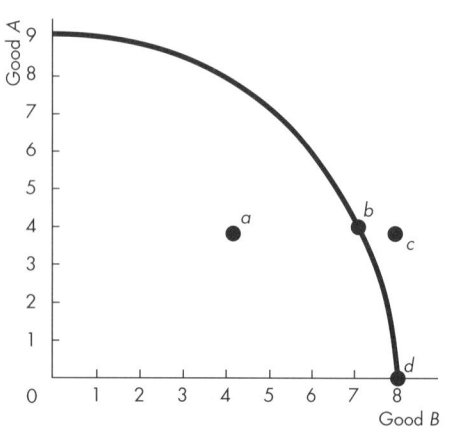

Refer to the production possibility frontier in Fig. 3.1 for Questions 2–7.

___ **2** At point *d*, 9 units of good *A* and 8 units of good *B* are produced.

___ **3** Point *a* is not attainable.

___ **4** The opportunity cost of increasing the production of good *B* from 7 to 8 units is 4 units of good *A*.

___ **5** Point *c* is not attainable.

___ **6** In moving from point *b* to point *d*, the opportunity cost of increasing the production of good *B* equals the absolute value of the slope of the production possibility frontier between *b* and *d*.

___ **7** The bowed out (concave) shape of a *PPF* reflects decreasing opportunity cost as we increase production of either good.

___ **8** Reducing the current production of consumption goods in order to produce more capital goods will shift the production possibility frontier inward in the future.

___ **9** Consider an economy with two goods, *X* and *Y*, and two producers, Bill and Joe. If Bill has a comparative advantage in the production of *X* then Joe must have a comparative advantage in the production of *Y*.

___ **10** Any time two individuals have different opportunity costs they can both gain from specialization and trade.

___ **11** The incentives for specialization and exchange do not depend on property rights but only on differing opportunity costs.

MULTIPLE CHOICE

1 If Harold can increase production of good *X* without decreasing the production of any other good, then Harold
  a is producing on his production possibility frontier.
  b is producing outside his production possibility frontier.
  c is producing inside his production possibility frontier.
  d must have a linear production possibility frontier.
  e must prefer good *X* to any other good.

2 The bowed out (concave) shape of a production possibility frontier
  a is due to the equal usefulness of resources in all activities.
  b is due to capital accumulation.
  c is due to technological improvement.
  d reflects the existence of increasing opportunity cost.
  e reflects the existence of decreasing opportunity cost.

3 The economy is at point *b* on the production possibility frontier in Fig. 3.2. The opportunity cost of producing one more unit of *X* is
  a 1 unit of *Y*.
  b 20 units of *Y*.
  c 1 unit of *X*.
  d 8 units of *X*.
  e 20 units of *X*.

4 The economy is at point *b* on the production possibility frontier in Fig. 3.2. The opportunity cost of increasing the production of *Y* to 50 units is
  a 2 units of *X*.
  b 6 units of *X*.
  c 8 units of *X*.
  d 20 units of *Y*.
  e 30 units of *Y*.

Figure 3.2

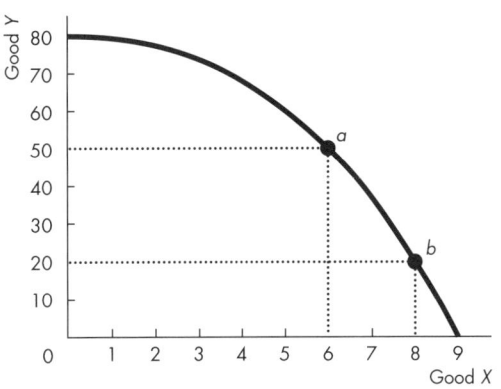

5 Because productive resources are scarce, we must give up some of one good in order to acquire more of another. This is the essence of the concept of
a specialization.
b monetary exchange.
c comparative advantage.
d absolute advantage.
e opportunity cost.

6 In general, the higher the proportion of resources devoted to technological research in an economy the
a greater will be current consumption.
b faster the production possibility frontier will shift outward.
c faster the production possibility frontier will shift inward.
d closer it will come to having a comparative advantage in the production of all goods.
e more bowed out will be the shape of the frontier.

In an 8-hour day, Andy can produce either 24 loaves of bread or 8 pounds of butter. In an 8-hour day, Rolfe can produce either 8 loaves of bread or 8 pounds of butter. Use this information to answer Questions 7 and 8.

7 Which of the following statements is true?
a Andy has an absolute advantage in butter production.
b Rolfe has an absolute advantage in butter production.
c Andy has an absolute advantage in bread production.

d Andy has a comparative advantage in butter production.
e Rolfe has a comparative advantage in bread production.

8 Andy and Rolfe
a can gain from exchange if Andy specializes in butter production and Rolfe specializes in bread production.
b can gain from exchange if Andy specializes in bread production and Rolfe specializes in butter production.
c cannot gain from exchange.
d can exchange, but only Rolfe will be able to gain.
e can exchange, but only Andy will be able to gain.

9 Anything that is generally acceptable in exchange for goods and services is
a a commodity.
b a medium of exchange.
c private property.
d a barter good.
e called an exchange resource.

10 Which of the following is an advantage of a monetary exchange system over barter?
a A monetary exchange system eliminates the basis for comparative advantage.
b A monetary exchange system does not require a medium of exchange.
c Only in a monetary exchange system can gains from trade be realized.
d A monetary exchange system does not require a double coincidence of wants.
e All of the above are advantages of a monetary exchange system over barter.

11 Norway and the United Kingdom each produce both oil and apples using labour only. A barrel of oil can be produced with 4 hours of labour in Norway and 8 hours of labour in the United Kingdom; and 18 kilograms of apples can be produced with 8 hours of labour in Norway and 12 hours of labour in the United Kingdom. The United Kingdom has
a an absolute advantage in oil production.
b an absolute advantage in apple production.
c a comparative advantage in oil production.
d a comparative advantage in apple production.
e none of the above.

Suppose a society produces only two goods – guns and butter. Three alternative combinations on its production possibility frontier are given in Table 3.1.

Table 3.1   Production Possibilities

Possibility	Units of butter	Units of guns
a	8	0
b	6	1
c	0	3

Use the information in Table 3.1 to answer Questions 12 and 13.

12 In moving from combination *b* to combination *c*, the opportunity cost of producing *one* additional unit of guns is
   a 2 units of butter.
   b 1/2 unit of butter.
   c 6 units of butter.
   d 1/6 unit of butter.
   e 3 units of butter.
   f 1/3 unit of butter.

13 According to this production possibility frontier
   a a combination of 6 units of butter and 1 unit of guns would not employ all resources.
   b a combination of 0 units of butter and 4 units of guns is attainable.
   c resources are homogeneous.
   d the opportunity cost of producing guns increases as more guns are produced.
   e the opportunity cost of producing guns decreases as more guns are produced.

14 In Germany, the opportunity cost of a bale of wool is 3 bottles of wine. In the United Kingdom, the opportunity cost of 1 bottle of wine is 3 bales of wool. Given this information,
   a the United Kingdom has an absolute advantage in wine production.
   b the United Kingdom has an absolute advantage in wool production.
   c Germany has a comparative advantage in wine production.
   d Germany has a comparative advantage in wool production.
   e no trade will occur.

15 Which of the following is *not* a resource used to produce goods?
   a capital equipment.
   b money in the bank.
   c land.
   d labour.

16 Which of the following does *not* help organize trade?
   a the production possibility frontier.
   b markets.
   c property rights.
   d none of the above, since they all help organize trade.

SHORT ANSWER

1 a Why is a production possibility frontier negatively sloped?
   b Why is it bowed out?

2 a In an economy with no tool-making possibilities (constant capital goods), what is the opportunity cost of moving from a point inside the production possibility frontier to a point on the frontier? Explain.
   b In a tool-making economy, what is the opportunity cost of current consumption?

3 Lawyers earn £100 per hour while secretaries earn £8 per hour. Use the concepts of absolute and comparative advantage to explain why a lawyer, who is a better typist than her secretary, will still 'specialize' in doing only legal work and will 'trade' with the secretary for typing services.

4 Explain, using a specific example of exchange, why a monetary exchange system is more efficient than barter.

5 Apply the concept of opportunity cost to the *Reading Between the Lines* material to analyse your own decision to become a student.

PROBLEMS

1 Suppose that an economy with unchanged capital goods (no tool-making) has the production possibility frontier shown in Table 3.2.

Table 3.2 Production Possibilities

Possibility	Maximum units of butter per week	Maximum units of guns per week
a	200	0
b	180	60
c	160	100
d	100	160
e	40	200
f	0	220

a On graph paper, plot these possibilities, label the points and draw the production possibility frontier. (Put guns on the *x*-axis.)

b If the economy moves from possibility *c* to possibility *d*, the opportunity cost *per unit of guns* will be how many units of butter?

c If the economy moves from possibility *d* to possibility *e*, the opportunity cost *per unit of guns* will be how many units of butter?

d In general terms, what happens to the opportunity cost of guns as the output of guns increases?

e In general terms, what happens to the opportunity cost of butter as the output of butter increases? What do the results for possibilities *e* and *f* imply about resources?

f If (instead of the possibilities given) the production possibility frontier were a straight line joining points *a* and *f*, what would that imply about opportunity costs and resources?

g Given the original production possibility frontier you have plotted, is a combination of 140 units of butter and 130 units of guns per week attainable? Would you regard this combination as an efficient one? Explain.

h If the following events occurred (each is a separate event, unaccompanied by any other event), what would happen to the production possibility frontier?

  i A new, easily exploited energy source is discovered.

  ii A large number of skilled workers immigrate into the country.

  iii The output of butter is increased.

  iv A new invention increases output per person in the butter industry but not in the guns industry.

  v A new law is passed compelling workers, who could previously work as long as they wanted, to retire at age 60.

2 France and Germany each produce both wine and beer, using a single homogeneous input – labour. Their production possibilities are:

France has 100 units of labour and can produce a maximum of 200 bottles of wine *or* 400 bottles of beer.

Germany has 50 units of labour and can produce a maximum of 250 bottles of wine *or* 200 bottles of beer.

Table 3.3

	Bottles produced by 1 unit of labour		Opportunity cost of 1 additional bottle	
	Wine	Beer	Wine	Beer
France				
Germany				

a Complete Table 3.3.

Use the information in part (a) to answer the following questions.

b Which country has an absolute advantage in wine production?

c Which country has an absolute advantage in beer production?

d Which country has a comparative advantage in wine production?

e Which country has a comparative advantage in beer production?

f If trade is allowed, describe what specialization, if any, will occur.

DISCUSSION QUESTIONS

1 Why bother to learn about production possibility curves with only two goods when every country produces millions?

2 Why does economic growth inevitably involve some costs?

DATA QUESTIONS

The Tailor and the Shoemaker

It is the maxim of every prudent master of a family never to attempt to make at home what it will cost him more to make than to buy. The tailor does not attempt to make his own shoes, but buys them off the shoemaker. The shoemaker does not attempt to make his own clothes, but employs a tailor.... What is prudence in the conduct of a private family can scarce be folly in that of a great kingdom.... If a foreign country can supply us with a commodity cheaper than we ourselves can make it, better buy it off them with some part of the produce of our own industry...

Source: Adam Smith, *The Wealth of Nations*, 1776.

1 Explain what is meant by 'absolute advantage' and 'comparative advantage'. Do either of these concepts relate to the passage above? If so, how?

2 Draw production possibility curves for the shoemaker and the tailor.

3 How would they each benefit from specialization?

ANSWERS

CONCEPT REVIEW

1 economic problem

2 land; labour; capital, entrepreneurship

3 natural; human; capital

4 production possibility frontier

5 opportunity cost

6 technological; capital

7 consumption

8 comparative

9 capitalism

10 marginal cost

11 marginal benefit

12 barter

13 coincidence

TRUE OR FALSE

1 F Unequal usefulness.

2 F At d, 0 units of good A and 8 units of good B produced.

3 F Attainable but not a maximum.

4 T Moving from b to d, production of good A falls by 4 units.

5 T Outside *PPF.*

6 T See Helpful Hint 1.

7 F Reflects the increasing opportunity cost as increased production of either good.

8 F It will shift the *PPF out*ward.

9 T Because comparative advantage measures *relative* advantages.

10 T Different opportunity cost means different comparative advantage.

11 F Property rights are a prerequisite for specialization and exchange.

MULTIPLE CHOICE

1 c For zero opportunity cost, there must be unemployed resources.

2 d **a** would be true if *un*equal resources, **b** and **c** shift *PPF.*

3 b To increase quantity X to 9, must cut quantity Y from 20 to 0.

4 a To move from b to a quantity X falls from 8 to 6.

5 e Definition.

6 b Technological progress shifts *PPF* outward at cost of current consumption.

7 c Andy is three times as efficient in producing bread.

8 b Andy is more efficient in producing bread.

9 b Definition.

10 d Double coincidence of wants is a principal limitation of barter.

11 d The United Kingdom uses relatively few hours to produce apples.

12 e Give up 6 units of butter to get 2 units of guns: 6/2 = 3 units of butter per gun.

13 d Opportunity cost of a gun between a and b = 2 units of butter. Between b and c = 3 units of butter. **a** is on *PPF*, **b** outside *PPF*.

14 c Opportunity cost of wine in terms of bales of wool is Germany 1/3, United Kingdom 3. Opportunity cost of wool in terms of wine is Germany 3, United Kingdom 1/3.

15 b Money in the bank is *not* a resource. It just represents the ability to buy a resource.

16 a The production possibility frontier shows the limits to production and does not help organize trade.

SHORT ANSWER

1 a The negative slope of the production possibility frontier reflects opportunity cost: in order to have more of one good, some of the other must be forgone.

b It is bowed out because the existence of non-homogeneous resources creates increasing opportunity cost as we increase the production of either good.

2 a In an economy with no tool-making possibilities, a point inside the production possibility frontier represents unemployed or underutilized resources. By moving to a point on the frontier, more output can be produced from the same resources, simply by utilizing the resources more efficiently. Since resources do not have to be withdrawn from the production of any other good, the opportunity cost of moving to a point on the frontier is zero. This is the closest we get to a 'free lunch' in the discipline of economics.

b In a tool-making economy, we can forgo current consumption to produce capital goods which subsequently increase future production and consumption. By consuming all that is currently produced, we forgo tool-making and, ultimately, increase future consumption.

3 The lawyer has an absolute advantage in producing both legal and typing services relative to the secretary. Nevertheless, she has a comparative advantage in legal services, and the secretary has a comparative advantage in typing. To demonstrate these comparative advantages, we can construct a table of opportunity costs.

Table 3.4 Opportunity Cost of 1 Additional Hour (pounds)

	Legal services	Typing
Lawyer	100	100
Secretary	>100	8

Consider first the lawyer's opportunity costs. The lawyer's best forgone alternative to providing 1 hour of legal services is the £100 she could earn by providing another hour of legal services. If she provides 1 hour of typing, she is also forgoing £100 (1 hour) of legal services. What would the secretary have to forgo to provide 1 hour of legal services? She would have to spend several years as a student, forgoing years of income in addition to the tuition she must pay. Her opportunity cost is a large number, certainly greater than £100. If she provides 1 hour of typing, her best forgone alternative is the £8 she could have earned at another secretarial job. Thus Table 3.4 shows that the lawyer has a lower opportunity cost (comparative advantage) of providing legal services, and the secretary has a lower opportunity cost (comparative advantage) of providing typing services. It is on the basis of comparative advantage (not absolute advantage) that trade will take place from which both parties gain.

4 The principal reason for the efficiency of a monetary exchange system relative to barter is that the monetary system does not require a double coincidence of wants to complete a successful exchange. For example, suppose you specialize in the production of apples but like to eat bananas. In a barter economy, you would probably not be able to complete an exchange with the first person you found who had bananas to trade. It would be necessary for that person also to want to trade the bananas for apples and not for carrots or some other good. In a monetary economy, you would always be able to make a successful exchange with the first person you found with bananas to trade since that person would be willing to accept money in exchange. Similarly, in a money exchange system, you would be able to sell your apples for money to the first person you found who wanted apples (even if that person did not have bananas to sell).

5 The opportunity cost of becoming a student is what you would have been doing if you had not made this decision. The answer will be personal to you, but may include a job (and money) and life with your family and friends.

PROBLEMS

1 a The graph of the production possibility frontier follows:

Figure 3.3

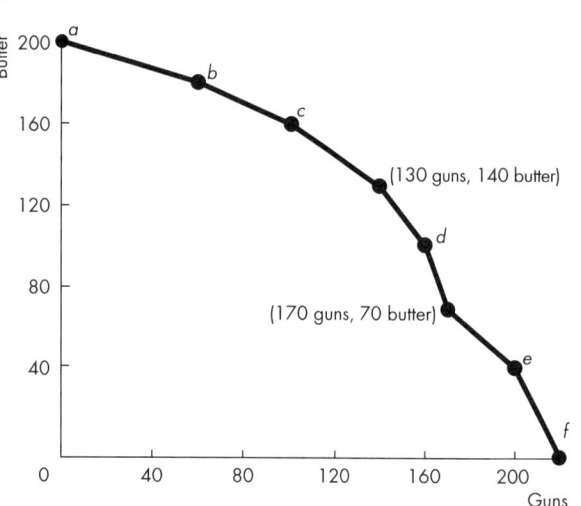

b In moving from *c* to *d*, in order to gain 60 units of guns, we must give up 160 − 100 = 60 units of butter. The opportunity cost per unit of guns is:

$$\frac{60 \text{ units butter}}{60 \text{ units guns}} = \frac{1 \text{ unit of butter per}}{\text{unit of guns}}$$

c In moving from *d* to *e*, in order to gain 40 units of guns, we must give up 100 − 40 = 60 units of butter. The opportunity cost per unit of guns is:

$$\frac{60 \text{ units butter}}{40 \text{ units guns}} = \frac{1.5 \text{ units of butter per}}{\text{unit of guns}}$$

d The opportunity cost of producing more guns increases as the output of guns increases.

e Likewise, the opportunity cost of producing more butter increases as the output of butter increases.

Increasing opportunity costs imply that resources are non-homogeneous, that is, they are not equally useful in gun and butter production.

f Opportunity costs would always be constant, regardless of the output of guns or butter. The opportunity cost per unit of guns would be:

200/220 = 10/11 units of butter

The opportunity cost per unit of butter would be:

220/200 = 1.1 units of guns

Constant opportunity costs imply that resources are homogeneous, that is, they are equally useful in gun and butter production.

g This combination is outside the frontier and, therefore, is not attainable. Since the economy cannot produce this combination, the question of efficiency is irrelevant.

h i Assuming that both goods require energy for their production, the entire frontier shifts out to the north-east.

Figure 3.4

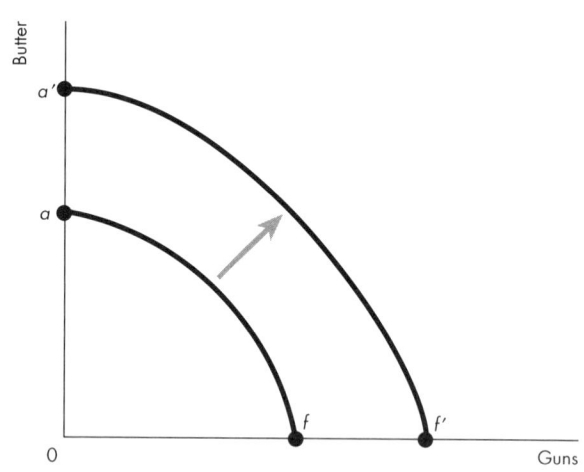

ii Assuming that both goods use skilled labour in their production, the entire frontier shifts out to the north-east.

iii The frontier does not shift. An increase in the output of butter implies a movement *along* the frontier to the left, not a shift of the frontier itself.

iv The new invention implies that for every level of output of guns, the economy can now produce more butter. The frontier swings to the right, but remains anchored at point *f*.

v The entire frontier shifts in towards the origin.

Figure 3.5

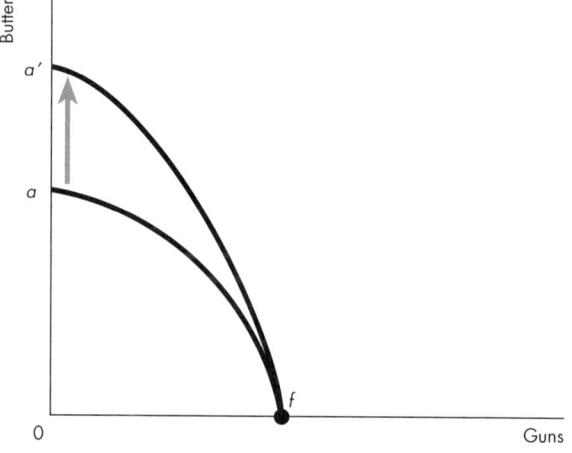

2 a The completed table is shown as Table 3.5.

Table 3.5

	Bottles produced by 1 unit of labour		Opportunity cost of 1 additional bottle	
	Wine	Beer	Wine	Beer
France	2	4	2.0 beer	0.5 wine
Germany	5	4	0.8 beer	1.25 wine

b Germany, which can produce more wine (5 bottles) per unit of input, has an absolute advantage in wine production.

c Neither country has an absolute advantage in beer production, since beer output (4 bottles) per unit of input is the same for both countries.

d Germany, with the lower opportunity cost (0.8 beer), has a comparative advantage in wine production.

e France, with the lower opportunity cost (0.5 wine), has a comparative advantage in beer production.

f The incentive for trade depends only on differences in comparative advantage. Germany will specialize in wine production and France will specialize in beer production.

DISCUSSION QUESTIONS

1 All economic models involve simplification. The lessons that can be learned from the simple two-good *PPF* carry over into the real world; for example, the two-good *PPF* shows that there are limits to production, and this applies whether or not there are two goods or 2 million goods.

The simple model also illustrates that production can be efficient or inefficient – just like the real world.

Lastly, the two-good *PPF* shows that once production is efficient – a point on the *PPF* – increasing the production of one good has an opportunity cost because the production of the other good must be curtailed. This also applies to countries. Once a country is producing efficiently, if it wishes to produce more of a particular good, it has to give up the production of other goods.

2 There is an opportunity cost to economic growth. As more and more of particular goods are produced, resources are being used that could have been used to produce other goods. In addition, some people would argue that economic growth imposes costs in terms of pollution.

DATA QUESTIONS

1 Absolute advantage occurs when one person or country has greater productivity than another in the production of all goods. A person has comparative advantage if that person can produce a good at a lower opportunity cost than another person. In the case in question, the shoemaker has a comparative advantage in producing shoes and the tailor in producing clothes.

2 The production possibility curves are shown in Fig. 3.6.

Figure 3.6

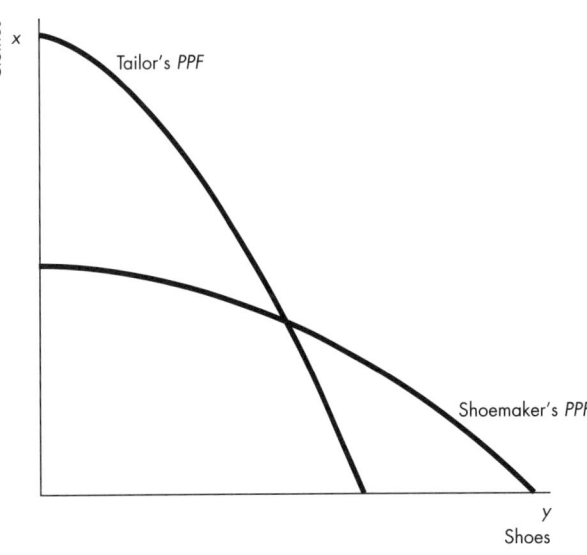

3 Both tailor and shoemaker would benefit if they specialized and exchanged their products. In Fig. 3.6, total output would be *x* units of clothes and *y* shoes. This exceeds the output if both tailor and shoemaker produced both clothes and shoes. Self-sufficiency means lower levels of output.

Part 2 What is Economics?

Looking back at Part 1 (Chapters 1–3)

Part 1 has three chapters that form a background to your course. The first chapter sets out to discuss what economics is, and what economists do. Remember the five big questions? (What? How? When? Where? Who?) This chapter also introduced some general points about the subject such as the divisions into *micro* economics – dealing with small-scale issues such as decisions made by individual firms, and *macro*economics which examines large-scale issues such as economic policy. In this book we begin with the small scale and build up to the macro.

Chapter 2 focused on a crucial technique – how to use graphs. You may have found this easy, but if not, it is worth while working on it because graphs are a very useful technique.

In Chapter 3 the authors concentrated on the fundamental economic problem – that of scarcity. We cannot all have everything that we would like, so we have to choose. This involves a basic economic concept – that of opportunity cost. The opportunity cost of any action is the best alternative forgone. For example, when you read this, you could have been doing something else; so the opportunity cost of reading this is what you would have been doing otherwise. On a larger scale, the opportunity cost to you of becoming a student is what you would have been doing if you had not chosen to become a student. These opportunity costs can sometimes be measured in monetary terms, but frequently they cannot. This chapter also introduces another important concept, that of comparative advantage. You will meet this again when we discuss international trade. Its application is one reason why living standards today are higher than they have ever been before in history, so it is worth while making sure that you understand it.

Questions (the answers are at the end of this section)

1 This is a good time to explore the material that is available on the internet. This changes over time, but a good start would be to look up the Parkin, Powell and Matthews website (www.econ100.com) and the bized (www.bized.com) sites (details are given in the introduction). Newspapers are another useful source. Look at the Economist (www.economist.com) and Financial Times (news.ft.com/ft/gx.cgi/ftc?pagename=View&c= Collection &cid=ZZZLLCHPDOC) sites. Jot down what is available so that you can access it quickly at appropriate times on the course.

2 Re-read the *Understanding the Sources of Economic Wealth* article. What did Adam Smith think were the two sources of economic wealth?

Looking forward to Part 2 (Chapters 4–7)

Chapter 4 on supply and demand is perhaps the most important chapter in the entire book. That is because supply and demand analysis can be used to analyse a huge range of issues from the price of fish and chips to the wages of pop stars and the value of the pound. You will meet these concepts many times during your economics course. They are as fundamental to the subject as addition and subtraction are to arithmetic, so whatever else you feel like skimming – or even skipping – you must master this.

Chapter 5 is also important It is concerned with elasticity. In essence this is about whether one variable (such as price) has a large or a small effect on another variable (such as quantity). For example, if Ford puts up the price of its cars, what will happen to sales of Ford cars? And what will be the effect on sales of competing cars?

Chapter 6 steps back a little to examine two main ideas – efficiency and equity (i.e. fairness).

Answers

1 The answer will depend on what you found in your search.

2 Adam Smith believed that the sources of economic wealth were the division of labour and free markets.

Chapter 4 Demand and Supply

Chapter in Perspective, Text Pages 68–95

This is perhaps the most important chapter in the book. The concepts of demand and supply are so powerful they can be applied to a wide variety of situations. It is therefore important that you master the ideas in this chapter.

Most formal exchange takes place in 'markets' at prices determined by the interaction of buyers (demanders) and sellers (suppliers) in those markets. There are markets for goods (such as wheat or textbooks), for services (such as haircuts or tattoos), for financial assets (such as IBM shares, pounds sterling or government bonds), and also for labour. Demand and supply are powerful tools that economists use to explain how much will be traded and at what price. Careful use of these tools will allow us to explain a wide array of economic phenomena and even predict changes in prices and quantities traded.

Helpful Hints

1 Specific examples will help you understand economic ideas. For example, when analysing complementary goods, think about hamburgers and chips; when discussing substitute goods, think about hamburgers and hot dogs. This will help reduce the 'abstractness' of the economic theory.

   Similarly, a useful way to get a grip on the idea of supplies to picture yourself as the owner of a firm. What factors will influence your decision to produce more or less? One factor will be a rise in wages. Other things remaining equal, this will increase your costs and cause you to supply less at a given price.

2 The statement 'price is determined by demand and supply' is a shorthand way of saying that price is determined by all of the factors affecting demand (such as prices of other goods, income, population, preferences) and all of the factors affecting supply (such as prices of other goods, prices of factors of production, technology). The benefit of using demand and supply *curves* is that they allow us systematically to sort out the influences on price of each of these separate factors. Changes in the factors affecting demand shift the demand curve and move us up or down the given supply curve. Changes in the factors affecting supply shift the supply curve and move us up or down the given demand curve.

   Any demand and supply problem requires you to sort out these influences carefully. In so doing, *always draw a graph*, even if it is just a small graph in the margin of a true–false or multiple-choice problem. As you become comfortable with graphs, you will find that they are effective and powerful tools for systematically organizing your thinking.

Note that when you draw a graph, you should be sure to *label* the *axes*. As the course progresses, you will encounter many graphs with different variables on the axes. It is easy to become confused if you do not develop the habit of labelling the axes.

3 Another common mistake among students is a failure correctly to *distinguish between a shift in a curve and a movement along a curve*. This distinction applies to both demand and supply curves.

Consider demand curves. The quantity of a good demanded depends on its own price, the prices of related goods, income, population and preferences. The term 'demand' refers to the relationship between the price of a good and the quantity demanded, holding constant all the other factors on which the quantity demanded depends. This demand relationship is represented graphically by the demand curve. Thus the effect of a change in price on quantity demanded is already reflected in the slope of the demand curve; that is, the effect of a change in the price of the good itself is given by a movement along the demand curve. This is referred to as a change in quantity demanded.

On the other hand, if one of the other factors affecting the quantity demanded changes, the demand curve itself will shift; that is, the quantity demanded at each price will change. This shift of the demand curve is referred to as a change in demand. The critical thing to remember is that a change in the price of a good will not shift the demand curve, it will only cause a movement along the demand curve. Similarly, it is just as important to distinguish between shifts in the supply curve and movements along the supply curve.

Remember: it is shifts in demand and supply curves that cause the market price to change, not changes in the price that cause demand and supply curves to shift.

4 When analysing the shifts of demand and supply curves in related markets (for example, for substitute goods like beer and wine), it often seems as though the feedback effects from one market to the other can go on endlessly. To avoid confusion, stick to the rule that each curve (demand and supply) for a given market can shift a maximum of *once*.

5 Remember that changes in demand do *not* cause changes in supply. Neither do changes in supply cause changes in demand.

SELF-TEST

CONCEPT REVIEW

1 The _____ _____ of a good or service is the amount that consumers are willing and able to purchase at a particular price.

2 The law of demand states that, other things remaining the same, the higher the_____ of a good, the _____ is the quantity demanded.

3 A demand _____ is a list of the quantities of a good demanded at different _____.

4 A demand curve illustrates the _____ price that consumers are willing to pay for the last unit of a good purchased.

5 The demand curve for most goods will shift to the right if income _____ , or if the price of a substitute _____, or if the price of a complement _____, or if the size of the population_____ .

6 A good is said to be _____ if the demand for it increases as income increases and _____ if demand decreases as income increases.

7 The amount of a good or service that producers plan to sell at a particular price is called the _____ _____ .

8 The law of supply states that the_____ the price of a good, the _____ the quantity supplied.

9 A supply curve shows the quantity supplied at each given _____ .

10 A decrease in supply is represented by a shift to the _____ in the supply curve.

11 The supply curve will shift to the right if the price of a complement in production —————————— , or if the price of a substitute in production —————————— , or if there is a technological ——————————, or if the price of a productive resource —————————— .

12 An increase in the price of a good will cause an increase in the —————————— ——————————; this is represented by a(n) —————————— movement along the supply curve.

13 The price at which the quantity demanded equals the quantity supplied is called the—————————— price.

14 If the price is above equilibrium, a(n) —————————— will exist, causing the price to —————————— .

15 When demand increases, the equilibrium price will —————————— and the quantity traded will —————————— .

16 When supply increases, the equilibrium price will —————————— and the quantity traded will —————————— .

17 If demand increases and supply increases, then we know that the quantity traded must —————————— ; but the equilibrium price may increase, decrease or remain unchanged.

TRUE OR FALSE

1 The law of demand tells us that as the price of a good rises the quantity demanded decreases.

2 The negative slope of a demand curve is a result of the law of demand.

3 An increase in the price of apples will shift the demand curve for apples to the left.

4 Hamburgers and chips are complements. If Burger Bar reduces the price of chips, the demand for hamburgers will increase.

5 A supply curve shows the maximum price at which the last unit will be supplied.

6 A demand curve is a graphical representation of the relationship between the price of a good and quantity demanded given the level of income, prices of other goods, population and preferences.

7 A cost-reducing technological improvement will shift a supply curve to the right.

8 If we observe a doubling of the price of mozzarella cheese (an ingredient in pizza), we will expect the supply curve for pizzas to shift to the left.

9 When a cow is slaughtered for beef, its hide becomes available to make leather. Thus beef and leather are substitutes in production.

10 If the price of beef rises, we would expect to see an increase in the supply of leather and in the quantity of beef supplied.

11 If the current price is such that the quantity demanded exceeds the quantity supplied, the price will tend to rise.

12 If demand increases, we would predict an increase in equilibrium price and a decrease in quantity traded.

13 If potatoes are inferior goods, we would expect an increase in income to result in a fall in the price of potatoes.

14 A decrease in the supply of a good will result in a decrease in both the equilibrium price and the quantity traded.

MULTIPLE CHOICE

1 Which of the following could *not* cause an increase in demand for a commodity?
 a an increase in income
 b a decrease in income
 c a decrease in the price of a substitute
 d a decrease in the price of a complement
 e an increase in preferences for the commodity

2 A rise in the price of beer shifts the
 a demand curve for crisps to the left.
 b demand curve for crisps to the right.
 c supply curve for crisps to the left.
 d supply curve for crisps to the right.

3 If Hamburger Helper is an inferior good, then, *ceteris paribus*, a decrease in income will cause

a a leftward shift of the demand curve for Hamburger Helper.

b a rightward shift of the demand curve for Hamburger Helper.

c a movement up along the demand curve for Hamburger Helper.

d a movement down along the demand curve for Hamburger Helper.

e none of the above.

4 Good A is a normal good if

a an increase in the price of a complement causes the demand for A to decrease.

b an increase in income causes the demand for A to increase.

c an increase in the price of a substitute causes the demand for A to increase.

d it satisfies the law of demand.

e income and the demand for A are negatively correlated.

5 A decrease in quantity demanded is represented by a

a rightward shift of the supply curve.

b rightward shift of the demand curve.

c leftward shift of the demand curve.

d movement upward and to the left along the demand curve.

e movement downward and to the right along the demand curve.

6 The price of a good will tend to fall if

a there is a surplus at the current price.

b the current price is above equilibrium.

c the quantity supplied exceeds the quantity demanded at the current price.

d all of the above are true.

e none of the above is true.

7 The fact that a decline in the price of a good causes producers to reduce the quantity of the good supplied illustrates

a the law of supply.

b the law of demand.

c a change in supply.

d the nature of an inferior good.

e technological improvement.

8 A shift of the supply curve for salami will be caused by

a a change in preferences for salami.

b a change in the price of a related good that is a substitute in consumption for salami.

c a change in income.

d a change in the price of salami.

e none of the above.

9 An increase in the number of suppliers of mobile phones _____ the supply of mobile phones and shifts the supply curve _____

a increases; rightward.

b increases; leftward.

c decreases; rightward.

d decreases; leftward.

10 Which of the following will shift the supply curve for good X to the left?

a a decrease in the wages of workers employed to produce X

b an increase in the cost of machinery used to produce X

c a technological improvement in the production of X

d a situation where quantity demanded exceeds quantity supplied

e all of the above

11 If a resource can be used to produce either good A or good B, then A and B are

a substitutes in production.

b complements in production.

c substitutes in consumption.

d complements in consumption.

e normal goods.

12 If the market for pencils is in equilibrium, then

a pencils must be a normal good.

b producers would like to sell more at the current price.

c consumers would like to buy more at the current price.

d there will be a surplus.

e quantity traded equals quantity demanded.

13 A shortage is the amount by which quantity

a demanded exceeds quantity supplied.

b traded exceeds quantity supplied.

c traded exceeds quantity demanded.

d demanded exceeds the equilibrium quantity.

e supplied exceeds the equilibrium quantity.

14 A surplus can be eliminated by

a increasing supply.

b government raising the price.

c decreasing the quantity demanded.

d allowing the price to fall.

e allowing the quantity traded to fall.

The market for coffee is initially in equilibrium with supply and demand curves of the usual shape. Pepsi is a substitute for coffee; cream is a complement for coffee. Questions 15–17 concern the market for *coffee*.

Assume that all *ceteris paribus* assumptions continue to hold *except* for the event(s) listed. Answer each question without considering the others.

15 Coffee is a normal good. A decrease in income will
   a increase the price of coffee and increase the quantity demanded of coffee.
   b increase the price of coffee and increase the quantity supplied of coffee.
   c decrease the price of coffee and decrease the quantity demanded of coffee.
   d decrease the price of coffee and decrease the quantity supplied of coffee.
   e cause none of the above.

16 An increase in the price of Pepsi will
   a increase the price of coffee and increase the quantity demanded of coffee.
   b increase the price of coffee and increase the quantity supplied of coffee.
   c decrease the price of coffee and decrease the quantity demanded of coffee.
   d decrease the price of coffee and decrease the quantity supplied of coffee.
   e cause none of the above.

17 A technological improvement lowers the cost of producing coffee. At the same time, preferences for coffee decrease. The *quantity traded* of coffee will
   a rise.
   b fall.
   c remain the same.
   d rise or fall depending on whether the price of coffee falls or rises.
   e rise or fall depending on the relative shifts of demand and supply curves.

18 If both demand and supply increase, then
   a price will rise and quantity traded will increase.
   b price will fall and quantity traded will increase.
   c price could either rise or fall and quantity traded will increase.
   d price will rise and quantity traded could either increase or decrease.
   e price will fall and quantity traded could either increase or decrease.

19 Which of the following will definitely cause an increase in the equilibrium price?
   a an increase in both demand and supply
   b a decrease in both demand and supply
   c an increase in demand combined with a decrease in supply
   d a decrease in demand combined with an increase in supply
   e none of the above

SHORT ANSWER

1 Explain the difference between wants and demands.

2 Suppose we observe that the consumption of peanut butter increases at the same time as its price rises. What must have happened in the market for peanut butter? Is the observation consistent with the law of demand?

3 The price of personal computers has continued to fall even in the face of increasing demand. Explain.

4 Brussels sprouts and carrots are substitutes in consumption and, since they can both be grown on the same type of land, substitutes in production too. Suppose there is an increase in the demand for Brussels sprouts. Trace through the effects on price and quantity traded in both the Brussels sprout and carrot markets. (Keep in mind Helpful Hint 4.)

5 Use the information in the *Reading Between the Lines* article to analyse the effects of changing student numbers in the market for fast food.

PROBLEMS

1 The information given in Table 4.1 is about the behaviour of buyers and sellers of fish at the market on a particular Saturday.

Table 4.1 Demand and Supply Schedules for Fish

Price per fish	Quantity demanded	Quantity supplied
£0.75	270	45
£1.00	260	135
£1.25	245	185
£1.50	225	225
£1.75	200	250
£2.00	170	265
£2.25	135	280
£2.50	105	290
£2.75	80	300
£3.00	60	310
£3.25	45	315
£3.50	35	320

a On graph paper, draw the demand curve and the supply curve. Be sure to label the axes. What is the equilibrium price?

b We will make the usual *ceteris paribus* assumptions about the demand curve so that it does not shift. List four factors that we are assuming do not change.

c We will also hold the supply curve constant by assuming that three factors do not change. List them.

d Explain briefly what would happen if the price were initially set at £2.75.

e Explain briefly what would happen if the price were initially set at £1.

f Explain briefly what would happen if the price were initially set at £1.50.

2 The market for wine in the United Kingdom is initially in equilibrium with supply and demand curves of the usual shape. Beer is a close substitute for wine; cheese and wine are complements. Use demand and supply diagrams to analyse the effect of each of the following (separate) events on the equilibrium price and quantity traded in the UK wine market. Assume that all of the *ceteris paribus* assumptions continue to hold except for the event listed. For both price and quantity traded, you should indicate in each case whether the variable rises, falls, remains the same, or moves ambiguously (may rise or fall).

a The income of consumers falls (wine is a normal good).

b Early frost destroys a large part of the world grape crop.

c A new churning invention reduces the cost of producing cheese.

d A new fermentation technique is invented that reduces the cost of producing wine.

e A government study is published which suggests that wine drinking is linked to higher rates of heart disease.

f Costs of producing both beer and wine increase dramatically.

3 Table 4.2 lists the demand and supply schedules for cases of peanuts.

Table 4.2 Demand and Supply Schedules for Cases of Peanuts per Week

Price per case	Quantity demanded (cases)	Quantity supplied (cases)
£70	20	140
£60	60	120
£50	100	100
£40	140	80
£30	180	60

a Draw the demand and supply curves for peanuts. Be sure to label the axes properly. Label the demand and supply curves D_0 and S_0 respectively.

b What are the equilibrium price and quantity traded in the peanut market? On your diagram, label the equilibrium point *a*.

c Is there a surplus or a shortage at a price of £40? How much?

d Suppose the population grows sufficiently that the demand for peanuts increases by 60 cases per week at every price.
  i Construct a table (price, quantity demanded) of the new demand schedule.
  ii Draw the new demand curve on your original graph and label it D_1.
  iii Label the new equilibrium point *b*. What are the new equilibrium price and quantity traded?

DISCUSSION QUESTIONS

1 What is the difference between a move along a curve and a movement of a curve?

2 The law of demand and supply says that a fall in demand will lead to a fall in price. But observation would suggest that in the real world prices hardly ever fall. So how do we explain this difference?

DATA QUESTION

Do You Eat Beef?
The discovery of BSE in cattle had a devastating effect on the market for beef in the 1990s. After a good deal of prevarication, the British government announced that the disease could spread to humans. This caused the EU to ban the sale of British beef in the EU outside the UK. The ban was only lifted in 1999, and then only subject to very strict conditions. In the UK, the effect on consumption seemed only short-term, but it nudged many people into becoming vegetarians.

1 Draw a diagram to show the effect of BSE on the market for beef.

2 Who benefited from these developments?

ANSWERS

CONCEPT REVIEW

1 quantity demanded

2 price; lower

3 schedule; prices

4 highest

5 increases; increases; decreases; increases

6 normal; inferior

7 quantity supplied

8 higher; higher

9 price

10 left

11 increases; decreases; improvement; decreases

12 quantity supplied; upward

13 equilibrium

14 surplus; fall

15 increase; increase

16 decrease; increase

17 increase

TRUE OR FALSE

1 T As price rises, quantity demanded decreases.

2 T The law of demand states that as price falls, quantity increases.

3 F It will cause a movement *along* the curve.

4 T A meal of hamburger and chips is now cheaper.

5 F Supply curve shows minimum price at which last unit supplied.

6 T The demand curve holds constant all factors except quantity and price.

7 T More will be supplied at each price.

8 T An increase in the price of a factor of production leads to a fall in supply.

9 F Beef and leather are complements in production because they are produced together.

10 T For complements in production, an increase in the price of one good leads to an increase in quantity supplied and an increase in the supply of the other good.

11 T Price rises when demand exceeds supply.

12 F An increase in demand will lead to an increase in quantity.

13 T For inferior goods, an increase in income leads to a fall in demand and a fall in price.

14 F A decrease in supply will lead to a rise in price.

MULTIPLE CHOICE

1 c A fall in the price of a substitute causes an increased demand for the substitute and therefore a fall in demand for the other good.

2 a Beer and crisps can be regarded as complementary goods, hence a rise in the price of beer will mean a fall in demand for crisps.

3 b Changes in income shift the demand curve rather than causing moves along it.

4 b Definition.

5 d Decrease in quantity is caused by a change in price and a movement along a curve.

6 d Demand shifts left.

7 a Definition.

8 e **a**, **b** and **c** affect demand. **d** would cause a move along the supply curve.

9 a An increase in supply will shift the supply curve rightwards (more phones will be supplied at each price).

10 b A rise in the price of a factor shifts the supply curve left.

11 a As alternatives, they are substitutes.

12 e Definition.

13 a Shortage occurs when demand exceeds supply.

14 d Other answers make surplus larger.

15 d Demand shifts left.

16 b Demand shifts right.

17 e Supply shifts right and demand shifts left.

18 c Both shifts will increase quantity but have opposite effects on price.

19 c Both shifts will increase price.

SHORT ANSWER

1 Wants reflect our unlimited desires for goods and services without regard to our ability or willingness to make the sacrifices necessary to obtain them. The existence of scarcity means that many of those wants will not be satisfied. On the other hand, demands refer to plans to buy and, therefore, reflect decisions about which wants to satisfy.

2 The observation that the consumption of peanut butter increases at the same time as the price of peanut butter rises is entirely consistent with the law of demand (that is, a negatively-sloped demand curve). It simply reflects the fact that the demand for peanut butter has increased (that is, the demand curve has shifted out to the right).

3 Owing to the tremendous pace of technological advance, not only has the demand for personal computers been increasing, but the supply has been increasing as well. Indeed, supply has been increasing much more rapidly than demand, which has resulted in falling prices. Thus *much* (but not all) of the increase in sales of personal computers reflects a movement down along a demand curve rather than a shift in demand.

4 The answer to this question requires us to trace through the effects on the two graphs in Fig. 4.1(a) and (b) – one for the Brussels sprout market and one for the carrot market. The sequence of effects occurs in order of the numbers on the graphs.

Figure 4.1

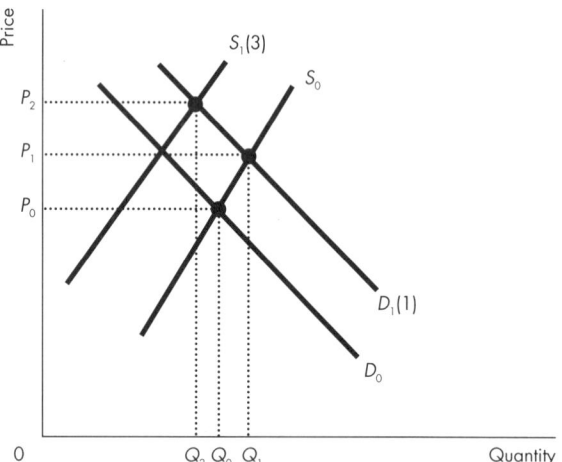

(a) Brussels sprouts

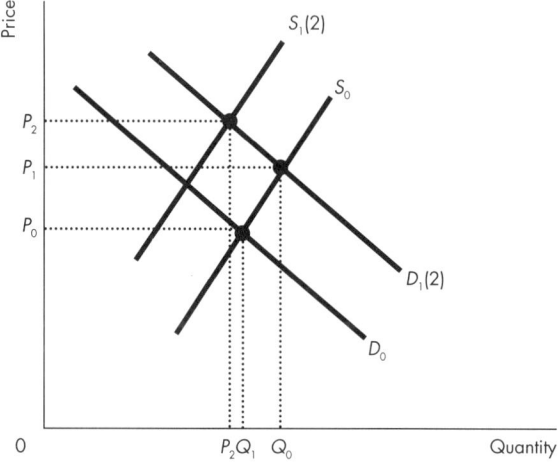

(b) Carrots

Look first at the market for Brussels sprouts. The increase in demand shifts the demand curve to the right from D_0 to D_1 (1), and the price of Brussels sprouts rises. This price rise has two effects (2) on the carrot market. Since Brussels sprouts and carrots are substitutes in consumption, the demand curve for carrots shifts to the right from D_0 to D_1. And, since Brussels sprouts and carrots are substitutes in production, the supply curve of carrots shifts to the left from S_0 to S_1. Both of these shifts in the carrot market raise the price of carrots, causing feedback effects on the Brussels sprout market. But remember the rule (Helpful Hint 4) that each curve (demand and supply) for a given market can shift a maximum of *once*. Since the demand curve for Brussels sprouts has already shifted, we can only shift the supply curve from S_0 to S_1 (3) because of the substitutes in production relationship. Each curve in each market has now shifted once and the analysis must stop. We can predict that the net effects are increases in the equilibrium prices of both Brussels sprouts and carrots, and indeterminate changes in quantities traded in both markets.

5 Most students consume fast food rather than cook every day. Hence other factors remaining unchecked, we would expect that more students would mean a shift in the demand curve for fast food to the right, leading to a rise in both price and quantity supplied.

PROBLEMS

1 a The demand and supply curves are shown in Fig. 4.2. The equilibrium price is £1.50 per fish.

Figure 4.2

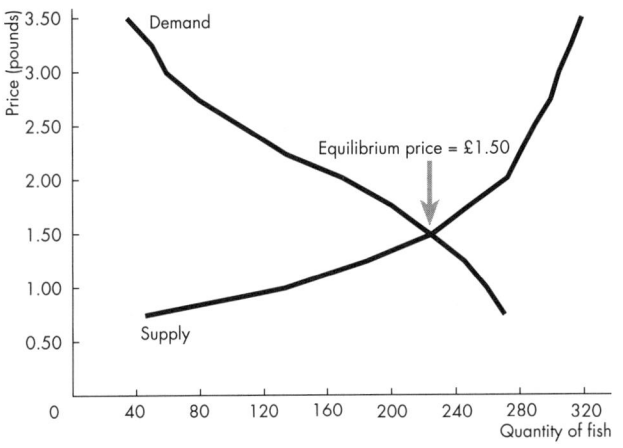

b Prices of other (related) goods; income; population; preferences.

c Prices of other (related) goods; prices of factors of production; technology.

d At a price of £2.75, quantity supplied (300) exceeds quantity demanded (80). Fish sellers find themselves with surplus fish. Rather than be stuck with unsold fish (which yield no revenue), some sellers cut their price in an attempt to increase the quantity of fish demanded. Competition forces other sellers to follow suit, and the price falls until it reaches the equilibrium price of £1.50, while quantity demanded increases until it reaches the equilibrium quantity of 225 units.

e At a price of £1, the quantity demanded (260) exceeds the quantity supplied (135) – there is a shortage. Unrequited fish buyers bid up the price in an attempt to get the 'scarce' fish. As prices continue to be bid up as long as there is excess demand, quantity supplied increases in response to higher prices. Price and quantity supplied both rise until they reach the equilibrium price (£1.50) and quantity (225 units).

f At a price of £1.50, the quantity supplied exactly equals the quantity demanded (225). There is no excess demand (shortage) or excess supply (surplus), and, therefore, no tendency for the price or quantity to change.

2 The demand and supply diagrams for parts (a) to (e) are shown in Fig. 4.3.

Questions like part (f) require the examination of two separate but related markets – the beer and wine markets. Since this kind of question often causes confusion for students, here is a more detailed explanation of the answer.

Figure 4.3

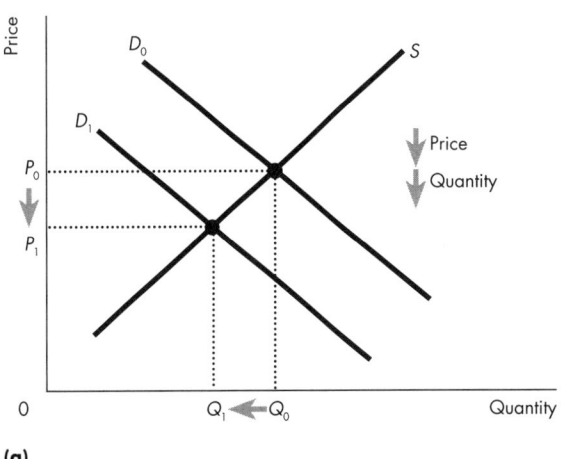

(a)

Figure 4.3

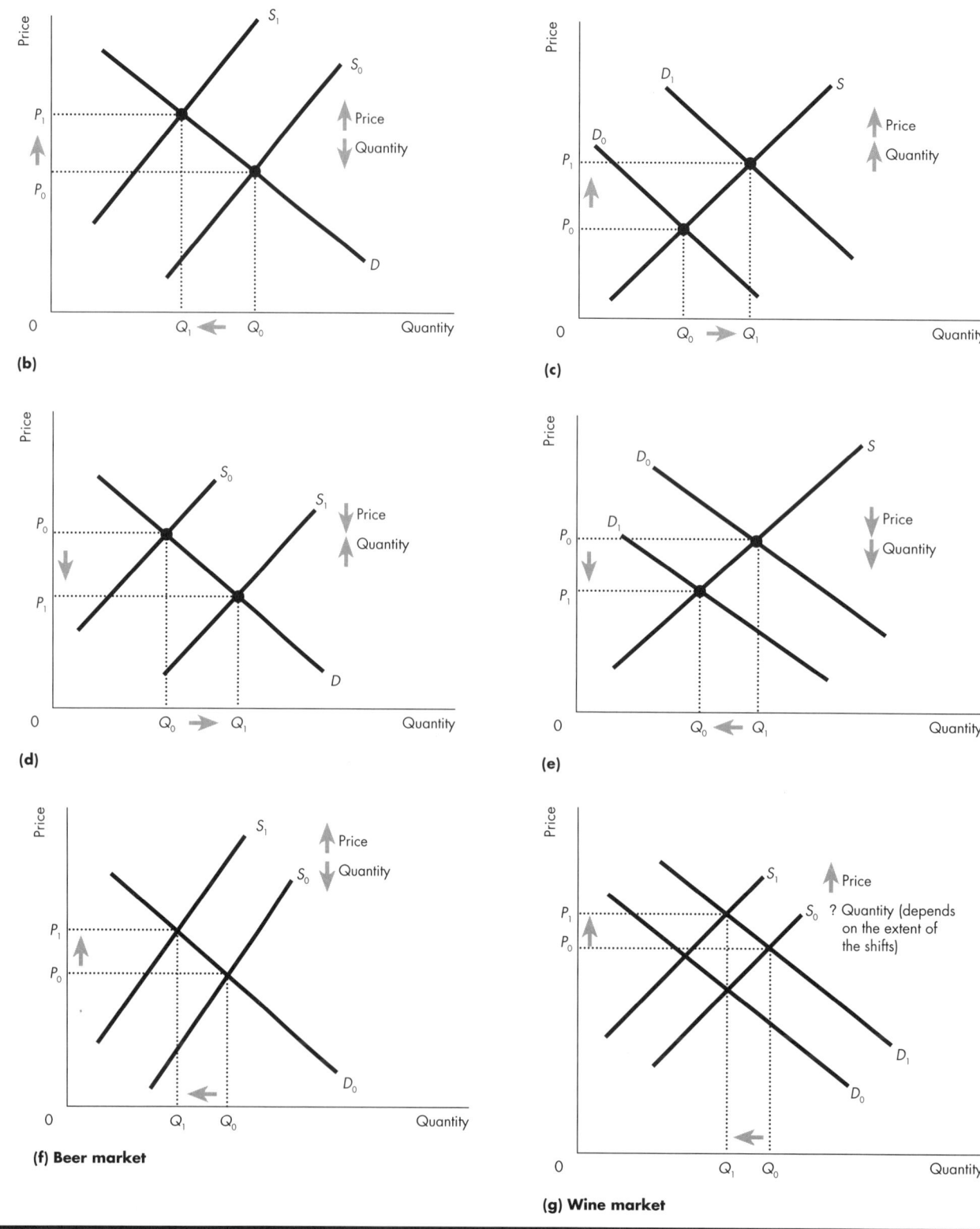

(b)

(c)

(d)

(e)

(f) Beer market

(g) Wine market

Look first at the beer market. The increase in the cost of beer production shifts up the supply curve of beer from S_0 to S_1. The resulting rise in the price of beer affects the wine market since beer and wine are substitutes (in consumption).

Turning to the wine market, there are two shifts to examine. The increase in beer prices causes the demand for wine to shift out from D_0 to D_1. The increase in the cost of wine production shifts up the supply curve of wine from S_0 to S_1. This is the end of the analysis, since the question asks only about the wine market. The final result is a rise in the price of wine and an ambiguous change in the quantity traded of wine.

Many students rightfully ask: 'But doesn't the rise in wine prices then shift out the demand curve for beer, causing a rise in beer prices and an additional increase in the demand for wine?' This question, which is correct in principle, is about the dynamics of adjustment, and these graphs are capable only of analysing once-over shifts of demand or supply. We could shift out the demand for beer, but the resulting rise in beer prices would lead us to shift the demand for wine a *second time*. In practice, stick to the rule that each curve (demand and supply) for a given market can shift a maximum of *once*.

3 a The demand and supply curves for peanuts are shown in Fig. 4.4.
  b The equilibrium is given at the intersection of the demand and supply curves (labelled point *a*). The equilibrium price is £50 per case and the equilibrium quantity traded is 100 cases per week.
  c At a price of £40 there is a shortage of 60 cases per week.
  d **i** Table 4.3 also contains the (unchanged) quantity supplied, for reference purposes.
  ii The graph of the new demand curve is shown in Fig. 4.4.
  iii The new equilibrium price is £60 per case and the quantity traded is 120 cases of peanuts per week.

Table 4.3   Demand and Supply Schedules for Cases of Peanuts per Week

Price per case	Quantity demanded (cases)	Quantity supplied (cases)
£70	80	140
£60	120	120
£50	160	100
£40	200	80
£30	240	60

Figure 4.4

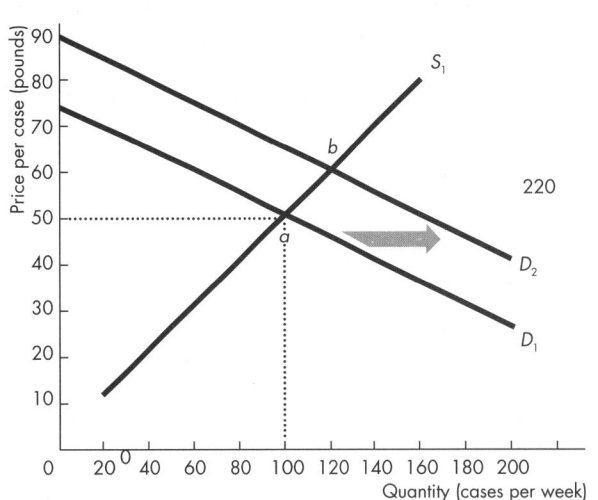

DISCUSSION QUESTIONS

1 The distinction between a shift in a curve and a movement along a curve is important.

The demand curve shows the relationship between two variables: price and quantity. A change in price will cause a movement along the demand curve. For example, a rise in price will cause a move down the demand curve. However, if there is a change in any of the other variables that affect the quantity of goods we buy (for example, incomes, competing or substitute goods or advertising in the case of demand) this will shift the entire curve. For example, a fall in our income will mean that we buy less of most goods. The demand curve's slope cannot show us this effect because the slope indicates the relationship between the price and the quantity demanded. Instead, the whole curve shifts, showing that (in this case) we will buy less whatever the price.

In this answer we have discussed the difference between a movement along the demand curve and a shift in the demand curve. Exactly the same arguments apply to the supply curve. A change in price will cause a movement along the curve. A change in something like the cost of production will cause the whole curve to shift.

2 The point about prices not usually falling in the real world but often doing so in economic models is explained by the fact that in the model we are predicting what will happen to *relative* prices. For example, if prices as a whole are rising by 5 per cent and the price of a particular good rises by only 2 per cent, then its relative price will have fallen. This is what the economic model predicts and, as relative price changes are frequent in the real economy, the model is extremely useful.

What causes prices as a whole to change is discussed later in the book when we talk about inflation.

DATA QUESTIONS

1 The effect is shown in Figure 4.5.

The result was a fall in the quality and the price of beef. Without government and EU support, beef farmers would have had greatly reduced income and large numbers would have gone out of business.

2 Beef producers outside the UK benefited. So did suppliers of foods which replaced beef.

Figure 4.5

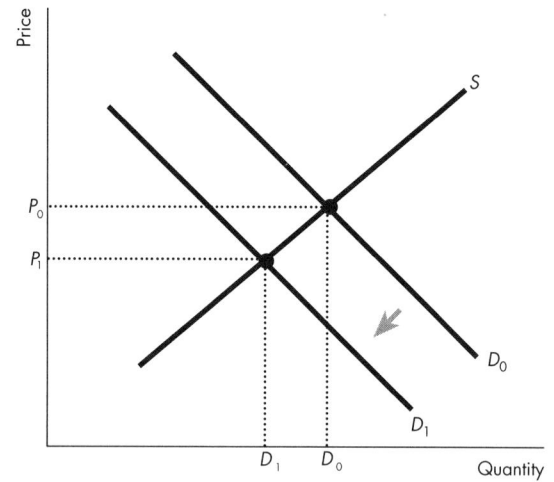

Chapter 5   **Elasticity**

Chapter in Perspective, Text Pages 96–117

Elasticity is a measure of the quantitative *responsiveness* of quantity demanded or supplied to changes in other key economic variables. Using different applications of elasticity, we can calculate how much quantity demanded will respond to changes in price, income, or changes in the prices of substitutes or complements, and by how much quantity supplied will respond to a change in price. Similarly, we can use the idea of elasticity to calculate the effect of a change in price on the quantity of a good that firms will be willing to supply.

    The elasticity concept is one of the most practical concepts in economics. It can help a company decide whether lowering the price of its product will increase or decrease total revenue from sales. It can also help a government policy maker estimate how much revenue a sales tax will raise.

Helpful Hints

1 There are many elasticity formulae in this chapter, but they are all based on *responsiveness*. All of the demand and supply elasticity formulae measure the *responsiveness (sensitivity) of quantity* (demanded or supplied) to changes in something else. Thus percentage change in quantity is always in the numerator of the relevant formula.

2 The complete formula for calculating the price elasticity of demand between two points on the demand curve is:

$$\eta = \left| \frac{\% \, \Delta \text{ quantity demanded}}{\% \, \Delta \text{ price}} \right|$$

$$= \left| \left(\frac{\Delta Q}{Q_{ave}} \right) \Big/ \left(\frac{\Delta P}{P_{ave}} \right) \right|$$

The law of demand assures us that price and quantity demanded always move in opposite directions along any demand curve. Thus without the absolute value sign, the formula for the price elasticity of demand would yield a negative number. Whenever you see the often-used shorthand term, *elasticity of demand*, remember that it means the absolute value of the *price* elasticity of demand.

3 Elasticity is *not* the same as slope (although they are related). Along a straight-line demand curve the slope is constant, but the elasticity varies from infinity to zero as we move down the demand curve.

4 One of the most practical and important uses of the concept of price elasticity of demand is that it allows us to predict the *effect on total revenue* of a change in price. A fall in price will increase total revenue if demand is elastic, leave total revenue unchanged if demand is unit elastic, and decrease total revenue if demand is inelastic. Because price and quantity demanded always move in opposite directions along a demand curve, a fall in price will cause an increase in quantity demanded. Since total revenue equals price × quantity, the fall in price will tend to decrease total revenue, while the increase in quantity demanded will increase total revenue. The net effect depends on which of these individual effects is larger.

The concept of price elasticity of demand conveniently summarizes the net effect. For example, if demand is elastic, the percentage change in quantity demanded is greater than the percentage change in price. Hence with a fall in price, the quantity effect dominates and total revenue will increase. If, however, demand is inelastic, the percentage change in quantity demanded is less than the percentage change in price. Hence with a fall in price, the price effect dominates and total revenue will decrease.

5 Two other important elasticity concepts are the income elasticity of demand and the cross elasticity of demand.

Income elasticity of demand:

$$\eta_Y = \frac{\% \, \Delta \text{ quantity demanded}}{\% \, \Delta \text{ income}}$$

$$= \left(\frac{\Delta Q}{Q_{ave}}\right) \Big/ \left(\frac{\Delta Y}{Y_{ave}}\right)$$

Cross elasticity of demand:

$$\eta_X = \frac{\% \, \Delta \text{ quantity demanded of good } A}{\% \, \Delta \text{ price of good } B}$$

$$= \left(\frac{\Delta Q^A}{Q^A_{ave}}\right) \Big/ \left(\frac{\Delta P^B}{P^B_{ave}}\right)$$

Notice that these two elasticity formulae do *not* have absolute value signs and can take on either positive or negative values. In the case of income elasticity of demand, the response of quantity demanded to an increase in income will be positive for a normal good and negative for an inferior good. In the case of cross elasticity of demand, the response of the quantity demanded of good A to an increase in the price of good B will be positive if the goods are substitutes and negative if the goods are complements.

6 We see the magnitude of the change when considering the price elasticity of demand. For other elasticities we use the actual number. That is because price elasticity is always negative. Other elasticities can be positive or negative. For example, a negative income elasticity indicates that the product is an inferior good.

SELF-TEST

CONCEPT REVIEW

1 A units-free measure of the responsiveness of quantity demanded to price changes is given by the _____ _____ of demand.

2 The (price) elasticity of demand is calculated as the percentage change in the _____ _____ divided by the percentage change in the _____ .

3 If the (price) elasticity of demand is between 0 and 1, demand is said to be _____ ; if it is greater than 1, demand is said to be _____ ; if it is equal to 1, demand is said to be _____ _____ .

4 A good that has many good substitutes is likely to have demand that is _____ . If only a small proportion of income is spent on a good, its demand is likely to be _____ .

5 As time passes after a change in the price of a good, demand will tend to become more _____ .

6 If demand is elastic, an increase in the price implies that revenue (expenditures) will _____ .

7 A measure of the responsiveness of the quantity demanded of a good to changes in income is given by the _____ _____ of demand.

8 The income elasticity of demand is calculated as the percentage change in the _____ _____ divided by the percentage change in _____ .

9 The income elasticity is _____ for inferior goods.

10 The responsiveness of the quantity demanded of one good to a change in the price of a complement or substitute is given by the _____ _____ of demand.

11 The cross elasticity of demand with respect to the price of a substitute is _____ . The cross elasticity of demand with respect to the price of a complement is _____ .

12 The elasticity of supply is a measure of the responsiveness of the _____ _____ to changes in _____ .

13 To illustrate the initial change in quantity supplied induced by a sudden change in price we use the _____ supply curve. To illustrate the response of quantity supplied after all technologically possible long-run adjustments in the production process have been made we use the _____ supply curve.

14 The long-run supply curve will generally be more _____ than a short-run supply curve, which will be more _____ than the momentary supply curve.

TRUE OR FALSE

1 The price elasticity of demand measures how responsive prices are to changes in demand.

2 A horizontal demand curve is perfectly inelastic.

3 The demand for petrol is likely to become more inelastic with the passage of time after a price increase.

4 If substitutes for a good are more readily available, demand for it will be more inelastic.

5 If total revenue falls following an increase in price, demand must be inelastic.

6 If your expenditures on toothpaste are a small proportion of your total income, your demand for toothpaste is likely to be inelastic.

7 The more narrowly we define a good, the more elastic is its demand.

8 Long-run demand is more inelastic than short-run demand because there is more opportunity for substitution.

9 If the income elasticity of the demand for turnips is positive, then turnips are an inferior good.

10 The effect of the change in the price of one good on the quantity demanded of another good is measured by the cross elasticity of demand.

11 We would expect the cross elasticity of demand between hamburgers and hot dogs to be negative.

12 If goods *A* and *B* are substitutes, then a decrease in the demand for *A* will lead to a decrease in the equilibrium price of *B*.

13 Supply will generally be more inelastic in the long run than in the short run.

14 For a linear demand curve, demand is more elastic at higher price ranges than at lower price ranges.

15 If a 10 per cent increase in the price of good *A* causes a 6 per cent decrease in the quantity of good *B* demanded, the cross elasticity of demand between *A* and *B* is 0.6.

16 If a 9 per cent increase in price leads to a 5 per cent decrease in quantity demanded, total revenue has decreased.

MULTIPLE CHOICE

1 Two points on the demand curve for volleyballs are shown in Table 5.1.

Table 5.1

Price per volleyball (pounds)	Quantity demanded
19	55
21	45

What is the elasticity of demand between these two points?

a 2.5
b 2.0
c 0.5
d 0.4
e none of the above

2 The fact that butter has margarine as a close substitute in consumption
a makes the supply of butter more elastic.
b makes the supply of butter less elastic.
c makes the demand for butter more elastic.
d makes the demand for butter less elastic.
e does not affect butter's elasticity of supply or demand.

3 If the price elasticity of demand is 2, then a 1 per cent decrease in price will
a double the quantity demanded.
b reduce the quantity demanded by half.
c increase the quantity demanded by 2 per cent.
d reduce the quantity demanded by 2 per cent.
e increase the quantity demanded by 0.5 per cent.

4 A good will have a more price inelastic demand
a the higher its price.
b the larger the percentage of income spent on it.
c the longer the time elapsed.
d if it is a luxury good.
e if it has no close substitutes.

5 If the demand for frozen orange juice is price elastic, then a severe frost that destroys large quantities of oranges is likely to
a reduce the equilibrium price of juice but increase total consumer spending on it.
b reduce the equilibrium quantity of juice as well as total consumer spending on it.
c reduce both the equilibrium quantity and the price of juice.
d increase the equilibrium price of juice as well as total consumer spending on it.
e increase the equilibrium price of juice but leave total consumer spending on it constant.

6 If a 4 per cent rise in the price of peanut butter causes the total revenue from peanut butter sales to fall by 8 per cent, then demand for peanut butter
a is elastic.

b is inelastic.
c is unit elastic.
d has an elasticity of 0.5.
e has an elasticity of 2.

7 Tina and Brian work for the same recording company. Tina claims that they would be better off by increasing the price of their tapes while Brian claims that they would be better off by decreasing the price. It can be concluded that
a Tina thinks the demand for tapes has price elasticity of zero and Brian thinks price elasticity equals one.
b Tina thinks the demand for tapes has price elasticity equal to one and Brian thinks price elasticity equals zero.
c Tina thinks the demand for tapes is price elastic and Brian thinks it is price inelastic.
d Tina thinks the demand for tapes is price inelastic and Brian thinks it is price elastic.
e Tina and Brian should stick to singing and forget about economics.

8 Given the relationship shown in Fig. 5.1 between total revenue from the sale of a good and the quantity of the good sold, then
a this is an inferior good.
b this is a normal good.
c the elasticity of demand is zero.
d the elasticity of demand is infinity.
e the elasticity of demand is one.

Figure 5.1

9 If an increase in price causes a decrease in total revenue then price elasticity of demand is

a negative.

b zero.

c greater than zero but less than one.

d equal to one.

e greater than one.

10 If a 4 per cent decrease in income (at a constant price) causes a 2 per cent decrease in the consumption of books then

a the income elasticity of demand for books is negative.

b books are a necessity and a normal good.

c books are a luxury and a normal good.

d books are an inferior good.

e **a** and **d** are true.

11 Luxury goods tend to have income elasticities of demand which are

a greater than one.

b greater than zero but less than one.

c positive.

d negative.

e first positive and then negative as income increases.

12 If a 10 per cent increase in income causes a 5 per cent increase in quantity demanded (at a constant price), what is the income elasticity of demand?

a 0.5

b −0.5

c 2.0

d −2.0

e none of the above

13 The cross elasticity of the demand for white tennis balls with respect to the price of yellow tennis balls is probably

a negative and high.

b negative and low.

c positive and high.

d positive and low.

e zero.

14 A decrease in the price of X from $6 to $4 causes an increase in the quantity of Y demanded (at the current price of Y) from 900 to 1,100 units. What is the cross elasticity of demand between X and Y?

a 0.5

b −0.5

c 2

d −2

e **a** or **b**, depending on whether X and Y are substitutes or complements

15 When price goes from $1.50 to $2.50, quantity supplied increases from 9,000 to 11,000 units. What is the price elasticity of supply?

a 0.4

b 0.8

c 2.5

d 4.0

e none of the above

16 The magnitude of *both* the elasticity of demand and the elasticity of supply depend on

a the ease of substitution between goods.

b the proportion of income spent on a good.

c the time elapsed since the price change.

d the technological conditions of production.

e none of the above factors.

17 The long-run supply curve is likely to be

a more elastic than momentary supply but less elastic than the short-run supply curve.

b less elastic than momentary supply but more elastic than the short-run supply curve.

c less elastic than both momentary and short-run supply curves.

d more elastic than both momentary and short-run supply curves.

e vertical.

18 All normal goods have

a income elasticities of demand greater than 1.0.

b price elasticities of demand greater than 1.0.

c negative price elasticities of demand.

d positive income elasticities of demand.

19 Suppose that the price elasticity of supply of pencils is 0.1. Then, if the price of pencils rises by 20 per cent, the quantity of pencils supplied will rise by

a 200 per cent.

b 20 per cent.

c 2 per cent.

d 0.2 per cent.

SHORT ANSWER

1 In each of the following, compare the price elasticity of demand for each pair of goods and explain why demand for one of the goods is more elastic than demand for the other.

a IBM personal computers before the development of other 'clone' personal computers versus IBM personal computers after the production of such clones

b Television sets versus matches

c Electricity just after an increase in its price versus electricity two years after the price increase

2 Why does demand tend to be more elastic in the long run?

3 Why does supply tend to be more elastic in the long run?

4 Which demand curve in Fig. 5.2 (D_A or D_B) is more elastic in the price range P_1 to P_2? Explain why. [*Hint:* use the formula for price elasticity of demand.]

Figure 5.2

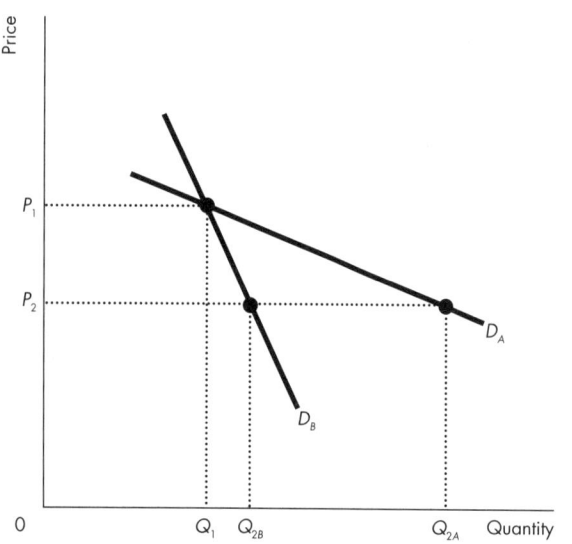

5 In *Reading Between the Lines*, explain

a why some markets can be described as 'cut throat'.

b how knowledge of price elasticity can lead to the 'rewards of a better pricing strategy'.

PROBLEMS

1 a Given the demand curve in Fig. 5.3, complete the second and third columns of the table in

this figure: η (the price elasticity of demand) and ΔTR (the change in total revenue) as the price falls from the higher price to the lower price. Describe the relationship between elasticity and change in total revenue as price falls (moving down the demand curve).

Figure 5.3

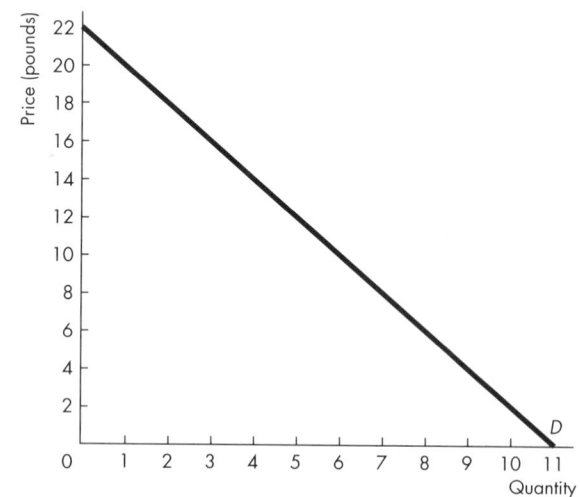

ΔP (pounds)	η	ΔTR (pounds)	η	$\Delta TR'$ (pounds)
16–14				
14–12				
12–10				
10–8				
8–6				

b Suppose income, which initially was £10,000, increases to £14,000, causing an increase in demand: at every price, quantity demanded increases by 2 units. Draw the new demand curve and label it D'. Use this new demand curve to complete the last two columns of the table in Fig. 5.3 for η (the new price elasticity of demand) and $\Delta TR'$ (the new change in total revenue).

c Using the price range between £16 and £14, explain why D' is more inelastic than D.

d Calculate the income elasticity of demand, assuming the price remains constant at £12. Is this a normal or an inferior good? Explain why you could have answered the question even without calculating the income elasticity of demand.

2 Table 5.2 gives the demand schedules for good A when the price of good B (P_B) is £8 and when the price of good B is £12. Complete the last column of the table by computing the cross elasticity of demand between goods A and B for each of the three prices of A. Are A and B complements or substitutes?

Table 5.2 Demand Schedules for Good A

	$P_B = £8$	$P_B = £12$	
P_A	Q_A	Q'_A	η_X
8	2,000	4,000	
7	4,000	6,000	
6	6,000	8,000	

DISCUSSION QUESTION

1 'The mathematics for calculating the elasticity of demand are not necessary; the slope of a diagram will do just as well.' Discuss.

DATA QUESTIONS

Table 5.3 gives figures of income elasticity of various foods.

Table 5.3

	Income elasticity
All foods	−0.01
Frozen convenience meats	−0.36
Fresh fruit	0.48
Fruit juices	0.94
Bread	−0.25
Tea	−0.56
Coffee	0.23

Source: Adapted from *Household Food Consumption and Expenditure Report*, Ministry of Agriculture, Fisheries and Food, 1990.

1 Explain what is meant by 'income elasticity of demand'.

2 What is meant by saying that the income elasticity of all foods is −0.01?

3 Assume that incomes continue to rise in the next few years and that income elasticities of demand remain constant. What will be the effect on firms producing the goods mentioned in the table?

ANSWERS

CONCEPT REVIEW

1 price elasticity

2 quantity demanded; price

3 inelastic; elastic; unit elastic

4 elastic; inelastic

5 elastic

6 decrease

7 income elasticity

8 quantity demanded; income

9 negative

10 cross elasticity

11 positive; negative

12 quantity supplied; price

13 momentary; long-run

14 elastic; elastic

TRUE OR FALSE

1 F It measures the responsiveness of quantity to changes in price.

2 F Definition.

3 F Elasticity increases as time passes.

4 F More substitutes lead to greater elasticity.

5 F Revenue increases when price rises and demand is elastic.

6 T The smaller the proportion of income spent on a good, the lower the elasticity.

7 T Narrow definitions are associated with more substitutes.

8 F In the long run more substitutes will be produced.

9 F For inferior goods, as income increases less is demanded.

10 T Definition.

11 F Cross elasticity is positive for substitutes.

12 T Follows from definition.

13 F Supply becomes more elastic in the long run.

14 T Elasticity changes along a straight line.

15 F Cross elasticity is *minus* 0.6.

16 F Percentage increase in price is greater than the percentage fall in quantity, so total revenue increases.

MULTIPLE CHOICE

1 b $(-10/50)/(2/20) = -2$

2 c Closer substitutes lead to more elastic demand.

3 c Q and P are always inversely related on demand curve.

4 e a and **d** irrelevant, elasticity falls with smaller proportion of income spent on a good and shorter elapsed time.

5 b Supply curve will shift to the left; the rise in price will lead to a bigger fall in demand.

6 a If increase in price leads to a fall in total revenue, elasticity must be greater than one.

7 d Better off means increased total revenue. If demand is elastic a price cut will increase revenue.

8 e Note total revenue on y-axis. Since total revenue is constant as quantity increases (and presumably price falls), elasticity = 1.

9 e Definition.

10 b Income elasticity >0, so normal good. Necessities tend to have income elasticity <1.

11 a See previous answer. **c** is correct, but **a** is best answer.

12 a Positive, because income and price move in the same direction.

13 c Close substitutes, so cross elasticity is positive and high.

14 b Substituting into formula gives $(200/1,000)/(-2/5)$ $= -0.5$.

15 a Substituting into formula gives $(2,000/10,000)/(1/2) =$ 0.4.

16 c a and **b** affect price elasticity only; **d** affects supply elasticity only.

17 d Definition. Momentary supply curve most vertical.

18 d An increase in income increases the demand for a normal good.

19 c Percentage change in quantity supplied = price elasticity of supply × percentage change in price = $(0.1) × (20$ per cent$) = 2$ per cent.

SHORT ANSWER

1 a The demand for IBM personal computers will be more elastic after the production of clone personal computers since there would then be more readily available substitutes.

b The demand for television sets will be more elastic since they will generally take a larger proportion of consumer income.

c The demand for electricity after the passage of two years will be more elastic since consumers will have more time to find substitutes for electricity (for example, a gas stove).

2 Demand is more responsive to price changes (more elastic) in the long run because more substitutes become available to consumers. Not only are new goods invented but consumers also learn about and begin to use new substitutes.

3 Supply is more elastic in the long run because the passage of time allows producers to find better (more efficient) ways of producing that are not available in the short run. The responsiveness of production to an increase in price will increase as firms have time to discover and implement new technologies or to increase the scale of operation.

4 D_A is more elastic than D_B. To see why, look at the formula for price elasticity of demand:

$$\eta = \left| \frac{\% \Delta \text{ quantity demanded}}{\% \Delta \text{ price}} \right|$$

The percentage change in price is the same for the two demand curves. But the percentage change in quantity is greater for D_A. At P_1, the initial quantity demanded is the same for both demand curves (Q_1). With the fall in price to P_2, the increase in quantity demanded is greater for D_A (to Q_{2A}) than for D_B (to Q_{2B}). Therefore D_A is more elastic than D_B. (See Fig. 5.4.)

5 a 'Cut throat' implies that sellers are forced to cut prices. This would be the case where competition is strong, and also where price elasticity of demand is high. This would mean that any seller with higher prices would sell very little.

b Where demand for a good is inelastic, firms can increase their prices without losing much custom. Hence revenue will rise when they increase prices. Where demand is elastic, total revenue will be increased if prices are cut, but whether or not this is profitable will depend on other factors such as what happens to costs when output rises.

PROBLEMS

1 a The completed columns of the table attached to Fig. 5.3 are shown here in Table 5.4. The second and third columns of the table show that as price falls, total revenue increases when demand is elastic; total revenue remains constant when demand is unit elastic; total revenue falls when demand is inelastic.

Figure 5.4

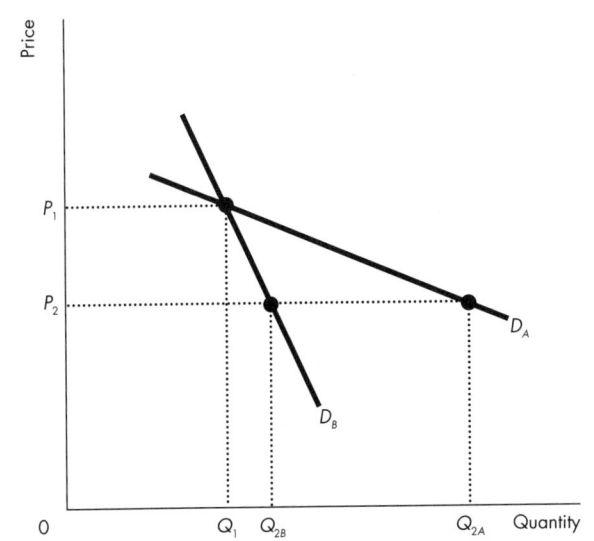

Table 5.4

ΔP (pounds)	η	ΔTR (pounds)	η	ΔTR' (pounds)
16–14	2.14	+8	1.36	+4
14–12	1.44	+4	1.00	0
12–10	1.00	0	0.73	−4
10–8	0.69	−4	0.53	−8
8–6	4.67	−8	0.37	−12

Figure 5.5

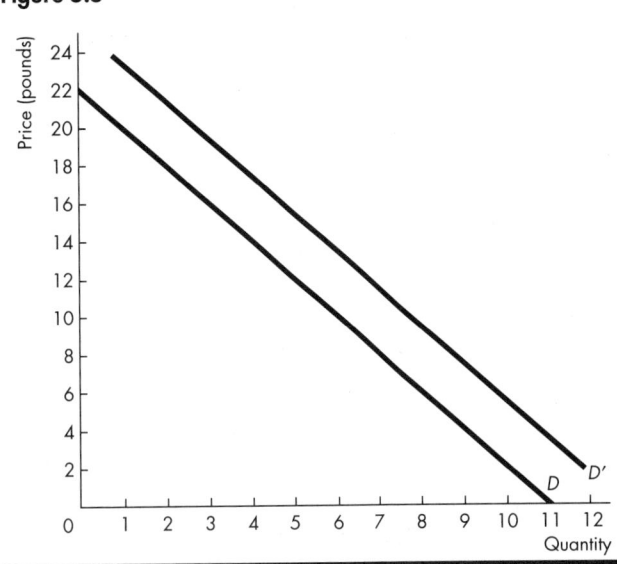

b The new demand curve is labelled D' (Fig. 5.5). The last two columns of the table have been completed on the basis of the new demand curve.

c Since they are parallel, D' and D have exactly the same slope. Thus we know that for a given change in price, the change in quantity demanded will be the same for the two curves. However, elasticity is determined by *percentage* changes, and the percentage change in quantity demanded is different for the two curves (although the percentage change in price will be the same). For a given percentage change in price, the percentage change in quantity demanded will always be less for D'. For example, as the price falls from £16 to £14 (a 13 per cent change), the quantity demanded increases from 5 to 6 units along D' but from 3 to 4 units along D. The percentage change in quantity demanded is only 18 per cent along D' and 29 per cent along D. Since the percentage change in price is the same for both curves, D' is more inelastic than D.

d Income increases from £10,000 to £14,000. At a constant price of £12, the increase in income, which shifts out the demand curve to D', increases the quantity consumers will demand from 5 units to 7 units. Substituting these numbers into the formula for the income elasticity of demand yields:

$$\eta_Y = \left(\frac{\Delta Q}{Q_{ave}}\right) \bigg/ \left(\frac{\Delta Y}{Y_{ave}}\right)$$

$$= \left(\frac{2}{6}\right) \bigg/ \left(\frac{4,000}{12,000}\right) = +1$$

The income elasticity of demand is a positive number, since both Q and Y are positive. Therefore this is a normal good. We already knew that from the information in part (b), which stated that the demand curve shifted out to the right with an increase in income. If this were an inferior good, the increase in income would have shifted the demand curve in to the left, and the income elasticity of demand would have been negative.

2 The cross elasticities of demand between A and B are listed in the table. Since the cross elasticities are positive, we know that A and B are substitutes.

DISCUSSION QUESTION

1 It is true that the slope of a diagram is a useful quick way to discuss elasticity, but it is imprecise. Changing the scale on the axes will change the slope of the curve and so might give a misleading impression. Numerical answers avoid this difficulty.

Table 5.5 Demand Schedules for Good A

P_A	$P_B = £8$ Q_A	$P_B = £12$ Q'_A	η_X
8	2,000	4,000	1.67
7	4,000	6,000	1.00
6	6,000	8,000	0.71

DATA QUESTIONS

1 Income elasticity of demand is a measure of the responsiveness of demand for a good to a change in income.

2 When we say that the income elasticity of demand for all food is –0.01 we mean that as incomes rise there is little effect on the demand for foods as a whole, although this conceals some significant changes in the demand for particular foods. This is not surprising; if our incomes doubled, most of us would not double our food consumption, although we might eat more of some luxury foods.

3 If incomes rise while income elasticities remain unchanged, then sales of goods such as fresh fruit and fruit juice will rise faster than incomes. Hence producers of such goods will prosper, other things remaining the same. However, producers of goods with negative income elasticities will find that their sales fall.

Chapter 6 — Efficiency and Equity

Chapter in Perspective, Text Pages 118–139

This chapter considers two of the most important concepts in modern life. An inefficient economy would mean that we were all poorer, since the economy would be producing fewer goods, or the wrong sort of goods. Equity is also important, since fairness is clearly more desirable than the alternative. Behind the seemingly simple ideas of efficiency and equity lie some interesting ideas that are clarified in this chapter.

Helpful Hints

1 This chapter states that producing where marginal benefit (MB) equals marginal cost (MC) gives the efficient level of production. It might seem more reasonable to produce where MB exceeds MC. However, producing where MB exceeds MC does not give the efficient level of output. The reason is that as long as people value another unit of the good more than it costs to produce the good, that is MB>MC, society's total surplus increases if the good is produced.

Figure 6.1 illustrates this conclusion. In it, the first unit has a large difference between MB and MC, equal to the length of a long grey arrow. The second unit also has MB greater than MC but by less than the first unit, as indicated by the shorter grey arrow. However, producing this unit still adds to society's *total* net surplus; it just adds less than the first unit. As long as MB is larger than MC, the

Figure 6.1

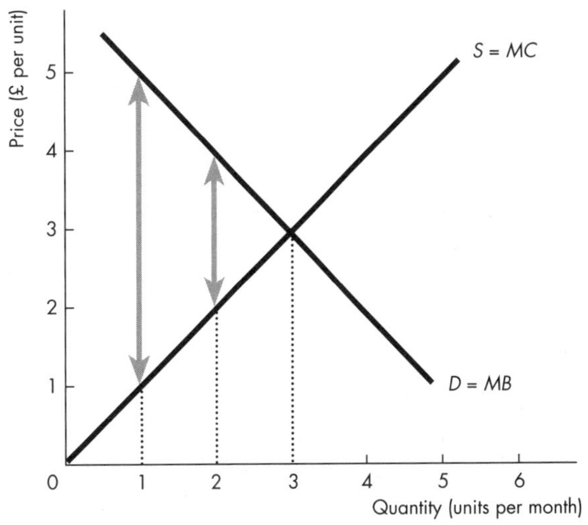

unit has a greater value to someone than its cost of production, so the unit should be produced. When MB=MC production should stop expanding because beyond this point the marginal benefit from more units falls short of their marginal costs.

2 In casual conversion we talk about 'how much a good cost us'. We also talk about 'how much a

firm benefited by selling us the good'. But be careful not to confuse conversation with the precise language of economic science. In particular, the marginal benefit from a good is received by the consumer and the marginal cost is paid by the producer. It is the consumer of the good who benefits from the product. You, when you drive your car, benefit from your car. It is the producer of the good who pays for the production.

SELF-TEST

CONCEPT REVIEW

1 An efficient allocation of resources occurs when we produce the _____ and _____ that people value most highly.

2 The marginal _____ from a good or service is the maximum amount that a person is willing to pay for one more unit of it.

3 If the marginal benefit of producing a good exceeds the marginal _____ , we can use resources more efficiently by producing more of it and decreasing the production of goods _____ .

4 _____ surplus is the value of a good minus the price paid for it.

5 The demand curve shows _____ benefit.

6 _____ surplus is the price of a good minus the opportunity cost of producing it.

7 Price _____ and floors, taxes, monopoly, public _____ and externalities all result in a market producing an inefficient quantity.

8 John Rawls says that the fair distribution of the economic pie is the one that makes the _____ person as well off as possible.

9 Resources will be allocated efficiently if private _____ rights are enforced; if exchange takes place in a _____ market and there are no market or government failures.

TRUE OR FALSE

___ **1** Resource use is efficient when the goods with the lowest opportunity costs are produced.

___ **2** As more of a product is consumed, its marginal benefit decreases.

___ **3** Resource efficiency requires that the marginal benefit of a good equal its marginal cost.

___ **4** Consumer surplus equals the area above the demand curve and below the market price.

___ **5** The supply curve and the marginal benefit curve are the same.

___ **6** Producer surplus equals the price of the good minus the opportunity cost of producing the unit.

___ **7** A competitive market is always efficient.

___ **8** Deadweight loss comprises a loss of consumer surplus and/or producer surplus.

___ **9** Utilitarianism says that a competitive market producing the efficient quantity is always fair.

MULTIPLE CHOICE

1 In general, resources are used efficiently when
 a the opportunity cost of the goods being produced is as low as possible.
 b marginal benefits from a good exceed its marginal cost by as much as possible.

c the goods produced are those valued most highly.

d none of the above.

2 The marginal benefit curve for a product is the same as the good's

a marginal cost curve.

b supply curve.

c demand curve.

d consumer surplus curve.

3 Susan is willing to pay £3.00 for the second slice of pizza she eats. The price she actually pays is £2.00. Susan's consumer surplus for this slice of pizza equals

a £3.00.

b £2.00.

c £1.50.

d £1.00.

4 Because of decreasing marginal benefit, the consumer surplus from the first unit of a good is _____ the consumer surplus from the second unit.

a greater than

b equal to

c less than

d not comparable to

5 The cost of producing one more unit of a good is the good's

a price.

b marginal benefit.

c marginal cost.

d producer surplus.

6 The supply curve shows the

a minimum price suppliers must receive in order to produce another unit of the good.

b maximum price suppliers must receive in order to produce another unit of the good.

c amount of producer surplus suppliers receive.

d profit that suppliers receive from producing another unit of the good.

7 The producer surplus from a good is equal to the

a maximum amount a consumer is willing to pay for the good minus the price that actually must be paid.

b actual price of the good minus the maximum amount a consumer is willing to pay for the good.

c opportunity cost of producing the good minus its price.

d price of the good minus its opportunity cost of production.

Is the competitive market efficient?

Figure 6.2 illustrates a perfectly competitive market without any external costs, external benefits, taxes, subsidies, quotas, price ceilings, or price floors. Use Fig. 6.2 for the next two questions.

Figure 6.2

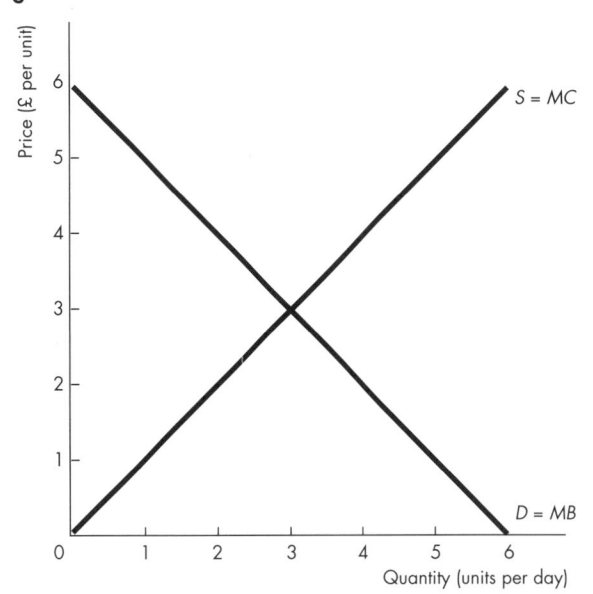

8 The equilibrium quantity produced equals

a 0 units.

b 3 units.

c 6 units.

d none of the above.

9 The efficient quantity equals

a 0 units.

b 3 units.

c 6 units.

d none of the above.

10 A deadweight loss

a is possible only if the good is underproduced, but is not possible if the good is overproduced.

b subtracts only from producer surplus.

c is a loss to consumers and a gain to producers.

d is a loss inflicted on the entire society.

11 Suppose consumers decide they value a product more highly than before. Then the efficiency quantity to produce of that product

a increases.
b does not change.
c decreases.
d perhaps changes, but without more information the direction of the change cannot be told.

SHORT ANSWER

1 What is the relationship between the marginal benefit of a good, its value and the maximum amount that a consumer is willing to pay for the good?

2 What is a deadweight loss?

3 Use the *Reading Between the Lines* article to argue the case for and against retail price maintenance in the case of over-the-counter drugs.

PROBLEMS

1 **a** Table 6.1 presents the marginal benefit and marginal cost schedules for video games. There are no external cost or benefits. Based on Table 6.1, complete Table 6.2.
b In Fig. 6.3 draw the marginal benefit and marginal cost curves from Table 6.1.
c What is the efficient number of video games to produce?

Figure 6.3

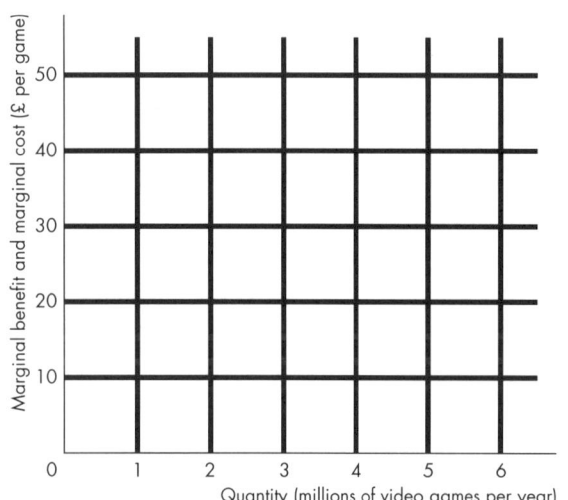

Table 6.1
Marginal Benefit and Marginal Cost of Video Games

Quantity (millions of video games)	Marginal benefit (pounds per game)	Marginal cost (pounds per game)
1	50	10
2	40	20
3	30	30
4	20	40
5	10	50

Table 6.2

Quantity (millions of video games)	Marginal benefit minus marginal cost
1	
2	
3	
4	
5	

2 **a** Use the data in Table 6.1 to draw the demand curve for video games and the supply curve for video games in Fig. 6.3.
b There are no price ceilings, price floors, taxes, subsidies, or quotas in this market. The market is also competitive, that is, it is not a monopoly. What quantity of video games will be produced?
c Compare your answer to part [c] of problem 2 with your answer to part [c] of problem 1.

3 **a** The market for mushrooms is competitive. There are no external benefits or external costs and there are no government policies, such as taxes or subsidies, affecting the market. The equilibrium quantity of mushrooms is 10 million kilos a year. If resources are being used efficiently, what is the efficient quantity of mushrooms?
b What would be the loss if 11 million kilos of mushrooms are grown?
c If someone claims that the efficient quantity isn't fair because it is too small, what concept of fairness is this?

DISCUSSION QUESTION

1 Can you reconcile the ideas that resources are limited and that we overproduce some goods?

DATA QUESTION

Post codes chart growing income divide
Paul Baldwin
Liverpool is the poorest place in the country according to a new survey. Way over 80 per cent of households in parts of Liverpool, in Middlesbrough, Leicester and central Belfast get by on less than £13,000 a year.

In contrast, households in some areas of London such as the Barbican and Blackfriars have incomes of over £47,000. The postcode area with the highest household incomes was EC4Y7 – the Temple area of London with average incomes of £51,900 per household. The poorest postcode area was Birkenhead where average household income was only £9,000.
Source: *The Guardian*, 25 October 1999, p. 5.

1 Do you think that this distribution of income is fair?

ANSWERS

CONCEPT REVIEW

1 goods; services

2 benefit

3 cost; forgone

4 consumer

5 marginal

6 producer

7 ceilings; goods

8 poorest

9 property; competitive

TRUE OR FALSE

1 F Resources are used efficiently when they produce goods valued most highly.

2 T The principle of decreasing marginal benefit states that as more of a good is consumed its marginal benefit decreases.

3 T The fact that marginal benefit equals marginal cost shows that resources are being used efficiently.

4 F Consumer surplus equals the area under the demand curve and above the price.

5 F The supply curve is the same as the marginal cost curve.

6 T Definition.

7 F A competitive market is not always efficient; for example, if the government has imposed taxes or if there are externalities.

8 T A deadweight loss is a total loss to society.

9 F Utilitarianism suggests that income should be redistributed from rich to poor. It does not claim that efficiency is fair.

MULTIPLE CHOICE

1 c Efficiency occurs when the goods people value most highly are the goods being produced.

2 c The marginal benefit is the maximum that someone is willing to pay for an extra unit. It is therefore the same as the demand curve which also shows this.

3 d Consumer surplus is the difference between the maximum she is willing to pay minus what she actually pays.

4 a The maximum a consumer is willing to pay for the first unit of a good is greater than the amount that they are willing to pay for additional amounts.

5 c Definition.

6 a The supply curve shows the minimum price for which a unit of output will be produced. Because the minimum price is the marginal cost of the unit, it is the same as the marginal cost curve.

7 d Producer surplus accrues to suppliers. Answer *d* is the definition of producer surplus.

8 b The quantity produced is determined by the intersection of the demand and supply curves.

9 b The efficient quantity is determined by the intersection of the marginal benefit and marginal cost curves.

10 d No one benefits from a deadweight loss.

11 a When a good is valued more highly, the marginal benefit increases so efficiency requires more of the good to be produced.

SHORT ANSWER

1 The marginal benefit of a good is defined as the good's value. The value of a good is the maximum that someone is willing to pay for it. So, the three terms are interchangeable.

2 A deadweight loss is the loss to society when resources are used inefficiently. No one benefits from a deadweight loss.

3 The case for maintaining prices is that without it many small chemists would go out of business, causing unemployment. This would make it more difficult for many people to buy these drugs and all the other things that people buy from chemists.

On the other hand, these drugs have a high mark-up; allowing supermarkets to sell them would lead to lower prices.

PROBLEMS

Table 6.3

Quantity (millions of video games)	Marginal benefit minus marginal cost
1	40
2	20
3	0
4	−20
5	−40

1 a See completed Table 6.3. For each quantity, the answer in the table is obtained by subtracting the marginal benefit from the marginal cost.

b Figure 6.4 shows the marginal benefit and marginal schedules.

c Both the table and the figure demonstrate that the efficient number of video games is 3 million because this quantity sets the marginal benefit from an additional game equal to the game's marginal cost.

Figure 6.4

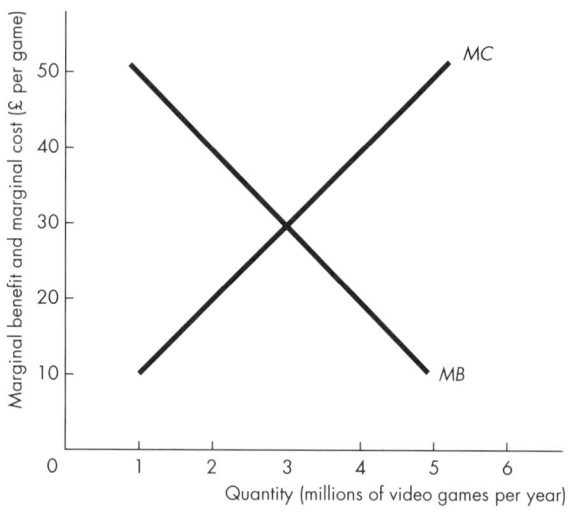

2 a Figure 6.5 shows the demand and supply curves for video games. The key point in drawing Fig. 6.5 is the fact that the demand curve, D, is the same as the marginal benefit curve, MB, and the supply curve, S, is the same as the marginal cost curve, MC. These equivalencies are noted in the figure.

b The quantity produced is 3 million video games, determined by where the supply and demand curves cross.

c The two answers are identical, 3 million video games. In other words, the efficient quantity of video games is the same as the quantity actually produced.

Figure 6. 5

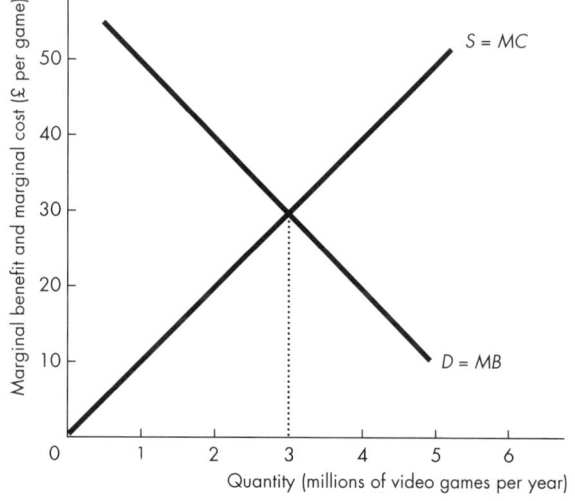

3 **a** The efficient quantity of mushrooms to produce is 10 million kilos a year. Why? The mushroom market meets all the criteria to be efficient: it is a competitive market, there are no externalities, and there are no government policies (such as price controls or taxes) that cause the amount produced to differ from the equilibrium quantity. So the amount produced, the equilibrium quantity, is the efficient amount.

 b Figure 6.6 shows the deadweight loss from producing 11 million kilos of mushrooms. The deadweight loss exists because past 10 million kilos of mushrooms, the value people place on an additional kilo of mushrooms – their marginal benefit – is less than the cost to produce an additional kilo – the marginal cost. Hence all the kilos past 10 million subtract from the gains from trade, and the amount subtracted is equal to the deadweight loss.

 c This argument is using the result (not enough mushrooms) to judge fairness; i.e. the concept of 'it isn't fair if the result isn't fair'.

DISCUSSION QUESTION

1 It is clear that goods and services are limited – we can all think of things that we would like but can't have. But if society produced more of the goods that you or I want, then we would produce less of other goods – remember the production possibility cure? The crucial concept here is opportunity cost.

DATA QUESTION

1 There is no right or wrong answer to this question. Some people would answer instinctively that such gross disparities of income are not desirable whilst others would suggest that income differences are essential in market economies.

More sophisticated answers would bring in the ideas of writers such as Rawls who suggests that the incomes of rich people should be taxed and income transferred to the poor. However, taxes should not be so high that they result in falling national income, which would make poor people even poorer.

On the other hand, Nozick suggests that fairness means that the state should protect private property and that this should only be transferred from one person to another by voluntary agreement. You must decide which approach leads to fairness.

Figure 6.6

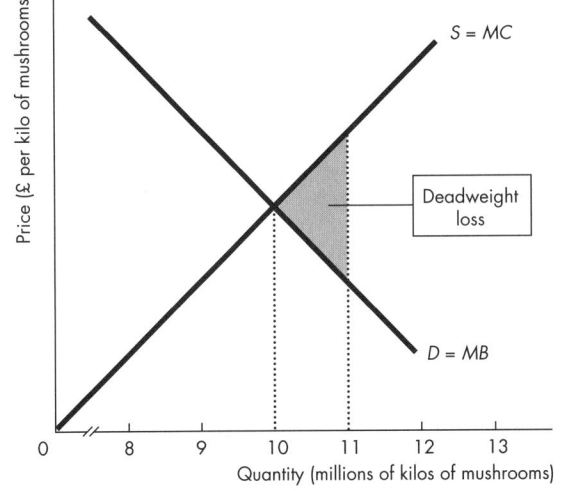

Chapter 7   **Markets in Action**

Chapter in Perspective, Text Pages 140–165

This chapter extends the theory of demand and supply by focusing on markets in action. In particular, it examines various types of government intervention in the economy. This can take several forms. Governments intervene in markets such as housing and labour because they believe that markets fail. Hence they introduce schemes such as minimum wage legislation to help low-paid workers. They intervene on a huge scale by imposing taxes on goods and services. Governments also affect markets by prohibiting some products, particularly drugs, and the chapter examines the effect that this has on the quantity and price of such products.

    The chapter also examines another type of intervention: that of the European Union in the market for agricultural products.

Helpful Hints

1 In the real world we frequently observe market regulation by governments in the form of price constraints of one type or another so it is important to study the effects of such regulation in its own right. Another significant benefit of exploring the effects of government regulation, however, is a clearer and deeper understanding of how markets work when, by contrast, the government does *not* affect the normal operation of markets.

    Whenever something happens to disturb an equilibrium in an unregulated (free) market, the desires of buyers and sellers are brought back into balance by price movements. If prices are controlled by government regulation, however, the price mechanism can no longer serve this purpose. Thus 'balance' must be restored in some other way. In the case of price ceilings, black markets are likely to arise. If black markets cannot develop because of strict enforcement of the price ceiling, then demanders will be forced to bear the costs of increased search activity, waiting in queues, or something else.

2 In any market with a legal price ceiling set below the market-clearing price, we will observe excess quantity demanded, because the price cannot increase to eliminate it. As a consequence, the value of the last unit of the good available will exceed the controlled price, and therefore demanders are willing to engage in costly activities up to the value of that last unit (for example, search activity, queuing and black market activity) in order to obtain the good.

Furthermore, if the price is allowed to increase in response to a decrease in supply or an increase in demand, there are incentive effects for suppliers to produce more and demanders to purchase less (that is, movements along the supply and demand curves). Indeed, it is the response to these incentives that restores equilibrium in markets with freely adjusting prices. If, however, the price cannot adjust, these price-induced incentive effects do not have a chance to operate.

3 Many people believe that when the government imposes or increases a sales tax (such as VAT), consumers pay all the tax. This is a fallacy. If firms tried to put up prices to include all the tax, some consumers would cease to buy the product. This is particularly true when demand is very elastic. In this case, supplies absorb most of the tax.

SELF-TEST

CONCEPT REVIEW

1 In an unregulated housing market, a sudden decrease in the supply of housing would cause rent to _____ in the short run and thus create an incentive for the construction of new housing to _____ in the long run.

2 A(n) _____ _____ is a regulation making it illegal to charge a rent higher than a specified level.

3 If a price ceiling is below the market clearing price, an excess quantity _____ of the relevant good will exist. In such a situation two mechanisms will tend to arise in order to achieve equilibrium. We will observe an increase in _____ activity as demanders spend more time trying to find a seller. In addition, illegal markets, called _____ markets, may arise in order to satisfy demand.

4 The invention of a new labour-saving technology will cause the demand curve for unskilled labour to shift to the _____. If the labour market is unregulated, the wage rate will _____ .

5 Unemployment will be created if a legal minimum wage is established, which is _____ the market clearing wage rate.

6 A tax on expenditure will lead to a(n) _____ in price and a(n) _____ in quantity.

7 Taxes can create a _____ loss and inefficiency.

TRUE OR FALSE

—— **1** In an unregulated housing market, higher rents will result in an increase in the quantity of housing supplied.

—— **2** When rents in an unregulated housing market rise owing to a decrease in supply, people who are unable to pay the higher rents will not get housing.

—— **3** In a housing market with rent ceilings, there will be a strong incentive to construct new housing.

—— **4** If a rent ceiling exceeds people's willingness to pay, search activity and black markets will arise.

—— **5** Search activity will tend to be greater in unregulated markets than in markets with price ceilings.

—— **6** The black market price of a good is usually below the regulated price.

—— **7** An increase in the minimum wage will reduce the number of workers employed.

—— **8** In an unregulated labour market a decline in the demand for labour causes the wage rate to increase.

—— **9** The impact of minimum wage laws on unemployment among young workers tends to be about the same as it is for older workers.

—— **10** A specific tax is set as a fixed amount per unit of the commodity.

—— **11** The imposition of a sales tax shifts the supply curve upward by the amount of the tax.

—— **12** The CAP shifts income from consumers to farmers.

—— **13** If penalties are imposed on both sellers and buyers in a market for prohibited goods, the price remains constant and the quantity bought decreases.

MULTIPLE CHOICE

1 The short-run supply curve for rental housing is positively sloped because
  a the supply of housing is fixed in the short run.
  b the current stock of buildings will be used more intensively as rents rise.
  c the cost of constructing a new building increases as the number of buildings increases.
  d the cost of constructing a new building is about the same regardless of the number of buildings in existence.
  e new buildings will be constructed as rents rise.

2 Rent ceilings imposed by governments
  a keep rental prices below the unregulated market price.
  b keep rental prices above the unregulated market price.
  c keep rental prices equal to the unregulated market price.
  d increase the stock of rental housing.
  e increase the intensity of use of the current stock of rental housing.

3 Which of the following is *not* a likely outcome of rent ceilings?
  a a black market for rent-controlled housing
  b long waiting lists of potential renters of rent-controlled housing
  c a short-run shortage of housing
  d black market prices below the rent ceiling prices
  e increased search activity for rent-controlled housing

4 In an unregulated market which of the following is *not* a likely result of the sudden destruction of a large proportion of the stock of housing?

  a higher rental prices
  b a shortage of rental housing
  c more basement apartments offered for rent
  d more families sharing living quarters
  e the construction of new rental housing

5 A price ceiling set below the equilibrium price will result in
  a excess supply.
  b excess demand.
  c the equilibrium price.
  d an increase in supply.
  e a decrease in demand.

6 A price floor set below the equilibrium price results in
  a excess supply.
  b excess demand.
  c the equilibrium price.
  d an increase in supply.
  e a decrease in demand.

7 If the minimum wage is set at $2 per hour in Fig. 7.1, what is the level of unemployment in millions of hours?
  a 50
  b 40
  c 20
  d 10
  e 0

8 In Fig. 7.1, if the minimum wage is set at $6 per hour, what is the level of unemployment in millions of hours?
  a 50
  b 40
  c 20
  d 10
  e 0

9 Which of the following types of labour would be most significantly affected by an increase in the legal minimum wage?
  a professional athletes
  b young, unskilled labour
  c skilled union workers
  d university professors
  e self-employed labour

Figure 7.1

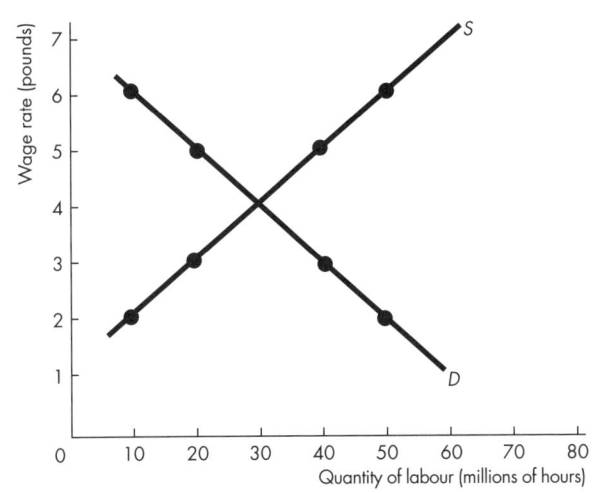

10 A minimum wage law creates
  a gainers
  b losers
  c gainers and losers
  d a decrease in supply
  e an increase in hours worked

11 The burden of a sales tax falls on
  a consumers
  b governments
  c consumers and governments
  d producers
  e consumers and producers

12 The more elastic the supply of a good, the
  a more likely the government is to tax the product.
  b more likely the government is to impose a price ceiling.
  c smaller the amount of any tax on the product paid by supplier.
  d more elastic is the demand.

13 A tax on cigarettes will discourage consumption most when the elasticity of demand is
  a 2.00.
  b 1.00.
  c 0.50.
  d 0.

14 The Common Agricultural Policy of the European Union
  a forces the Union to buy surplus food
  b increases farm incomes
  c increases the price paid by consumers
  d sets a common external tariff
  e all of the above

15 Which of the following combinations would generally yield the greatest price fluctuations?
  a large supply shifts and inelastic demand
  b large supply shifts and elastic demand
  c large supply shifts and perfectly elastic demand
  d small supply shifts and inelastic demand
  e small supply shifts and elastic demand

SHORT ANSWER

1 a Suppose there is a significant reduction in the supply of petrol. Explain how an unregulated market adjusts.
  b What is it that induces consumers willingly to reduce their consumption of petrol?

2 Explain the effects of the imposition of a minimum wage.

3 Explain what happens when the government imposes an expenditure tax.

4 Suppose the Nudist party wins the next election and passes a law making clothes illegal. Unfortunately for the Nudists, the police don't take the law seriously and put little effort into enforcement. Use a diagram to explain why the black market price of now illegal clothes will be close to the unregulated equilibrium price.

5 With reference to the *Reading Between the Lines* article,
  a why do governments tax alcohol and tobacco?
  b who benefits and who loses from the smuggling?

PROBLEMS

1 Suppose that the market for rental housing is initially in long-run equilibrium. Use graphs to answer the following:
  a Explain how an unregulated market for rental housing would adjust if there is a sudden

significant increase in demand. Consider what will happen to rent and the quantity of units rented in the short run and in the long run. Be sure to discuss the effect on incentives (in both the short run and the long run) as the market-determined price (rent) changes.

b Now explain how the market would adjust to the increase in demand if rent ceilings are established at the level of the initial equilibrium rent. What has happened to supplier incentives in this case?

2 Answer the following, given the information about the demand for and supply of mineral water in Table 7.1.

a What is the equilibrium price of mineral water and the equilibrium quantity of mineral water traded?

Table 7.1

Price (pounds per litre)	Quantity demanded (millions of litres per day)	Quantity supplied
1.40	8	24
1.30	10	22
1.20	12	20
1.10	14	18
1.00	16	16
0.90	18	14

b Suppose that the quantity of mineral water supplied suddenly declines by 8 million litres per day at every price. Construct a new table of price, quantity demanded and quantity supplied, and draw a graph of the demand curve and the initial and new supply curves. Assuming that the market for mineral water is unregulated, use either your table or your graph to find the new equilibrium price of mineral water and the new equilibrium quantity of mineral water traded.

c How has the change in price affected the behaviour of demanders? the behaviour of suppliers?

d Suppose that the government imposes a price ceiling of £1 per litre of mineral water at the same time as the decrease in supply reported in part **b**.

i What is the quantity of mineral water demanded?

ii What is the quantity of mineral water supplied?

iii What is the quantity of mineral water actually sold?

iv What is the excess quantity of mineral water demanded?

v What is the highest price demanders are willing to pay for the last litre of mineral water available?

vi Consider someone who values mineral water as in **d**. How long would that consumer be willing to queue to buy 10 litres of mineral water if the best alternative was to work at a wage rate of £8 per hour?

DISCUSSION QUESTION

1 'It seems to me that when taxes rise, the poor consumer pays all the tax. Am I right?' Discuss.

DATA QUESTIONS

The cost of the Common Agricultural Policy (CAP)

The costs of the CAP are considerable and include:

◆ The cost of buying and storing surplus produce
◆ Payments to farmers for structural improvements
◆ Transfers from consumers in the form of higher prices

It is not possible to make precise calculations of these costs because these depend in part on the effect of European surpluses on the world price of food. These surpluses are sold on the world market and force down the world price of many commodities. Thus one result is that there is a fall in the incomes of developing country farmers.

Within Europe, the costs and benefits are not distributed evenly since large farmers benefit much more than those with only small farms.

1 What are the aims of the CAP?

2 Draw a diagram to show the effect of European food exports on the world price of food.

3 Who benefits and who loses from the CAP system?

4 How can the surpluses be eliminated?

ANSWERS

CONCEPT REVIEW

1 increase; increase

2 rent ceiling

3 demanded; search; black

4 left; fall

5 above

6 rise; fall

7 deadweight

TRUE OR FALSE

1 T Movement up supply curve is unobstructed by the ceiling.

2 T At equilibrium, all who can afford housing get it, but not necessarily all who need it.

3 F Returns on investment in housing will be low.

4 F The rent ceiling will have little effect.

5 F Because people will search for bargains.

6 F Black market prices are higher.

7 T Increase in minimum wage leads to a fall in quantity demanded.

8 F Wage will fall.

9 F Greater impact on young workers because they have lower wages.

10 T Definition.

11 T Taxes reduce supply since they are similar to an increase in raw material prices.

12 T Consumers face higher prices, farmers receive more than the equilibrium price.

13 F Supply shifts to the right.

MULTIPLE CHOICE

1 b c, d, and e refer to the long run.

2 a Definition d and e result of increase in rent in unregulated market.

3 d Black markets cause shortages and lead to prices above the official price.

4 b Price would rise and stimulate supply as after Gelderland province flood.

5 b Draw a graph. No change in *ceteris paribus* assumptions so no shift in supply or demand.

6 c A price floor below the equilibrium will have no effect.

7 e Floor below equilibrium price does not prevent market from reaching equilibrium.

8 b Quantity supplied (50) > quantity demanded (10).

9 b Lowest wage labour.

10 c Some will gain from higher wages, some will not find employment at higher wage.

11 e Both consumers and producers bear tax burden depending on elasticity.

12 c The more elastic the demand, the greater the proportion of the tax paid by customers.

13 a The greater the elasticity, the more a tax cuts demand.

14 e These are the effects of intervention.

15 a Draw graph to see.

SHORT ANSWER

1 a If the market for petrol is initially in equilibrium and there is a significant reduction in the supply of petrol, there will be excess quantity demanded at the existing price. As a result, the price of petrol will rise, which will cause movements along the new supply curve and the demand curve. As the price rises there will be a price-induced increase in quantity supplied and a price-induced decrease in quantity demanded. The price will continue to rise until the excess quantity demanded is eliminated.

b It is the price increase that causes consumers to reduce their desired consumption of petrol.

2 Minimum wage legislation stops employers paying their workers wages lower than a minimum set by government. The result is that some people benefit and others lose. Employers lose because they have to pay higher wages. Other losers include those who cannot find work since the higher wages cause firms to reduce their demand for labour. The main benefit accrues to those low-paid workers who receive higher wages as a result of the pay increase. The exact results will depend on the level at which the minimum wage is set and on the elasticity of demand and supply of labour. If these are both inelastic, the result will be only a small fall in employment. If they are elastic, there will be a considerable fall in employment.

3 An expenditure tax results in a rise in prices and a fall in the quantity of goods bought and sold. This is illustrated in Fig. 7.2.

Figure 7.2

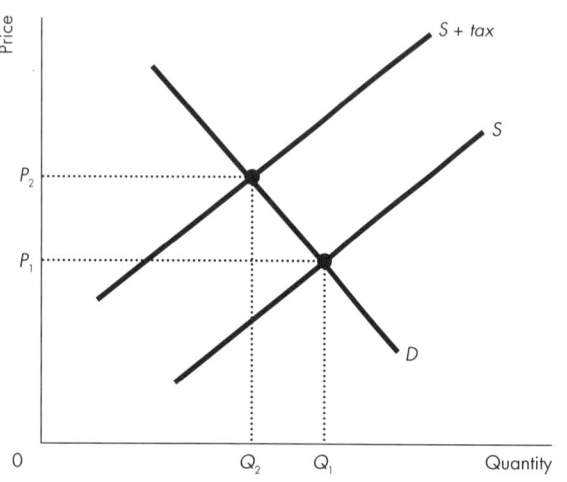

The tax will shift the supply curve to the left (the vertical distance between the supply curves measures the extent of the tax). The result is a rise in price from P_1 to P_2 and a fall in quantity from Q_1 to Q_2. The extent of these changes depends on the shape of the demand curve, that is, on its elasticity.

4 The clothing market is illustrated in Fig. 7.3. The demand curve is D and the supply curve is S. Since police enforcement is lax, the cost of breaking the law *(CBL)* is small for both buyers and sellers, so the demand and supply curves move only a short distance and the effect is small.

5 a Governments tax alcohol and tobacco because demand is inelastic (since they have few substitutes and are addictive). Hence taxes raise large sum of money and have little effect on quantity sold.

   b The smugglers and their customers clearly benefit from lower prices. So do foreign suppliers and governments. The losers are the UK government (and taxpayers) and also shops and pubs in the UK.

PROBLEMS

1 a Figure 7.4 corresponds to an unregulated market for rental housing. The initial demand, short-run supply

Figure 7.3

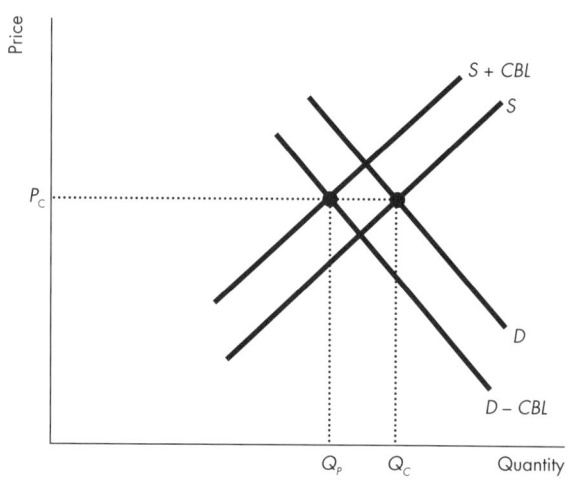

Figure 7.4

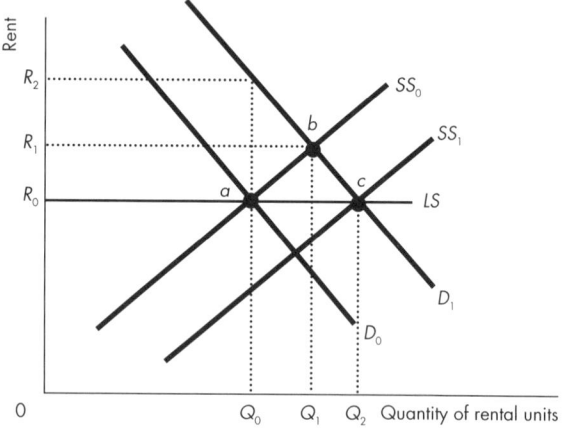

and long-run supply curves are D_0, SS_0 and LS respectively. The market is initially in long-run equilibrium at point a corresponding to rent R_0 and quantity of rental units Q_0. Demand then increases to D_1, creating excess quantity demanded of $Q_2 - Q_0$ at the initial rent. In the short run, in an unregulated market, rent will rise to R_1 to clear the market and the equilibrium quantity of housing rented is Q_1 (point b). Note that as the rent rises, the quantity of rental housing supplied increases (a movement from point a to point b along supply curve SS_0) as the existing stock of housing is used more intensively. Also the quantity of housing demanded decreases (a movement from point c to point b along demand curve D_1). Together, these movements eliminate the excess quantity demanded. The higher rent also provides an incentive to construct new housing in the long run. This is illustrated by the shift in the supply curve from SS_0 to SS_1. Lastly, a new long-run equilibrium is achieved at point c, with rent restored to its original level and the number of units rented equal to Q_2.

b We now use the graph in Fig. 7.4 to discuss the behaviour of a market with a rent ceiling set at R_0. Again we start in the same long-run equilibrium at point a. Once again we observe an increase in demand from D_0 to D_1. In this case, however, the rent cannot rise to restore equilibrium. There will be no incentive to use the existing stock of housing more intensively in the short run or to construct new housing in the long run. The quantity of rental housing supplied will remain at Q_0. Since the last unit of rental housing is valued at R_2, but rent is fixed at R_0, demanders of rental housing will be willing to bear additional costs up to $R_2 - R_0$ (in the form of additional search activity or illegal payments) in order to obtain rental housing.

2 a The equilibrium price of mineral water is £1 per litre since, at that price, the quantity of mineral water demanded is equal to the quantity supplied (16 million litres per day). The equilibrium quantity of mineral water traded is 16 million litres of mineral water per day.

b The new table and graph are shown in Table 7.2 and Fig. 7.5.

Figure 7.5

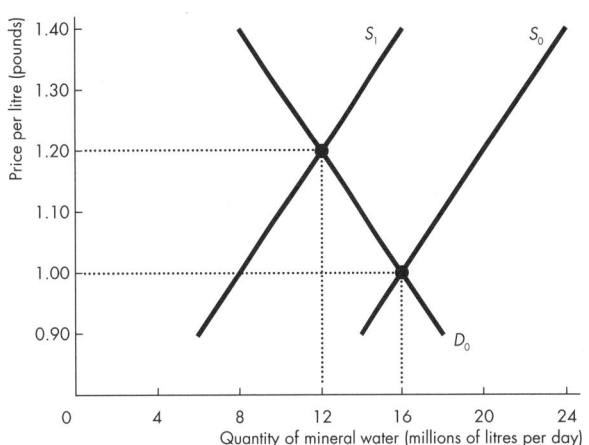

Table 7.2

Price (pounds per litre)	Quantity demanded (millions of litres per day)	Quantity supplied
1.40	8	16
1.30	10	14
1.20	12	12
1.10	14	10
1.00	16	8
0.90	18	6

The new equilibrium price is £1.20 per litre since, at that price, the quantity of mineral water demanded equals the new quantity supplied (12 million litres per day). The new equilibrium quantity traded is 12 million litres of mineral water per day.

c The increase in price has caused the quantity of mineral water demanded to decrease by 4 million litres per day (from 16 to 12 million). Given the new supply curve S_1, the increase in price from £1 to £1.20 per litre increases the quantity of mineral water supplied by 4 million litres per day (from 8 to 12 million).

d i At the ceiling price of £1, the quantity demanded is 16 million litres per day.

ii The quantity supplied is 8 million litres per day.

iii The quantity of mineral water actually sold is 8 million litres per day. When, at a given price, quantity demanded and quantity supplied differ, whichever quantity is the *lesser* will determine the quantity actually sold.

iv The excess quantity of mineral water demanded is 8 million litres per day.

v The highest price consumers are willing to pay for the last unit of mineral water supplied (the 8 millionth litre per day) is £1.40. You can obtain this answer from your graph by imagining a vertical line from the quantity 8 million litres up to where it intersects the demand curve at £1.40. The demand curve shows the highest price consumers would be willing to pay for that last litre supplied.

vi The regulated price of mineral water is £1 per litre but the value to the consumer of the last litre is £1.40, so the consumer would be willing to bear costs of £4 above the regulated price of mineral water to obtain 10 litres (£0.40 × 10 litres). If the best alternative is to earn £8 per hour, the consumer would be willing to spend up to half an hour queuing to buy the 10 litres.

DISCUSSION QUESTION

1 Appearances can be deceptive. Prices certainly rise after the imposition of a tax, although usually not by the full amount of the tax. When firms show the full amount of value added tax (VAT) to be paid, this may conceal a fall in the price before tax.

DATA QUESTIONS

1 The objectives of the CAP are to increase agricultural productivity, to increase farm incomes, to stabilize prices and to ensure reasonable prices for agricultural products.

2 The effects of the European Union's food surpluses on the world market are shown in Fig. 7.6. The result is a fall in world prices and an increase in quantity.

3 Large farmers in particular benefit. The biggest losers are consumers and developing country farmers who cannot compete with subsidized European exports.

4 Several measures can be used to reduce surpluses. These include cutting the price at which the European Union buys agricultural products, selling surpluses abroad at low prices, imposing quotas which limit the quantity of food farmers are allowed to produce, and paying farmers to set aside land, that is, to let land lie fallow.

Figure 7.6

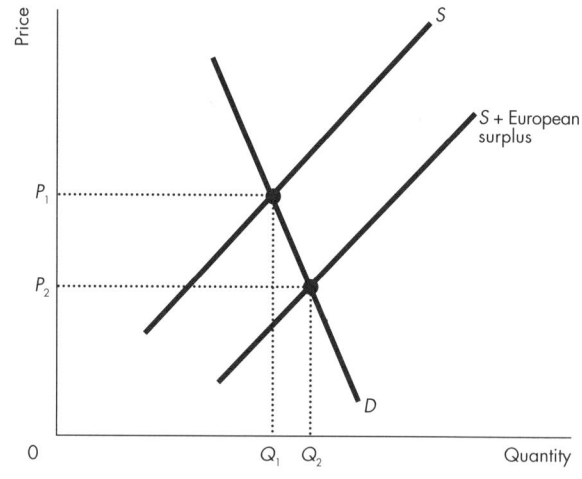

In recent years the European Union has taken some of these measures, and as a result surplus stocks have fallen.

Part 3 How Markets Work

Looking back at Part 2 (Chapters 4–7)

These chapters are at the heart of the subject.

Demand and supply are fundamental concepts in economics. They were introduced in Chapter 4; a chapter well worth looking at again and again to make sure that you understand it. The questions on that chapter in this *Study Guide* are a good indication of this. If you got several wrong, then it is well worth your time to look again at the chapter. Another important concept in Chapter 4 is the distinction between money price and real price. The distinction between real and nominal is most easily explained in the context of wages. If wages rise by five per cent and prices also rise by five per cent, then real wages have not changed because the quantity of goods that the wage can buy has not changed.

Chapter 5 is also important, dealing as it does with elasticity. The essential idea behind this is *responsiveness*; for example, in the case of price elasticity, does quantity fall a lot as price rises? If so, then we say that demand for the good is elastic. In some cases, such as salt or cigarettes, price rises have relatively little effect on sales; hence demand is inelastic.

Chapter 6 deals with one of the main concerns of Will Hutton in the *Talking with* article on pages 66–7. That is equity, or fairness. It also deals with another important concept – efficiency and the reasons why market economies can be inefficient.

Chapter 7 examines markets in the real world, making use of the theoretical concepts introduced earlier. For example, what is the effect when the government imposes a tax?

If you have mastered these chapters, you will have laid an excellent foundation for your course.

Questions

(The answers are at the end of this section.)

1 Re-read the Will Hutton interview. There he picks out three central concepts. Can you explain these?

2 This is another good time to explore the Internet. Look up the Parkin, Powell and Matthews site and classify the material that you find as micro or macro. Two general sites of useful sources: Resources for Economists on the Internet (rfe.wustl.edu/EconFAQ.html) and Econ Links: student resources (www.ncat.edu/~simkinss/studentres.html). Material on EU agriculture is available from ECDGVI (europa.eu.int/comm/dg06/publi/index_en.htm).

3 Look again at the *Discovering the Laws of Demand and Supply* article. Who laid out the first thorough and complete statement of the theory of demand and supply?

Looking forward to Part 3 (Chapters 8–11)

These chapters take a closer look at supply and demand. You may find Chapters 8 (on Utility) and 9 (on Possibilities, Preferences and Choices) rather difficult. That is because they are very theoretical. They could well be sub-titled 'What lies behind the demand curve' because they give a theoretical underpinning to consumer choice.

Chapters 10 and 11 change the focus from consumers to firms. They discuss issues such as different forms of business organization and the relationship between a firm's costs and its output.

Answers

1 The three concepts that Will Hutton believes are fundamental are incentives, opportunity cost and trade-offs at the margin. 'Incentives' are inducements to take particular actions. They are often financial, such as paying higher wages for

increased productivity, but they need not be. (For example, why do people become blood donors?) 'Opportunity cost' is the cost of the best alternative forgone. 'Trade-offs' are similar. They can be defined as a constraint that involves giving up one thing to get another. It differs from opportunity cost in that the cost element is not explicit.

2 The answers to this depend on what you find. Material about individual firms will be classified as micro; data on unemployment and prices as macro.

3 Alfred Marshall first developed the complete theory of demand and supply.

Chapter 8 Utility and Demand

Chapter in Perspective, Text Pages 168–187

The fundamental economic concept of demand was introduced in Chapter 4. There we assumed that as the price of a good rises, the quantity demanded will decline. Assuming this law of demand allowed us to draw a number of useful conclusions, and make predictions about the behaviour of prices and quantity traded. Our confidence in these results would be enhanced if it were not necessary to assume the law of demand – if this could be derived as a prediction of a more fundamental theory. This is the major task of this chapter. Not only is the law of demand derived as a prediction of the marginal utility theory, but other results that had previously been assumed (for example, a change in income causes a shift in demand) also turn out to be predictions.

This chapter and the next greatly deepen our understanding of the forces underlying the law of demand and associated concepts.

Helpful Hints

1 The concept of utility is an extremely useful abstract device that allows us to think more clearly about consumer choice. Marginal utility theory assumes that an individual is able to judge whether the additional satisfaction per pound spent on good X is greater or less than the additional satisfaction per pound spent on Y. If it is greater, then the decision is to consume an additional unit of X. How much greater is irrelevant for the decision.

2 Consumer equilibrium requires that all income is spent and that the marginal utility per pound spent on a good must equal the marginal utility per pound spent on all other goods. When this occurs, there is no incentive for change.

3 The marginal utility per pound spent on good X can be written as MU_X / P_X where MU_X is the marginal utility of the last unit of X consumed and P_X is the price of a unit of good X. The consumer equilibrium (utility-maximizing) condition for goods X and Y can thus be written:

$$\frac{MU_X}{P_X} = \frac{MU_Y}{P_Y}$$

This implies that, in consumer equilibrium, the ratio of marginal utilities will equal the ratio of prices of the two goods:

$$\frac{MU_X}{MU_Y} = \frac{P_X}{P_Y}$$

4 If an individual is not in consumer equilibrium, then the equation above is not satisfied. For example, consider spending all of your income on a consumption plan where:

$$\frac{MU_X}{P_X} > \frac{MU_Y}{P_Y}$$

or, equivalently

$$\frac{MU_X}{MU_Y} > \frac{P_X}{P_Y}$$

Since P_X and P_Y are given, this means that MU_X is 'too large' and MU_Y is 'too small'. Utility can be increased by increasing consumption of X (and thereby decreasing MU_X owing to the principle of diminishing marginal utility) and decreasing consumption of Y (and thereby increasing MU_Y owing to diminishing marginal utility).

5 Table 8.7 in the text on page 179 is a good review device.

SELF-TEST

CONCEPT REVIEW

1 The _____ demand curve is the sum of the quantities demanded by each individual at each _____ .

2 The benefit or satisfaction a person receives from the consumption of a good or a service is called _____ .

3 The additional utility a person receives from consuming one more unit of a good is called _____ _____ .

4 As consumption increases, marginal utility _____ . This is called the principle of _____ marginal utility.

5 We assume that a household will choose quantities to consume so as to _____ utility subject to its income and the prices it faces.

6 The marginal utility per pound spent is the marginal utility of the last unit of a good consumed divided by its _____ .

7 Utility will be maximized if the marginal utility per pound spent is _____ for all goods.

8 Marginal utility theory predicts that if the price of one good rises, _____ of it will be consumed and _____ of other goods will be consumed.

9 Marginal utility theory predicts that the higher household income is, the _____ is the quantity consumed of all normal goods.

10 The difference between the value of a good and its price is called _____ _____ .

TRUE OR FALSE

1 Market demand is the sum of all individual demands.

2 Total utility equals the sum of the marginal utilities for all units consumed.

3 The principle of diminishing marginal utility means that as consumption of a good increases, total utility declines.

4 The principle of diminishing marginal utility means that as consumption of a good increases, total utility increases but at a decreasing rate.

5 A consumer equilibrium exists when a consumer has allocated his or her income in a way that maximizes total utility.

6 A household will be maximizing utility if the marginal utility per pound spent is equal for all goods and all its income is spent.

7 When the price of good X rises, the marginal utility from the consumption of X decreases.

___ **8** If the marginal utilities from consuming two goods are not equal, then the consumer cannot be in equilibrium.

___ **9** If the marginal utility per pound spent on good X exceeds the marginal utility per pound spent on good Y, total utility will increase by increasing consumption of X and decreasing consumption of Y.

___ **10** Marginal utility theory predicts that if the price of a good falls, consumption of substitute goods will rise.

___ **11** Utility cannot be observed or measured.

___ **12** The value of a good is always the price of the good.

___ **13** The principle of diminishing marginal utility guarantees that consumers will always make some consumer surplus.

___ **14** Consumer surplus is the difference between the value of a good and its price.

___ **15** If a shift in supply decreases the price of a good, consumer surplus increases.

___ **16** The diamond–water paradox illustrates that relative prices actually reflect total utility rather than marginal utility.

MULTIPLE CHOICE

1 A household's consumption choices are determined by
  a prices of goods and services.
  b its income.
  c its preferences.
  d all of the above.

2 Marginal utility equals
  a total utility divided by price.
  b total utility divided by the total number of units consumed.
  c the slope of the total utility curve.
  d the inverse of total utility.
  e the area below the demand curve but above market price.

3 If Ms Petersen is maximizing her utility in the consumption of goods A and B, which of the following statements must be true?

  a $MU_A = MU_B$

  b $\dfrac{MU_A}{P_A} = \dfrac{MU_B}{P_B}$

  c $\dfrac{MU_A}{P_B} = \dfrac{MU_B}{P_A}$

  d $TU_A = TU_B$

  e $\dfrac{TU_A}{P_A} = \dfrac{TU_B}{P_B}$

4 If a consumer is in equilibrium, then
  a total utility is maximized given the consumer's income and the prices of goods.
  b marginal utility is maximized given the consumer's income and the prices of goods.
  c marginal utility per pound spent is maximized given the consumer's income and the prices of goods.
  d the marginal utility of the last unit of each good will be the same.
  e none of the above is true.

5 If Renata is maximizing her utility and two goods have the same marginal utility then
  a she will buy only one of them.
  b she will buy equal quantities of them.
  c she will be willing to pay the same price for each of them.
  d she will get the same total utility from each of them.
  e none of the above is true.

6 Shelley is maximizing her utility in her consumption of mink coats and Porsches. If the marginal utility of her last purchased mink coat is twice the marginal utility of her last purchased Porsche, then we do not know with certainty that
  a Shelley buys twice as many mink coats as Porsches.
  b Shelley buys twice as many Porsches as mink coats.
  c Shelley buys more Porsches than mink coats, but we do not know how many more.
  d the price of a mink coat is twice the price of a Porsche.
  e the price of a Porsche is twice the price of a mink coat.

7 Total utility equals
  a the sum of the marginal utilities of each unit consumed.

b the area below the demand curve but above the market price.

c the slope of the marginal utility curve.

d the marginal utility of the last unit divided by price.

e the marginal utility of the last unit consumed multiplied by the total number of units consumed.

8 Samir consumes apples and bananas and is in consumer equilibrium. The marginal utility of the last apple is 10 and the marginal utility of the last banana is 5. If the price of an apple is £0.50, then what is the price of a banana?

a £0.05

b £0.10

c £0.25

d £0.50

e £1

9 The value of a good is defined as the

a market price.

b average price paid by individuals in a market.

c cost of producing the good.

d highest price an individual is willing to pay.

e total utility to an individual of all units of the good.

10 The difference between the value of a good and its price is known as

a excess demand.

b excess supply.

c consumer surplus.

d consumer excess.

e marginal utility.

11 The demand schedule for marbles is shown in Table 8.1.

Table 8.1 Demand Schedule for Marbles

Price per marble (pounds)	Quantity demanded
10	1
9	2
8	3
7	4
6	5

If the actual price is £7, what is total consumer surplus?

a £3

b £4

c £6

d £12

e £27

12 The high price of diamonds relative to the price of water reflects the fact that at typical levels of consumption

a the total utility of water is relatively low.

b the total utility of diamonds is relatively high.

c the marginal utility of water is relatively high.

d the marginal utility of diamonds is relatively low.

e none of the above is true.

13 Marginal utility theory predicts that a rise in the price of apples causes

a the demand curve for apples to shift to the right.

b the demand curve for apples to shift to the left.

c a movement upward along the demand curve for apples.

d a movement downward along the demand curve for apples.

SHORT ANSWER

1 A consumer is initially maximizing his or her utility in the consumption of goods *A* and *B* so that:

$$\frac{MU_A}{P_A} = \frac{MU_B}{P_B}$$

The price of *A* then rises as a result of the shift in supply shown in Fig. 8.1. Use the above condition for utility maximization to explain how the consumer will move to a new utility-maximizing equilibrium. Show the connection between your explanation and the change on the diagram.

2 Explain why the consumer equilibrium condition and the principle of diminishing marginal utility imply the law of demand.

3 How does marginal utility theory resolve the diamond–water paradox of value?

4 In the *Reading Between the Lines* article, explain why Karen will maximise her utility by making the marginal utility per dollar spent on can packs equal to the marginal utility per dollar spent on bottles.

Figure 8.1

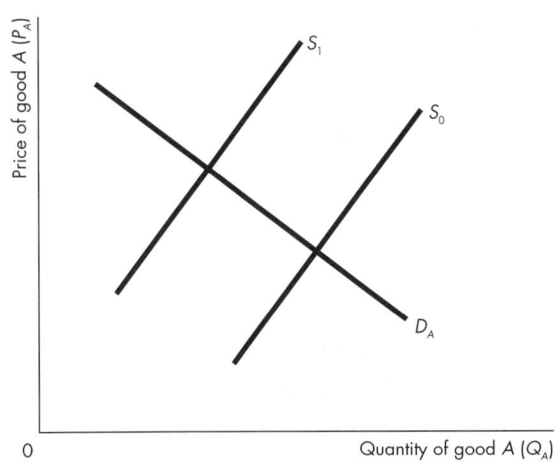

Table 8.3

| | Marginal utility | |
Quantity	Books	Rackets
1	20	36
2	18	32
3	16	20
4	8	16

b If John's income rises to £24, how many units of each good should he purchase?

c Using the information above, calculate John's income elasticity of demand for books.

3 Andy's weekly demand schedule for pizzas is shown in Table 8.4.

Table 8.4 Demand Schedule for Pizzas

Price per pizza (pounds)	Quantity demanded
15	1
12	2
10	3
9	4
8	5

If the price of a pizza is £9, what is Andy's consumer surplus for the following number of pizzas that he buys at that price?

a first pizza

b second pizza

c total number of pizzas

PROBLEMS

1 Table 8.2 gives the demand schedules for broccoli for three individuals: Tom, Jana and Ted.

Table 8.2 Individual Demand for Broccoli

Price per kilogram (pounds)	Quantity demanded (kilograms per week)		
	Tom	Jana	Ted
0.50	10	4	10
0.75	9	2	7
1.00	8	0	4
1.25	7	0	1

a Calculate the market demand schedule.

b On a single diagram, draw the individual demand curves for Tom, Jana and Ted, as well as the market demand curve.

2 Suppose that John spends his entire income of £8 on tennis rackets and books. The price of a tennis racket is £2 and the price of a book is £4. The marginal utility of each good is independent of the amount consumed of the other good.

a If John is maximizing his utility, how many units of each good should he purchase?

DISCUSSION QUESTIONS

1 What is the point of learning something so remote from reality as marginal utility theory?

2 'Marginal utility theory suggests that as the price of a good rises, less will be consumed'. But I rent only one flat. How does marginal utility theory explain this?

DATA QUESTIONS

Music, love and utility

Duke Orsino. 'If music be the food of love, play on:
  Give me excess of it, that, surfeiting,
  The appetite may sicken, and so die.
  … Enough! no more:
  'Tis not so sweet now as it was before.'

Source: Shakespeare, *Twelfth Night*, Act I, Scene 1.

1 Explain the effect of music on love in terms of utility theory.

2 In the play Orsino wants his love to die because his love for Olivia is not returned. What would be the effect on the utility of music for him if she also loved him?

ANSWERS

CONCEPT REVIEW

1 market; price

2 utility

3 marginal utility

4 decreases; diminishing

5 maximize

6 price

7 equal

8 less; more

9 greater

10 consumer surplus

TRUE OR FALSE

1 T Definition.

2 T Definition.

3 F *Marginal* utility falls as more is consumed.

4 T Because marginal utility is positive but diminishing.

5 T Because any change would reduce utility.

6 T Definition.

7 F Rise in price leads to a fall in quantity and hence a rise in marginal utility.

8 F If prices are unequal, then marginal utilities must be unequal for consumers to be in equilibrium.

9 T Because it moves the ratio of marginal utility/price towards equality.

10 F More of the good will be consumed and less of substitute goods.

11 T Utility is an abstract concept.

12 F Price can be greater or less than value.

13 T Willingness to pay is greater than price for all units consumed except the last.

14 T Definition.

15 T The shift in supply leads to an increase in quantity consumed, so there are more units where consumers are willing to pay more than the price.

16 F Relative prices reflect marginal utility.

MULTIPLE CHOICE

1 d A household's consumption is determined by the interplay of all these factors.

2 c Definition.

3 b Definition.

4 a Consumers maximize total utility. **c** and **d** are wrong because MU/P are equal for total utility maximization.

5 c From maximum condition of equal MU/P. There is no necessary relation between MU and quantity or total utility.

6 d From maximum condition of equal MU/P. No necessary relation between MU and quantity.

7 a **b** is consumer surplus. For **c**, MU = slope of the total utility curve. **d** and **e** are nonsense.

8 c Solve $10/0.5 = 5/P_b$ for P_b.

9 d Definition.

10 c Definition.

11 c For four marbles consumed, consumer surplus = $(10 − 7) + (9 − 7) + (8 − 7) + (7 − 7)$.

12 e For diamonds: *TU* is relatively low, *MU* relatively high. For water: *TU* is relatively high, *MU* relatively low.

13 c Higher prices for apples cause consumers to decrease their consumption, raising their marginal utility.

SHORT ANSWER

1 When the price of *A* rises, *ceteris paribus*:

$$\frac{MU_A}{P_A} = \frac{MU_B}{P_B}$$

The consumer is no longer in equilibrium. In order to restore the equality in the equilibrium condition, the consumer must change his consumption to make MU_A rise and MU_B fall. (The consumer cannot change the prices of *A* and *B*.) Since marginal utility diminishes with increases in quantity consumed, the consumer must decrease consumption of *A* and increase consumption of *B*. Decreased consumption of *A* moves the consumer up to the left on the demand curve, from the initial intersection of *D* and S_0 to the new intersection of *D* and S_1. In the new consumer equilibrium, equality will be restored in the equilibrium condition.

2 Suppose we observe an individual in consumer equilibrium consuming X_0 units of good *X* and Y_0 units of good *Y* with the prices of *X* and *Y* given by P_X and P_Y respectively. This means that at consumption levels X_0 and Y_0, the marginal utility per pound spent on *X* equals the marginal utility per pound spent on *Y*. Now let the price of *X* increase to P_X^1. This increase implies that the marginal utility per pound spent on *X* declines and thus is now less than the marginal utility per pound spent on *Y*. To restore equilibrium, our consumer must increase the marginal utility of *X* and decrease the marginal utility of *Y*. From the principle of diminishing marginal utility we know that the only way to do this is to decrease the consumption of *X* and increase the consumption of *Y*. This demonstrates the law of demand since an increase in the price of *X* has been shown to require a decrease in the consumption of *X* to restore consumer equilibrium.

3 The paradox of value is resolved by recognizing that while the total utility from consumption of water is large, the marginal utility from the last unit of water is small. Likewise, the total utility from the consumption of diamonds is small, but the marginal utility of the last unit of diamonds is large. If consumers are in equilibrium, then the requirement that the marginal utility per pound spent be the same for water and diamonds means that the price of water must be low and the price of diamonds must be high.

4 If consumers gained more utility per pound of money by buying packs than they did by buying other goods such as bottles, they would increase their utility by buying more packs. As they consumed more packs, its utility would gradually decline until the utility per pound spent equalled that spent on other goods such as bottles. They would then be maximizing their utility.

PROBLEMS

1 a The market demand schedule is obtained by adding the quantities demanded by Tom, Jana and Ted at each price.

Table 8.5 Market Demand Schedule for Broccoli

Price per kilogram (pounds)	Quantity demanded (kilograms per week)
0.50	24
0.75	18
1.00	12
1.25	8

b Figure 8.2 illustrates the individual demand curves for Tom, Jana and Ted as well as the market demand curve.

Figure 8.2

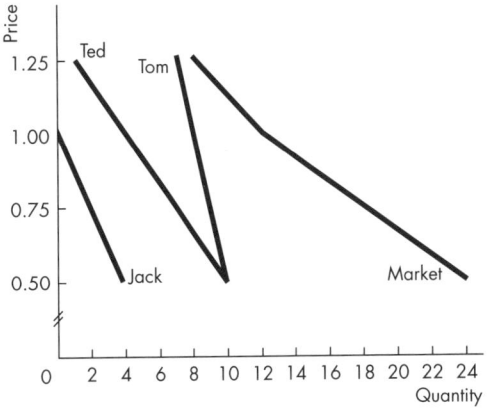

2 a The utility-maximizing combination of goods is shown in Table 8.6.

Table 8.6

	MU/P	
Quantity	Books	Rackets
1	10	9
2	9	8
3	8	5
4	4	4

John should purchase 2 books and 1 racket. John spends all of his income (£8) and the marginal utility per pound spent is the same for books and rackets (9).

b John should purchase 4 books and 4 rackets. He spends all of his income (£24) and the marginal utility per pound spent is the same for books and rackets (4).

c The income elasticity of demand for books is:

$$\eta_y = \frac{\Delta Q/Q_{ave}}{\Delta Y/Y_{ave}}$$

3 a The most Andy would be willing to pay for the first pizza is £15, but the price is only £9. Therefore his consumer surplus is £6 (£15–£9).

b Andy's consumer surplus on the second pizza is the difference between the most he would be willing to pay (£12) and the price (£9). His consumer surplus is £3.

c At a price of £9, Andy will buy 4 pizzas. He will receive consumer surplus on the first three pizzas in the amount of £6, £3 and £1, respectively. Thus his total consumer surplus is £10.

DISCUSSION QUESTIONS

1 It is certainly true that no one goes into a shop and calculates marginal utility before buying. But that is not the point. Marginal utility theory is *not* trying to explain how people make decisions about what to buy. Instead it assumes that people attempt to maximize their utility and tries to explain how they respond to changes in prices and incomes. It is a theory of peoples' actions, not of their thoughts.

2 The answer is that not all flats are identical. A rise in price would mean that some people would move to smaller flats or would be forced to share, so 'consuming' fewer flats.

DATA QUESTIONS

1 If we eat too many cakes the marginal utility of cakes will fall, and eventually we will be surfeited – turned off cakes altogether. Orsino hopes this will also be the case with the effect of music on love. More music means an increase in love, but eventually the marginal utility of love will diminish and become zero. Hence he will no longer want love.

2 If Olivia falls in love with Orsino, the position will change (just as a drink may change the utility of another cake). Now he will want love – and music, but not too much. He will choose additional amounts of music until the satisfaction he gets from love is maximized. Note that this assumes that the music is free. If he was paying for the music, he would buy more music until the cost of the music equalled the benefit he obtained from it.

Chapter 9 Possibilities, Preferences and Choices

Chapter in Perspective, Text Pages 188–211

This chapter provides an alternative analysis of consumer choice and the law of demand that complements the marginal utility analysis of Chapter 8. Here, the analysis uses a model of consumer behaviour based on a budget equation that represents *possible choices* given a consumer's income and an indifference curve representation of *preferences*.

The model allows more systematic analysis of what happens to quantity demanded when the price of a good changes and when income changes, as well as more insight into the distinction between normal and inferior goods. Compared with the marginal utility analysis, the budget equation/indifference curve model has the advantage that it does not depend on the abstract notion of utility.

Helpful Hints

1 The consumer's problem is to do the best given the constraints faced. These constraints, which limit the range of possible choices, depend on income and the prices of goods and are represented graphically by the budget line. 'Doing the best' means finding the most preferred outcome consistent with those constraints. In this chapter, preferences are represented graphically by indifference curves. Thus, graphically, the consumer problem is to find the highest indifference curve attainable given the budget line. To make graphical analysis feasible, we restrict ourselves to choices between only two goods, but the same principles apply in the real world where the array of choices is much broader.

2 Remember that indifference curves plot people's preferences and do not depend on their incomes or the prices of goods. They just indicate how much – or how little – a person likes or dislikes a particular good.

3 Each of the two endpoints (the intercepts) of a budget line is just income divided by the price of the good on that axis. Connecting those endpoints with a straight line yields the budget line. The slope of the budget line provides additional information relevant for the consumer's choice between goods. The magnitude (absolute value) of the slope equals the relative price (or opportunity cost) of films in terms of cola. To put it in different words, the magnitude of the slope equals the number of units of cola it takes to buy one cinema ticket. More generally, the magnitude of the slope of the budget line (P_X/P_Y) equals the relative price (or opportunity cost) of the good on the horizontal x-axis in terms of the good on the vertical y-axis; or the number of units of vertical-axis goods it takes to buy one unit of the horizontal-axis good.

4   The marginal rate of substitution (*MRS*) is the rate at which a consumer gives up good Y for an additional unit of good X and still remains indifferent. The *MRS* equals the magnitude of the slope of the indifference curve, Q_Y/Q_X.

Because indifference curves are bowed towards the origin (convex), the magnitude of the slope and, hence, the *MRS* diminish as we move down an indifference curve. The diminishing *MRS* means that the consumer is willing to give up less of good Y for each additional unit of good X. As the consumer moves down an indifference curve, the consumer is coming to value good Y more and value good X less. This is easily explained by the principle of diminishing marginal utility.

At the top of the indifference curve, the consumer is consuming little X and much Y, so the marginal utility of X (MU_X) is high and the mar-

ginal utility of Y (MU_Y) is low. Moving down the curve, as the quantity of X consumed increases, MU_X decreases; and as the quantity of Y consumed decreases, MU_Y increases. Thus the principle of diminishing marginal utility provides an intuitive understanding of why the *MRS* diminishes as we move down an indifference curve.

5   At the consumer's best affordable point, the budget line is just tangent to the highest affordable indifference curve, so the magnitude of the slope of the budget line equals the magnitude of the slope of the indifference curve.

6   Understanding the distinction between the income and substitution effects of a change in the price of a good is sometimes a challenge for students. Consider a decrease in the price of good A. This has two effects that will influence the consumption of A. First, the decrease in the price of A will reduce the relative price of A and, second, it will increase real income. The substitution effect is the answer to the question: how much would the consumption of A change as a result of the relative price decline if we also (hypothetically) reduce income by enough to leave the consumer indifferent between the new and original situations? The income effect is the answer to the following question: how much more would the consumption of A change if we (hypothetically) restore the consumer's real income but leave relative prices at the new level?

SELF-TEST

CONCEPT REVIEW

1   A _____ line describes the maximum amounts of consumption a household can undertake given its income and the prices of the goods it buys.

2   Real income is income expressed in units of _____ .

3   The price of one good divided by the price of another is called a(n) _____ price.

4   If the quantity of good A consumed is measured on the horizontal axis and the quantity of good B consumed is measured on the vertical axis, an increase in the price of good a will make the budget line _____ . An increase in income will shift the budget line _____ .

5   A(n) _____ curve shows all combinations of goods that would leave a consumer indifferent.

6   Suppose we measure good A on the horizontal axis and good B on the vertical axis. The rate at

which a person would give up good B to obtain more of good A is called the ＿＿＿＿＿ rate of ＿＿＿＿＿ . As the consumer increases consumption of good A (and decreases consumption of good B so as to remain indifferent), this rate ＿＿＿＿＿ .

7 The best affordable consumption point will be on both the ＿＿＿＿＿ line and the highest attainable ＿＿＿＿＿ curve.

8 If the price of good A rises, the ＿＿＿＿＿ effect will always imply that less of A will be consumed, while the ＿＿＿＿＿ effect reinforces this only if A is a normal good.

9 If a decrease in income causes an increase in the consumption of good B, then B is a(n)＿＿＿＿＿ good.

10 As the wage rate rises, the substitution effect encourages ＿＿＿＿＿ leisure and the income effect encourages ＿＿＿＿＿ leisure.

TRUE OR FALSE

___ **1** At any point on the budget line, all income is spent.

___ **2** An increase in the price of the good measured on the horizontal axis will make the budget line flatter.

___ **3** *Ceteris paribus*, an increase in the price of goods means that real income falls.

___ **4** An increase in income will cause an inward parallel shift of the budget line.

___ **5** Preferences depend on income and the prices of goods.

___ **6** We assume that more of any good is preferred to less of the good.

___ **7** An indifference curve shows all combinations of two goods which the consumer can afford.

___ **8** It is logically possible for indifference curves to intersect each other.

___ **9** The principle of the diminishing marginal rate of substitution explains why indifference curves are bowed towards the origin.

___ **10** The magnitude of the slope of an indifference curve is equal to the marginal rate of substitution.

___ **11** The marginal rate of substitution falls as consumption of the good measured on the y-axis falls and consumption of the good measured on the x-axis rises.

MULTIPLE CHOICE

1 Which of the following statements best describes a consumer's budget line?
 a the amount of each good a consumer can purchase
 b the limits to a consumer's set of affordable consumption choices
 c the desired level of consumption for the consumer
 d the consumption choices made by a consumer
 e the set of all affordable consumption choices

2 If the price of the good measured on the vertical axis increases, the budget line will
 a become steeper.
 b become flatter.
 c shift inward but parallel to the original budget line.
 d shift outward but parallel to the original budget line.
 e shift inward and become steeper.

3 If income increases, the budget line will
 a become steeper.
 b become flatter.
 c shift inward but parallel to the original budget line.
 d shift outward but parallel to the original budget line.
 e shift parallel but outward or inward depending on whether a good is normal or inferior.

4 A change in income changes which aspect(s) of the budget equation?
 a slope and y-intercept
 b slope and x-intercept
 c x- and y-intercepts but not slope
 d slope only
 e none of the above

5 Bill consumes apples and bananas. Suppose Bill's income doubles and the prices of apples and bananas also double. Bill's budget line will

a shift inward but not change slope.
b remain unchanged.
c shift outward but not change slope.
d shift outward and become steeper.
e shift outward and become flatter.

6 Suppose good X is measured on the horizontal axis and good Y on the vertical axis. The marginal rate of substitution is best defined as the
a relative price of good X in terms of good Y.
b relative price of good Y in terms of good X.
c rate at which a consumer will give up good Y in order to obtain more of good X and remain indifferent.
d rate at which a consumer will give up good X in order to obtain more of good Y and remain indifferent.
e slope of the budget line.

7 In general, as a consumer moves down an indifference curve, increasing consumption of good X (measured on the horizontal axis),
a more of Y must be given up for each additional unit of X.
b a constant amount of Y must be given up for each additional unit of X.
c less of Y must be given up for each additional unit of X.
d the relative price of Y increases.
e the relative price of Y decreases.

8 Consider the budget line and indifference curve in Fig. 9.1. If the price of good X is $2, what is the price of good Y?
a $0.37
b $0.67
c $1.50
d $2.67
e impossible to calculate without additional information

9 When the price of a good changes, the change in consumption that leaves the consumer indifferent is called the
a utility effect.
b substitution effect.
c income effect.
d price effect.
e Giffen effect.

10 When the price of a normal good rises, the income effect

Figure 9.1

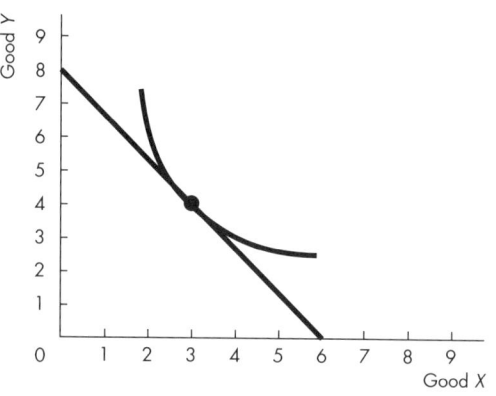

a increases consumption of the good and the substitution effect decreases consumption.
b decreases consumption of the good and the substitution effect increases consumption.
c and the substitution effect both increase consumption of the good.
d and the substitution effect both decrease consumption of the good.
e is always larger than the substitution effect.

11 The initial budget line labelled RS in Fig. 9.2 would shift to RT as a result of
a an increase in the price of good X.
b a decrease in the price of good X.
c a decrease in preferences for good X.
d an increase in the price of good Y.
e an increase in real income.

12 When the initial budget line labelled RS in Fig. 9.2 shifts to RT, the substitution effect is illustrated by the move from point
a a to b.
b a to c.
c a to d.
d b to d.
e d to c.

13 When the initial budget line labelled RS in Fig. 9.2 shifts to RT, the income effect is illustrated by the move from point
a a to b.
b a to c.
c a to d.
d b to c.
e b to d.

Figure 9.2

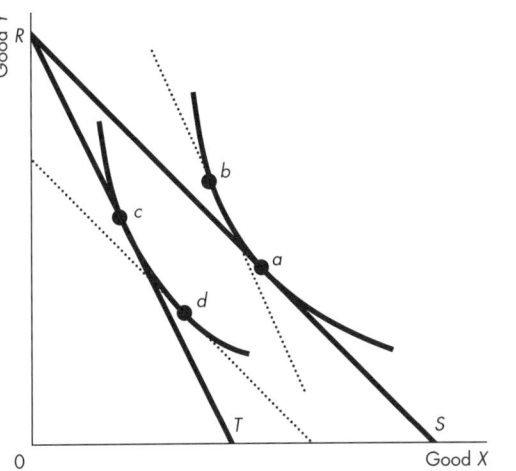

14 Over the last 100 years, the quantity of labour supplied has fallen as wages have increased. This indicates that the income effect
   a and the substitution effect have both discouraged leisure.
   b and the substitution effect have both encouraged leisure.
   c discouraging leisure has been dominated by the substitution effect encouraging leisure.
   d encouraging leisure has dominated the substitution effect discouraging leisure.
   e has not affected the labour–leisure choice.

15 When CDs fall in price, the substitution effect
   a increases the consumption of CDs if they are a normal good.
   b increases the consumption of CDs if they are an inferior good.
   c always increases the consumption of CDs.
   d always decreases the consumption of CDs.

SHORT ANSWER

1 Why is an indifference curve negatively sloped?

2 Use the principle of diminishing marginal utility to explain why the marginal rate of substitution diminishes as we move down an indifference curve.

3 Suppose the price of a normal good falls. Without the use of graphs, distinguish between the income and substitution effects of this price decline.

4 Turn to the *Reading Between the Lines* article. Use the ideas in this chapter to explain the consequences for Belgian mayonnaises and chocolates.

PROBLEMS

1 Jan and Dan both like bread and peanut butter and have the same income. Since they each face the same prices, they have identical budget lines. Currently, Jan and Dan consume exactly the same quantities of bread and peanut butter; they have the same best affordable consumption point. Jan, however, views bread and peanut butter as close (although not perfect) substitutes, while Dan considers bread and peanut butter to be quite (but not perfectly) complementary.
   a On the same diagram, draw a budget line and representative indifference curves for Jan and Dan. (Measure the quantity of bread on the horizontal axis.)
   b Now suppose the price of bread declines. Graphically represent the substitution effects for Jan and Dan. For whom is the substitution effect greater?

2 Kurt consumes both coffee and whisky. The initial price of coffee is £1 per unit and the price of whisky is £1.50 per unit. Kurt's initial income is £12.
   a What is the relative price of coffee?
   b Derive Kurt's budget equation and draw his budget line on a graph. (Measure coffee on the horizontal axis.)
   c On your graph, draw an indifference curve so that the best affordable point corresponds to 6 units of coffee and 4 units of whisky.
   d What is the marginal rate of substitution of coffee for whisky at this point?
   e Show that any other point on the budget line is inferior.

3 Given the initial situation described in Problem 2, suppose Kurt's income now increases.
   a Illustrate graphically how the consumption of coffee and whisky are affected if both goods are normal. (Numerical answers are not necessary. Just show whether consumption increases or decreases.)

b Draw a graph showing the effect of an increase in Kurt's income if whisky is an inferior good.

4 Return to the initial circumstances described in Problem 2. Now suppose the price of coffee doubles to £2 per unit while the price of whisky remains at £1.50 per unit and income remains at £12.

a Draw the new budget line.

b Why is the initial best affordable point (label it point *r*) no longer the best affordable point?

c Using your graph, show the new best affordable point and label it *t*. What has happened to the consumption of coffee?

d Decompose the effect on the consumption of *X* into the substitution effect and the income effect. On your graph, indicate the substitution effect as movement from point *r* to point *s* (which you must locate) and indicate the income effect as movement from point *s* to point *t*.

DISCUSSION QUESTIONS

1 Why should we bother to use indifference curves to derive demand curves? Why not just use demand curves?

2 What is the difference between demand curves and indifference curves?

DATA QUESTION

Age and mobility

Look at almost any bus. The passengers will not be a cross-section of the public as a whole because those with high incomes will tend to travel by car. Hence those on the bus will usually be from the poorer sections of society, particularly old people.

People that want to increase the mobility of old people make two suggestions. The first is a subsidy that allows old people to travel at a reduced price. The second is to increase the pensions paid to old people so that they have more money to spend on goods, including buses.

1 Draw budget lines and indifference curves to illustrate:

a the effect of a subsidy on the choice between bus travel and all other goods.

b the effect of an increase in income for old people.

ANSWERS

CONCEPT REVIEW

1 budget

2 goods

3 relative

4 steeper; outward

5 indifference

6 marginal; substitution; diminishes

7 budget; indifference

8 substitution; income

9 inferior

10 less; more

TRUE OR FALSE

1 T Definition.

2 F The budget line will move to the left.

3 T Real income = income/price of goods.

4 F Rightward parallel shift.

5 F Definition.

6 T One of three fundamental assumptions about preferences.

7 F Definition of budget line.

8 F Logically impossible.

9 T Definition.

10 T Definition.

11 T Describes downward movement along indifference curve.

MULTIPLE CHOICE

1 b **a** should be combinations of goods, **c** about indifference curves, **d** about best affordable point, **e** includes area inside budget line.

2 b y-intercept shifts down, x-intercept is unchanged.

3 d Increase in income does not change slope, but increase in x- and y-intercepts.

4 c Change in income does not change slope but does change intercepts.

5 b Numerators and denominators of both intercepts double, so intercepts do not change.

6 c Definition. **a** and **b** relate to the slope of the budget line. *MRS* = **e** only at best affordable point.

7 c Owing to diminishing *MRS*. **d** and **e** are wrong since relative price relates to budget line, not indifference curve.

8 c Income = £12 (£2 × 6 units X) so price of Y = £12/8 units Y.

9 b Definition.

10 d Both work in same direction. Rise in price leads to fall in consumption.

11 b With the same income there is a fall in quantity of X that can be purchased.

12 a Budget line with new prices tangent to original indifference curve.

13 d Hypothetically restore original income (reverse increase in real income), but keep prices constant at new level.

14 d Substitution effect always discourages leisure. But rise in wages leads to rise in income and an increase in leisure (since leisure is a normal good).

15 c The substitution effect from a lower price always motivates an increase in the consumption of a relatively cheaper good.

SHORT ANSWER

1 An indifference curve tells us how much the consumption of one good must change as the consumption of another good decreases in order to leave the consumer indifferent (no better or worse off). It is negatively sloped because the goods we measure on the axes are both desirable. This means that as we *decrease* the consumption of one good, in order to not be made worse off, consumption of the other good must *increase*. This implies a negative slope.

2 As we move down an indifference curve we change the combination of goods consumed by increasing the quantity of one good consumed and decreasing the quantity of the other good consumed. As consumption of a good increases its marginal utility falls because of the principle of diminishing marginal utility. Thus the value of the numerator on the right-hand side of the equation below decreases:

$$\text{Marginal rate of substitution} = \frac{\text{Marginal utility of } X}{\text{Marginal utility of } Y}$$

As consumption of Y decreases, each previous X consumed yields higher marginal utility. Thus the value of the denominator on the right-hand side of the equation increases. The effect of both a decrease in the numerator and an increase in the denominator is that the ratio MU_X/MU_Y falls as we move down an indifference curve, corresponding to a diminishing marginal rate of substitution on the left-hand side of the equation.

3 A decrease in the price of a good will have two effects on the consumption of the good. First, if all other prices remain constant, when the price of one good falls, real income increases. The substitution effect is the increase in consumption of the good resulting from the fall in its relative price accompanied by a hypothetical reduction in real income, which leaves the consumer indifferent between the new and initial situations. The income effect for a normal good is the further increase in consumption of the good when we hypothetically restore the consumer's real income but leave relative prices unchanged at the new level.

4 In the short run there will be a fall in the consumption of these products and a strong substitution effect. People will buy mayonnaise and chocolate from other countries. In the longer term, people may forget about the food scare and there may be a move back; a substitution effect in the opposite direction.

PROBLEMS

1 a Initially, Jan and Dan are at point c on the budget line labelled AB in Fig. 9.3. Jan's indifference curve is illustrated by I_J. Note that her indifference curve is

Figure 9.3

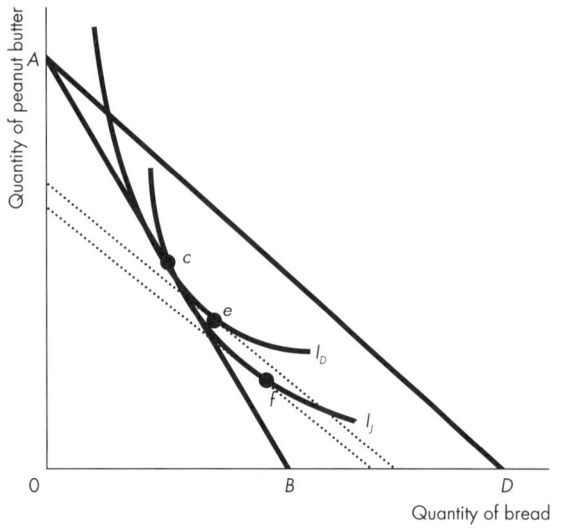

close to a straight line reflecting the fact that bread and peanut butter are close substitutes. On the other hand, since Dan considers bread and peanut butter to be complementary, his indifference curve, I_D, is more tightly curved.

b If the price of bread declines, the budget line will become flatter, such as the line labelled *AD* in Fig. 9.3. In order to measure the substitution effect we find the point on the original indifference curve that has the same slope as the new budget line. Since Dan's indifference curve is more sharply curved, it becomes flatter quite rapidly as we move away from point *c*. Thus the substitution effect is quite small: from *c* to point *e*. Since Jan's indifference curve is almost a straight line, the substitution effect must be much larger: from point *c* to point *f*.

2 a The relative price of coffee is the price of coffee divided by the price of whisky:

$$\frac{£1}{£1.50} = \frac{2}{3}$$

b Let P_c be the price of coffee, P_w be the price of whisky, Q_c be the quantity of coffee, Q_w be the quantity of whisky, and let y be income. The budget equation, in general form, is:

$$Q_w = \frac{y}{P_w} - \frac{P_c}{P_w} Q_c$$

Since $P_c = £1$, $P_w = £1.50$, and $y = £12$, Kurt's budget equation is specifically given by:

$$Q_w = 8 - \tfrac{2}{3} Q_c$$

The graph of this budget equation, the budget line, is given by the line labelled *AB* in Fig. 9.4.

Figure 9.4

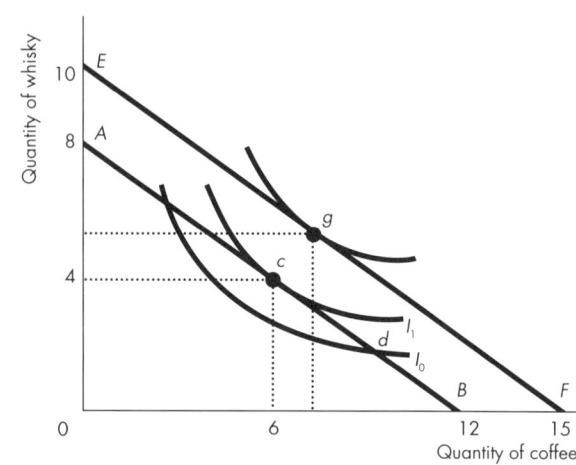

c If the best affordable point corresponds to 6 units of coffee and 4 units of whisky, then the relevant indifference curve must be tangent to (just touch) the budget line *AB* at *c*, which is indifference curve I_1.

d The marginal rate of substitution is given by the magnitude of the slope of the indifference curve at point *c*. We do not know the slope of the indifference curve directly but we can easily compute the slope of the budget line. Because at point *c* the indifference curve and the budget line have the same slope, we can obtain the marginal rate of substitution of coffee for whisky. Since the slope of the budget line is –2/3, the marginal rate of substitution is 2/3. For example, Kurt is willing to give up 2 units of whisky in order to receive 3 additional units of coffee and still remain indifferent.

e Since indifference curves cannot intersect each other and since indifference curve I_1 lies everywhere above the budget line (except at point *c*), we know that every other point on the budget line is on a lower indifference curve. For example, point *d* lies on indifference curve I_0. Thus every other point on the budget line is inferior to point *c*.

3 a An increase in income will cause a parallel outward shift of the budget line, for example, to *EF* in Fig. 9.4. If both coffee and whisky are normal goods, Kurt will move to a point like *g* at which the consumption of both goods has increased.

b If whisky is an inferior good, then its consumption will fall as income rises. This is illustrated in Fig. 9.5. Once again the budget line shifts from *AB* to *EF*, but Kurt's preferences are such that his new consump-

Figure 9.5

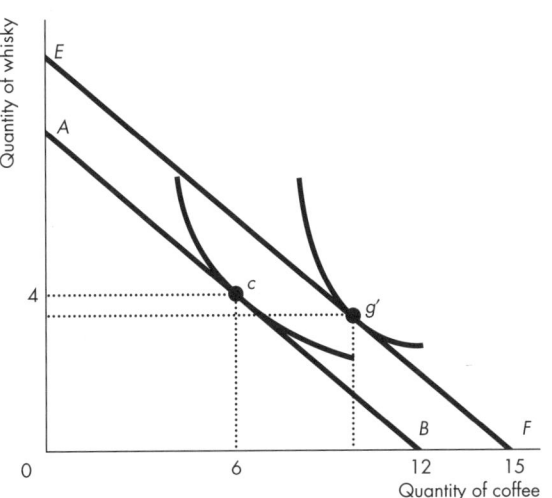

tion point is given by a point like *g'* where the consumption of whisky has actually declined.

4 a Kurt's initial budget line is given by *AB* and the initial best affordable point by *r* in Fig. 9.6. The new budget line following an increase in the price of coffee to £2 (income remains at £12) is represented by *AH*.

b After the price increase, point *r* is no longer the best affordable point since it is no longer even affordable.

c The new best affordable point (labelled *t* in Fig. 9.6) indicates a decrease in the consumption of coffee.

d The substitution effect of the increase in the price of coffee is indicated by the movement from *r* to *s* in Fig. 9.6. This gives the effect of the change in relative prices while keeping Kurt on the same indifference curve. The income effect is indicated by movement from point *s* to point *t*.

DISCUSSION QUESTIONS

1 There are two main reasons for using indifference curves. First, economists usually assume that rational individuals attempt to maximize their satisfaction, and indifference curves make use of this assumption to derive demand curves by rational argument.

Second, the indifference curve approach allows us to analyse income and substitution effects, and these concepts are important in several areas of economics. So indifference curves are a useful tool of analysis.

2 Demand curves show us how much of a good will be bought at different prices. Indifference curves show us different combinations of goods that give a consumer equal satisfaction.

DATA QUESTION

1 a Old people's original budget line is *AB* in Fig. 9.7, and they will maximize satisfaction at point *x* on indifference curve I_1. A subsidy for bus travel will shift the

Figure 9.6

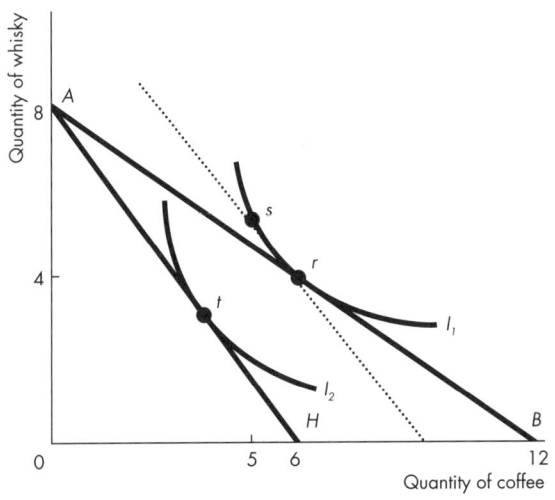

Figure 9.7

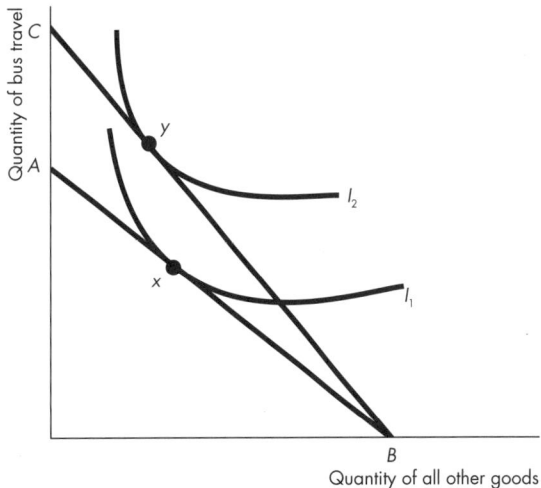

budget line to *CB* and satisfaction will be maximized at point y on I_2. They will consume considerably more bus travel and a little more of other goods.

b An increase in income will shift the entire budget line from *AB* to *CD* as shown in Fig. 9.8. However, since bus travel is an inferior good, they will move along budget line *CD* to position *y* on indifference curve I_2. The result will be a fall in the consumption of bus travel and an increase in the consumption of other goods such as taxis and private motoring.

Figure 9.8

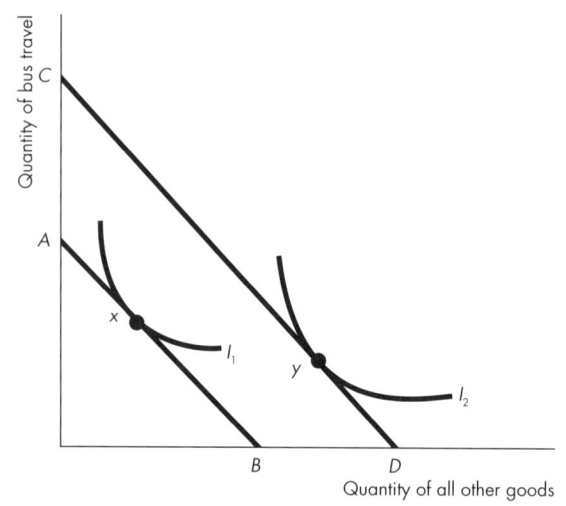

Chapter 10 Organizing Production

Chapter in Perspective, Text Pages 212–235

This chapter begins the analysis of firms' choices and the principles underlying supply. The analysis here focuses on key differences that exist in how firms organize production.

The first difference relates to types of firms. While there are common characteristics shared by all firms, there are different forms of business organization, each with pros and cons. The second difference relates to types of business finance. Concepts you read about every day in the business press – bonds, shares, present value, price–earnings ratios – are examined, as well as a difference between the accountant's and the economist's concepts of cost that depend crucially on opportunity cost. The third difference relates to the concepts of technological versus economic efficiency and the concepts of firm versus market coordination. The efficiency of firms (as institutions) makes them a primary coordinating mechanism through which market economies tackle the problem of scarcity.

Helpful Hints

1 The principal purpose of this chapter is to develop a fundamental understanding of why firms exist. Since it is obvious they do exist, it might seem better simply to begin with that fact and turn immediately to a study of their behaviour. Taking firms for granted, however, would eliminate an opportunity to acquire significant insights.

2 The chapter defines several important economic concepts.

a The concept of present value is fundamental in thinking about the value today of an investment or of future amounts of money. The intuition behind present value is that a pound today is worth more than a pound in the future because today's pound can be invested to earn interest. To calculate the value *today* of a sum of money that will be paid in the future, we must discount that future sum to compensate for the forgone interest. The *present value* of a future sum of money is the amount that, if invested today, will grow as large as that future sum, taking into account the interest that it will earn.

b In this chapter, we again meet our old friend opportunity cost. Here we look at the costs firms face with a special emphasis on the differences between historical cost measures used by accountants and opportunity cost measures used by economists. Historical cost includes only explicit, out-of-pocket costs. Opportunity cost, which is the concept of cost relevant for economic decisions, includes *explicit costs and imputed costs*. Important examples of imputed costs include the owner's/investor's forgone interest, forgone rent and forgone income. These differences in cost measures between accountants and economists lead to differences in profit measures as well, as outlined here.

Accountants
Historical costs = Explicit costs
Accounting profits = Revenues − Explicit costs

Economists
Opportunity costs = Explicit costs +
                    Imputed costs

Economic profits = Revenues − (Explicit costs
                    + Imputed costs)

Imputed costs, which economists include but accountants exclude, are the key difference between accountants' and economists' measures of cost and profit.

c It is important to distinguish between technological efficiency and economic efficiency. The difference is critical since economic decisions will be made only on the basis of economic efficiency. Technological efficiency is an engineering concept and occurs when it is not possible to increase output without increasing inputs. There is no consideration of input costs. Economic efficiency occurs when the *cost* of producing a given output is at a minimum. All technologically efficient production methods are not economically efficient. But all economically efficient methods are also technologically efficient.

SELF-TEST

CONCEPT REVIEW

1 An institution that organizes resources it has purchased or hired to produce and sell goods and services is called a(n) _____ .

2 There are three main forms of business organizations. The two simpler forms are a(n) _____ (which has a single owner) and a(n) _____ . In these two forms owners face_____ liability. The third more complicated form is a(n) _____ in which owners face _____ liability.

3 Firms can raise money by selling _____, which are legal obligations to pay specified amounts at specified future dates. Companies can also raise money by issuing _____ .

4 An agent is a person or firm hired by a _____ to do a specified job.

5 The four main ways of coping with the principal–agent problem are: ownership, _____ _____, _____-_____ _____ and _____ _____.

6 A _____ is a legally enforceable debt obligation to pay specified amounts of money at specified future dates.

7 In assessing costs, accountants measure _____ cost, which values resources at the prices originally paid for them. Economists measure _____ cost.

8 The change in the market price of a durable input over a given period is called economic _____ .

9 _____ efficiency is achieved when the cost of producing a given output is as low as possible. _____ efficiency is achieved when no more output can be produced without increasing inputs.

10 Firms coordinate economic activity when they can do so more efficiently than _____.

11 The costs associated with finding a buyer, reaching agreement about exchange and ensuring the fulfilment of the agreement are_____ costs.

12 _____ of _____ exist when the cost of producing a unit of output falls as we produce more.

13 Economies that are derived from the size of the firm rather than from the amount of machinery are called economies of _____ .

TRUE OR FALSE

__ **1** A firm purchases or hires factors of production and organizes production of goods and services.

__ **2** A partnership has joint unlimited liability.

__ **3** The residual claimants of a company are its bond holders.

__ **4** The perpetual 'life' of a company is an advantage over other forms of business organizations when it comes to raising large sums of money.

__ **5** A cooperative is a firm that has equal total costs and total revenue.

__ **6** Historical cost is more likely to be the same as opportunity cost when firms use their own funds rather than borrow.

__ **7** In general, opportunity cost will be greater than historical cost.

__ **8** When a firm produces using a machine it owns, its opportunity cost is lower than if it had rented the machine.

__ **9** The opportunity cost of using stocks is the current replacement cost.

__ **10** A production process that is economically efficient may become economically inefficient if the relative prices of inputs change.

MULTIPLE CHOICE

1 Which of the following statements is *not* true of firms?

a Firms are like markets in that they are an institution for coordinating economic activity.

b Firms organize factors of production in order to produce goods and services.

c Firms sell goods and services.

d Technologically efficient firms can eliminate scarcity.

e Firms include Crown corporations.

2 What is a firm called that has two or more owners with joint unlimited liability?

a a proprietorship

b a partnership

c a conglomerate

d a company

e none of the above

3 What is a *disadvantage* of a company relative to a proprietorship or partnership?

a owners have unlimited liability

b profits are taxed as corporate profits and as dividend income to shareholders

c there is difficulty in raising money

d perpetual life

e none of the above

4 The owner's stake in a business is called

a present value.

b redemption value.

c historical cost.

d equity capital.

e preferred stock.

5 Historical cost calculates the value of resources at the

a original purchase price.

b original purchase price minus depreciation.

c original purchase price minus economic depreciation.

d current market price.

e value of the best forgone alternative.

6 The construction cost of a building is $100,000. The conventional depreciation allowance is 5 per cent per year. At the end of the first year the market value of the building is $80,000. For the first year, the depreciation cost is

a $20,000 to an accountant or an economist.

b $5,000 to an accountant or an economist.

c $5,000 to an accountant but $20,000 to an economist.

d $20,000 to an accountant but $5,000 to an economist.

e none of the above.

7 John operates his own business and pays himself a salary of $20,000 per year. He was offered a job that pays $30,000 per year. What is the opportunity cost of John's time in the business?
a $10,000
b $20,000
c $30,000
d $50,000
e zero

8 The rate of interest is 10 per cent per year. If you invest $50,000 of your own money in a business and earn *accounting* profits of $20,000 after one year, what are your *economic* profits?
a $20,000
b $15,000
c $5,000
d $2,000
e −$15,000

9 Which of the following statements is *true*?
a All technologically efficient methods are also economically efficient.
b All economically efficient methods are also technologically efficient.
c Technological efficiency changes with changes in relative input prices.
d Technologically efficient firms will be more likely to survive than economically efficient firms.
e None of the above statements is true.

10 Firms will be more efficient than the market as a coordinator of economic activity when firms have
a lower transactions costs.
b lower monitoring costs.
c economies of scale.
d economies of team production.
e all of the above.

11 Economies of scale exist when
a transactions costs are high.
b transactions costs are low.
c hiring additional inputs does not increase the price of inputs.
d the cost of producing a unit of output falls as the output rate increases.
e the firm is too large and too diversified.

12 Which of the following is *not* a reason for the existence of firms?
a lower transactions costs.
b principal–agent problems.

c economies of scope.
d economies of team production.

13 McDonald's can use its labour and capital to sell hamburgers, fries and drinks cheaper than would be the case if each had to be produced seperately in a market. This demonstrates
a economies of scale.
b economies of scope.
c long-term contracts.
d none of the above.

SHORT ANSWER

1 Compare the historical cost and opportunity cost approaches in each of the following cases:
a depreciation cost
b the firm borrows money to finance its operation
c the firm uses its own funds rather than borrowing

2 Distinguish between technological efficiency and economic efficiency.

3 Markets and firms are alternative ways of co-ordinating economic activity that arises because of scarcity. Why is it that both firms and markets exist?

4 What is the differences between 'normal profit' and 'economic profit'?

PROBLEMS

1 Suppose that there are two technologically efficient methods of producing 1 tonne of wheat.

Method 1 requires 20 machine hours plus 20 human hours.

Method 2 requires 100 human hours.

Country *A* has a highly developed industrial economy, while country *B* is less developed. In country *A* the price of an hour of human labour (the wage rate) is $8, while the wage rate in country *B* is $4. The price of a machine hour is $20 in both countries. Which method is economically efficient in country *A*? in country *B*? Explain.

2 Consider countries *A* and *B* described in Problem 1.
a What wage rate in country *B* would make the two methods equally efficient in country *B*?

b What price of a machine hour would make the two methods equally efficient in country *A*?

DISCUSSION QUESTIONS

1 What is the difference between a 'normal profit' and an 'economic profit'? Why does the difference matter?

2 How can a situation be technologically efficient and not economically efficient?

DATA QUESTIONS

Firms and markets

No one knows who invented firms, or even markets, but both play crucial roles in the modern economy. In addition to conventional, privately owned 'firms', there are many kinds of formal organizations that play a part in the economic life of the country, for example, charities such as War on Want, educational institutions such as schools and other bodies such as athletics clubs. All have economic influences. Nevertheless, it is true that firms have a profound effect on the economy. Many of these are small. In 1998 there were over 3,600,000 enterprises in the UK. In construction 86 per cent of employment was in firms categorized as small or medium whilst in finance it was only 23 per cent.

In some circumstances, firms will be used to allocate resources. This will occur when they represent a more efficient method of organizing production. In other circumstances, markets will be used to allocate resources.

1 List some economic agents that are not firms.

2 Comment on the variation in the size of firms given in the text.

3 When will firms 'represent a more efficient method of organizing production'?

4 When are markets used to allocate resources?

ANSWERS

CONCEPT REVIEW

1 firm

2 proprietorship; partnership; unlimited; company; limited

3 bonds; shares

4 principal

5 incentive pay; long-term contracts and internal restructuring

6 bond

7 historical; opportunity

8 depreciation

9 Economic; technological

10 markets

11 transactions

12 Economies; scale

13 scope

TRUE OR FALSE

1 T Definition.

2 T This is the legal status.

3 F Bond holders have priority status.

4 T The legal status gives confidence to lenders.

5 F A cooperative is a form of organization where owners have equal shares.

6 F More likely to be different.

7 T Usually true, but it depends on the existence of imputed costs.

8 F Opportunity cost is equal whether the machine is owned or rented.

9 T Definition of opportunity cost.

10 T Economic efficiency depends on prices; if these change so does the efficiency of the process.

MULTIPLE CHOICE

1 d Scarcity can never be eliminated.

2 b Definition.

3 b d is an advantage; **a**, **c** are disadvantages of proprietorship and partnership.

4 d Definition.

5 a Definition.

6 c Accountant's depreciation = (5 per cent) × $100,000. Economist's depreciation = change in market value.

7 c Forgone income.

8 b Economic profits = accounting profits – imputed costs = $20,000 – (0.10 × $50,000).

9 b c is true for economic efficiency; the reverse of **d** is true.

10 e Definition.

11 d Definition.

12 b The principal–agent problem is a *difficulty* that firms must face.

13 b Economics of scope occur when producing several products lowers the cost of producing each unit.

SHORT ANSWER

1 a From the historical cost approach, depreciation cost is computed as a prespecified percentage of the original purchase price of the capital good, with no reference to current market value. The opportunity cost approach measures economic depreciation cost as the change in the market value of the capital good over the period in question.

b If a firm borrows money, the historical and opportunity cost approaches will be the same; both will include the explicit interest payments.

c If a firm uses its own funds rather than borrowing, the historical and opportunity cost approaches will again differ. The historical cost will be zero since there are no explicit interest payments. The opportunity cost approach recognizes that those funds could have been loaned out and thus the (imputed) interest income forgone is the opportunity cost.

2 A method is technologically efficient if it is not possible to increase output without increasing inputs. A method is economically efficient if the cost of producing a given level of output is as low as possible. Technological efficiency is independent of prices while economic efficiency depends on the prices of inputs. An economically efficient method of production is always technologically efficient, but a technologically efficient method is not necessarily economically efficient.

3 As we saw in the text example on page 229, car repair can be coordinated by the market or by a firm. The institution (market or firm) that actually coordinates in any given case will be the one that is more efficient. In cases where there are significant transactions costs, economies of scale, or economies of team production, firms are likely to be more efficient, and we will see firms dominate the coordination of economic activity. But the efficiency of firms is limited and there are many circumstances in which we observe market coordination of economic activity because it is more efficient.

4 Normal profit is the payment for the services of the entrepreneur. Because it is for services rendered (perhaps implicitly), it is part of the firm's opportunity costs. Economics profit equals the firm's revenues minus its opportunity costs. Because opportunity costs include normal profit, economic profit is on above-average profit.

PROBLEMS

1 Both production methods are technologically efficient. To find the economically efficient production method we want to know which of the methods has the lower cost of producing 1 tonne of wheat. In country A, the price of an hour of labour is $8 and the price of a machine hour is $20. Thus the cost of producing 1 tonne of wheat is $560 using method 1 and $800 using method 2. Therefore method 1 is economically efficient for country A.

The price of an hour of labour is $4 in country B and thus it will face different costs of producing 1 tonne of wheat. Under method 1, the cost will be $480 but under method 2, which uses only labour, the cost will be $400. So method 2 is economically efficient for country B.

The reason for this difference is that economic efficiency means producing at lowest cost. If the relative prices of inputs are different in two countries, there will be differences in the relative costs of production using alternative methods.

2 a If the wage rate in country B were to increase to $5 an hour, then production of 1 tonne of wheat would be $500 under either method. How did we obtain this answer? Express the cost under method 1 (C_1) and the cost under method 2 (C_2) as follows:

$$C_1 = 20 P_m + 20 P_h$$
$$C_2 = 100 P_h$$

where P_m is the price of a machine hour and P_h is the price of a human hour (the wage rate). We are given that $P_m = $20 and asked to find the value of P_h that makes the two methods equally efficient; the value of P_h that makes $C_1 = C_2$. Thus we solve the following equation for P_h:

$$20P_m + 20P_h = 100P_h$$
$$20(\$20) + 20P_h = 100P_h$$
$$\$400 = 80P_h$$
$$\$5 = P_h$$

b If the price of a machine hour is $32, production of 1 tonne of wheat would be $800 under either method in country A. This question asks: given the wage rate of $8 ($P_h$) in country A, what value of P_m makes $C_1 = C_2$? Thus we solve the following equation for P_m:

$$20P_m + 20P_h = 100P_h$$
$$20P_m + 20(\$8) = 100(\$8)$$
$$20P_m = \$640$$
$$P_m = \$32$$

DISCUSSION QUESTIONS

1 Every business owner supplies some input into the business. One of these inputs is entrepreneurial talent, and normal profit is the payment for these services. Because normal profit is a payment for services rendered (perhaps implicitly), it is part of the firm's opportunity costs.

An economic profit equals the firm's revenues minus its opportunity costs. Because opportunity costs already include normal profit, an economic profit is a profit over and above a normal profit.

2 Technological efficiency merely reflects a firm's inputs and the resulting outputs. A situation is technologically efficient when producing more output without using more inputs is impossible.

Economic efficiency occurs when the cost of producing a given amount of output is as low as possible. A firm which is economically efficient will also be technologically efficient, but it is possible for a firm to be technologically efficient but not economically efficient. This will occur if it uses the wrong mix of inputs. For example, if the local McDonald's employed economics professors to cook its burgers it might be technologically efficient, but it would not be economically efficient because the cost of wages would be too high.

DATA QUESTIONS

1 Other economic agents include cooperatives, nationalized industries and government departments.

2 In some industries there are economies of scale. These exist when the cost of producing a unit of output falls as the quantity produced increases. Hence in industries such as car production, firms tend to be large. When the product does not permit economies of scale – for example, in hairdressing or plumbing – the enterprise remains small.

3 Firms achieve lower transactions costs, economies of scale and economies of team production.

4 Markets are used to allocate resources when firms do not provide an optimal solution.

Chapter 11 Output and Costs

Chapter in Perspective, Text Pages 236–265

In a modern market economy, goods and services are produced primarily by firms. In Chapter 9 we saw that firms exist because they provide economically efficient ways of organizing factors of production for producing and selling goods and services. In this chapter we begin to analyse the production and cost constraints that firms face, and thus how efficiency is pursued.

What kinds of costs do firms face? How do these costs change as a firm's planning horizon changes? How will a firm, motivated by the desire to maximize profit, decide how much output to produce? When will a firm hire more labour? When will it increase its plant size? This chapter begins to answer these questions.

Helpful Hints

1 Be sure you understand the difference between 'marginal cost' and 'average cost' – the two are very different. 'Marginal' means additional, so if it costs £1,000 to produce 10 tables and £1,050 to produce 11, then the marginal cost of the eleventh table is 1,050 – 1,000 = £50. The averge cost is £1,050 ÷ 11 = £95.45.

2 There is a simple and fundamental relationship between production functions and cost functions.

The chapter begins with the short-run production function and the concepts of total product, marginal product and average product. This is followed by the short-run cost function and the concepts of total cost, marginal cost, average variable cost and average total cost.

All of these seemingly disparate concepts are related to the law of diminishing returns. The law states that as a firm uses additional units of a variable input, while holding constant the quantity of fixed inputs, the marginal product of the variable input will eventually diminish. This law explains why the marginal product and average product curves eventually fall, and why the total product curve becomes flatter. When productivity falls, costs increase, and the law explains the eventual upward slope of the marginal cost curve. The marginal cost curve, in turn, explains the U-shape of the average variable cost and average total cost curves. When the marginal cost curve is below the average variable (or total) cost curve, the average variable (or total) cost curve is falling. When marginal cost is above the average variable (or total) cost curve, the average variable (or total) cost curve is rising. The marginal cost curve intersects the average variable (or total) cost curve at the minimum point on the average variable (or total) cost curve.

Use the law of diminishing returns as the key to understanding the relationships between the many short-run concepts and graphs in the chapter. Pay most attention to the unit cost concepts and graphs – especially marginal cost, average variable cost and average total cost – because these will be used the most in later chapters to analyse the behaviour of firms. Be sure to thoroughly understand text Figure 11.5(b) on page 245. It is the most important figure in the chapter.

3 You will probably draw the unit cost graph with the marginal cost, average variable cost and average total cost curves many times in this course. Here are some hints on drawing the graph quickly and easily.

   a Be sure to label the axes; quantity of output (Q) on the horizontal axis and average cost on the vertical axis.

   b Draw a shallow U-shaped curve (see Fig. 11.1) and mark its minimum point. Then pick a second point above and to the right of that first minimum point. Draw another shallow U-shaped curve whose minimum point passes through your second point. Draw an upward-sloping marginal cost curve which passes through the two minimum points. The marginal cost curve can have a small downward-sloping section at first, but this is not important for subsequent analysis. Finally, label the curves.

   c Any time a test question asks about these curves, *draw a graph* before you answer.

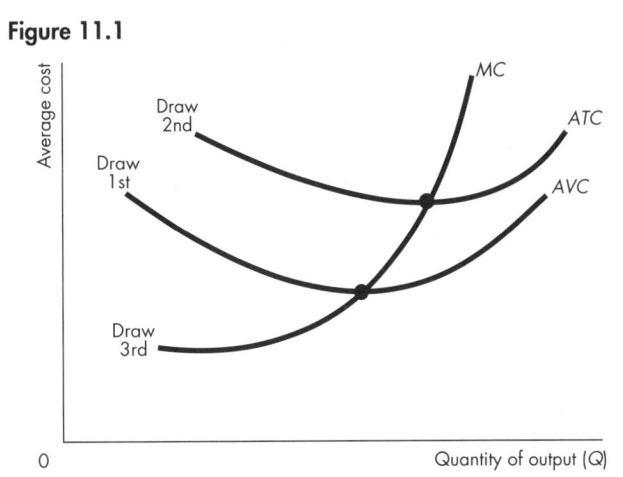

Figure 11.1

3 Be sure to understand how economists use the terms *short run* and *long run*. These terms do not refer to any notion of calendar time. They are better thought of as planning horizons. The short run is a planning horizon short enough for, while some inputs are variable, at least one input to be fixed not varied. The long run refers to a planning horizon that is long enough for all inputs to be varied.

4 The later sections of the chapter explain the long-run production function and cost function when plant size is variable. While diminishing returns was the key for understanding short-run costs, the concept of returns to scale is the key for understanding long-run costs. Returns to scale are the increase in output relative to the increase in inputs when *all inputs* are increased by the same percentage. Returns to scale can be increasing, constant, or decreasing, and correspond to the downward-sloping, horizontal and upward-sloping sections of the long-run average cost curve.

SELF-TEST

CONCEPT REVIEW

1 The profits of a firm are limited by two types of constraints: _____ constraints, which are conditions under which the firm can buy its inputs and sell its output, and _____ constraints, which limit the feasible ways in which inputs can be converted into output.

2 A production process that uses large amounts of capital relative to labour is called a(n) _____ - _____ technique while a(n) _____ - _____ technique uses a large amount of labour relative to capital.

3 The term economists use for a period of time in which the quantities of some inputs are fixed while others can be varied is the _____ _____ . The period of time in which all inputs are variable is the_____ _____ .

4 The total product curve is a graph of the maximum output attainable at each level of a _____ input, given the amount of fixed inputs. The change in total product resulting from a one-unit increase in labour input, holding the quantity of capital constant, is called the_____ _____ of labour. The average product of labour is _____ _____ divided by the units of _____ .

5 If marginal product is greater than average product, then average product must be _____ . Marginal product _____ average product when average product reaches a maximum.

6 The shape of the marginal product curve can be described as follows: it first _____ , reaches a _____ and then _____ as labour inputs increase.

7 Increasing marginal returns occur when the marginal product of an additional worker is _____ than the marginal product of the previous workers. As more of a variable input is used, holding other inputs fixed, the marginal product of the variable input begins to decline. This is a statement of the law of _____ _____ .

8 $TC = FC +$ _____ .

9 Marginal cost is the increase in total cost resulting from a one-unit increase in _____ .

10 If the average variable cost curve is decreasing, then the marginal cost curve must be _____ the average variable cost.

11 If output increases by 20 per cent when all inputs are increased by 10 per cent, the production process is said to display _____ _____ to _____ .

12 If a firm is experiencing constant returns to scale, a 10 per cent increase in inputs will result in a _____ per cent _____ in output. When the long-run average cost curve rises, there are _____ returns to scale.

13 A technological advance will tend to _____ product curves and _____ cost curves.

TRUE OR FALSE

___ **1** All economically efficient production methods are also technologically efficient.

___ **2** The short run is a time period in which there is at least one fixed input and at least one variable input.

___ **3** All inputs are fixed in the long run.

___ **4** Marginal product is given by the slope of the total product curve.

___ **5** Average product can be measured as the slope of a line drawn from the origin to a point on the total product curve.

___ **6** The average product curve cuts the marginal product curve from above at the maximum point on the marginal product curve.

___ **7** Average total cost, average variable cost and average fixed cost are all U-shaped.

___ **8** Average variable cost reaches its minimum at the level of output at which average product is a maximum.

___ **9** In the real world, marginal cost curves are rarely upward sloping.

___ **10** A firm producing on the downward-sloping part of its average total cost curve is said to have excess capacity.

___ **11** By capacity, economists mean the physical limits of production.

___ **12** If average total cost is greater than marginal cost, then average total cost must be increasing.

___ **13** Increasing returns to scale means that the long-run average cost curve is negatively sloped.

___ **14** In the long run, the total cost and total variable cost curves are the same.

MULTIPLE CHOICE

1 In economics, the short run is a time period
  a of one year or less.
  b in which all inputs are variable.
  c in which all inputs are fixed.
  d in which there is at least one fixed input and at least one variable input.
  e in which all inputs are variable but the technology is fixed.

2 The average product of labour can be measured as the
  a slope of a straight line from the origin to a point on the total product curve.
  b slope of the total product curve.
  c slope of a straight line from the origin to a point on the marginal product curve.
  d slope of the marginal product curve.
  e change in output divided by the change in labour input.

3 A field of ripe corn is waiting to be harvested. Labour is the only variable input, and the total product (in kilograms) of various numbers of workers is given in the table.

Table 11.1

Number of workers	Total product
0	0
1	300
2	700
3	1,000
4	1,200

Diminishing returns *begin* when you add which worker?
  a 1st worker
  b 2nd worker
  c 3rd worker
  d 4th worker
  e there are no diminishing returns since total product always rises

4 When the marginal product of labour is less than the average product of labour
  a the average product of labour is increasing.
  b the marginal product of labour is increasing.
  c the total product curve is negatively sloped.
  d the firm is experiencing diminishing returns.
  e none of the above is true.

5 The vertical distance between the *TC* and *TVC* curves is
  a decreasing as output increases.
  b increasing as output increases.
  c equal to *AFC*.
  d equal to *TFC*.
  e equal to *MC*.

6 The marginal cost *(MC)* curve intersects the
  a *ATC*, *AVC* and *AFC* curves at their minimum points.
  b *ATC* and *AFC* curves at their minimum points.
  c *AVC* and *AFC* curves at their minimum points.
  d *ATC* and *AVC* curves at their minimum points.
  e *TC* and *TVC* curves at their minimum points.

7 Marginal cost is the amount by which
  a total cost increases when one more worker is hired.
  b fixed cost increases when one more worker is hired.
  c variable cost increases when one more worker is hired.
  d total cost increases when one more unit of output is produced.
  e fixed cost increases when one more unit of output is produced.

8 A firm's fixed costs are £100. If total costs are £200 for one unit of output and £310 for two units, what is the marginal cost of the second unit?
  a £100
  b £110
  c £200
  d £210
  e £310

Use Table 11.2 for the next three questions.

Table 11.2

Output	Total variable cost (£)	Totoal cost (£)
3	15	21
4	18	24

9 The marginal cost of producing the fourth unit is
a £6.
b £5.
c £3.
d £2.

10 The average total cost of the fourth unit is
a £6.
b £5.
c £3.
d £2.

11 The average fixed cost of the third unit is
a £6.
b £5.
c £4.
d £3.

12 If *ATC* is falling then *MC* must be
a rising.
b falling.
c equal to *ATC*.
d above *ATC*.
e below *ATC*.

13 In the long run
a only the scale of plant is fixed.
b all inputs are variable.
c all inputs are fixed.
d a firm must experience decreasing returns to scale.
e none of the above is true.

14 The marginal cost curve slopes upward because of
a diminishing marginal utility.
b diminishing returns.
c technological inefficiency.
d economic inefficiency.
e none of the above statements.

15 Constant returns to scale means that as all inputs are increased
a total output remains constant.
b average total cost remains constant.
c average total cost increases at the same rate as inputs.
d long-run average cost remains constant.
e long-run average cost rises at the same rate as inputs.

16 The long-run average cost curve
a shifts upward when fixed costs increase.

b shifts downward when fixed costs increase.
c is the short-run average total cost curve with the lowest cost.
d traces the minimum points on all the short-run average total cost curves for each scale of plant.
e traces the minimum short-run average total cost for each output.

17 A firm will want to increase its scale of plant if
a it persistently produces on the upward-sloping part of its short-run average total cost curve.
b it persistently produces on the downward-sloping part of its short-run average total cost curve.
c it is producing below capacity.
d marginal cost is below average total cost.
e marginal cost is below average variable cost.

The following questions relate to the Appendix to this chapter (text pages 257–263).

18 Figure 11.2 shows a series of isoquants. Which of the following combinations of labour and capital could *not* produce 30 units of output?
a 8 units of labour and 1 unit of capital
b 7 units of labour and 2 units of capital
c 5 units of labour and 3 units of capital
d 2 units of labour and 6 units of capital
e 1 unit of labour and 8 units of capital

Figure 11.2

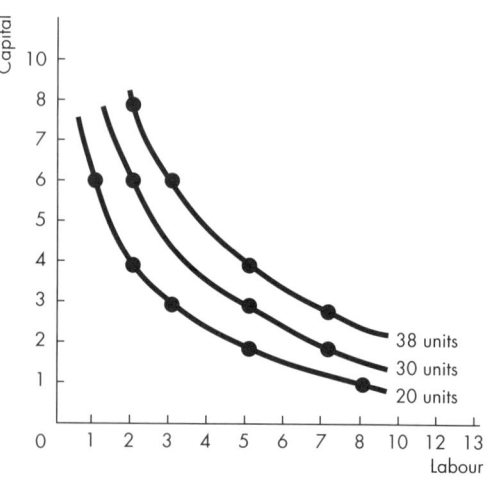

19 In Fig. 11.2, what is the marginal rate of substitution of capital for labour as labour is increased from 2 to 3 units if output is kept constant at 38 units?

a 1/2
b 1
c 2
d 3
e 6

20 In Fig. 11.2, 6 units of capital and 2 units of labour are currently in use. What is the marginal product of an additional unit of labour?

a 6
b 8
c 10
d 18
e cannot be determined without additional information

SHORT ANSWER

1 What market constraints does a firm face on its ability to make profits?

2 Why does a steeper slope of the total product curve imply a higher level of the marginal product curve?

3 Why is it the case that the marginal product curve must intersect the average product curve at its maximum point?

4 What is the difference, if any, between diminishing returns and decreasing returns to scale?

PROBLEMS

1 For a given scale of plant, Table 11.2 gives the total monthly output of golf carts attainable using varying quantities of labour.

Table 11.2   Monthly Golf Cart Production

Workers (per month)	Output (units per month)	Marginal product	Average product
0	0		
1	1		
2	3		
3	6		
4	12		
5	17		
6	20		
7	22		
8	23		

a Complete the table for the marginal product and average product of labour. (Note that marginal product should be entered midway between rows to emphasize that it is the result of *changing* inputs – moving from one row to the next. Average product corresponds to a *fixed* quantity of labour and should be entered on the appropriate row.)

b Label the axes and draw a graph of the total product curve *(TP)*.

c On a separate piece of paper, label the axes and draw a graph of both marginal product *(MP)* and average product *(AP)*. (Marginal product should be plotted midway between the corresponding units of labour, as in text Figure 11.2 on page 240, while average product should be plotted directly above the corresponding units of labour, as in text Figure 11.3 on page 242.)

2 Now let's examine the short-run costs of golf cart production. The first two columns of Table 11.2 are reproduced in the first two columns of Table 11.3. The cost of 1 worker (the only variable input) is £2,000 per month. Total fixed cost is £2,000 per month.

Table 11.3   Short-run Costs

Workers (per month)	Output (units per month)	TFC (£)	TVC (£)	TC (£)	MC (£)	AFC (£)	AVC (£)	ATC (£)
0	0	2,000						
1	1							
2	3							
3	6							
4	12							
5	17							
6	20							
7	22							
8	23							

a Given this information, complete Table 11.3 by computing total fixed cost *(TFC)*, total variable cost *(TVC)*, total cost *(TC)*, marginal cost *(MC)*, average fixed cost *(AFC)*, average variable cost *(AVC)* and average total cost *(ATC)*. Your completed table should look like text Table 11.2 on page 244, with marginal cost entered midway between the rows.

b Label the axes and draw the *TC*, *TVC* and *TFC* curves on a single graph.

c Label the axes and draw the *MC*, *ATC*, *AVC* and *AFC* curves on a single graph. Be sure to plot *MC* midway between the corresponding units of output.

d Now suppose that the price of a worker increases to £2,500 per month. Construct a table for the new *MC* and *ATC* curves (output, *MC*, *ATC*). Label the axes and draw a graph of the new *MC* and *ATC* curves. What is the effect of the increase in the price of the variable input on these curves?

3 Figure 11.3 gives a sequence of short-run *ATC* curves numbered 1 to 7 corresponding to seven different factory sizes.

  a Draw the long-run average cost curve on Fig. 11.3.

  b If the desired level of output is 100 units per day, what is the best factory size? (Give the number of the associated short-run *ATC* curve.)

  c If the desired level of output is 200 units per day, what is the best factory size?

Figure 11.3

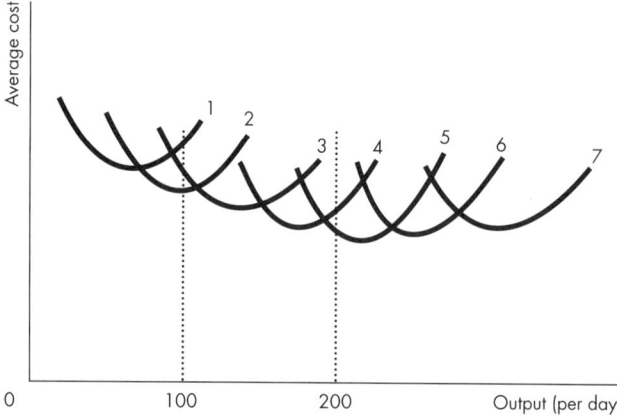

4 This question relates to the Appendix to this chapter (text pages 257–263).

  In country *A* the price of labour is £8 per unit and the price of capital is also £8 per unit. In country *B*, the price of labour is £4 per unit and the price of capital is £8 per unit. Country *B* is a low-wage economy. Consider the production problem faced by two firms, one in each country, which both produce the same good. Firm 1 is in country *A* and firm 2 is in country *B*. Both firms

have access to the same production technology, and therefore the same production function.

  a Draw a graph of an isoquant and isocost line for firm 1 which illustrates the least-cost production techniques for some level of output.

  b Now consider firm 2. As the firms have the same production function, their isoquants are identical. On the same graph as part **a**, illustrate the least-cost production technique for firm 2, using the same level of output.

  c Using the same graph, show that the combinations of labour and capital used by

  i firm 1 is more expensive than the combination used by firm 2 when the price of labour is as in country *B*.

  ii firm 2 is more expensive than the combination used by firm 1 when the price of labour is as in country *A*.

DISCUSSION QUESTION

1 Why is marginal cost an important concept?

DATA QUESTION

Enlarging the European Union

In December 1999 the Council of Ministers of the European Union met to dicuss enlarging the Union from 15 members to a possible 26 to include Central European countries such as Poland, Hungary and the Czech Republic.

  The resulting market integration will lead to increased trade enabling firms to make savings linked to larger-scale production. Empirical studies show that the bigger the market, the greater is the move towards the size needed to achieve substantial economies of scale.

There are three complicating factors:

  a In addition to economies in the production process, firms may realize economies in areas such as research and finance.

  b The enlargement of the EU will take several years to complete.

  c Potential gains vary significantly by industry. Doubling output may cut unit costs by 10 per cent in car manufacturing and 20 per cent in aircraft manufacture.

1 Explain what is meant by 'economies of scale'.

2 Why do you think some industries benefit more from economies of scale than others?

3 Draw points on average cost curves for (a) cars, and (b) aircraft manufacture.

4 If large firms benefit from substantial economies of scale, why are not all industries made up of enormous firms?

ANSWERS

CONCEPT REVIEW

1 market; technological

2 capital-intensive; labour-intensive

3 short run; long run

4 variable; marginal product; total product (output); labour

5 rising; equals

6 increases; maximum; decreases

7 greater; diminishing returns

8 VC

9 output

10 below

11 increasing returns; scale

12 10; increase; decreasing

13 raise; lower

TRUE OR FALSE

1 T Definition.

2 T Definition.

3 F All inputs are variable in the long run.

4 T Change in TP/Change in L.

5 T Geometrical relationship.

6 F This would be true if the terms 'average product' and 'marginal product' were switched.

7 F See cost curve diagrams.

8 T $AVC = TVC/Q = WL/Q = W/(Q/L) = W/AP$

9 F Marginal costs sometimes fall, sometimes rise.

10 T Could increase output up to capacity (quantity associated with minimum ATC).

11 F Capacity = capacity associated with minimum ATC.

12 T Draw curves to check.

13 T Definition.

14 T All costs are variable in the long run.

MULTIPLE CHOICE

1 d Definition.

2 a Equals TP/L.

3 c MP 1st = 3. MP 2nd = 4. MP 3rd = 3.

4 d When $MP < AP$, MP is falling (diminishing returns), AP is falling and TP is positively sloped.

5 d $TC = TFC + TVC$. Distance is constant.

6 d AFC always falls, TC and TVC always rise.

7 d Definition.

8 b Fixed costs are irrelevant. Change in TC/Change in quantity = (£310 – £200) / (2 – 1).

9 c Marginal cost of the fourth item is the difference between the total cost of producing the fourth item (£24) minus the total cost of producing the third item (£21) = £3.

10 a Average total cost equals total cost divided by output = £24 ÷ 4 = £6.

11 d Total cost equals total fixed cost plus total variable cost, so total fixed cost equals £21 – £15 = £6. To find average fixed cost, we divide this by the output (3) so average fixed cost is 6 ÷ 3 = £2.

12 e MC could be rising or falling below ATC when ATC is falling.

13 b Definition. All returns to scale possible in long run.

14 b Diminishing returns will cause marginal costs to rise.

15 d $LRAC$ is horizontal.

16 e Definition. **a** and **b** apply to the short run since fixed costs.

17 a **b** and **c** plant too big. **d** and **e** relate to short run.

18 a This isoquant would produce only 20 units.

19 c Read off from move along 38-unit isoquant.

20 b Read off from move along 30-unit isoquant.

SHORT ANSWER

1 Every firm is constrained by the supply of inputs it uses and by the demand for the output it produces. Because of the law of supply, firms, in general, can obtain more inputs only if they are willing to pay more for them. On the other hand, given the law of demand, firms, in general, can sell more of their output only if they are willing to drop the price.

2 Marginal product is equal to the slope of the total product curve since it is defined as the change in total product resulting from an increase in the variable input. Since a steeper slope means a larger slope, it also means a higher marginal product.

3 Since the average product curve first rises and then falls, when average product is rising, marginal product must be greater than average product, and when average product is falling, marginal product must be lower than average product. If this is the case, then the marginal product curve intersects the average product curve at its maximum point. In order for average product to increase, it must have been *pulled up* by a larger increase in product from the last unit of input. Therefore the marginal product is higher than average product. Similarly, when average product is falling, it must have been *pulled down* by a lower marginal product. When average product is at its maximum, it is neither rising nor falling, so marginal product cannot be higher or lower than average product. Therefore marginal product must be equal to average product.

4 The law of diminishing returns states that as a firm uses additional units of a variable input, *while holding constant the quantity of fixed inputs*, the marginal product of the variable input will eventually diminish. Decreasing returns to scale occur when a firm increases *all of its inputs by an equal percentage*, and this results in a lower percentage increase in output. Diminishing (marginal) returns is a short-run concept since there must be a fixed input. Decreasing returns to scale is a long-run concept since all inputs must be variable.

PROBLEMS

1 a The completed table is shown as Table 11.4.
  b Figure 11.4 gives the graph of the total product curve.
  c Figure 11.5 gives the graphs of marginal product and average product.

Table 11.4 Monthly Golf Cart Production

Workers (per month)	Output (units per month)	Marginal product	Average product
0	0		0
		...1	
1	1		1.00
		...2	
2	3		1.50
		...3	
3	6		2.00
		...6	
4	12		3.00
		...5	
5	17		3.40
		...3	
6	20		3.33
		...2	
7	22		3.14
		...1	
8	23		2.88

Figure 11.4

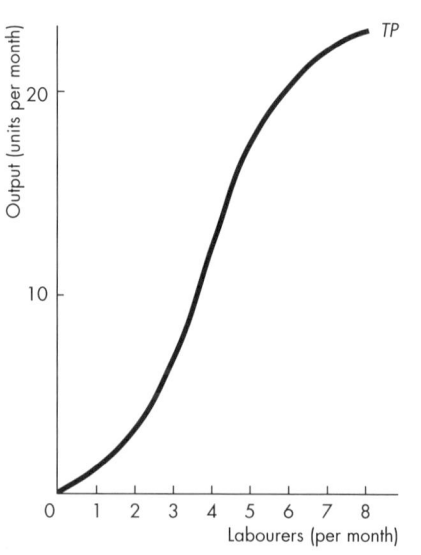

Figure 11.5

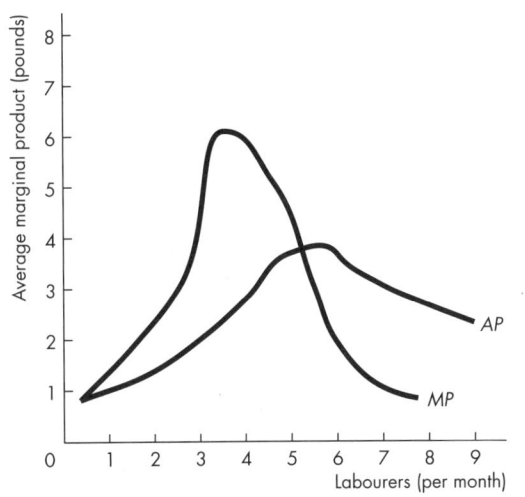

2   a The completed table is given as Table 11.5.

Table 11.5   Short-run Costs

Workers (per month)	Output (units per month)	TFC (£)	TVC (£)	TC (£)	MC (£)	AFC (£)	AVC (£)	ATC (£)
0	0	2,000	0	2,000				
					2,000			
1	1	2,000	2,000	4,000		2,000	2,000	4,000
					1,000			
2	3	2,000	4,000	6,000		667	1,333	2,000
					667			
3	6	2,000	6,000	8,000		333	1,000	1,333
					333			
4	12	2,000	8,000	10,000		167	667	833
					400			
5	17	2,000	10,000	12,000		118	588	706
					667			
6	20	2,000	12,000	14,000		100	600	700
					1,000			
7	22	2,000	14,000	16,000		91	636	727
					2,000			
8	3	2,000	8,000	18,000		87	696	783

b The *TC*, *TVC* and *TFC* curves are graphed in Fig. 11.6.
c The *MC*, *ATC*, *AVC* and *AFC* curves are graphed in Fig. 11.7.
d The new *MC* and *ATC* curves (and the associated table) are given in Fig. 11.8. The original curves, MC_1 and ATC_1, are indicated for reference. The new curves are labelled MC_2 and ATC_2. Both curves have shifted upward as a result of an increase in the price of labour.

Figure 11.6

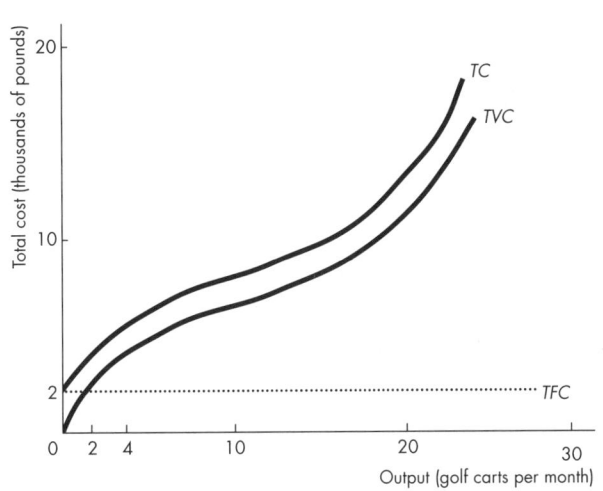

Figure 11.7

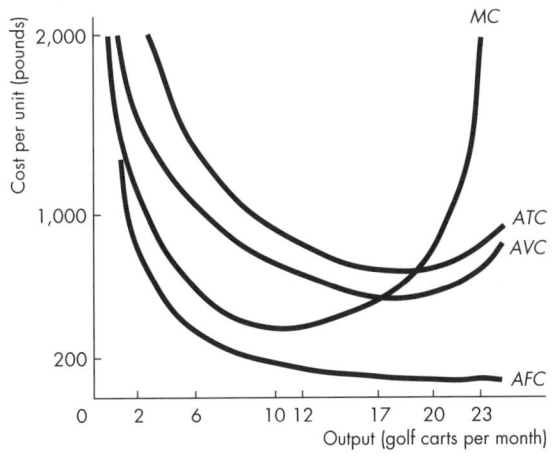

3   a The long-run average cost curve is indicated in Fig. 11.9 by the heavy line tracing out the lowest short-run average total cost of producing each level of output.
b If the desired level of output is 100 units, the best plant size is the one associated with short-run average total cost curve 2.
c If the desired level of output is 200 units, the best plant size is the one associated with short-run average total cost curve 5.

Figure 11.8

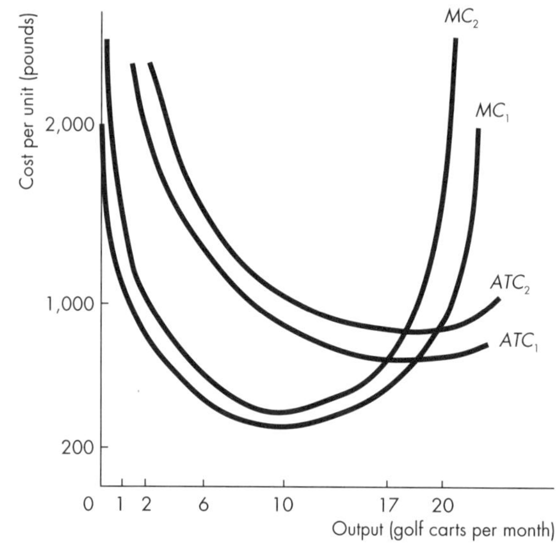

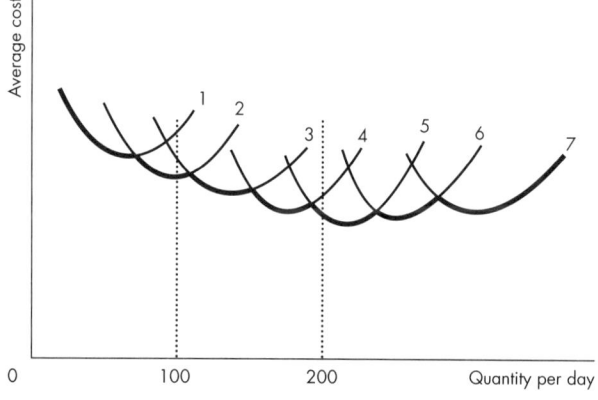

Output	MC (£)	ATC (£)
0		0
1	...2,500	4,500
3	...1,250	2,333
6	833	1,583
12	417	1,000
17	500	853
20	833	850
22	...1,250	886
23	...2,500	957

Figure 11.9

4 **a** See Fig. 11.10. The isoquant for the chosen level of output is the curve Q. Since firm 1 is in country A where the prices of labour and capital are the same, the slope of the isoquant line is 1 in absolute value. The least-cost isoquant line for firm 1 is given by the line labelled AA, which is tangent to the isoquant at point a. Thus for firm 1, the least-cost combination is L_1 units of labour and K_1 units of capital.

b The isoquant for firm 2 is the same as for firm 1. In this case the slope of the isoquant lines is 1/2 in absolute value and the least-cost isoquant for firm 2 is the line labelled BB, which is tangent to the isocost at point b. Thus for firm 2 the least cost combination is L_2 units of labour and K_2 units of capital.

c **i** The input combination represented by point a is more costly than the input combination represented by point b.

ii Point b lies above the AA isocost line and therefore must lie on a higher isocost line. This means that the input combination represented by point a is more costly than the input combination represented by point b.

Figure 11.10

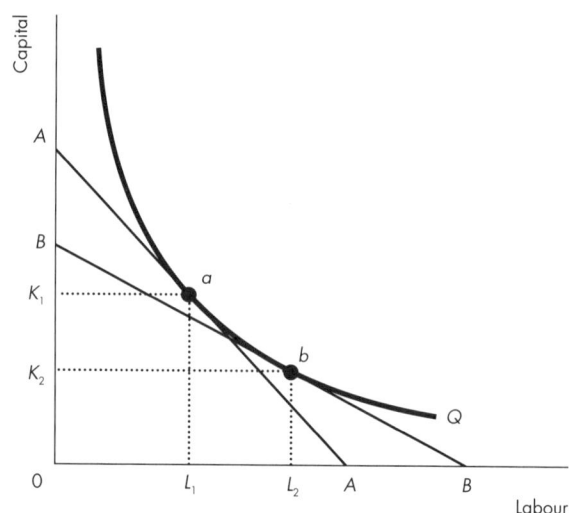

DISCUSSION QUESTION

1 The idea of the margin is fundamental in economics. Here we have been analysing marginal cost – the additional cost which a firm incurs when it expands production by one unit. When a firm is considering expansion, it will maximize profit if it continues to expand as long as the marginal revenue obtained by selling an additional unit exceeds the marginal cost of making that unit. This idea is fundamental to much economic analysis of firms.

DATA QUESTIONS

1 Economies of scale exist when the cost of producing a unit of a good falls as the level of output increases.

2 Some industries (such as car manufacture) enjoy considerable economies of scale, but in other industries (such as hairdressing and other personal services) there are few economies of scale.

3 The cost curves are shown in Fig. 11.11.

4 There are two main reasons why the economy is not completely dominated by large firms. First, there are often substantial diseconomies of scale so that growth may mean less efficiency. This is discussed in the text on page 252. Second, there is only a small market for some products so firms in these industries are inevitably small.

Figure 11.11

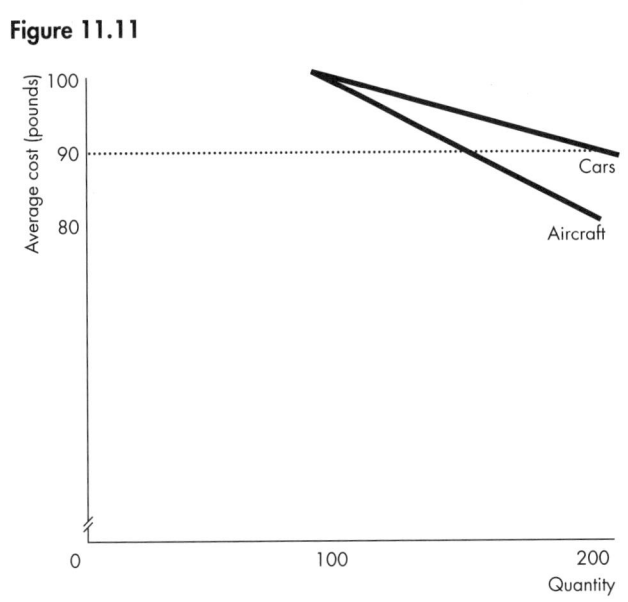

Part 4 Competition versus Monopoly

Looking back to Part 3 (Chapters 8–11)

One way to see if you have understood the main ideas in Chapter 8 (in addition to seeing if you can explain the key terms listed in the main text on page 183) is to see if you understand the paradox of value. Why are diamonds expensive and water cheap? Explaining this brings in many of the main ideas in the chapter.

Chapter 9 is constructed round two main ideas. One is the idea of a budget line. You should know by now that this is a way of saying that a household's consumption is limited by its income and by prices. This can be shown in the form of a line. The other idea is that of an indifference curve, showing all the combinations of goods about which the consumer is indifferent. These two – the budget line and indifference curves – can be used in many advanced areas of economics and will be useful if you continue to study the subject. Here they have been used to predict the effects of changes in prices and income on consumer choice.

Again, in Chapter 10, look at the key terms (page 231) and see if you can explain them. The beginning of the chapter suggests that after reading it you will be able to explain why firms coordinate some economic activities whilst others are left to markets. A good test of your understanding is to see if you can do this. If not, look back at the chapter.

This part of the text concludes in Chapter 11, focusing on the relationship between a firm's costs and its output. Here it is important that you understand notions such as returns to scale, marginal cost and product and the difference between various concepts of cost such as fixed cost and variable cost. Which of these is the cost of the paper used to produce this book? If you are not sure, look back at the chapter. Also note the difference between the short run and the long run. These words have a meaning in economics that differs from that in everyday life.

This chapter has an appendix. Your tutor will tell you if it appropriate for you to study this.

Questions

1 Re-read the *How Markets Work* article. What policy areas does Sheila Dow suggest are suitable for contributions from economists? What concept does she single out as being particularly important?

2 Look again at the *Understanding Human Behaviour* article. How does the economic approach explain the changes in the way in which women allocate their time?

3 Use the bized Web site to look up company reports. Try to classify their costs.

If you want to make greater use of the Internet, look at the links to economic resources sites (www.estima.com/weblinks.htm) and the Gateway for UK official sites (www.open.gov.uk). These can lead you to other sources.

Looking forward to Part 4 (Chapters 12–14)

Part 4 looks at different types of markets. These have a profound effect on our lives. At one extreme is monopoly – literally one seller. This applies to the supply of goods such as water. In this market, I can't choose my supplier. This gives the supplier power to cut output and put up prices; hence the need for regulation. At the other extreme is 'perfect' competition. This is a hypothetical construct, but one that enables us to explain how prices and output are determined in certain conditions.

Between these two extremes come two other types of market. One is monopolistic competition. This gets its name because it has characteristics of both monopoly and competition. A good example is hairdressing.

No two hairdressers are identical, so in a sense they have some monopoly power, but the market is very competitive because there are so many hairdressers. This keeps prices down (unless, like Vidal Sassoon, you can persuade customers that your 'product' is very different from that of other hairdressers). Also in between competition and monopoly is 'oligopoly'. This word is derived from the Greek meaning a few, so an oligopoly is a type of market with only a few suppliers. This is probably the most important type of market. Just think of banks, or cars or airlines. These industries are dominated by only a few firms. The crucial thing about this is that the actions of one firm are affected by what the others do – or might do. For example, when Shell is deciding whether or not to put up its prices, it needs to consider how other firms in the industry will respond.

As always, a good way to begin your study of a chapter is to read the *After studying this chapter you will be able to ...* preamble. Bear this in mind as you read because it will help structure your reading.

Answers

1 Sheila Dow suggests that economists can contribute to policy in areas such as the design of the international financial system and innovations in taxation. She picks out opportunity cost as being particularly important.

2 Economists would explain the changes in the way women allocate their time as the consequences of changing constraints, for example, by increasing the wages women can earn.

3 The answer depends on what you have discovered on the Internet.

Chapter 12 **Competition**

Chapter in Perspective, Text Pages 268–293

This chapter combines the cost information of Chapters 10 and 11 with new revenue information in order to analyse the profit-maximization decisions of firms in a perfectly competitive market. The analysis includes derivations of both the individual firm supply curve and the industry supply curve. While we have previously simply assumed that supply curves are upward sloping, this chapter derives upward-sloping supply curves as a prediction of the theory of perfect competition. The theory also allows us to make precise predictions about the behaviour of firms and their responses to changes in market conditions. Although perfect competition does not occur frequently in the real world, the theory allows us to isolate the effects of competitive forces that are at work in *all* markets, even in those that do not match the assumptions of the theory of perfect competition.

Helpful Hints

1 Although perfectly competitive markets are quite rare in the real world, there are three important reasons to develop a thorough understanding of their behaviour.

First, many markets closely approximate perfectly competitive markets. Thus the analysis developed in this chapter gives direct and useful insights into the behaviour of these markets.

Second, the theory of perfect competition allows us to isolate the effects of competitive forces that are at work in *all* markets, even in those that do not match the assumptions of perfect competition.

Third, the perfectly competitive model serves as a useful benchmark against which to evaluate relative allocative efficiency.

2 In the short run, a perfectly competitive firm cannot change the scale of its plant – it has fixed inputs. The firm is also a price *taker*; it always sells at the market price, which it cannot influence. Thus the only variable that the firm controls is its level of output. The short-run condition for profit maximization is to choose the level of output at which marginal revenue equals marginal cost. This is a general condition which, as we will see in subsequent chapters, applies to other market structures such as monopoly and monopolistic competition. Since for the perfectly competitive firm, marginal revenue is equal to price, this profit-maximizing condition takes a particular form: choose the level of output at which price is equal to marginal cost ($P = MC$).

3 Many students have trouble understanding why a firm continues to operate at the break-even point, where economic profits are zero. The key to understanding lies in the definition of which costs are included in the average total cost curve. Recall from Chapter 10 that a firm's total costs are defined by the economist as *opportunity costs*, which include both explicit costs and *imputed costs*.

Imputed costs include the owners'/investors' forgone interest, forgone rent and forgone income. Therefore, at the break-even point where total revenue equals total cost (or, equivalently, average revenue equals average total cost), the owners/investors of the firm are earning a return on their investment which is equal to the best return that they could earn elsewhere. That is the definition of opportunity cost – the best alternative forgone. Economists sometimes refer to these imputed costs or best alternative return on investment as 'normal profits'. As the phrase implies, these are profits that could normally be earned in any other industry. At the break-even point, the firm is earning 'normal profits' even though its economic profits (sometimes called 'extra-normal profits') are zero. In earning 'normal profits', the firm is earning just as much profit as it could anywhere else, and is therefore totally content to continue producing in this industry.

4 When the price of output falls below the break-even point, but is above the shutdown point, the firm will continue to produce even though it is making economic losses. In order to switch industries, the firm would have to shut down, which entails losing its total fixed costs.

As long as the price is above the shutdown point (minimum average variable cost), however, a firm will decide to produce since it will be cov-ering total variable cost and part of total fixed cost. Thus its loss will be less if it continues to produce at the output where $P = MC$ than if it shuts down.

If the price falls below the shutdown point, a firm which produces output will not only lose its total fixed costs, it will lose additional money on every unit of output produced, since average revenue is less than average variable cost. Thus when the price is less than average variable cost, the firm will choose to minimize its loss by shutting down.

5 In the long run, fixed costs disappear and the firm can switch between industries and change scale of plant without cost. Economic profits serve as the signal for the movement or reallocation of firm resources until long-run equilibrium is achieved. Firms will move out of industries with negative economic profits and into industries with positive economic profits. Only when economic profits are zero will there be no tendency for firms to exit or enter industries.

The fact that there are no restrictions on entry into the industry assures that economic profits will be zero and that firms will be producing at the minimum of their long-run average cost curves in long-run equilibrium.

6 In long-run equilibrium, three conditions are satisfied for each firm in a competitive industry:
  a $MR = P = MC$. This implies that profits are maximized for each firm.
  b $P = ATC$. This implies that economic profits are zero and each firm is just earning 'normal profits'.
  c $P = $ minimum $LRAC$. This implies that production takes place at the point of minimum long-run average cost.

SELF-TEST

CONCEPT REVIEW

1 Perfect competition occurs in a market under the following conditions.
  a There are ＿＿＿＿＿＿ firms, each selling a(n) ＿＿＿＿＿＿ product.
  b There are ＿＿＿＿＿＿ buyers.

  c There are no restrictions on ＿＿＿＿＿＿ into the industry.

2 A firm in a perfectly competitive market is said to be a price ＿＿＿＿＿＿ since it cannot influence the price of the good it produces. Such a firm faces a demand curve that is perfectly ＿＿＿＿＿＿ .

3 We assume that the firm's single objective is to maximize its _____ .

4 Total revenue divided by the total quantity sold is called _____ _____ . The change in revenue resulting from a one-unit increase in the quantity sold is called _____ _____ .

5 In the case of perfect competition, average revenue and marginal revenue are both equal to _____ .

6 An output at which total cost equals total revenue is called a _____ - _____ point. The point at which a firm's maximum profit (minimum loss) is the same regardless of whether the firm produces any output or not is called the _____ point.

7 Profit is maximized when marginal revenue equals _____ _____ .

8 Market price is determined by _____ demand and _____ supply.

9 In the range of prices greater than the minimum average variable cost, a perfectly competitive firm's supply curve is the same as its _____ _____ curve. At prices below minimum average variable cost, the firm will produce _____ and make a loss equal to its _____ _____ _____ .

10 New firms will enter a perfectly competitive industry if firms in the industry are making economic _____ . As new firms enter the industry, the price will _____ . If economic _____ are being made, firms will tend to exit the industry.

11 Long-run equilibrium occurs in a perfectly competitive industry when economic profits are _____ . Each firm will also be producing at the _____ point of its long-run average cost curve.

12 Factors beyond the control of an individual firm that lower its costs as industry output increases are called _____ _____ . Factors beyond the control of an individual firm that raise its costs as industry output increases are called _____ _____ .

13 _____ _____ occurs when no one can be made better off without making someone else worse off.

14 Costs that are not borne by the producer but are borne by other members of society are called _____ _____ . Benefits which accrue to people other than the buyer of a good are called _____ _____ .

TRUE OR FALSE

___ **1** In a perfectly competitive industry no single firm can exert a significant effect on the market price of a good.

___ **2** In a perfectly competitive industry there are no restrictions on entry into the industry.

___ **3** The industry demand curve in a perfectly competitive industry is horizontal.

___ **4** The objective of firms in a competitive industry is to maximize revenue.

___ **5** If marginal revenue is greater than marginal cost, a firm can increase profit by decreasing output.

___ **6** A firm is breaking even if its economic profit is zero.

___ **7** If the price is below the minimum average total cost, a firm will shut down.

___ **8** All firms in a competitive market will be maximizing profit in short-run equilibrium.

___ **9** The short-run industry supply curve is obtained as the horizontal sum of the supply curves of the individual firms.

___ **10** In long-run equilibrium, each firm in a perfectly competitive industry will be making zero economic profit.

___ **11** The entry of new firms into an industry will increase the price and increase the profit of each firm.

___ **12** Suppose a competitive industry is in long-run equilibrium when there is a substantial increase in total fixed costs. All firms will now be making economic losses and some firms will go out of business.

___ **13** If a firm is economically efficient, then it must be allocatively efficient.

___ **14** A firm is economically efficient if it is maximizing profit.

___ **15** Allocative efficiency occurs when marginal social benefit is greater than marginal social cost.

MULTIPLE CHOICE

1 If a firm faces a perfectly elastic demand for its product, then
  a it is not a price taker.
  b it will want to lower its price to increase sales.
  c it will want to raise its price to increase total revenue.
  d its marginal revenue curve is equal to the price of the product.
  e it will always earn zero economic profits.

2 A perfectly competitive firm is maximizing profit if
  a marginal cost equals price and price is above minimum average variable cost.
  b marginal cost equals price and price is above minimum average fixed cost.
  c total revenue is at a maximum.
  d average variable cost is at a minimum.
  e average total cost is at a minimum.

3 In which of the following situations will a perfectly competitive firm earn economic profits?
  a $MR > AVC$
  b $MR > ATC$
  c $ATC > MC$
  d $ATC > AR$
  e $AR > AVC$

4 The maximum loss a firm will experience in the short run is equal to
  a zero.
  b total costs.
  c total variable costs.
  d total fixed costs.
  e none of the above.

5 The short-run industry supply curve is
  a the horizontal sum of the individual firm's supply curves.
  b the vertical sum of the individual firm's supply curves.

  c vertical at the total level of output being produced by all firms.
  d horizontal at the current market price.
  e none of the above.

6 If a perfectly competitive firm in the short run is able to pay its variable costs and part, but not all, of its fixed costs, then it is operating in the range on its marginal cost curve that is
  a above the break-even point.
  b below the break-even point.
  c above the shutdown point.
  d below the shutdown point.
  e between the shutdown and break-even points.

7 In a perfectly competitive industry, the market price is $10. An individual firm is producing the output at which $MC = ATC = \$15$. AVC at that output is $10. What should the firm do to maximize its short-run profits?
  a shut down
  b expand output
  c contract output
  d leave output unchanged
  e insufficient information to answer

8 In a perfectly competitive industry, the market price is $5. An individual firm is producing the level of output at which marginal cost is $5 and is increasing, and average total cost is $25. What should the firm do to maximize its short-run profits?
  a shut down
  b expand output
  c contract output
  d leave output unchanged
  e insufficient information to answer

9 The maximum loss a firm will experience in long-run equilibrium is
  a zero.
  b its total cost.
  c its total variable cost.
  d its average total cost.
  e none of the above.

10 The long-run competitive industry supply curve will be positively sloped if there are
  a external economies.
  b external diseconomies.
  c no external economies or diseconomies.
  d external costs.
  e external benefits.

11 If an industry experiences external economies as the industry expands in the long run, the long-run industry supply curve will
   a be perfectly inelastic.
   b be perfectly elastic.
   c have a positive slope.
   d have a negative slope.
   e have allocative inefficiency.

12 Which of the following is *not* a characteristic of a perfectly competitive industry?
   a a downward-sloping market demand curve.
   b perfectly elastic demand for each firm.
   c each firm decides its quantity of output.
   d each firm produces slightly different goods.

SHORT ANSWER

1 Why will a firm in a perfectly competitive industry choose *not* to charge a price either above or below the market price?

2 Why is the perfectly competitive firm's supply curve the same as the marginal cost curve above minimum average variable cost?

3 Why will economic profits be zero in long-run equilibrium in a perfectly competitive industry?

4 Suppose output is at a level such that marginal social benefit is greater than marginal social cost. Explain why this level of output is allocatively *inefficient*.

5 Re-read the *Reading Between the Lines* article. Why do you think that car prices are higher in the UK than in the rest of the EU?

PROBLEMS

1 a Table 12.1 gives the total cost structure for one of many identical firms in a perfectly competitive industry. Complete the table by computing total variable cost, average total cost, average variable cost and marginal cost at each level of output. (Remember, as in the problems in *Study Guide* Chapter 11, marginal cost should be entered midway between rows.)

Table 12.1

Quantity (units per day)	Total cost (pounds)	Total variable cost (pounds)	Average total cost (pounds)	Average variable cost (pounds)	Marginal cost (pounds)
0	12				
1	24				
2	32				
3	42				
4	54				
5	68				
6	84				

b Complete Table 12.2 by computing the profit (per day) for the firm at each level of output if the price of output is £9, £11, or £15.

Table 12.2

Quantity (units per day)	Profit P = £9	Profit P = £11	Profit P = £15
0			
1			
2			
3			
4			
5			
6			

c Consider the profit-maximizing output decision of the firm at alternative prices. How much will the firm produce if the price of output is £9? £11? £15? Explain each of your answers.

2 A firm will maximize profit if it produces every unit of output for which marginal revenue exceeds marginal cost. This is sometimes called the marginal approach to profit maximization. Using the marginal approach, determine the profit-maximizing level of output for the firm of Problem 1 when the price of output is £15. How does your answer here compare with your answer in **1c**?

3 a Consider a perfectly competitive industry in long-run equilibrium. All the firms in the industry are identical. Draw a two-part graph illustrating the long-run equilibrium for the industry (part

(a) on the left) and for the typical firm (part (b) on the right). The graph of the firm should include the *MC*, *ATC*, *MR* and *LRAC* curves.

Assume that the *LRAC* curve is U-shaped. Label the equilibrium price P_0, the equilibrium industry quantity traded Q_0 and the output of the firm q_0.

b Now suppose there is a decline in industry demand. Using your graphs from part (a),

   i show what happens to market price, firm output, firm profits and industry quantity traded in the short run (assume that the shutdown point is not reached).

   ii show what happens to market price, firm output, firm profits and industry quantity traded in the long run (assume that there are no external economies or diseconomies). What has happened to the number of firms?

DISCUSSION QUESTIONS

1 Why do firms produce where $MR = MC$? Wouldn't it make more sense to produce where MR exceeds MC so that revenue exceeds costs?

2 Why should a business operate even though it incurs an economic loss?

DATA QUESTIONS

Perfect competition in the lead mining industry – a nineteenth-century case study

The structure of the lead mining industry has changed enormously over the last couple of centuries and today large firms account for great proportions of output. But the price at which they sell their product is still determined by market forces, and the producers have little control over the price of their product and are therefore price takers.

The Snailbeach Company worked a vein of ore in Shropshire. It took a lease in 1783 and continued to produce lead until 1912. Before analysing the firm it is worthwhile to outline the features of lead mining which made for a perfect market.

First, there were a large number of firms; in the early years of the eighteenth century most mines were worked as partnerships and needed only small amounts of capital to work what were in effect little more than shallow holes in the ground. The fixed costs of the company were therefore small.

The normal method of sale was for the company to put a sample of its ore into the market; buyers would inspect it and then make an offer for the whole lot. The price of lead was therefore determined by the market, thus satisfying the condition of perfect competition, which requires that the firm has no control over the price of the product it sells. In times of scarcity the price of lead was high, and in times of surplus or demand deficiency it fell. In consequence the price of lead exerted an enormous influence on the whole structure of the industry, determining profits, wages, and the opening up and closing down of enterprises.

During the 1860s demand increased to such an extent that a shortage of ore occurred. However, it was only a matter of time before the bubble burst. In the early 1870s lead ore was selling at between £13 and £14 a ton, but by 1890 the price had fallen to £7 a ton. The reason for the fall was an increased supply from overseas sources in Australia and America. With falling prices it was impossible for many firms to stay profitable, and many companies went out of business.

Source: Adapted from E. Brook, 'Perfect competition in the lead mining industry', *Economics*, Autumn 1970, **8**(5) No 35, 240–255. Reproduced by kind permission of EBEA (Economics and Business Education Association).

1 Outline the characteristic features of perfect competition. To what extent did the lead mining industry of the period satisfy the criteria needed for perfect competition?

2 Draw diagrams to show the effect on the industry and the firm of an increase in demand for lead.

3 Draw diagrams for the industry and the firm to show why prices fell between 1880 and 1890.

ANSWERS

CONCEPT REVIEW

1 many; identical; many; entry

2 taker; elastic

3 profit

4 average revenue; marginal revenue

5 price

6 break-even; shutdown

7 marginal cost

8 industry; industry

9 marginal cost; nothing; total fixed cost

10 profits; fall; losses

11 zero; minimum

12 external economies; external diseconomies

13 Allocative efficiency

14 external costs; external benefits

TRUE OR FALSE

1 T Each firm is a price taker.

2 T Definition.

3 F The individual firm's demand curve is horizontal. The industry demand curve is downward sloping.

4 F Firm aims to maximize total profit.

5 F Profits will increase if it increases output since each additional unit's revenue is greater than its cost.

6 T Definition.

7 F It would be true if $P <$ minimum AVC.

8 T Otherwise they would be making losses.

9 T Definition.

10 T Otherwise new firms would enter and bring down profits till they reached zero.

11 F New firms will lead to lower prices and profits.

12 T ATC will rise with no change in marginal cost. This will lead to losses and some firms will go bust.

13 F It would be true if there are no external costs or benefits, otherwise it is false.

14 T Maximizing profit means minimizing costs.

15 F Allocative efficiency occurs when marginal social benefit equals marginal social cost.

MULTIPLE CHOICE

1 d Firm can increase quantity without changing price, so MR from additional quantity = price.

2 a AFC is irrelevant. Maximizing profit does not equal maximizing revenue. **d, e** might be true, depending on P.

3 b Since $MR = AR$, $AR > ATC$. Multiply by Q gives $TR > TC$, so economic profits.

4 d Equals shutdown cost. Any potentially greater loss, firm will shut down.

5 a Definition. **c** is momentary supply curve. **d** is demand curve facing individual firm.

6 e If couldn't pay variable costs → below shutdown. If paying all variable and fixed costs → break even.

7 c Draw a graph. Firm should choose lower Q where $P = MC$. If AVC at current $Q = \$10$, minimum AVC must be $< \$10$, so new $Q >$ minimum AVC.

8 e Firm is at Q where $P = MC$, but is losing money since $AR < ATC$. Need AVC information to determine if **a** or **d** is correct.

9 a Definition. Long-run equilibrium leads to zero economic profits.

10 b Rise in costs as industry quantity increases.

11 d Because fall in costs as industry Q rises.

12 d In perfect competition, each firm produces identical goods. The *market* demand curve for the industry slopes down, though the individual firm's demand curve is perfectly elastic.

SHORT ANSWER

1 If a firm in a perfectly competitive industry charged a price even slightly higher than the market price, it would lose all of its sales. Thus it will not charge a price above the market price. Since it can sell all it wants at the market price, it would not be able to increase sales by lowering its price. Thus it would not charge a price below the market price since this would decrease total revenue and hence profits.

2 A perfectly competitive firm will want to supply the quantity that will maximize profit. This is done by equating marginal revenue and marginal cost. Since marginal revenue is equal to price for a perfectly competitive firm, the firm will produce the level of output at which price equals marginal cost. Since this is true for each price above minimum *AVC*, the firm's supply curve is the same as its marginal cost curve above minimum *AVC*. For prices below minimum *AVC*, the firm will maximize profit (actually minimize loss) by shutting down. The loss from shutting down will be equal to total fixed cost. If the firm continued to produce at a price below minimum *AVC*, its loss would exceed total fixed cost.

3 In a perfectly competitive industry, the existence of positive economic profits will attract the entry of new firms, which will shift the industry supply curve to the right, causing the market price to fall and firm profits to decline. This tendency will exist as long as there are positive economic profits. Similarly, the existence of economic losses will cause firms to exit from the industry, which will shift the industry supply curve to the left, causing the market price to rise and firm profits to rise (losses to decline). This tendency will exist as long as losses are being made. Thus the only point of rest in the long run (the only equilibrium) is one in which economic profits are zero.

4 A level of output at which marginal social benefit is greater than marginal social cost is allocatively inefficient, because some people can be made better off without making anyone worse off if more is produced. Since the production of an additional unit of output will add more to social benefit than to social cost, those who bear the additional costs can be compensated out of the additional benefits (and thus be left no worse off) with some additional benefits left over (making those who receive the additional benefits better off).

5 There is some disagreement about the extent of high car prices in the UK. Manufacturers argue that cars in the UK have higher specifications (e.g. better radios), plus benefits such as free insurance and servicing. This makes comparisons difficult.

On the other hand, consumer groups argue that manufacturers are restricting competition. This prevents the demand curve moving to the right. Hence prices remain high.

PROBLEMS

1 a The completed Table 12.1 is shown here as Table 12.3.

b The completed Table 12.2 is given here as Table 12.4. The values for profit are computed as total revenue minus total cost, where total revenue is price times quantity and total cost is given in Table 12.1.

Table 12.3

Quantity (units per day)	Total cost (pounds)	Total variable cost (pounds)	Average total cost (pounds)	Average variable cost (pounds)	Marginal cost (pounds)
0	12	0	–	–	
					…12
1	24	12	24.00	12.00	
					…8
2	32	20	16.00	10.00	
					…10
3	42	30	14.00	10.00	
					…12
4	54	42	13.50	10.50	
					…14
5	68	56	13.60	11.20	
					…16
6	84	72	14.00	12.00	

Table 12.4

Quantity (units per day)	Profit P = £9	Profit P = £11	Profit P = £15
0	−12	−12	−12
1	−15	−13	−9
2	−14	−10	−2
3	−15	−9	3
4	−18	−10	6
5	−23	−13	7
6	−30	−18	6

c If the price is £9, profit is maximized (actually loss is minimized) when the firm shuts down and produces zero units. If the firm chooses to produce, its loss will be at least £14, which is greater than the fixed cost loss of £12. Therefore the firm will minimize losses by shutting down. If the price is £11, the firm is still unable to make a positive economic profit. The loss is minimized (at £9) if the firm produces 3 units. At this price all of variable cost and part of fixed cost can be recovered. At a price of £15, the firm will maximize profit (at £7) at an output of 5 units per day.

2 The marginal approach to profit maximization states that the firm should produce all units of output for which marginal revenue exceeds marginal cost. For a perfectly competitive firm, marginal revenue equals price, so the approach states (equivalently) that the firm should produce every unit for which price exceeds marginal cost. If the price of output is £15, we can see from Table 12.3 that the firm should produce 5 units. Since the marginal cost of moving from the 4th to the 5th unit (£14) is less than price (£15), the 5th unit should be produced. The marginal cost of moving to the 6th unit (£16), however, is greater than price. It should not be produced. The answer obtained here is the same as the answer obtained in **1c**.

3 a A long-run equilibrium in a perfectly competitive industry is illustrated in Fig. 12.1.

Part (a) illustrates industry equilibrium at the intersection of industry demand (D_0) and industry supply (S_0): point a. The equilibrium industry quantity traded is labelled Q_0 and the equilibrium market price is labelled P_0.

Part (b) illustrates the situation for a single firm in long-run equilibrium. The firm is at point a', the minimum point of both the short-run average total cost curve (*ATC*) and the long-run average cost curve (*LRAC*). The firm is producing the output labelled q_0 and earning zero economic profit.

b i The new short-run equilibrium is also illustrated in Fig. 12.1. The decrease in demand shifts the market demand curve to the left, from D_0 to D_1. The new market equilibrium is at point b. The price has fallen from P_0 to P_1 and the industry quantity traded has fallen from Q_0 to Q_1. The fall in price induces firms to reduce output as shown by the move from point a' to point b' on the *MC* curve in part (b). Since P_1 is less than minimum *ATC*, firms are making losses in the new short-run equilibrium.

ii The new long-run equilibrium is also illustrated in Fig. 12.1. Since losses are experienced in short-run equilibrium, firms will exit from the industry in the long run.

This will make the industry supply curve shift to the left causing the price to rise and thus reducing losses. Firms will continue to leave until the industry supply curve has shifted enough to eliminate losses, from S_0 to S_1. This gives a new long-run industry equilibrium at point c and the price has returned to its initial level, P_0, but industry quantity traded has fallen to Q_2. As firms exit and the market price rises, remaining firms will increase their output (moving up the *MC* curve from point b' to point a') and their losses will be reduced. When sufficient firms have left the industry, the price will have risen (returned) to P_0 and firms will have returned to point a' in part (b). At this point, each firm is again earning zero economic profit and firm output has returned to Q_0. But since there are now fewer firms, industry quantity traded is less.

Figure 12.1

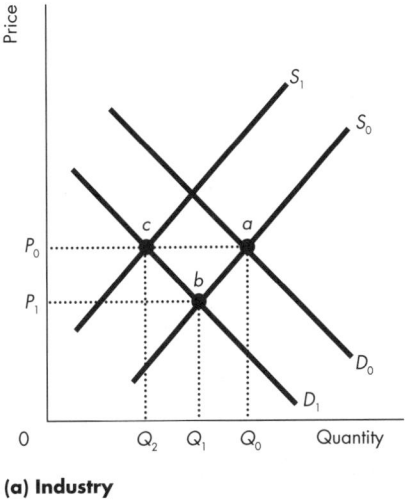

(a) Industry

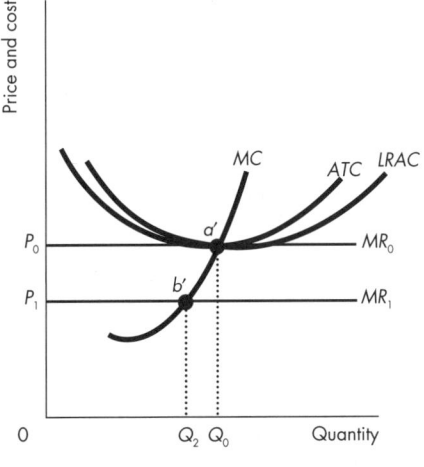

(b) Firm

DISCUSSION QUESTIONS

1 The basic assumption underlying most economic analysis is that firms attempt to maximize *total* profit; that is the difference between total costs and total revenue. This will occur if a firm expands output until $MR = MC$. If it ceased to expand while marginal revenue exceeded marginal cost, it would be losing some profit which it could obtain from producing one more unit of output, as long as the costs of producing that unit did not exceed the revenue obtained by selling it.

2 Whenever the price of output falls below the break-even point (the minimum average total cost) but remains above the shutdown point (the minimum average variable cost), the firm continues to produce even though it is making an economic loss. The key idea here is that since a loss is inevitable, the owner wants to make it as low as possible. If the firm were to shut down it would still have to pay its fixed costs. The owner compares this loss to the loss incurred by continuing to operate. If the price exceeds the average variable cost, the owner loses less by continuing to operate. This is because some of the revenue obtained can be used to pay some of the fixed costs.

DATA QUESTIONS

1 The characteristic features of perfect competition are: many firms, identical product, many buyers, easy entry and perfect knowledge, and that existing firms have no advantage over new entrants. The lead industry in the nineteenth century satisfied many of these criteria, but we do not know that those involved had perfect knowledge about the product and the industry.

Moreover, the product was not identical – different samples of lead ore differed in quality. However, it is safe to conclude that the industry exhibited many of the characteristics of perfect competition.

2 The position is shown in Fig. 12.2. In this figure the demand curve for the firm is horizontal because the Snailbeech Company has to take the price determined by the supply and demand for lead in the industry as a whole. It can then sell all the lead ore it wants at this price because it is only a small firm in a large industry. The original equilibrium is at price P_0 and quantity Q_0. The increase in demand will cause the demand curve to shift and a new equilibrium at price P_1 and quantity Q_1.

3 Prices fell because there was a large increase in supply from overseas firms. This caused the supply curve to shift and the result was that price fell from P_0 to P_1 while quantity rose from Q_0 to Q_1 as shown in Fig. 12.3.

Figure 12.2

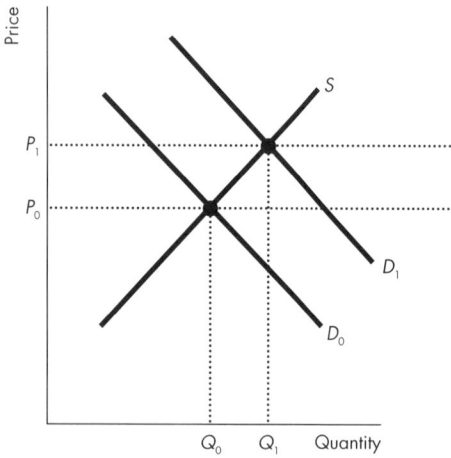

(a) Industry

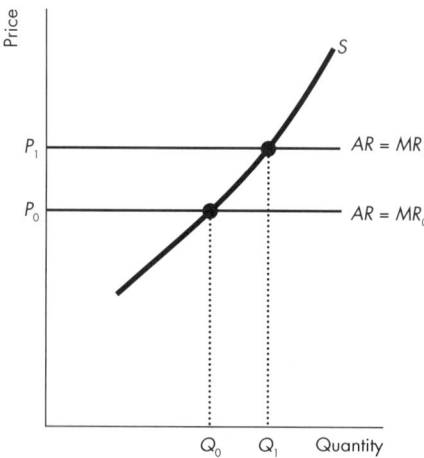

(b) Snailbeach Company

Figure 12.3

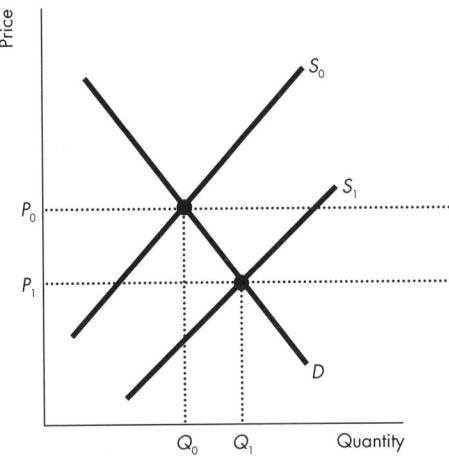

(a) Industry

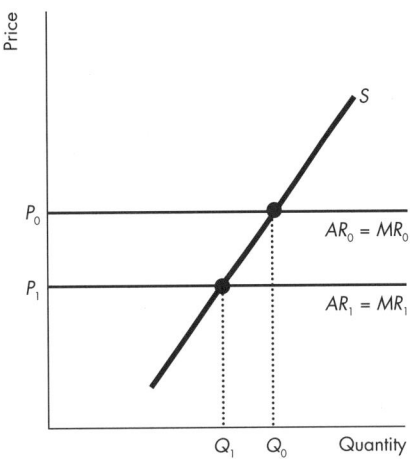

(b) Snailbeach Company

Chapter 13 **Monopoly**

Chapter in Perspective, Text Pages 294–319

The perfectly competitive firms of Chapter 12 are price takers. At the opposite extreme are industries in which there is a single firm, a monopoly. Unlike a perfectly competitive firm, a monopoly's output decision has a direct effect on price; it cannot sell more output unless it drops its price.

This chapter pursues the answers to numerous questions about monopoly. Why does monopoly exist? How does a monopoly choose how much to produce? What constraints on behaviour does a monopoly face? How much profit will a monopoly make? When will a monopoly charge different prices to different customers for the same good or service? How does a monopoly compare with perfect competition in terms of efficiency? Is monopoly always 'bad'?

Helpful Hints

1 A monopoly is a single firm with the ability to set both quantity and price. Because there is only one firm, the industry demand curve is also the firm demand curve. In order to sell additional output, the monopoly must lower the price. A single-price monopoly must lower the price on all units of output, not just the additional unit. As the following explanation for Fig. 13.1 states, this means that marginal revenue is less than price. Combining this new revenue situation with our familiar cost curves from Chapter 11 yields the important diagram shown in Fig. 13.1.

Notice the following:

a The rule for profit maximization is to find the quantity of output where $MR = MC$. This is the same rule that applies to a perfectly competitive firm.

Figure 13.1

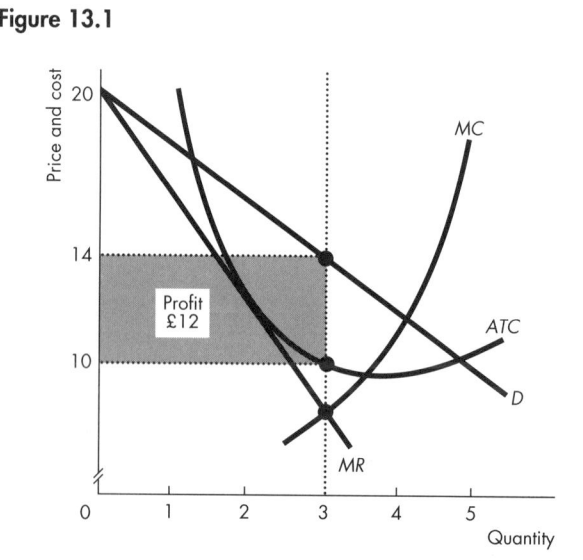

For a perfectly competitive firm *MR* is also equal to price, so the intersection of *MR* and *MC* yields the profit-maximizing output and price. That is not true for the monopolist. *MR* is not equal to price, and once the profit-maximizing output is identified, the monopolist still has to set the price.

b The reason why *MR* is not equal to price for the monopolist (as it was in perfect competition) is that the monopolist has to cut prices to sell more. Moreover, it must lower the price on all units sold – not just an additional units. This means marginal revenue is less than price.

c To find the profit-maximizing price, draw an imaginary vertical line up to the demand curve from the intersection of *MR* and *MC*. Then draw an imaginary horizontal line to the price axis to read the price.

d Understanding what the vertical and horizontal distances of the total profit area represent will make you less likely to make mistakes in drawing that area. The vertical distance is between the demand (or average revenue) curve and the average total cost curve. That distance measures average revenue minus average total cost, which equals average profit, or profit per unit. The horizontal distance is just the number of units produced. So the area of the rectangle (vertical distance × horizontal distance) = profit per unit × number of units = total profit. Do *not* make the mistake of drawing the vertical distance down to the intersection of *MC* and *MR*. That intersection has no economic meaning for the calculation of total profit.

2 There is an easy trick for drawing the marginal revenue curve corresponding to any linear demand curve. The price intercept (where $Q = 0$) is the same as for the demand curve, and the quantity intercept (where $P = 0$) is exactly *half* of the output of the demand curve. The marginal revenue curve is, therefore, a downward-sloping straight line whose slope is twice as steep as the slope of the demand curve.

3 Price discrimination can only be profitable for a monopoly if different groups have different elasticities of demand for the good. The monopoly can then treat each group as a separate market and produce where $MR = MC$ for each group.

SELF-TEST

CONCEPT REVIEW

1 A firm that is the single supplier of a good in an industry is called a(n) _____ . The key feature of such an industry is the existence of _____ preventing the entry of new firms.

2 A monopoly that charges the same price for every unit of output it sells is called a(n) _____ -_____ monopoly.

3 The demand curve facing a monopoly firm is the _____ demand curve.

4 For a monopoly charging a single price, the average revenue curve is the _____ curve and the marginal revenue curve is _____ the average revenue curve.

5 The output range over which total revenue is rising is the same as that over which marginal revenue is _____ . This is the same range of input over which the (price) elasticity of demand is _____ than 1. If elasticity of demand is _____ than 1, marginal revenue is _____ . This implies that a profit-maximizing monopoly will never produce an output in the _____ range of its demand curve.

6 Unlike a perfectly competitive firm, a monopoly's decision to produce more or less of a good will affect the _____ of the good.

7 A profit-maximizing monopoly will want to produce less if, at the current level of output, marginal _____ is greater than marginal _____ .

8 Unlike a perfectly competitive firm, a monopoly can be making positive economic _____ in the long run.

9 The practice of charging some customers a higher price than others for exactly the same good is called _____ _____. This kind of pricing policy can be seen as an attempt by the monopoly to capture all or part of the consumer _____ .

10 Charging different prices to different groups of customers will increase the profits of a monopoly only if the groups of customers have different _____ of demand for the product. A monopoly that charges different prices to different groups of customers will produce _____ than would a monopoly that charges a single price.

11 If a perfectly competitive industry is taken over by a single monopoly firm, output will _____ and the price will _____. The reduction in consumer and producer surplus resulting from this new monopoly is called the _____ loss.

12 The activity of creating monopoly is called _____ _____ . If there are no barriers to such activity, the value of the resources used up in the process will, in equilibrium, be _____ _____ the monopoly's profit.

13 A firm that has a decrease in average total cost when it increases the number of different goods it produces is said to have economies of _____ .

TRUE OR FALSE

— **1** Natural monopoly can arise because of economies of scale.

— **2** For a single-price monopoly, average revenue always equals price.

— **3** Over the output range where total revenue is decreasing, marginal revenue is positive.

— **4** The marginal revenue curve lies below the demand curve for a single-price monopoly because when the price is lowered to sell additional units of output, it must be lowered on all units of output.

— **5** A profit-maximizing single-price monopoly will produce only in the elastic range of its demand curve.

— **6** The supply curve of a monopoly firm is its marginal cost curve.

— **7** A monopoly will always make economic profits.

— **8** Price discrimination occurs when a firm charges one group of customers more than another or when a firm gives quantity discounts.

— **9** A monopoly can acquire all of the consumer surplus for itself if it practises perfect price discrimination.

— **10** Price discrimination is an attempt by a monopolist to capture the producer surplus.

— **11** For a perfect price-discriminating monopolist, the demand curve is also the marginal revenue curve.

— **12** A monopoly industry with large economies of scale and scope may produce more output and charge a lower price than does a perfectly competitive industry.

MULTIPLE CHOICE

1 Which of the following is a natural barrier to the entry of new firms in an industry?
a licensing of professions
b economies of scale
c issuing a patent
d a public franchise
e all of the above

2 In order to increase sales from 7 units to 8 units, a single-price monopoly must drop the price from $7 per unit to $6 per unit. What is marginal revenue in this range?
a $48
b $6
c $1
d −$1
e none of the above

3 A single-price monopoly will maximize profits if it produces the output where
a price equals marginal cost.
b price equals marginal revenue.
c marginal revenue equals marginal cost.
d average revenue equals marginal cost.
e average revenue equals marginal revenue.

4 If a profit-maximizing monopoly is producing at an output at which marginal cost exceeds marginal revenue, it
  a should raise price and lower output.
  b should lower price and raise output.
  c should lower price and lower output.
  d is making losses.
  e is maximizing profit.

5 A single-price monopoly never operates
  a on an elastic portion of the demand curve.
  b on a portion of the demand curve that is unit elastic.
  c on an inelastic portion of the demand curve.
  d at a quantity where marginal revenue is positive since total revenue is not at a maximum.
  e under any of the above conditions.

6 For the single-price monopoly depicted in Fig. 13.2, when profit is maximized quantity is
  a 3 and price is $3.
  b 3 and price is $6.
  c 4 and price is $4.
  d 4 and price is $5.
  e 5 and price is $4.

Figure 13.2

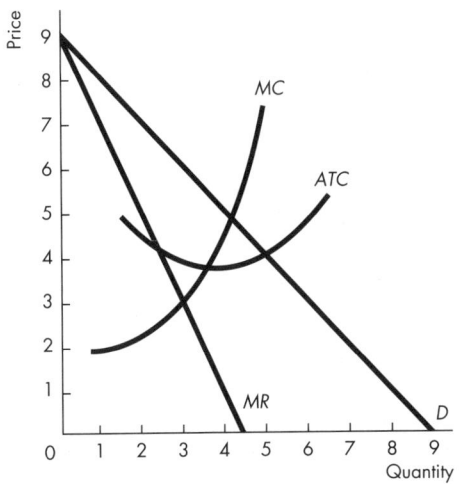

7 If the monopoly depicted in Fig. 13.2 is maximizing profit, what is the total profit?
  a $3
  b $4
  c $6
  d $9
  e none of the above

8 A perfect price-discriminating monopoly
  a has a demand curve which is also its average revenue curve.
  b will maximize revenue.
  c is assured of making a profit.
  d will produce the quantity at which the marginal cost curve intersects the demand curve.
  e will be allocatively inefficient.

9 Table 13.1 lists marginal costs for the XYZ firm. If XYZ sells 3 units at a price of $6 each, what is its producer surplus?
  a $2
  b $6
  c $7
  d $9
  e $12

Table 13.1

Quantity	Marginal cost
1	2
2	3
3	4
4	5

10 Consider the industry demand curve in Fig. 13.3. Which area in the diagram indicates the deadweight loss from a single-price monopoly?
  a *eacf*
  b *acd*
  c *abd*
  d *bcd*
  e none of the above

Figure 13.3

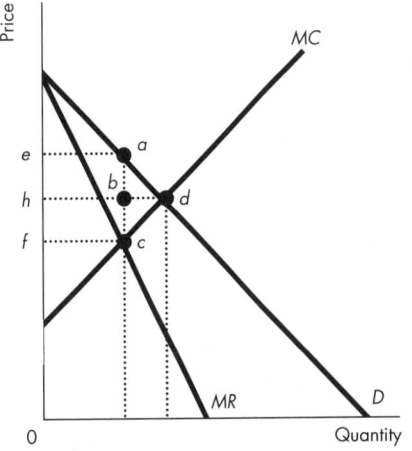

11 Which area in Fig. 13.3 indicates the dead-weight loss from a perfect price-discriminating monopoly?
  a *eacf*
  b *acd*
  c *abd*
  d *bcd*
  e none of the above

12 Why is the quantity of output produced by a single-price monopoly allocatively inefficient?
  a average social cost exceeds average social benefit
  b marginal social cost exceeds marginal social benefit
  c average social benefit exceeds average social cost
  d marginal social benefit exceeds marginal social cost
  e none of the above

13 Activity for the purpose of creating monopoly is
  a called rent seeking.
  b illegal in the United Kingdom.
  c called price discrimination.
  d called legal monopoly.
  e costless.

14 A monopoly finds that its *ATC* and *MC* have risen. If it continues in business, it will _____ its price and _____ the quantity it produces
  a raise; increase
  b raise; decrease
  c lower; increase
  d lower, decrease

SHORT ANSWER

1 Does a single-price monopoly produce in the elastic or inelastic range of its demand curve? Why?

2 Explain why the output of a competitive industry will always be greater than the output of the *same* industry under single-price monopoly.

3 Under what circumstances would a monopoly be more efficient than a large number of competitive firms? Illustrate graphically such a situation where a monopoly produces more and charges a lower price than would be the case if the industry consisted of a large number of perfectly competitive firms.

4 Study the *Reading Between the Lines* article. Why can BSkyB decide the prices it charges?

PROBLEMS

1 Keith's Lunch has two kinds of customers for lunch: stockbrokers and retired senior citizens. The demand schedules for lunches for the two groups are given in Table 13.2.

Keith has decided to price discriminate between the two groups by treating each demand separately and charging the price that maximizes profit in each of the two submarkets. Marginal cost and average total cost are equal and constant at £2 per lunch.
  a Complete Table 13.2 by computing the total and marginal revenue associated with stockbroker demand (TR_{SB} and MR_{SB}) as well as the total and marginal revenue associated with senior citizen demand (TR_{SC} and MR_{SC}). (Remember that marginal revenue should be entered midway between rows.)
  b What are the profit-maximizing output and price for stockbrokers?
  c What are the profit-maximizing output and price for senior citizens?
  d What is total profit?
  e Show that the total profit in part (d) is the maximum by comparing it with total profit if instead Keith served
    i 1 additional lunch *each* to stockbrokers and senior citizens.
    ii 1 less lunch *each* to stockbrokers and senior citizens.

2 Figure 13.4 gives the demand, marginal revenue and marginal cost curves for a certain industry. In this problem we consider how consumer and producer surplus are distributed under each of four ways of organizing the industry. In each case redraw any relevant part of Fig. 13.4 and then **(1)** indicate the region of the graph corresponding to consumer surplus by drawing horizontal lines through it; **(2)** indicate the region corresponding to producer surplus by drawing vertical lines through it; and **(3)** indicate the region (if any) corresponding to deadweight loss by putting dots in the area.

a The industry consists of many perfectly competitive firms.

b The industry is a single-price monopoly.

c The industry is a price-discriminating monopoly charging two prices: P_1 and P_3.

d The industry is a perfect price-discriminating monopoly.

DISCUSSION QUESTIONS

1 Can you think of a couple of rules that you can use to determine, first, how much is produced, and second, how much is charged?

2 How does price discrimination reduce the amount of consumer surplus?

Table 13.2

Price (P) (pounds)	Stockbrokers				Senior citizens			
	Quantity demanded (Q_D) (lunches)	Total revenue (TR_{SB}) (pounds per lunch)		Marginal revenue (MR_{SB}) (pounds per lunch)	Quantity demanded (Q_D) (lunches)	Total revenue (TR_{SC}) (pounds per lunch)		Marginal revenue (MR_{SC}) (pounds per lunch)
8	0				0			
7	1				0			
6	2				0			
5	3				1			
4	4				2			
3	5				3			
2	6				4			
1	7				5			
0	8				6			

DATA QUESTIONS

Table 13.3 Return Rail Fares from Preston to London, 1999

Ticket type	Fare (£)
First	205
Standard open	143
Supersaver	46
Three-day advance	32
Seven-day advance	25

Young Persons and Senior Citizens railcards give a discount of one-third on most fares.

1 Explain how the conditions required for successful price discrimination apply to this market.

2 Show how the rail company benefits from charging different prices for similar services (similar, but in this case not identical, because, for example, the seats in a first class carriage differ from those in standard class).

Figure 13.4

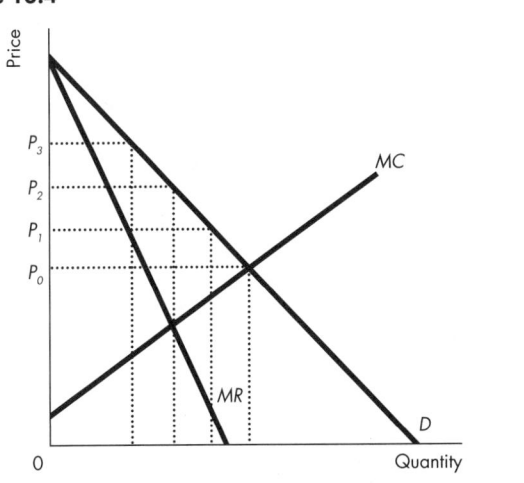

ANSWERS

CONCEPT REVIEW

1 monopoly; barriers

2 single-price

3 industry

4 demand; below

5 positive; greater; less; negative; inelastic

6 price

7 cost; revenue

8 profits

9 price discrimination; surplus

10 elasticities; more

11 decrease; increase; deadweight

12 rent seeking; equal to

13 scope

TRUE OR FALSE

1 T Natural monopolies have high fixed costs.

2 T Average of all (equal) prices of a product = price.

3 F MR is negative.

4 T Draw curves to verify this.

5 T If it produced in the inelastic range it would increase profits by increasing price.

6 F Monopoly has no supply curve.

7 F Monopoly gives no guarantee of profits if consumers are unwilling to buy the product.

8 T Definition.

9 T Definition.

10 F It is an attempt to capture consumer surplus.

11 T Demand curve gives revenue for each successive unit.

12 T This is one of the advantages of monopoly.

MULTIPLE CHOICE

1 b Others are legal barriers.

2 d TR $(P = \$7) = \$7 \times 7 = \$49$. TR $(P = \$6) = \$6 \times 8 = \$48$, MR = change in TR = $\$48 - \$49$.

3 c All firms will maximize profits if they produce where $MR = MC$.

4 a Draw graph. If MC exceeds MR firm should cut production, so increasing MR and cutting MC.

5 c Since TR falls needlessly, MR must always be > 0 to intersect (positive) MC.

6 b Profit is maximized where $MR = MC$.

7 c $(AR - ATC) \times Q = (\$6 - \$4) \times 3$

8 d Same outcome as perfectly competitive industry, so **e** wrong. $D = MR$ so **a** wrong. Profit maximizing, so **b** wrong.

9 d Sum of $(P - MC)$ for each unit of output.

10 b Sum of lost producer *(bcd)* and consumer *(abd)* surplus compared to competitive outcome.

11 e Deadweight loss is zero.

12 d MSB measured on demand curve, MSC on MC curve.

13 a Definition. Activity has costs.

14 b The rise in MC shifts this curve to the left, so the firm decreases quantity and raises price.

SHORT ANSWER

1 A single-price monopoly will always produce in the elastic range of the demand curve. The reason is straightforward. Marginal cost is always positive. Thus the profit-maximizing condition that marginal cost equals marginal revenue must be satisfied over the range of output for which marginal revenue is positive, the elastic range.

2 A competitive industry will produce the level of output at which the industry marginal cost curve intersects the demand curve facing the industry. A single-price monopoly will produce at the level of output at which the industry marginal cost curve intersects the monopoly marginal revenue curve. Since the marginal revenue curve lies below the demand curve, this implies a lower level of output in the monopoly industry.

3 A monopoly would be more efficient than perfect competition if the monopoly had sufficient economies of scale and/or scope. These economies must be large enough for the monopoly to produce more than the competitive industry and sell it at a lower price. Figure 13.5 illustrates such a situation. The important feature is that the marginal cost curve for the monopoly must not only be lower than the supply curve of the competitive industry, but it must also be sufficiently lower so that it intersects the *MR* curve at an output greater than *C* (the competitive output). Such a situation could arise if there are extensive economies of scale and/or scope.

4 BSkyB can decide the prices that it charges because it is a monopoly supplier of certain programmes. Because it buys sole rights to televise certain football matches (for instance) it creates a barrier to entry. Demand to watch these programmes is high; hence BSkyB can charge high prices.

Figure 13.5

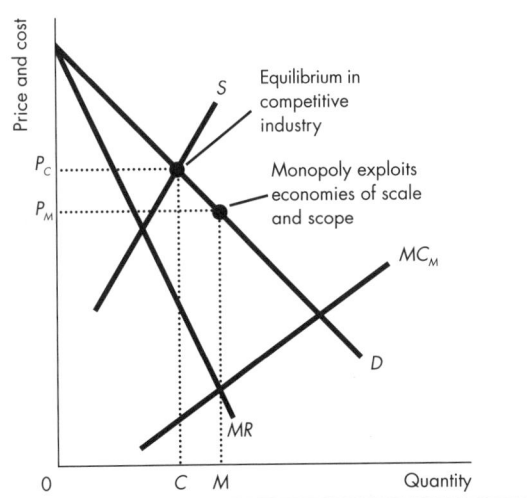

PROBLEMS

1 a The completed table is given in Table 13.4.
　For stockbrokers, equilibrium output occurs where $MC = MR = 2$, $Q_{SB} = 3$, $P_{SB} = 5$.
　For senior citizens, equilibrium output occurs where $MC = MR = 2$, $Q_{SC} = 2$, $P_{SC} = 4$.
b The profit-maximizing output for stockbrokers occurs when $MC = £2 = MR_{SB}$. This is at 3 lunches and the price is £5 per lunch to stockbrokers.
c The profit-maximizing output for senior citizens occurs when $MC = £2 = MR_{SC}$. This occurs at 2 lunches and the price to senior citizens is £4 per lunch.
d Since average total cost is also £2 per lunch, the total cost is £2 × 5 lunches = £10. Total revenue is £15 from stockbrokers and £8 from senior citizens, or £23. Thus total profit is £13.

Table 13.4

	Stockbrokers				Senior citizens		
Price (P) (pounds)	Quantity demanded (Q_D) (lunches)	Total revenue (TR_SB) (pounds per lunch)	Marginal revenue (MR_SB) (pounds per lunch)		Quantity demanded (Q_D) (lunches)	Total revenue (TR_SC) (pounds per lunch)	Marginal revenue (MR_SC) (pounds per lunch)
8	0	0			0	0	
			...7				...0
7	1	7			0	0	
			...5				...0
6	2	12			0	0	
			3				...0
5	3	15			1	5	
			1				3
4	4	16			2	8	
			−1				1
3	5	15			3	9	
			3				−1
2	6	12			4	8	
			−5				−3
1	7	7			5	5	
			−7				−5
0	8	0			6	0	

e i If Keith served 1 additional lunch each to stock-brokers and senior citizens, that would make 4 lunches for stockbrokers (at $4/lunch) and 3 lunches for senior citizens (at $3/lunch). Since average total cost is $2 per lunch, the total cost is $2 × 7 lunches = $14. Total revenue is $16 from stockbrokers and $9 from senior citizens, or $25. Thus total profit is $11, less than the $13 in part **d**.

ii If Keith served 1 less lunch each to stockbrokers and senior citizens, that would make 2 lunches for stockbrokers (at $6/lunch) and 1 lunch for senior citizens (at $5/lunch). Since average total cost is $2 per lunch, the total cost is $2 × 3 lunches = $6. Total revenue is $12 from stockbrokers and $5 from senior citizens, or $17. Thus total profit is $11, less than the $13 in part **d**.

2 a Under perfect competition, price equals marginal cost. The amount of consumer surplus is given by the area under the demand curve but above the price (P_0) while the amount of producer surplus is given by the area above the MC curve but below the price. See Fig. 13.6(a).

b If the industry is a single-price monopoly, price will be greater than MC and output will be less than under competition. Consumer surplus is still given by the area under the demand curve but above the price (P_2), while producer surplus is given by the area above the MC curve but below the price up to the monopoly level of output. The remaining part of the large triangle is a deadweight loss since it is the amount of surplus under competition that is lost under a single-price monopoly. See Fig. 13.6(b).

Figure 13.6

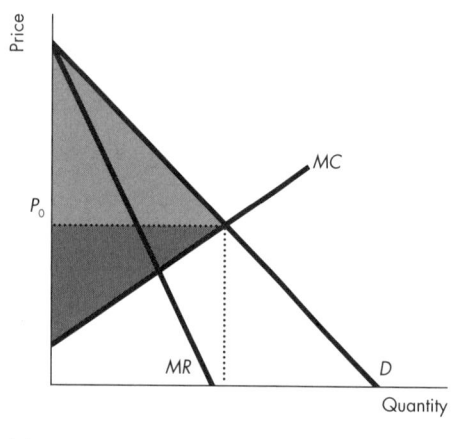

(a)

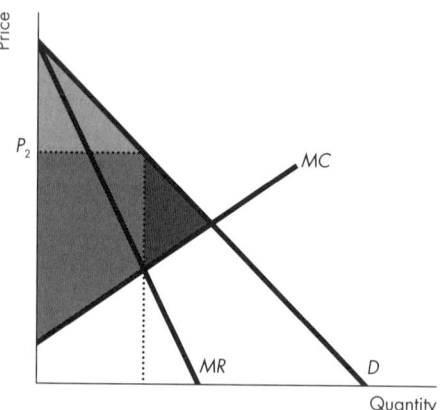

(b)

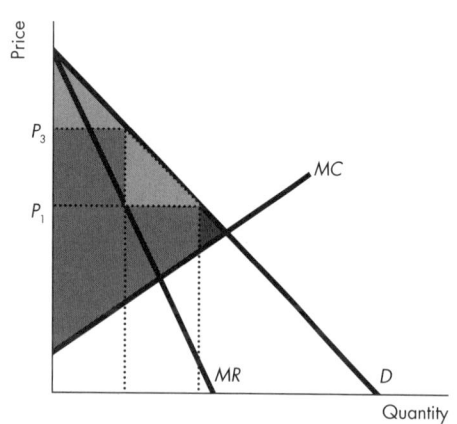

(c)

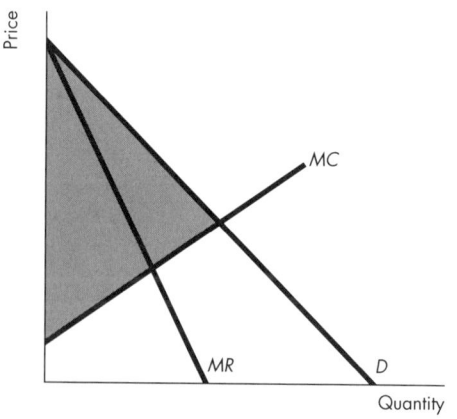

(d)

c Similar reasoning allows us to establish regions in Fig. 13.6(c) corresponding to consumer surplus, producer surplus and deadweight loss.

d Under perfect price discrimination, all of the potential surplus is captured by the producer and there is no deadweight loss (or consumer surplus). See Fig. 13.6(d).

DISCUSSION QUESTIONS

1 Two mechanical rules help you to remember how a profit-maximizing monopolist selects price and output. First, find the output by using the $MR = MC$ rule. Second, find the price. To do this draw a vertical line up from where the MR and MC curves intersect until you reach the demand curve. Then draw a horizontal line to the vertical axis to find the price.

2 Price discrimination measures the difference between how much consumers actually pay and how much they would be willing to pay. Through price discrimination, the monopoly can reduce this difference. Consumers who value the service a lot and are willing to pay high prices do pay high prices. Those who do not value it so much and are not willing to pay high prices obtain it for less. Thus a price-discriminating monopolist moves the price closer to what consumers are willing to pay, and so reduces consumer surplus.

DATA QUESTIONS

1 Price discrimination is the practice of charging a higher price to some customers than to others for an identical item, or charging an individual customer a higher price on a small purchase than on a large one. It can be used only when it is impossible for a buyer to sell the good and when customers have different elasticities. In the case of rail journeys, the company can easily differentiate among people sitting in first class or standard class seats; similarly it can distinguish among people travelling on early trains who have to pay the full standard fare and those travelling later.

2 The rail company benefits by obtaining a higher revenue (price times quantity) by charging a higher price when demand is inelastic and a lower price when demand is elastic.

Chapter 14 **Monopolistic Competition and Oligopoly**

Chapter in Perspective, Text Pages 320–349

Perfect competition and strict monopoly are quite rare. Most firms that we observe seem to lie somewhere between these two polar cases.

This chapter explores the behaviour of the in-between firms that populate the real world. We will discover that the tools of analysis developed in the previous two chapters will take us a long way.

Helpful Hints

1 It is important not only to know the different key characteristics of the alternative forms of market structure (see Table 14.2 on text page 324 for a review) but also to understand how these characteristics explain differences in firm behaviour.

2 We continue to assume that all firms are profit-maximizers and produce the level of output so that $MR = MC$. In spite of this common objective, the equilibrium price and level of output will be different for each of the market structures. This is because of differences in the nature of constraints faced by firms in each of the four types of market structures. For example, except in the case of perfect competition, firms face downward-sloping demand curves and thus have

some control over the price of the good they sell. In these cases, profit-maximizing firms will (typically) produce less than would have been produced in the competitive case and will charge a price higher than the competitive price.

3 Free entry leads to zero economic profits in the long run in both perfect competition and monopolistic competition. That is because new firms would enter the market, bringing down prices and profits. It is barriers to entry that enable firms to earn economic profit in the long run.

4 In graphing a monopolistically competitive firm in long-run equilibrium, be sure that the ATC curve is tangent to the demand curve at the same level of output at which the MC and MR curves intersect. Also be sure that the MC curve intersects the

ATC curve at the minimum point on the *ATC* curve.

5 This chapter explains the use of elementary game theory to help understand oligopoly. Be sure to understand the prisoners' dilemma game because it illustrates the most important game theory concepts (rules, strategies, payoffs), which are then used in more complex game theory models like those of repeated games.

Understand the incentives faced by the players and why a particular outcome is an equilibrium. The key to finding the equilibrium of a simple game is carefully to construct and examine the payoff matrix.

SELF-TEST

CONCEPT REVIEW

1 The most commonly used measure of concentration is called the five-firm _____ _____ . This is the percentage of _____ accounted for by the largest five firms in the industry.

2 The market structure characterized by a large number of firms that compete with each other by making similar but slightly different products is called _____ _____ . The market structure characterized by a small number of producers competing with each other is called _____ .

3 When profits are being made in a monopolistically competitive industry, firms will _____ . If losses are being made, firms will _____ . As a result, in a monopolistically competitive industry, in long-run equilibrium, each firm will make a(n) _____ economic profit and will have _____ capacity.

4 The modern approach to understanding oligopoly uses _____ theory, a method of analysing strategic interaction invented by John von Neumann. In such a theory all the possible actions of each player are called _____ and the score of each player is called the _____ .

5 A market structure in which only two producers of a commodity compete with each other is called _____ .

6 The table that shows the payoffs for every possible action by each player for every possible action by the other player is called a(n) _____ _____ .

7 The equilibrium of a game like the prisoners' dilemma is called a(n) _____ equilibrium. A special case of such an equilibrium occurs when the best strategy for each player is the same regardless of the action taken by the other player. This is called a(n) _____ equilibrium.

8 A group of firms that has entered into a collusive agreement to restrict output and increase price and profits is called a(n) _____ . Each firm in the group can pursue one of two strategies: it can either comply or _____ .

9 In a repeated game, the strategy in which a player begins by cooperating and then cheats only if the other player cheated the previous time the game was played is called a(n) _____ - _____ - _____ strategy.

10 In a repeated game, the strategy in which a player cooperates if the other player cooperates, but plays the Nash equilibrium strategy forever thereafter if the other player cheats is called a _____ _____ .

11 The equilibrium which results from each player responding rationally to a credible threat of a heavy penalty from the other player if the agreement is broken is called a(n) _____ equilibrium.

12 _____ pricing is the practice of charging a price below the monopoly profit-maximizing price.

TRUE OR FALSE

___ 1 A low concentration ratio indicates a low degree of competition.

2 In a monopolistically competitive industry, each firm faces a downward-sloping demand curve.

3 Product differentiation is what gives a monopolistically competitive firm some monopoly power.

4 A critical difference between monopoly and monopolistic competition is that in the latter case there is free entry.

5 If firms in a monopolistically competitive industry are making profits, we can expect to see their demand curves shift to the left as new firms enter.

6 In long-run equilibrium, a monopolistically competitive firm will produce more output than that associated with the minimum point on its average total cost curve.

7 An oligopolist will consider the reaction of other firms before it decides to cut its price.

8 A Nash equilibrium occurs when *A* takes the best possible action given the action of *B* and *B* takes the best possible action given the action of *A*.

9 If two players in a game face the same choices, there cannot be a dominant strategy equilibrium.

10 If duopolists agree to collude, they can (jointly) make as much profit as a single monopoly.

11 In the case of colluding duopolists in a non-repeated game, the dominant strategy equilibrium is for both firms to cheat.

MULTIPLE CHOICE

1 The four-firm concentration ratio measures the share of the largest four firms in total industry
a profits.
b sales.
c cost.
d capital.
e none of the above.

2 Under monopolistic competition, long-run economic profits tend towards zero *because of*

a product differentiation.
b the lack of barriers to entry.
c excess capacity.
d inefficiency.
e the downward-sloping demand curve facing each firm.

3 In the long run, the firm in monopolistic competition will
a face a perfectly elastic demand curve.
b produce more than the quantity that minimizes *ATC*.
c produce less than the quantity that minimizes *ATC*.
d produce the quantity that minimizes *ATC*.
e earn economic profits.

4 Figure 14.1 represents a monopolistically competitive firm in short-run equilibrium. What is the firm's level of output?
a Q_1
b Q_2
c Q_3
d Q_4
e zero

Figure 14.1

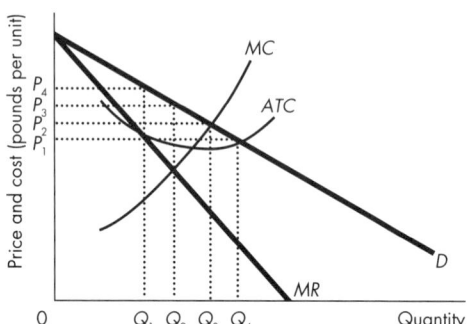

5 What will be the price charged by the monopolistic competitor of Fig. 14.1?
a P_1
b P_2
c P_3
d P_4
e zero, since the firm has shut down

6 Refer again to the short-run situation illustrated in Fig. 14.1. We know that in the long run

  a there will be entry of new firms and each existing firm's demand will shift to the left.

  b there will be entry of new firms and each existing firm's demand will shift to the right.

  c existing firms will leave and each remaining firm's demand will shift to the left.

  d existing firms will leave and each remaining firm's demand will shift to the right.

  e there will be no change from the short run.

7 A monopolistically competitive firm is like a perfectly competitive firm in that

  a both face perfectly elastic demand.

  b both earn an economic profit in the long run.

  c both have *MR* curver that lie below their demand curver.

  d neither is protected by barriers to entry.

8 Which of the following is true for perfect competition, monopolistic competition and single-price monopoly?

  a homogeneous product

  b zero long-run economic profits

  c short-run profit-maximizing quantity where $MC = MR$

  d easy entry and exit

  e none of the above

9 In the dominant firm model of oligopoly, the large firm acts like

  a an oligopolist.

  b a monopolist.

  c a monopolistic competitor.

  d a perfect competitor.

10 The kinked demand curve theory

  a suggests that price will remain constant even with fluctuations in demand.

  b suggests how the current price is determined.

  c assumes that marginal revenue sometimes increases with output.

  d assumes that competitors will match price cuts and ignore price increases.

  e suggests none of the above.

11 In the prisoners' dilemma with players Alf and Bob, the dominant strategy equilibrium is

  a both prisoners confess.

  b both prisoners deny.

  c Alf denies and Bob confesses.

  d Bob denies and Alf confesses.

  e indeterminate.

12 The firms Trick and Gear form a cartel to collude to maximize profit. If this game is non-repeated, the dominant strategy equilibrium is

  a both firms cheat on the agreement.

  b both firms comply with the agreement.

  c Trick cheats while Gear complies with the agreement.

  d Gear cheats while Trick complies with the agreement.

  e indeterminate.

13 Consider the same cartel consisting of Trick and Gear. Now, however, the game is repeated indefinitely and each firm employs a tit-for-tat strategy. The equilibrium is

  a both firms cheat on the agreement.

  b both firms comply with the agreement.

  c Trick cheats while Gear complies with the agreement.

  d Gear cheats while Trick complies with the agreement.

  e indeterminate.

14 The equilibrium in Question 13 is called a

  a credible strategy equilibrium.

  b dominant player equilibrium.

  c duopoly equilibrium.

  d trigger strategy equilibrium.

  e cooperative equilibrium.

SHORT ANSWER

1 **a** Considering the geographical scope of markets, how might concentration ratios *understate* the degree of competitiveness in an industry?

  b How might they *overstate* the degree of competitiveness in an industry?

2 Why will a firm in a monopolistically competitive industry always have excess capacity in long-run equilibrium?

3 Compare the advantages and disadvantages of perfect competition and monopolistic competition in terms of allocative efficiency.

4 Consider the case of two colluding duopolists in a non-repeated game. Why will both firms cheat on the agreement in equilibrium?

5 What type of market structure is described in the *Reading Between the Lines* article? What barriers to entry exist in this industry?

PROBLEMS

1 Consider a single firm in a monopolistically competitive industry in the short run. On a grid similar to the grid shown in Fig. 14.2, draw a new graph for each of the following situations.

Figure 14.2

a The firm is making a profit.
b The firm is making a loss that will cause shutdown.
c The firm is making a loss but is still producing.
d Starting from the situation in **c**, explain what will happen in this industry and how your graph in **c** will be affected. (A new graph is not required.)
e The firm is in long-run equilibrium.

2 A duopoly industry with no collusion consists of firms *A* and *B*, which are essentially identical. Currently, neither firm is advertising and each is making a profit of £5 million per year. If *A* advertises and *B* does not, *A* will make an annual profit of £12 million while *B* will make a loss of £5 million.

On the other hand, if *B* advertises and *A* does not, *B* will make a £12 million profit and *A* will make a loss of £5 million. If both advertise, each will make zero profit.
a Represent this duopoly as a game by identifying the players, strategies and possible outcomes.
b Construct the payoff matrix.
c What is the equilibrium outcome? Explain.

3 Use the graphs given in Fig. 14.3 to answer this question. Figure 14.3(a) gives the average total cost *(ATC)* curve for each of two identical firms (call them *A* and *B*) in a duopoly. Figure 14.3(b) gives the market demand curve and the firms' joint marginal cost curve. Suppose these firms collude to maximize profit and agree to divide output equally *for a single year*.

Figure 14.3

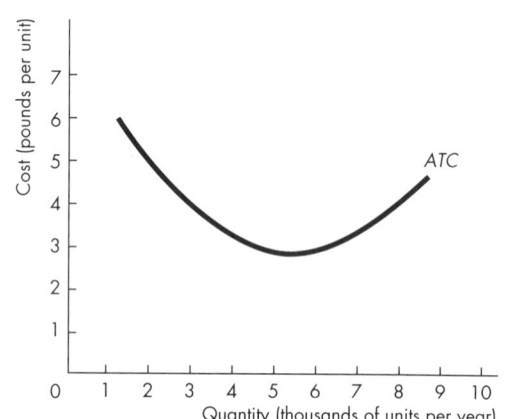

(a)

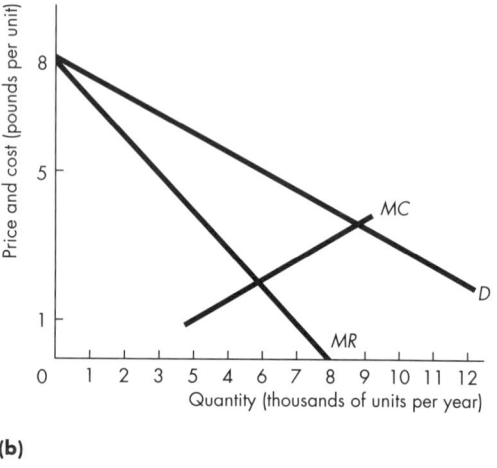

(b)

a How much will each firm produce by the agreement and what price will they charge?
b What is each firm's average total cost and profit?

c Now suppose that firm B convinces A that demand has decreased and they must reduce their price by £1 per unit in order to sell the quantity agreed upon. Of course, demand has *not* decreased but A produces its agreed amount and charges £1 less per unit. Firm B, the cheater, also charges £1 less than the original agreement price but increases output sufficiently to satisfy the rest of the demand at this price.

    i How much does B produce?

    ii What is firm A's average total cost and profit?

    iii What is firm B's average total cost and profit?

DISCUSSION QUESTION

1 Common rules make it easier to understand economics. One such rule is that firms will maximize profits if they produce where $MR = MC$. There is another rule that is common across all industries. Can you explain it? (Hint: it deals with when a firm earns an economic profit, that is, with the relationship between P and ATC.)

DATA QUESTIONS

1 In Table 14.1, classify this industry as to market type.

2 What is the five-firm concentration ratio in this industry?

3 Why are there so few firms in this European industry?

Table 14.1 Shares of the West European Car Market, 1996

Company	Market share (%)
Volkswagen	17
General Motors	13
Peugeot Group	12
Ford	12
Fiat	11
Renault	10
Daimler Benz	4
Rover (BMW)	3
Volvo	2
Others	16

Source: Derived from data from Society of Motor Manufacture Traders.

ANSWERS

CONCEPT REVIEW

1 concentration ratio; sales

2 monopolistic competition; oligopoly

3 enter; leave; zero; excess

4 game; strategies; payoff

5 duopoly

6 payoff matrix

7 Nash; dominant strategy

8 cartel; cheat

9 tit-for-tat

10 trigger strategy

11 cooperative

12 Limit

TRUE OR FALSE

1 F Low concentration ratio = high degree of competition.

2 T Firm will have to cut price to sell more.

3 T Creates a downward-sloping demand curve.

4 T Definition.

5 T Increase in supply moves curve to left.

6 F Profits would fall if it produced beyond the minimum point.

7 T Oligopoly involves strategic behaviour.

8 T Definition.

9 F Prisoners' dilemma players face same choices leading to dominant strategy equilibrium.

10 T With collusion they act like a monopoly.

11 T True for non-repeated game, but may be false for repeated game.

MULTIPLE CHOICE

1 b Definition.

2 b **a** and **e** lead to possible profits, **c** and **d** are outcomes.

3 c Excess capacity at Q where demand is tangent to downward slope ATC.

4 b Where $MR = MC$.

5 c Highest possible price to sell Q_2.

6 a Since firm is making profits, new firms will enter so each firm will sell less.

7 d There are many firms in the industry because there are no high barriers to entry.

8 c **b** and **d** false for monopoly, **a** false for monopolistic competition.

9 b The dominant firm acts like a monopoly to maximize profits.

10 d **a** is true if there are fluctuations in MC. **c** is false because MR always falls as quantity rises.

11 a Outcome of game.

12 a Similar to prisoners' dilemma outcome.

13 b Cooperative equilibrium; each player responds rationally to credible threat of the other.

14 e Definition.

SHORT ANSWER

1 a Since concentration ratios are calculated from a national perspective, if the actual geographical scope of the market is not national, the concentration ratio is likely to mis-state the degree of competitiveness in an industry. For example, if the actual market is global, the concentration ratio will understate the degree of competitiveness, and it will be too high. It is possible for a firm to have a concentration ratio of 100 because it is the only producer in the country, but to face a great deal of international competition.

b Similarly, when the scope of the market is regional, the degree of competitiveness is likely to be less than would be indicated by the simple concentration ratio.

2 A firm is defined to have excess capacity if it is producing in the negatively-sloped portion of its average total cost curve. At the long-run equilibrium level of output (sales) in a monopolistically competitive industry, each firm will be earning zero profit and its average total cost curve will be tangent to its demand curve. Since the demand curve of a monopolistic competitor is downward sloping, so is the average total cost curve at that level of output. Therefore, the monopolistically competitive firm will have excess capacity in long-run equilibrium.

3 The advantage of perfect competition is that it leads to production at minimum average total cost, while monopolistic competition leads to a higher average total cost with reduced output.

The advantage of monopolistic competition is that it leads to greater product variety, which consumers value, while in a perfectly competitive industry there is a single, identical product produced by all firms. Thus the loss in allocative efficiency (higher ATC) that occurs in monopolistic competition has to be weighed against the gain of greater product variety.

4 Each firm's best strategy is to cheat regardless of the strategy of the other firm. Call the firms A and B. Firm A knows that if firm B follows the collusive agreement, A can increase its profit by cheating. If firm B cheats, then firm A knows that it must also cheat to minimize its loss of profit. Thus cheating is the dominant strategy for firm A. Accordingly, it is also the dominant strategy for firm B.

5 The industry is a duopoly (two firms), a specific type of digopoly. The main barrier to entry is advertising, but others may include research and development as well as other forms of marketing.

PROBLEMS

1 a Figure 14.4(a) illustrates a monopolistically competitive firm making a profit in the short run. The important feature of the graph is that at the profit-maximizing output, price is greater than average total cost. Profit is given by the shaded area in the graph.

b Figure 14.4(b) illustrates a firm that will shut down in the short run since price is less than average variable cost at the profit-maximizing (loss-minimizing) level of output.

c Figure 14.4(c) illustrates a firm making a loss but continuing to produce. The loss is given by the shaded area in the graph. Note that, at the profit-maximizing output, price is less than ATC but greater than AVC.

d Since firms are typically experiencing a loss, firms will leave the industry. This means that the demand curves facing each of the remaining firms will begin to shift out as they each attract some of the customers of the departing firms. As the firm demand curves shift out, losses are reduced. Firms will continue to have an incentive to leave until losses have been eliminated. Thus firm demand curves will continue to shift out until they are tangent to the ATC curve.

e Figure 14.4(d) illustrates a typical monopolistically competitive firm in long-run equilibrium. The key feature is that the demand curve facing the firm is tangent to the ATC curve at the profit-maximizing output. Thus the firm is making zero profit.

Figure 14.4

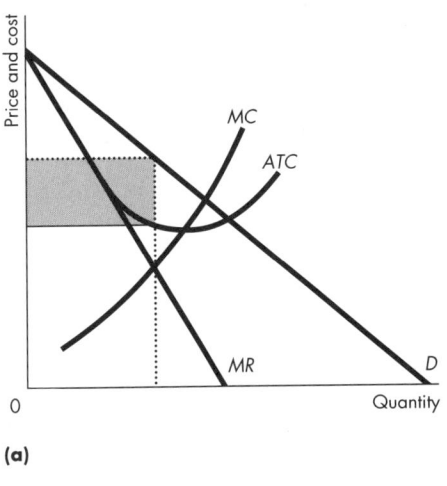

(a)

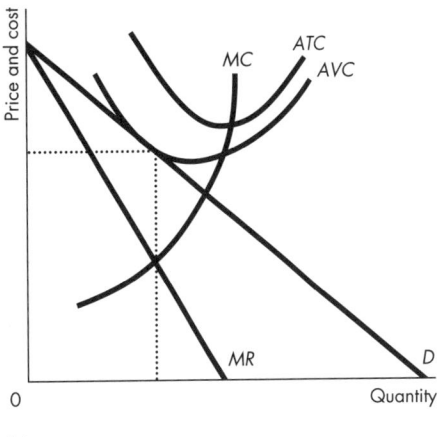

(b)

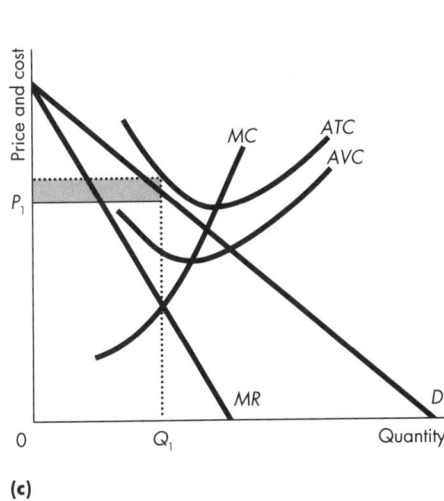

(c)

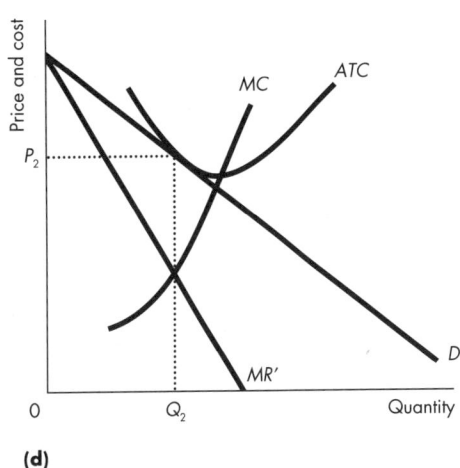

(d)

---

2 a The players are firms *A* and *B*. Each firm has two strategies: to advertise or not to advertise. There are four possible outcomes: (**1**) both firms advertise, (**2**) firm *A* advertises but firm *B* does not, (**3**) firm *B* advertises but firm *A* does not, and (**4**) neither firm advertises.

b The payoff matrix is given in Table 14.2. The entries give the profit earned by firms *A* and *B* under each of the four possible outcomes.

c First consider how firm *A* decides which strategy to pursue. If *B* advertises, *A* can advertise and make zero profit or not advertise and make a £5 million loss. Thus firm *A* will want to advertise if firm *B* does.

If *B* does not advertise, *A* can advertise and make a £12 million profit or not advertise and make a £5

Table 14.2

		Firm *B*	
		Advertise	**Not advertise**
Firm *A*	**Advertise**	A: 0 B: 0	A: £12 million B: −£15 million
	Not Advertise	A: −£5 million B: £12 million	A: £5 million B: £5 million

million profit. Therefore, firm *A* will want to advertise whether firm *B* advertises or not. *B* will come to the same conclusion. Thus the dominant strategy equilibrium is that both firms advertise.

3 a The firms will agree to produce 3,000 units each and sell at a price of £5 per unit. We determine this by noticing (Fig. 14.3b) that the profit-maximizing (monopoly) output is 6,000 units for the industry (*MR* = *MC* at 6,000) at a price of £5. Since the firms have agreed to divide output equally, each will produce 3,000 units.

b From Fig. 14.3(a) we determine that, at 3,000 units, each firm's average total cost is £4 per unit. Since price is £5, profit will be £3,000 for each firm.

c i At the new price of £4 the total quantity demanded is 8,000 units. Since *A* continues to produce 3,000 units this means that firm *B* will produce the remaining 5,000 units demanded.

  ii Since firm *A* continues to produce 3,000 units, its average total cost continues to be £4 per unit. With the new price also at £4, firm *A* will make a zero profit.

  iii Firm *B* has increased output to 5,000 units, which implies average total cost of £3 per unit. Thus given a price of £4, firm *B*'s profit will be £5,000.

DISCUSSION QUESTION

1 One other rule works for a firm in any type of industry structure. In particular:

◆ if *P* > *ATC* the firm earns an economic profit
◆ if *P* = *ATC* the firm earns a normal profit
◆ if *P* < *ATC* the firm suffers an economic loss.

DATA QUESTION

1 An industry dominated by a few firms such as this is characterized by oligopoly.

2 The five-firm concentration ratio for this industry is 17 + 13 + 12 + 12 + 11 = 65%.

   Note that these figures are for the European market. They would be different if a particular country was considered to be the market.

3 The reason that there are so few firms in the industry is because there are huge barriers to entry. These are largely made up of research and development costs and heavy fixed costs of production, but firms add to these barriers by large-scale advertising expenditure, which creates an additional barrier.

Part 5 Resource Markets

Looking back to Part 4 (Chapters 12–14)

After reading Chapter 12 on competition you should be able to define perfect competition. Remember that this is a hypothetical construct; you need to be able to differentiate this from 'competition' in general; for example, by explaining why firms enter and leave an industry. Can you do this?

After reading Chapter 13, try to draw a diagram showing how a monopoly determines its price and output. This is one of most difficult diagrams, so if you can draw this accurately, you are doing very well.

Chapter 14 discusses two types of market (monopolistic competition and oligopoly), and after reading this chapter you should now be able to compare how prices and output are determined in these two types of market. This chapter also makes use of game theory; some students find this fascinating, others are less impressed, but it is worth trying to master it.

Questions

1 Use the Parkin, Powell and Mathews Web site, or the bized equivalent, to look up some company reports. Try to find examples of monopoly and oligopoly. Also use the links listed earlier to find some reports of the Competition Commission or any EU report on monopolistic practices in the EU. Newspapers such as *The Times* (www.the-times.co.uk) and the *Guardian* (www.guardianunlimited.co.uk) give recent examples; and the Competition Commission (www.competition-commission.gov.uk) has its own site as does the Office of Fair Trading (www.oft.gov.uk).

2 Re-read the *Talking with Peter Mackie* article. Why does he suggest that in some cases competition may not be feasible?

3 The article on *Understanding Market Power* summarizes the contributions of several economists to our understanding of how firms operate in different market conditions. So, briefly, summarize the contributions of von Neumann, Smith and Cournot.

Looking forward to Part 5 (Chapters 15–17)

Chapters 15–17 are also concerned with markets, but the scene shifts from goods and services to the factors of production: land, labour, capital and entrepreneurs. The first of these chapters examines how firms and individuals decide to employ or supply factors of production. In turn these decisions determine prices. Note the meaning of 'economic rent' – another term which has a more precise meaning in economics than it has in everyday life.

Chapter 16 develops these ideas by looking at a market that affects us all – the labour market. It explains why, for example, on average graduates earn more than non-graduates and men earn more than women. 'Monopsony' is an important concept here. Just as 'monopoly' means a single seller, so 'monopsony' means a single buyer.

The final chapter in this part focuses on inequality and includes a section on how health care affects inequality.

Answers

1 The answer to this depends on what you find in your search.

2 Mackie suggests that whilst monopolists have strong incentives to earn monopoly rents, in some cases competition is not feasible. The reason is that in some cases economies of scale may be so large that it would be very inefficient to have two firms in an industry. In these cases (e.g. water distribution) regulation is necessary.

3 Von Neumann introduced game theory, Smith suggested (wrongly) that a monopolist would charge the highest price and Cournot corrected this by arguing that it would charge the price that maximized profit.

Chapter 15 Pricing and Allocating Factors of Production

Chapter in Perspective, Text Pages 352–381

This chapter explains how factor prices are determined. As with the prices of outputs of goods and services, the prices of productive inputs are determined in markets – markets for factors of production. These markets have many of the same characteristics as the markets for goods and services we examined in Chapters 12–14. Here we take a broad first look at markets for factors of production, leaving more detailed discussion of specific markets to later chapters.

Helpful Hints

1 The purpose of this chapter is to give a broad overview of the characteristics that are common to the markets for all factors of production. For example, the assumption that firms are profit-maximizers implies that they will hire each factor of production up to the point where marginal revenue product is equal to the marginal cost of the factor, regardless of whether the factor of production is labour, land or capital.

2 Be sure to distinguish carefully between the marginal revenue product of a factor of production and the marginal revenue of a unit of output. As noted in the text, the marginal revenue product of a factor of production can be calculated by multiplying marginal revenue and marginal product ($MRP = MR \times MP$). We can think of this intuitively as follows: marginal product tells us how much more output we receive from using more of a factor, and marginal revenue tells us how much more revenue we receive from each unit of that additional output. Therefore, MP times MR tells us how much more revenue we receive from using more of the factor (the MRP).

3 The most important graphic in this chapter shows that a firm's demand curve for labour is the same as its marginal revenue product curve of labour. For example, if the wage rate is £5 an hour and the marginal revenue product is £5 when five workers are employed, the firm will hire five workers.

SELF-TEST

CONCEPT REVIEW

1 The four factors of production are _____, _____, _____ and _____.

2 An increase in the demand for a factor of production will _____ that factor's income. If the supply curve for a factor of production is very elastic, the resulting change in quantity traded will be _____ and the change in price will be _____ .

3 The demand for a factor as an input in the productive process rather than for its own sake is called a(n) _____ demand.

4 The change in total revenue resulting from _____ an additional unit of _____ is called the marginal revenue product of labour. If a profit-maximizing firm finds that the marginal revenue product of labour exceeds the wage, the firm should _____ the quantity of labour it hires.

5 The two conditions for profit maximization are that MR = _____ and MRP = _____ .

6 If the price of the good produced by firm A increases, the demand curve for labour hired by firm A will shift to the _____ . A technological change that increases the marginal product of labour will shift the demand curve for labour to the _____ .

7 The price of an exhaustible natural resource is expected to rise at a rate equal to the _____ rate on financial capital.

8 The total income of a factor of production is made up of its economic _____ and its _____ cost.

9 An increase in the wage will have two effects on the quantity of labour supplied by a household. The income effect will lead to a(n) _____ in the quantity of labour supplied and the substitution effect will lead to a(n) _____ in the quantity of labour supplied.

10 The income received by the owner of a factor of production that exceeds the amount just necessary to induce the owner to offer the factor for use is called _____ _____ . The income required to induce the supply of the factor is called _____ earnings.

TRUE OR FALSE

___ **1** When the elasticity of demand for labour is greater than 1, an increase in the supply of labour will lead to a decrease in labour income.

___ **2** As long as the labour supply curve is positively sloped, an increase in the demand for labour will increase total labour income.

___ **3** A profit-maximizing firm will hire the quantity of a factor of production for which the marginal revenue product equals the marginal cost of the factor.

___ **4** The firm's demand for labour curve is the same as the average revenue product curve.

___ **5** The market demand curve for labour is the horizontal sum of the individual firms' marginal revenue product of labour curves.

___ **6** When discussing the short-run demand for labour, labour is considered to be the only variable input.

___ **7** If the production of good A is labour intensive, the demand for labour used in the production of good A is likely to be rather inelastic.

___ **8** The steeper the marginal product curve for labour, the less elastic is the firm's demand for labour.

___ **9** The short-run elasticity of demand for labour depends on the substitutability of capital for labour in the production process.

___ **10** If the wage rate increases, the substitution effect results in the household increasing the time spent in market activities and decreasing the time spent in non-market activities.

___ **11** If the wage rate increases, the income effect results in the household increasing its demand for leisure.

___ **12** The household supply curve for capital shows the relationship between the interest rate and the quantity of capital supplied.

MULTIPLE CHOICE

1 The income received by owners of factors of production are wages paid for labour,
   a profit paid for capital and interest paid for money.
   b dividends paid for capital and interest paid for money.
   c dividends paid for capital and rent paid for land.
   d interest paid for capital and rent paid for land.
   e profit paid for capital and rent paid for land.

2 An increase in the supply of a factor of production will
   a increase the factor's income if the elasticity of factor demand is less than 1.
   b decrease the factor's income if the elasticity of factor demand is less than 1.
   c increase the factor's income if the elasticity of factor supply is less than 1.
   d decrease the factor's income if the elasticity of factor supply is less than 1.
   e always decrease the factor's income.

3 The change in total revenue resulting from employing an additional unit of capital is the
   a marginal product of capital.
   b marginal revenue of capital.
   c marginal revenue cost of capital.
   d marginal revenue product of capital.
   e average revenue product of capital.

4 When a firm is a price-taker in the labour market, its marginal revenue product of labour curve is also its
   a marginal cost curve for labour.
   b demand curve for labour.
   c supply curve of labour.
   d supply curve of output.
   e average revenue curve.

5 A profit-maximizing firm will continue to hire units of a variable factor of production until the

   a marginal cost of the factor equals its marginal product.
   b marginal cost of the factor equals its average revenue product.
   c average cost of the factor equals its marginal revenue product.
   d marginal cost of the factor equals its marginal revenue product.
   e factor's marginal revenue product equals zero.

6 Suppose a profit-maximizing firm hires labour in a competitive labour market. If the marginal revenue product of labour is greater than the wage, the firm should
   a increase the wage rate.
   b decrease the wage rate.
   c increase the quantity of labour it hires.
   d decrease the quantity of labour it hires.
   e shift to a more labour-intensive production process.

7 The demand curve for a factor of production will shift to the right as a result of
   a a decrease in the price of the factor.
   b an increase in the price of the factor.
   c a decrease in the price of a substitute factor.
   d an increase in the price of a substitute factor.
   e a decrease in the price of output.

8 A technological change that causes an increase in the marginal product of labour will shift
   a the labour demand curve to the left.
   b the labour demand curve to the right.
   c the labour supply curve to the left.
   d the labour supply curve to the right.
   e **b** and **d**.

9 Other things remaining the same, the larger the proportion of total cost coming from labour, the
   a more elastic is the demand for labour.
   b less elastic is the demand for labour.
   c more elastic is the supply of labour.
   d less elastic is the supply of labour.
   e lower is the demand for labour.

10 If the wage rate increases, the *substitution* effect will give a household an incentive to
   a raise its reservation wage.
   b increase its non-market activity and decrease its market activity.
   c increase its market activity and decrease its non-market activity.

d increase both market and non-market activity.

e decrease both market and non-market activity.

11 If the wage rate increases, the *income* effect will give a household an incentive to

a raise its reservation wage.

b increase its non-market activity and decrease its market activity.

c increase its market activity and decrease its non-market activity.

d increase both market and non-market activity.

e decrease both market and non-market activity.

12 If the desire for leisure increased, the wage rate would

a rise and the quantity of labour hired would fall.

b rise and the quantity of labour hired would rise.

c fall and the quantity of labour hired would fall.

d fall and the quantity of labour hired would rise.

e fall and the quantity of labour demanded would rise.

13 Economic rent is the

a price paid for the use of a hectare of land.

b price paid for the use of a unit of capital.

c income required to induce a given quantity of a factor of production to be supplied.

d income received that is above the amount required to induce a given quantity of a factor of production to be supplied.

e transfer earnings of a factor of production.

14 An exhaustible natural resource is

a labour.

b land.

c coal.

d water.

15 Mary will supply 40 hours of labour as an economist for £1,600. She actually receives £2,000. Her economic rent is

a £1,600.

b £2,000.

c £400

d 40 hours.

SHORT ANSWER

1 Why will an increase in the supply of a factor of production result in an increase in income if the demand for the factor has elasticity greater than 1, and result in a decrease in income if the elasticity of demand for the factor is less than 1?

2 Why is the demand for a factor of production given by its marginal revenue product curve?

3 Discuss the substitution and income effects on the quantity of labour supplied if the wage rate *decreases*.

4 Are prices of retail goods in central London high because rents are high, or are rents high because prices are high? Explain.

5 Explain present value by showing how £110 received one year from now has a present value of £100 if the interest rate is 10 per cent.

PROBLEMS

1 Table 15.1 gives the total and marginal product schedules for a firm that sells its output in a competitive market and buys labour in a competitive market. Initially the price at which the firm can sell any level of output is £5 per unit and the wage rate at which it can purchase any quantity of labour is £15 per unit.

a Complete the first two blank columns in Table 15.1 by computing the *TR* and *MRP$_L$* corresponding to price of output = £5.

b The text informs us that the values obtained for the marginal revenue product of labour (*MRP$_L$*) are the same when they are computed by either of the following formulae:

$$MRP_L = \Delta TR / \Delta L$$

$$MRP_L = MR \times MP_L$$

where ΔTR = the change in total revenue, ΔL = the change in labour, MR = marginal revenue and MP_L = marginal product of labour. Show that these two formulae are equivalent for the case when the quantity of labour changes from 1 to 2 units.

c If the firm maximizes profit, what quantity of labour will it hire? How much output will it produce?

d If total fixed cost is £125, what is the amount of profit?

e What is its profit if the firm hires one more unit of labour than the profit-maximizing quantity? One less unit of labour than the profit-maximizing quantity?

Table 15.1

Quantity of labour (L) (workers)	Output (Q) (units per hour)	Marginal product of labour $(MP_L = \Delta Q/\Delta L)$ (units per worker)	Total revenue $(TR = £5 \times Q)$ (pounds per hour)	Marginal revenue product $(MRP = \Delta TR/L)$ (pounds per worker)	Total revenue $(TR = £3 \times Q)$ (pounds per hour)	Marginal revenue product $(MRP_L = TR/L)$ (pounds per worker)
0	0					
		...12				
1	12					
		...10				
2	22					
		...8				
3	30					
		...6				
4	36					
		...4				
5	40					
		...2				
6	42					

f Draw a graph of the demand for labour and the supply of labour and illustrate labour market equilibrium.

2 Now suppose that the market demand for the output of the firm in Problem 1 decreases, causing the price of output to decrease to £3 per unit. The total and marginal product schedules remain unchanged.
   a Complete the last two blank columns in Table 15.1 by computing the *TR* and *MRP_L* corresponding to price of output = £3.
   b If the wage remains at £15 per unit of labour, what is the profit-maximizing quantity of labour that the firm will hire? How much output will it produce?
   c Total fixed cost continues to be £125. What is the amount of profit?
   d Will the firm shut down in the short run? Explain.
   e Draw a new graph of the new labour market equilibrium.

3 The price of output for the firm in Problem 2 remains at £3 but the wage now rises to £21 per unit of labour. The total and marginal product schedules remain unchanged.
   a What happens to the demand curve for labour (the *MRP* of labour curve)?

b Under these circumstances, what is the profit-maximizing quantity of labour that the firm will hire? How much output will it produce?
c Total fixed cost continues to be £125. What is the amount of profit?
d Draw a graph of the labour market equilibrium.

DISCUSSION QUESTION

1 What is the point of discussing the supply of labour when most people have no choice about the number of hours that they work?

DATA QUESTIONS

Increased supply of women in the labour force

Increased real wages Real wages for women have been rising since World War II. Since 1970, part of this rise has been a consequence of the Equal Pay Act.

Changes in demographic trends Labour force participation rates are higher for single women. In the United Kingdom, 40 per cent of all marriages end in divorce, and married women may choose to enter the labour market as a cushion against the financial loss of unearned income after divorce. In addition, the mean age of marriage has increased.

Changes in the value of non-market time Labour-saving devices, supermarket dinners and shops full of commodities mean that women do not have to devote as much time to non-market work. Market goods have been substituted for non-market time at low prices.

Changes in male earnings A rise in male earnings might reduce the participation of women as their unearned income will rise. However, this effect is overridden by the rise in women's earnings.

Keeping up with the Jones's As individuals require an ever rising standard of living and equate that with increased consumption of market commodities, the value of non-market time falls.

Source: Adapted from Anna Palmer, 'Changes in Labour Force Participation', in G.B.J. Atkinson (ed.), *Developments in Economics*, **13**, 1997, Causeway Press.

1 Why do you think women's real wages have been rising?

2 How do non-market activities affect market activities?

3 The extract deals with the supply of women's labour. What factors do you think might affect the demand for women's labour?

ANSWERS

CONCEPT REVIEW

1 land; labour; capital; entrepreneurship

2 increase; large; small

3 derived

4 hiring; labour; increase

5 *MC*; *PF*

6 right; right

7 interest

8 rent; opportunity

9 decrease; increase

10 economic rent; transfer

TRUE OR FALSE

1 F Fall in price leads to rise in income.

2 T Income is price times quantity.

3 T A specific example of the *MR* = *MC* rule.

4 F Same as *MRP* curve.

5 T The *MRP* curve is the firm's demand for labour curve.

6 T Definition.

7 F Tends to be elastic.

8 T Steep *MRP* curve means inelastic demand.

9 F Short-run elasticity of demand for labour depends on elasticity of demand for the product, labour intensity and slope of marginal product curve – capital cannot be substituted in short run.

10 T People will substitute work for leisure.

11 T Definition. Leisure is a normal good.

12 T Definition.

MULTIPLE CHOICE

1 d Definition.

2 b Increase in factor of production with inelastic demand leads to increase in $PF \times QF$.

3 d Revenue from selling marginal product of capital.

4 b Shows quantity of labour hired at each wage rate.

5 d Where supply curve of factor to firm *(MC)* intersects with demand curve for factor *(MRP)*.

6 c Hiring more labour leads to more profit since *MRP* > *MC*. Firm cannot change wage.

7 d Firm demands more of the now relatively cheaper factor. **a** and **b** move along curve, **e** shifts curve leftward.

8 b Definition.

9 a Increase in wage leads to greater increase in total costs and increase in price of product. This leads to greater fall in sales and labour hired.

10 c Substitute work for leisure.

11 b Consume more normal goods including leisure, which entails working less.

12 a Labour supply would shift leftward.

13 d Definition. Price paid for land use is rent.

14 c Coal cannot be replaced.

15 c $400 is the difference between a resource's total income and its opportunity cost.

SHORT ANSWER

1 An increase in the supply of a factor of production will cause the price of the factor to decrease and the quantity of the factor hired to increase. Income received by the factor is equal to the price of the factor times the quantity hired. If the percentage increase in the quantity hired is greater than the percentage decrease in price (if

PRICING AND ALLOCATING FACTORS OF PRODUCTION 149

the elasticity of demand for the factor is greater than 1), income will increase. Similarly, if the percentage increase in the quantity hired is less than the percentage decrease in price (if the elasticity of demand for the factor is less than 1), income will decrease.

2 The marginal revenue product curve for a factor of production gives its demand curve because firms are profit maximizers. As a consequence, they will hire an additional unit of a factor of production until the marginal cost of the factor (its price) is equal to the additional revenue from its use (its *MRP*). Thus the quantity of the factor demanded at each price (the demand curve) is given by the *MRP* curve.

3 If the wage rate decreases, households will have a tendency to shift from work to leisure (the substitution effect), thus reducing the quantity of labour supplied. The lower wage also decreases the household's income, causing the household to reduce its demand for leisure and other normal goods (the income effect) and thus increasing the quantity of labour supplied.

4 Rents are high because prices are high. Land in central London has a perfectly inelastic supply, so the price of land (its rent) is determined entirely by demand for the land.

Demand is high because shop owners know that the prime retail location will allow them to charge higher prices and potentially earn higher profits than in other locations.

5 The present value of £110 received one year in the future is the amount that £100 invested today would grow to at the prevailing interest rate of 10 per cent. Thus £110 a year hence has a present value of £100.

PROBLEMS

1 a The completed columns for *TR* and *MRP*$_L$ corresponding to price of output = £5 are shown in Table 15.2. The values for *TR* are obtained by multiplying the quantity of output by the price of output (£5). The values for *MRP*$_L$ between any two quantities of labour are obtained by dividing the change in *TR* by the change in quantity of labour.

b From **a**, the formula $MRP_L = TR/L$ yields a marginal revenue product of labour of 60 when the quantity of labour changes from 1 to 2 units. To confirm that the second formula ($MRP_L = MR \times MP_L$) gives the same answer when the quantity of labour changes from 1 to 2 units, substitute in the values for *MR* (£5, the price of an additional unit of output) and *MP*$_L$ (12 units of output). This yields the same marginal revenue product of labour as above; £5 × 12 units = £60.

c The firm maximizes profit by hiring labour up to the point where the *MRP* of labour is equal to the mar-

Table 15.2

Quantity of labour (L) (workers)	Output (Q) (units per hour)	Marginal product of labour (MP$_L$ = ΔQ/ΔL) (units per worker)	Total revenue (TR = £5×Q) (pounds per hour)	Marginal revenue product (MRP = ΔTR/L) (pounds per worker)	Total revenue (TR = £3×Q) (pounds per hour)	Marginal revenue product (MRP$_L$ = TR/L) (pounds per worker)
0	0		0		0	
		...12		...60		...36
1	12		60		36	
		...10		...50		...30
2	22		110		66	
		...8		...40		...24
3	30		150		90	
		...6		...30		...18
4	36		180		108	
		...4		...20		...12
5	40		200		120	
		...2		...10		...6
6	42		210		126	

ginal cost of labour (the wage rate). That point occurs at 5 units of labour. The *MRP* of moving from 4 to 5 units of labour is 20, and the *MRP* of moving from 5 to 6 units of labour is 10. Thus by interpolation the *MRP* at exactly 5 units of labour is 15 (midway between 20 and 10). So when 5 units of labour are hired, the *MRP* of labour is equal to the wage rate (£15). Given that 5 units of labour are hired, the profit-maximizing output will be 40 units (from Table 15.2).

d To calculate profit, we must first calculate total revenue and then subtract total cost. Total revenue is £200 (40 units of output × £5 per unit) and total cost is also £200 – the sum of total variable (labour) cost of £75 (5 units of labour × £15 per unit) and total fixed cost of £125. Thus profit is zero.

e If the firm hires one more unit of labour (6 units), total revenue will be £210 (42 units of output × the £5 price). Total cost will be the £125 fixed cost plus £90 in total variable cost (6 units of labour × the £15 wage rate) or £215. Thus profit will be a negative £5 (a £5 loss).

If the firm hires one less unit of labour (4 units), total revenue will be £180 (36 units of output × the £5 price). Total cost will be the £125 fixed cost plus £60 in total variable cost (4 units of labour × the £15 wage rate) or £185. Thus profit will be a negative £5 (a £5 loss).

f The graph of labour market equilibrium appears in Figure 15.1. The demand for labour is given by the firm's *MRP*$_L$ curve which is labelled D_0 (D_1 will be discussed in Problem 2).

Notice that the values for *MRP* are plotted midway between the corresponding quantities of labour. For example, *MRP* of 60 is plotted midway between 1 and 2 units of labour.

Since the firm purchases labour in a perfectly competitive labour market, the supply of labour to the firm is perfectly elastic at the market wage rate. The labour supply curve is labelled $W = £15$. The equilibrium is at the intersection of these curves, and corresponds to a wage rate of £15 and a quantity of labour hired of 5 units.

Figure 15.1

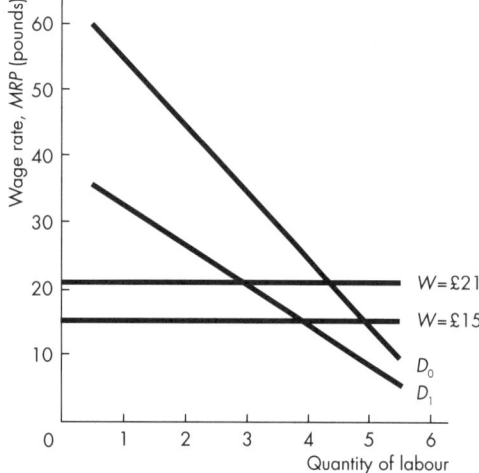

---

2 a The completed columns for *TR* and MRP_L corresponding to price of output = £3 are shown in Table 15.2. The values for *TR* are obtained by multiplying the quantity of output by the price of output (£3). The values for MRP_L between any two quantities of labour are obtained by dividing the change in *TR* by the change in quantity of labour.

b If the wage rate remains at £15, the profit-maximizing quantity of labour will fall to 4 units since MRP_L equals the wage rate at 4 units of labour. The *MRP* of moving from 3 to 4 units of labour is 18, and the *MRP* of moving from 4 to 5 units of labour is 12. Thus by interpolation the *MRP* at exactly 4 units of labour is 15 (midway between 18 and 12). Given that 4 units of labour are employed, the profit-maximizing output will be 36 units (from Table 15.2).

c Profit equals total revenue minus total cost. Total revenue is £108 (36 units of output × £3 per unit)

and total cost is £185 – the sum of total variable (labour) cost of £60 (4 units of labour × £15 per unit) and total fixed cost of £125. Thus profit is –£77, or a loss of £77.

d The firm will not shut down since total revenue (£108) is enough to cover total variable cost (£60) and part of fixed cost. If the firm decided to shut down, it would lose the £125 of fixed cost rather than just £77.

e The graph of labour market equilibrium appears in Fig. 15.1. The new demand for labour is given by the firm's new MRP_L curve, which is labelled D_1. The supply of labour has not changed; it continues to be horizontal at £15, the competitive market wage. The new equilibrium is at the intersection of these curves, and corresponds to a wage rate of £15 and a quantity of labour hired of 4 units.

3 a Since marginal revenue and the marginal product of labour are unaffected by a change in the wage rate, the demand curve for labour (the *MRP* of labour) will remain at D_1.

b If the wage rate rises to £21, the profit-maximizing quantity of labour will fall to 3 units since MRP_L equals the wage rate at 3 units of labour. Given that 3 units of labour are employed, the profit-maximizing output will be 30 units (from Table 15.2).

c Profit equals total revenue minus total cost. Total revenue is £90 (30 units of output × £3 per unit) and total cost is £188 – the sum of total variable (labour) cost of £63 (3 units of labour × £21 per unit) and total fixed cost of £125. Thus profit is –£98, or a loss of £98.

d See Figure 15.1. The relevant demand for labour curve continues to be D_1, but the labour supply curve reflects the rise in the competitive wage rate; it is now horizontal at a wage rate of £21 (labelled $W = £21$). The equilibrium is at the intersection of these curves and corresponds to a wage rate of £21 and a quantity of labour hired of 3 units.

DISCUSSION QUESTION

1 While it is true that some people have little choice over the number of hours they work, others do have a choice. Many employers allow overtime and there are part-time jobs where the hours are flexible, and some people have more than one part-time job. Self-employed people can also extend the hours that they work.

DATA QUESTIONS

1 Women's real wages have been rising for a number of reasons. One is that real wages as a whole have been rising (for example, because of increased technology), and women have benefited from this as well as men. In addition, higher education is associated with higher incomes, and women's educational standards have been rising, leading to higher wages. Equal pay legislation has also had an effect. Lastly, there has been increased demand for the goods produced and services provided by women, and this increased demand has led to higher wages. Despite this, women's wages remain below those of men.

2 Non-market activities, such as leisure, can have a strong effect on market activities, for example, a rise in incomes increases the demand for leisure. This will increase the demand for goods and services in the leisure industry, and it may also cause people to choose to do less work and to take more leisure.

3 A number of factors have affected the demand for women's labour. One is that the demand for labour is a derived demand, so as the demand for goods rises, so does demand for labour. In particular, there has been a rise in the importance of services, and many jobs in these areas are considered to be women's jobs. This is reinforced by the rise in part-time jobs, predominantly done by women. Lastly, the increased education of women has narrowed the gap between educated women and men and enabled many women to take jobs which were previously held by educated men.

Chapter 16 **Labour Markets**

Chapter in Perspective, Text Pages 382–403

Labour markets play an important role in the economic well-being of almost every household since household income is determined largely by the operation of these markets. This chapter looks more carefully at labour markets to explain how wage rates and employment levels are determined. We investigate why some groups earn more than other groups: why skilled workers earn more than unskilled workers; why union members earn more than non-union members; why, on average, men earn more than women; and why there are differences in the average earnings of people from different ethnic groups.

Helpful Hints

1 This chapter introduces the concept of a monopsonist, a firm that is the only buyer in a market such as labour, for example. The monopsonist faces an upward-sloping supply of labour curve and, as a result, its marginal cost of labour curve (*MCL*) is different from the labour supply curve.

    The monopoly, as the only seller in an output market, faces a downward-sloping demand curve. The marginal revenue from the sale of an additional unit of output is *less* than the selling price because the monopoly must *lower* the price on all previous units as well. Thus the *MR* curve lies *below* the demand curve for the monopoly. For the monopsonist in a labour market, the marginal cost of hiring an additional unit of labour is *higher* than the wage because the monopsonist must *raise* the wage on all previous units of

labour as well. Thus the *MCL* curve lies *above* the supply of labour curve for the monopsonist.

2 Both monopoly and monopsory cause inefficiency. The reason is the same – they exploit their market power by restricting their output. Thus, compared to a perfectly competitive firm, a monopsonist will hire less labour and so produce less output.

3 A particular labour market may *not* establish a wage rate and a level of employment in the simple sense of the intersection of demand and supply curves. The broader notion of labour market equilibrium includes determination of quantity and of the type of compensation scheme, of which time rates of pay (wage rates) are only one possibility. Equilibrium occurs when the market is at rest in the sense that no worker or firm has an incentive to change.

SELF-TEST

CONCEPT REVIEW

1 The demand curve for skilled labour lies _____ the demand curve for unskilled labour, because the marginal revenue product of skilled workers is _____ than that of unskilled workers. The supply curve for skilled labour lies _____ the supply curve for unskilled labour, because skills are costly to acquire.

2 Education and training can be viewed as investments in _____ capital. The value of that capital is the _____ _____ of the extra future earnings that result from the increased education or training.

3 A market in which there is only one buyer is called _____ . If there is only one firm that buys labour, the wage rate will be _____ than the marginal cost of labour. A situation in which a single seller of labour, such as a union, faces a single buyer of labour is called _____ monopoly.

4 Four possible explanations of wage differentials between the sexes are discussed in Chapter 16. The first is concerned with job types. The second is discrimination. The third is that the two groups have differences in _____ capital. The fourth is that there are differences in the degree of _____ in market and non-market activities.

5 A formula for calculating a person's income is called a(n) _____ rule. If the formula is based solely on the number of hours the person works, it is called a(n) _____ rate. If the formula is based on the amount of output the worker produces it is called a(n) _____ rate. A rule that allocates a certain fraction of the firm's profit to employees is called _____ - _____ .

6 Often, either worker effort or worker output are difficult, if not impossible, to observe. An individual who sets a rule for compensating workers, which motivates the worker to choose activities advantageous to the individual is called a(n) _____ . Each worker in such a situation is called a(n) _____ .

TRUE OR FALSE

___ **1** The marginal revenue product of unskilled workers is lower than that of skilled workers.

___ **2** The vertical distance between the labour supply curves for skilled and unskilled workers is the marginal revenue product of the skill.

___ **3** The larger the marginal revenue product of the skill and the more costly it is to acquire, the smaller is the wage differential between skilled and unskilled workers.

___ **4** Unions support minimum wage laws in part because they increase the cost of unskilled labour, a substitute for skilled union labour.

___ **5** A firm that is a monopsonist in the labour market must compete with other firms for the labour it hires.

___ **6** The more elastic is labour supply, the less opportunity a monopsonist has to make an economic profit.

___ **7** In a monopsonistic labour market, the introduction of a minimum wage that is above the current wage will raise the wage but reduce employment.

___ **8** The evidence suggests that, after allowing for the effects of skill differentials, union workers earn no more than non-union workers.

___ **9** Economic theory tells us that discrimination in employment will result in wage differentials.

___ **10** If males on average earn more than females, we can conclude that there must be discrimination.

MULTIPLE CHOICE

1 Which of the following is *not* a reason why the wage of skilled workers exceeds the wage of unskilled workers?
  a The market for skilled workers is more competitive than the market for unskilled labour.
  b The marginal revenue product of skilled workers is greater than that of unskilled workers.
  c The cost of training skilled workers is greater than the cost of training unskilled workers.
  d Skilled workers have acquired more human capital than unskilled workers.
  e The demand curve for skilled workers lies to the right of the demand curve for unskilled workers.

2 The economic value of the increase in human capital owing to additional education is
  a the money cost of the additional education.
  b the money cost of the additional education plus forgone earnings.
  c the present value of all expected future earnings.
  d the present value of all extra expected future earnings that are the result of the additional education.
  e none of the above.

3 Which of the following would unions be *least* likely to support?
  a increasing the legal minimum wage
  b restricting immigration
  c encouraging imports
  d increasing demand for the goods their workers produce
  e increasing the marginal product of union labour

4 The most important way in which unions increase wages is by
  a increasing the marginal (physical) product of labour.
  b increasing the marginal revenue product of labour.
  c increasing the demand for labour.
  d decreasing the supply of labour.
  e increasing the marginal cost of labour.

5 In order to hire an additional worker, a monopsonist must pay
  a a higher wage rate.
  b the same wage rate.
  c a lower wage rate

  d sometimes higher, sometimes lower or sometimes the same wage, depending on the supply curve of labour.

6 For a monopsony, the MCL curve
  a lies above the labour supply curve.
  b is the same as the labour supply curve.
  c lies below the labour supply curve.
  d is the same as the labour demand curve.

7 Figure 16.1 illustrates a monopsonist in the labour market (*MCL* = marginal cost of labour). The profit-maximizing wage rate and quantity of labour hired will be
  a $4 per hour and 800 hours of labour.
  b $4 per hour and 400 hours of labour.
  c $7 per hour and 600 hours of labour.
  d $9 per hour and 400 hours of labour.
  e none of the above.

Figure 16.1

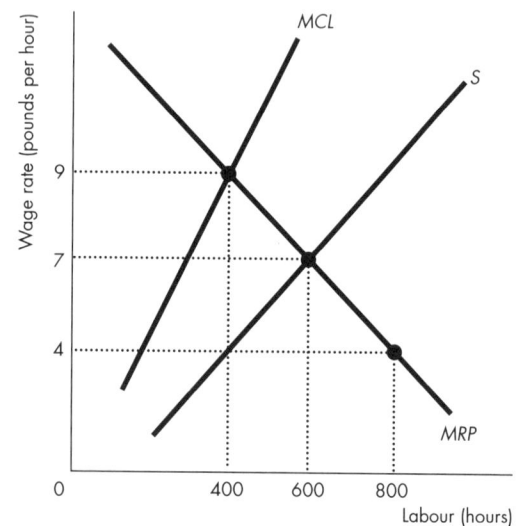

8 If the labour market illustrated in Fig. 16.1 became competitive, the equilibrium wage rate and quantity of labour hired would be
  a $4 per hour and 800 hours of labour.
  b $4 per hour and 400 hours of labour.
  c $7 per hour and 600 hours of labour.
  d $9 per hour and 400 hours of labour.
  e none of the above.

9 Wage differentials between males and females can be explained by
  a occupational differences.

b human capital differences.
c degree of specialization differences.
d discrimination.
e all of the above.

10 Which of the following cases is most likely to be characterized by a time rate of pay?
   a Individual effort is readily observed but individual contribution to output is not.
   b Individual effort is not readily observed but individual contribution to output is.
   c Neither individual effort nor individual contribution to output is readily observable.
   d Monitoring costs are high.
   e None of the above statements is most likely.

SHORT ANSWER

1 Members of trade unions earn wages well above the minimum wage. Even so, why is it in the interest of a union to support increases in the legal minimum wage?

2 Bob and Sue form a household. They have decided that Sue will fully specialize in market activity and Bob will pursue activities both in the job market and in the household. If most households are like Bob and Sue, why would the result be a difference between the earnings of men and women, even if there is no discrimination?

3 Many large firms are owned by a group of shareholders who hire managers to run the firm. Why is profit-sharing a good compensation scheme for top management in such a firm?

4 The *Reading Between the Lines* article shows that some television presenters and actors earn millions of pounds. So, why don't you go into this business?

PROBLEMS

1 Figure 16.2 shows the demand and supply of skilled and unskilled labour. S_U and S_S are the supply curves for unskilled and skilled workers, respectively, and D_U and D_S are the demand curves for unskilled and skilled workers, respectively.

Figure 16.2

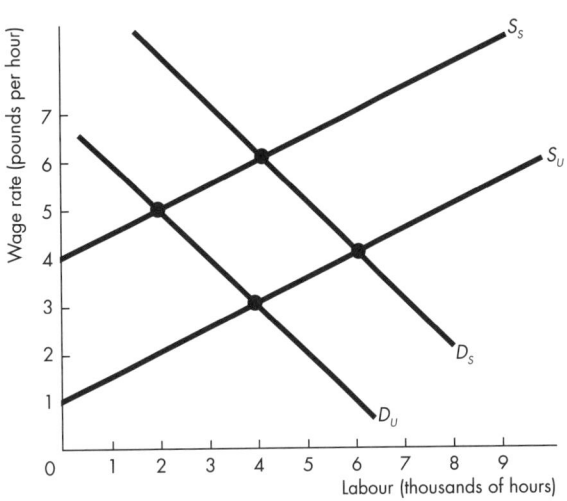

a What is the marginal revenue product of skill if 5,000 hours of each kind of labour are hired?
b What is the amount of extra compensation per hour required to induce the acquisition of skill at the same level of hiring?
c What are the equilibrium wage and quantity of labour in the market for skilled labour?
d What are the equilibrium wage and quantity of labour in the market for unskilled labour?

2 Yuri has an opportunity to increase his human capital by taking a training course that will raise his income by £100 every year for the rest of his life. Assume that there are no other benefits of the course. The cost of the course is £1,200 and Yuri's best alternative investment pays an interest rate of 10 per cent per year for the rest of his life. Should Yuri pay the £1,200 and take the course? Explain.

3 Figure 16.3 illustrates a profit-maximizing monopsonist in the labour market.
   a What wage rate will the monopsonist pay and how much labour will be employed? What is the value of labour's marginal revenue product at this level of employment?
   b If this were a competitive labour market with the same marginal revenue product curve, what would the equilibrium wage rate and the level of employment be?

Figure 16.3

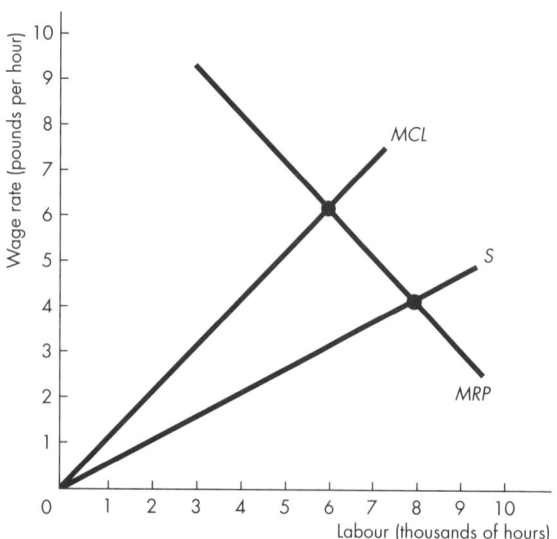

c Now suppose the government imposes a minimum wage of £4 per hour. What wage rate will the monopsonist pay and how much labour will be employed?

DISCUSSION QUESTION

1 Explain why it is possible for unions to lower the wages of workers who are not members of unions.

DATA QUESTIONS

You're only as insecure as you feel
It's official, apparently. One of Britain's largest recruitment agencies has declared that the 'job for life' is dead. We live in a hire and fire age where companies downsize their workforce at the drop of a management consultancy report.

Yet the facts contradict this. Surveys consistently show that when members of the public are questioned about how secure their own positions are, three-quarters of respondents say they are not worried about losing their jobs. The proportion who are worried about job security – under 10 per cent – has remained almost the same since the 1970s.
Source: *Guardian*, 2 November 1999, p. 27.

1 Why do companies 'downsize their workforce'?

2 Can you explain the disagreement about the existence of job insecurity?

ANSWERS

CONCEPT REVIEW

1 above; greater; above

2 human; present value

3 monopsonist; lower; bilateral

4 human; specialization

5 compensation; time; piece; profit-sharing

6 principal; agent

TRUE OR FALSE

1 T Demand for unskilled workers is to the left of the demand for skilled workers.

2 F Vertical distance is compensation for cost of acquiring skill.

3 F The larger is the wage differential.

4 T Increase in the price of a substitute leads to rise in demand for union labour.

5 F Definition. Monopsonist is sole buyer.

6 T Draw diagram to verify this.

7 F True for competitive market.

8 F Union members earn more than non-union members with similar skills.

9 T Discrimination means that those discriminated against earn less.

10 F Differences may be owing to discrimination, human capital differences and/or specialization.

MULTIPLE CHOICE

1 a Wage differences are not owing to competitive differences. In any case, an increase in competitiveness would lead to a fall in skilled wages.

2 d Return on investment in additional education.

3 c Increase in imports would lead to a fall in sales of domestic products and hence in demand for domestic labour.

4 d **a**, **b** and **c** are indirect ways.

5 a The monopsonist must pay a higher wage to recruit more labour.

6 a The *MCL* curve is above the labour supply curve.

7 b Quantity of labour is where *MCL* intersects *MRP*. Then the lowest wage required for labour to supply that quantity (on supply curve).

8 c Where *S* intersects *MRP*.

9 e All can contribute to differentials.

10 a Lazy individuals can be sacked so no need to pay by results.

SHORT ANSWER

1 An increase in the minimum wage will increase the cost of hiring unskilled labour, which will tend to increase the demand for skilled labour; which is a substitute.

2 If Sue specializes in market activity while Bob is diversified, it is likely that Sue's earning ability will exceed Bob's owing to the gains from her specialization. If most households followed this pattern of specialization, the income of women would exceed that of men even without discrimination.

3 In this case the owners (shareholders) are the principals and the top managers are the agents. Neither the effort nor the output of the managers can be easily monitored. But since the decisions of managers have a direct and significant bearing on the profit of the firm, their incentive is to make decisions that maximize profit if they share in any increase in profit through a profit-sharing compensation scheme.

4 This requires a personal answer. For most people in the industry, earnings are low. The main reason is that the supply of people wanting to be actors is much greater than the demand. Only a few people with exceptional talents (or luck) can differentiate themselves from others and so become monopolistic suppliers.

PROBLEMS

1 a The marginal revenue product of skill is the difference between the marginal revenue products of skilled versus unskilled labour; the vertical distance between the demand curves for skilled and unskilled labour. In Fig. 16.2, the marginal revenue product of skill is £3 per hour when 5,000 hours of each kind of labour are employed.

  b Since labour supply curves give the minimum compensation workers are willing to accept in return for supplying a given quantity of labour, the extra compensation for skill is the vertical distance between the supply curves of skilled and unskilled labour. At 5,000 hours of employment for both kinds of labour, this is £3 per hour.

  c In equilibrium in the market for skilled labour, the wage rate will be £6 per hour and employment will be 4,000 hours of labour. This occurs at the intersection of the D_S and S_S curves.

  d In equilibrium in the market for unskilled labour, the wage rate will be £3 per hour and employment will be 4,000 hours of labour. This occurs at the intersection of the D_U and S_U curves.

2 Yuri should take the course only if the value of the course exceeds the cost of the course. The cost of the course is £1,200 while the value of the course is the present value of the extra £100 in income Yuri can expect to receive each year for the rest of his life. The present value of this income stream is the amount of money which, if invested today at 10 per cent (Yuri's best alternative return), would yield an equivalent stream of income. Thus the present value of the extra income is £1,000. Since this is less than the cost of the training course, Yuri should not take it.

3 a The profit-maximizing monopsonist will hire additional labour up to the point where the marginal cost of labour *(MCL)* equals the marginal revenue product of labour *(MRP)*. Referring to Fig. 16.3, this means that the monopsonist will hire 6,000 hours of labour. The wage rate is given by the labour supply curve *S* and, for 6,000 hours of labour, will be £3 per hour. This is less than the £6 per hour marginal revenue product of labour.

  b In a competitive market, the wage rate would be £4 per hour and 8,000 hours of labour would be employed.

  c If the government establishes a minimum wage at £4 per hour, the marginal cost of labour to the monopsonist becomes constant at £4 per hour (up to 8,000 hours of labour). Thus equating the marginal cost of labour and the marginal revenue product of labour leads to a wage rate of £4 and 8,000 hours of labour employed.

DISCUSSION QUESTION

1 If unions are successful in their demands for higher wages, employers may respond by cutting the quantity of labour that they employ. The unemployed workers may then migrate to other industries, and this increase in supply may then lead to a fall in wages for these workers, some of whom will not be union members.

DATA QUESTIONS

1 Firms 'downsize their workforce' in order to increase profits. For example, in 1999 Marks & Spencer cut many management jobs because profits were falling. They also ended contracts with UK textile firms in order to source abroad.

2 One reason for the disagreement was that different methods were used. Surveys are a very useful source of information, but their usefulness depends on the size and representativeness of the sample, and also on the precise question asked.

Chapter 17 Inequality, Redistribution and Welfare

Chapter in Perspective, Text Pages 404–429

Income is the payment to owners of factors of production for the use of those resources. Individuals with more resources to sell or whose resources sell for a higher price will receive larger incomes. Thus the distribution of income depends on the distribution of ownership of resources used in production and the market prices of those resources.

This chapter discusses the distribution of income and wealth in the United Kingdom, and addresses the following questions. How unequally are income and wealth actually distributed? What accounts for this inequality? What are the consequences of government policies intended to redistribute income or wealth? What are the major ideas that constitute a 'fair' distribution of income?

The chapter also analyses one of the largest and most important industries – health. This industry has significant implications for equality.

Helpful Hints

1 The major tool used by economists to depict the degree of inequality of income or wealth in an economy is the Lorenz curve.

2 The crucial point to note about a Lorenz curve is that it measures *cumulative* percentages. So, for example, it might show that the richest 10 per cent of the population owns 30 per cent of the wealth of the country and the richest 20 per cent own 50 per cent.

3 A major message of this chapter is that statistics used to construct Lorenz curves do not always give an accurate picture of inequality.

For example, distribution of wealth that excludes the value of human capital will give a distorted picture relative to the distribution of income.

You should also understand why the distribution of annual (static) income will give a distorted picture relative to the distribution of lifetime (dynamic) income.

Finally, you should understand why the distribution of before-tax, before-transfer income will give a distorted picture relative to the distribution of after-tax, after-transfer income.

SELF-TEST

CONCEPT REVIEW

1 Of the three basic factors of production, _____ earns the largest share of total income.

2 The diagram used by economists to illustrate the cumulative percentage of households ranked from the poorest to the richest is called a(n) _____ _____ . The straight line running through the middle of the diagram is called the line of _____ .

3 The most important factor in determining whether a person receives a high income or a low income is _____ .

4 Differences in income and wealth arise partly from differences in individual _____ and partly from differences in _____ prices.

5 An income tax system in which the marginal tax rate rises as income rises is called a(n) _____ income tax. A(n) _____ income tax is one in which the marginal tax rate falls with the level of income while for a(n) _____ income tax, the marginal tax rate is constant for all levels of income.

6 The distribution of income that would prevail in the absence of government policies is called the _____ distribution. The distribution that takes account of government policies is called the distribution after _____ and _____ .

7 A gift from one generation to the next is called a(n) _____ .

8 The three types of health-care systems are _____ supply and finance, private supply and _____ finance and government finance and supply.

9 Private insurance faces _____ hazard and _____ selection problems. National health services face _____ problems but are the most equitable.

TRUE OR FALSE

— **1** In the United Kingdom income is more unequally distributed than wealth.

— **2** The further the Lorenz curve is from the line of equality, the more equal is the distribution of income.

— **3** Under a proportional income tax, the marginal tax rate does not change as income rises.

— **4** A regressive income tax redistributes income from rich people to poor people.

— **5** Compared with the market distribution of income, government benefits and taxes reduce the inequality of income distribution.

— **6** A national health service avoids the problems of third-party payments, economies of scale and insurance markets.

— **7** A normal distribution is bell-shaped and is symmetrical around the average.

MULTIPLE CHOICE

1 Differences in the wage rates received by different individuals reflect differences in
a marginal product of labour.
b natural ability.
c human capital.
d all of the above.
e none of the above.

2 The inequality in the distribution of wealth is
  a less than the inequality in the distribution of income.
  b decreased by the existence of assortative mating.
  c a better measure of the inequality in the distribution of economic resources than is the inequality in the distribution of income.
  d even greater if we look at the distribution of wealth among the richest 1 per cent of all families.
  e all of the above.

3 A reason for rising health-care prices is
  a decreased demand owing to higher health-care insurance premiums.
  b increased supply owing to lower labour costs.
  c increased demand owing to growth in number of ailments that can be treated.
  d increased supply owing to improved technology.

4 Consider the Lorenz curves in Fig. 17.1. Which Lorenz curve corresponds to the greatest income *inequality*?
  a *A*
  b *B*
  c *C*
  d *D*
  e impossible to tell without additional information

Figure 17.1

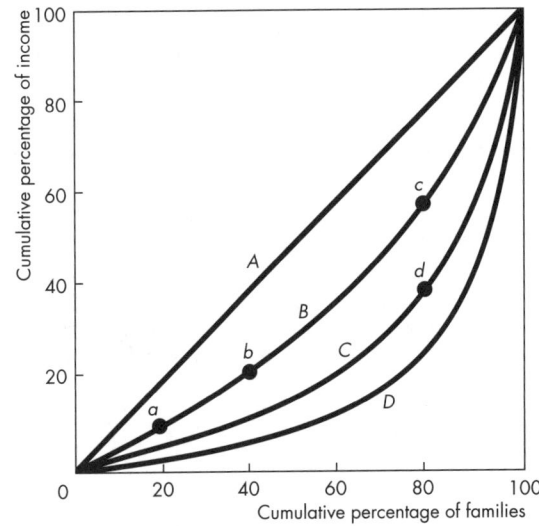

5 In Fig. 17.1, what is curve *A* (a straight line) called?
  a market distribution line
  b line of equality
  c fairness line
  d Okun trade-off curve
  e none of the above

6 Which point in Fig. 17.1 indicates that the richest 20 per cent of families earn 40 per cent of the income?
  a *a*
  b *b*
  c *c*
  d *d*
  e none of the above

7 If the marginal tax rate increases as income increases, the income tax is defined as
  a progressive.
  b proportional.
  c negative.
  d regressive.
  e excessive.

8 The distribution of *annual income*
  a understates the degree of inequality because it does not take into account the family's stage in its life cycle.
  b understates the degree of inequality because it does not take into account the distribution of human capital.
  c overstates the degree of inequality because it does not take into account the family's stage in its life cycle.
  d overstates the degree of inequality because it does not take into account the distribution of human capital.
  e is an accurate measure of the degree of inequality.

9 Which of the following *reduces* the inequality of income or wealth relative to the market distribution?
  a government payments to poor people
  b a regressive income tax
  c large bequests
  d assortative mating
  e all of the above

10 Even if the distribution of wages is symmetrical and bell-shaped, the distribution of income will be skewed because

a abilities are distributed symmetrically.
b abilities are distributed asymmetrically.
c individuals with higher wages tend to supply more labour.
d individuals with lower wages tend to supply less labour.

SHORT ANSWER

1 a What is a Lorenz curve?
  b What does it illustrate?

2 Explain the differences and connections between the concepts of wealth and income.

3 a What are the two factors that determine a person's income?
  b To what extent are these factors the result of forces beyond the control of the individual and to what extent are they the result of individual choice?

4 The two classes of theories of distributive justice are process theories and end-state theories.
  a What is the principal characteristic of a process theory of distributive justice?
  b Why is the utilitarian theory an end-state theory of distributive justice?

PROBLEMS

1 Table 17.1 gives information regarding the distribution of income in an economy which generates £100 billion in total annual income.

Table 17.1   Total Family Income

Percentage of families	Total income (billions of pounds)	Income share (per cent)	Cumulative percentage of families	Cumulative percentage of income
Poorest 20%	5			
Second 20%	10			
Third 20%	15			
Fourth 20%	20			
Richest 20%	50			

a Complete Table 17.1 by computing the entries in the last three columns.

b Draw the Lorenz curve for income in this economy and label it *A*.

2 Now suppose that a progressive income tax is levied on the economy. The distribution of after-tax income is given in Table 17.2. We have assumed that none of the revenue is redistributed to families in the economy. Note that total after-tax income is £71 billion.

Table 17.2   After-tax Family Income

Percentage of families	After-tax income (billions of pounds)	After-tax income share (per cent)	Cumulative percentage of families	Cumulative percentage of after-tax income
Poorest 20%	5			
Second 20%	9			
Third 20%	12			
Fourth 20%	15			
Richest 20%	30			

a Complete Table 17.2.
b Draw the Lorenz curve for after-tax income on the same graph you used for **1b** and label it *B*.
c What effect has the progressive income tax had on inequality?

3 Lastly, suppose that, in addition, the government redistributes all of the tax revenue so that the after-transfer (after-tax) income distribution is that given in Table 17.3. For example, those in the poorest group receive transfer income of £10 billion so that their after-transfer income becomes £15 billion.

Table 17.3   After-transfer Family Income

Percentage of families	After-transfer income (billions of pounds)	After-transfer income share (per cent)	Cumulative percentage of families	Cumulative percentage of after-transfer income
Poorest 20%	15			
Second 20%	16			
Third 20%	18			
Fourth 20%	20			
Richest 20%	31			

a Complete Table 17.3.

b Draw the Lorenz curve for after-transfer income on the same graph you used for **1b** and **2b** and label it *C*.

c What effect has income redistribution through transfer payments had on inequality?

DISCUSSION QUESTION

1 Discuss the proposition that no one ought to be denied the best health care possible.

DATA QUESTIONS

The redistribution of income through taxes and benefits in 1995–96

Table 17.4 shows how the wide range of household incomes is modified by the tax and benefit system in the United Kingdom. There are various measures of income used in the table; for example, original income, which shows income before benefits are received and taxes deducted. Cash benefits can be either contributory (such as old age pensions) or non-contributory (such as child benefit). Non-cash benefits such as free or subsidized education also affect the distribution of income.

1 a Use the data in the table to compare the distribution of original income with the distribution of final income.

b Account for the inequalities in original income which are shown in the table.

2 Compare the relative importance of the different categories of government expenditure and revenue as methods of reducing inequalities in the distribution of income.

3 Discuss the economic consequences of policies which result in a less equal distribution of income and wealth.

Table 17.4 Redistribution of income through taxes and benefits, 1995–96

	Quintile groups of households					All house-holds
	Bottom fifth	Next fifth	Middle fifth	Next fifth	Top fifth	
Average per household (£ per year)						
Wages and salaries	1,390	4,050	10,390	17,610	29,810	12,650
Imputed income from benefits in kind	30	30	100	290	890	270
Self-employment income	370	570	1,250	1,670	5,050	1,780
Occupational pensions, annuities	290	950	1,310	1,790	2,410	1,350
Investment income	200	340	580	830	2,640	920
Other income	150	160	170	250	460	240
Total original income	2,430	6,090	13,790	22,450	41,260	17,200
+ Benefits in cash						
Contributory	1,860	2,280	1,710	1,180	770	1,560
Non-contributory	3,050	2,380	1,650	950	430	1,690
Gross income	7,340	10,750	17,150	24,580	42,450	20,450
− Income tax and NIC	540	930	2,480	4,470	9,660	3,610
− Local taxes (gross)	590	590	650	710	820	670
Disposable income	6,210	9,230	14,020	19,400	31,980	16,170
− Indirect taxes	1,930	2,340	3,290	4,090	5,090	3,350
Post-tax income	4,280	6,890	10,730	15,310	26,890	12,820
+ Benefits in kind						
Education	1,810	1,300	1,420	1,070	830	1,290
National Health Service	1,890	1,830	1,730	1,520	1,330	1,660
Housing subsidy	90	80	40	20	10	50
Travel subsidies	50	70	60	60	140	70
School meals and welfare milk	100	30	10	—	—	30
Final income	8,230	10,200	13,990	17,980	29,200	15,920

Source: *Social Trends*, ONC, 1998.

ANSWERS

CONCEPT REVIEW

1 labour

2 Lorenz curve; equality

3 education

4 endowments; factor

5 progressive; regressive; proportional

6 market; taxes; transfers

7 bequest

8 private; government

9 moral; adverse; monopoly

TRUE OR FALSE

1 **F** Wealth distribution is more unequal.

2 **F** Further away = more unequal.

3 **T** Definition.

4 **F** Regressive = from poor to rich.

5 **T** See Table 17.4 in Data Question.

6 **T** But it has other forms of inefficiency.

7 **T** Definition.

MULTIPLE CHOICE

1 **d** All affect marginal revenue product of labour.

2 **d** The very rich are very rich!

3 **c** The health industry is characterized by rising demand.

4 **d** Curve furthest from 45° line.

5 **b** Definition.

6 **c** Moving from 80 per cent to 100 per cent of families (richest 20 per cent) moves income from 60 per cent of total to 100 per cent (40 per cent).

7 **a** Definition.

8 **c** People who are poor at some stage may be rich at other times.

9 **a** Others increase inequality.

10 **c** High wage earner incomes are higher because their wage rate is higher and also because they work longer hours.

SHORT ANSWER

1 **a** The Lorenz curve gives a graphical representation of the distribution of income or wealth across some population.

b The horizontal axis measures the cumulative percentage of families ranked from the poorest to the richest. The vertical axis measures the cumulative percentages of income or wealth. The further the Lorenz curve is from the line of equality, the more unequal is the distribution of income or wealth.

2 Wealth is the *stock* of assets owned by an individual while income is the *flow* of earnings received by an individual. The concepts are connected in that an individual's income is the earnings that flow from the person's stock of wealth.

3 **a** A person's income is determined by the market prices for productive resource services and the quantity of resource services the person is able and willing to sell at those prices.

b These two factors depend on a number of things, some of which are (at least partially) under the control of the individual and some of which are not.

The price of labour services, the wage rate, is determined in the market for labour. But the wage rate will depend on the marginal product of labour, which is affected by individual choices about training and education as well as inherent personal ability.

The quantity of labour services supplied will also depend on personal choices about how to spend one's time. The quantity of other resource services supplied will depend on personal choices as well as the individual's endowment of the factor.

4 **a** A process theory of distributive justice focuses on the fairness of the process or mechanisms by which results are achieved instead of focusing on the results themselves.

b The utilitarian theory suggests that the fairest system is one in which the sum of the utilities in the society is a maximum. Since the theory focuses on the outcome or the ends, it is an end-state theory of distributive justice.

PROBLEMS

1 **a** Table 17.1 is completed as Table 17.5. The income share for each group of families is the total income of that group as a percentage of total income in the economy (£100 billion). The cumulative percentage of income (last column) is obtained by adding the percentage income share of the group (from the third column) to the total percentage income share of all poorer groups of families.

Table 17.5 Total Family Income

Percentage of families	Total income (billions of pounds)	Income share (per cent)	Cumulative percentage of families	Cumulative percentage of income
Poorest 20%	5	5	20	5
Second 20%	10	10	40	15
Third 20%	15	15	60	30
Fourth 20%	20	20	80	50
Richest 20%	50	50	100	100

b The curve labelled *A* in Fig. 17.2 is the Lorenz curve for total family income. This simply plots the values in the last two columns of Table 17.5.

Figure 17.2

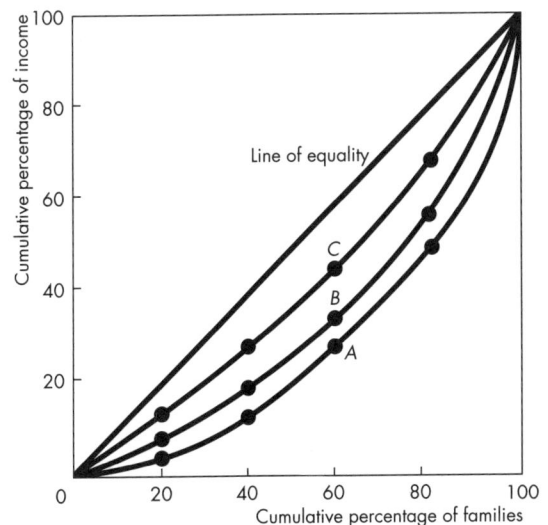

2 a Table 21.2 is completed as Table 17.6.

b The curve labelled *B* in Fig. 17.2 is the Lorenz curve for after-tax family income.

c The progressive income tax has reduced inequality by taking a larger percentage of income from higher income groups.

Table 17.6 Solution After-tax Family Income

Percentage of families	After-tax income (billions of pounds)	After-tax income share (per cent)	Cumulative percentage of families	Cumulative percentage of after-tax income
Poorest 20%	5	7	20	7
Second 20%	9	13	40	20
Third 20%	12	17	60	37
Fourth 20%	15	21	80	58
Richest 20%	30	42	100	100

3 a Table 17.3 is completed as Table 17.7.

b The curve labelled *C* in Fig. 17.2 is the Lorenz curve for (after-tax) after-transfer family income.

c Income redistribution through transfer payments has reduced inequality.

Table 17.7 After-transfer Family Income

Percentage of families	After-transfer income (billions of pounds)	After-transfer income share (per cent)	Cumulative percentage of families	Cumulative percentage of after-transfer income
Poorest 20%	15	15	20	15
Second 20%	16	16	40	31
Third 20%	18	18	60	49
Fourth 20%	20	20	80	69
Richest 20%	31	31	100	100

DISCUSSION QUESTION

1 The opportunity cost of providing everyone with the best health care possible would be the goods and services that could no longer be consumed. The best health care possible would mean many more doctors, nurses and other health-care workers, as well as many more buildings and more equipment. This would mean that other sectors of the economy would become poorer.

DATA QUESTIONS

1 a Final income is much more equally distributed than original income. For example, the bottom fifth saw their total original income rise from £2,430 to £8,230 as a result of taxes and benefits. The income of the richest fifth fell from £17,200 to £15,920.

b The main reason is the difference in earned income. This is caused by factors such as differences in human capital, which were discussed in Chapter 16. These differences are exacerbated by differences in investment income.

2 Benefits in cash and kind play a substantial part in increasing the incomes of the poorest sections of the community. However, these are outweighed by the income removed from the richest fifth by income tax (£3,610 per household) and indirect taxes (£3,350 per household).

3 Policies that result in a less equal distribution of income and wealth will increase economic growth if they create incentives to work hard and to invest and if people respond to these incentives. However, less equal distributions of income and wealth may mean that poor people suffer from ill health and become less productive, while better-off people may find that their income rises so much that they do not need to work so hard. Hence the result may be a slower rate of economic growth.

Part 6 Market Failure and Government

Looking back at Part 5 (Chapters 15–17)

After reading these chapters, you should have a good knowledge of factor markets. Chapter 15 set out the broad parameters, and you should be able to explain the topics listed at the beginning of the chapter; for example, how firms choose the quantities of labour, capital and land that they employ. You should also be able to explain 'economic rent' and 'net present value' to a friend.

Chapter 16 may have suggested to you that your financial prospects will be pretty good after you graduate, particularly if you are male. Can you explain why? You should also understand the equal pay laws.

Chapter 17 stepped back and took an analytical look at one particular issue: inequality. You should know how economists measure this, and how the tax and welfare system impacts on it.

Questions

1 The Frans Somers article gives reasons why the European Union adopted the Social Charter. Can you recall these reasons?

2 Briefly compare the ideas of Malthus and Hotelling as set out in the *Running Out?* article.

3 There is a lot of information on the Internet about labour markets. Try the Trades Union Congress site (www.tuc.org.uk), the Low Pay Unit Site (www.lowpay.gov.uk), the Confederation of British Industry (www.cbi.org.uk) and the official DfEE Sites (www.dfee.gov.uk). Are these sites one-sided?

Looking forward to Part 6 (Chapters 18–20)

So far the thrust of the book has been that markets are pretty marvellous – as indeed they are. But they sometimes fall short; there is market failure. After reading Chapter 18 you should be pretty clear about the distinction between public and private goods, and how markets are not very good at supplying the former. Chapter 19 is concerned with policy; in particular policy towards privatized industries and towards monopolies in general. The last chapter in this Part takes many of the concepts we have already met and applies them to the environment.

Answers

1 Somers suggests that the European Union adopted the Social Charter because otherwise there would be a danger of 'social dumping'. By that he means that some countries would cut such things as health and safety at work standards, enabling them to cut prices.

2 Malthus suggested that without constraints – such as late marriage – population would grow faster than food production, leading to starvation. Hotelling was more optimistic, suggesting that shortages would lead to price rises for exhaustible natural resources. This would lead to a fall in demand and also an increase in substitutes.

The answer is a normative one and will depend on your assessment.

Chapter 18   Market Failure and Public Choice

Chapter in Perspective, Text Pages 430–451

In this chapter we discover that there are circumstances in which markets fail to allocate goods and services efficiently. For example, if competitive markets are efficient, why is there so much pollution? As a result of such *market failure* to achieve efficiency, there are additional opportunities for government to improve allocation. This chapter begins a discussion of how an 'ideal' government might proceed to do so. In the next chapter we examine the behaviour of actual governments.

Helpful Hints

1 The criterion economists use to judge the success of the market is allocative efficiency. Allocative efficiency means that the economy is producing all goods and services up to the point at which the marginal cost is equal to the marginal benefit. In such a state, no one can be made better off without making someone else worse off.

When the market fails to achieve this 'ideal' state of efficiency, we call it *market failure*. The market can fail by producing too little if the marginal benefit of the last unit exceeds the marginal cost. On the other hand, the market can fail by producing too much if the marginal cost of the last unit exceeds the marginal benefit.

2 All goods provided by the government are not necessarily public goods. A public good is defined by the characteristics of non-rivalry and non-excludability, not by whether or not it is publicly provided. For example, local authorities provide swimming pools and residential refuse collection but neither of these is a pure public good in spite of the fact that they may be provided by the local government.

3 A private good is a rival in consumption. Therefore, to obtain the demand curve for the whole economy, we sum the individual marginal benefit (demand) curves *horizontally*. However, the economy's marginal benefit curve for a public good is obtained by summing the individual

marginal benefit curves *vertically*. This is the relevant marginal benefit curve for evaluating the efficient provision level of the public good.

4   A competitive market will result in the quantity being traded at which the marginal private cost is equal to the marginal private benefit. The efficient quantity is the quantity at which marginal social cost is equal to marginal social benefit.

The difference between *marginal social cost* and *marginal private cost* is external cost, and the difference between *marginal social benefit* and *marginal private benefit* is external benefit. When third parties are affected, there are external costs or benefits and competitive markets will not be efficient.

5   Competitive markets with externalities are not efficient because some of the costs or benefits are *external*. If these costs or benefits could be *internalized* somehow, then the market would be efficient. Two approaches to internalizing externalities are discussed in this chapter.

The first is to define clearly and strictly enforce property rights. Then costs imposed on non-participants in a transaction can be recovered through the legal process and will thus be borne by those making the transaction decision: the costs will become internal (private).

The second approach to internalizing externalities is to tax activities that generate external costs and subsidize activities that generate external benefits. By charging a tax equal to the external cost, the entire cost becomes internal. Similarly, by paying a subsidy in the amount of external benefits, the entire benefit becomes internal.

6   Public choice theory provides a theory of the political marketplace that parallels the economic theory of the market for goods and services. In political markets the demanders are voters while in ordinary markets the demanders are consumers. In both cases, demanders are concerned about their own costs and benefits. The suppliers in political markets are politicians and bureaucrats, and again they are concerned about their own costs and benefits.

One way to analyse this market is to use the median voter theorem. This predicts that successful politicians will appeal to the median voter.

SELF-TEST

CONCEPT REVIEW

1   If an unregulated market economy is unable to achieve allocative efficiency in all circumstances, we have _____ _____ .

2   There are two classes of economic theories of government behaviour. Public_____ theories predict that government will pursue actions that will achieve allocative efficiency. Public _____ theories study the behaviour of government as the outcome of individual choices made by voters, politicians and bureaucrats.

3   A good which, if consumed by one person, cannot be consumed by another is called a(n) _____ good. There are two important features of such a good. The fact that Bob's consumption of a good means that Sue cannot consume the same good illustrates the feature of _____ . If Sue has purchased a good, she owns it and can keep others from using it. This illustrates the feature of _____ .

4   A good which, if consumed by one person, is necessarily also consumed by everyone else is called a(n)_____ _____ good.

5   Someone who consumes a good without paying for it is called a(n)_____ _____ . When such individuals are prevalent in the consumption of a particular good, the amount of that good provided by the private market will be _____ than the allocatively efficient amount.

6   The maximum amount a person would be willing to pay for one more unit of a public good is the _____ _____ of that good to the individual.

7   A cost or a benefit arising from a transaction which affects someone other than the direct parties in the transaction is called a(n) _____ . When a chemicals firm dumps its waste into the river, it kills a large number of fish downstream. This is an example of an external _____ . When a neighbour plants flowers on the border of your property, you benefit. This is an example of an external _____ .

8 A legally established title to the sole ownership of a resource is a(n) _____ _____ _____ .

9 The marginal cost borne directly by the producer of a good is called the marginal _____ cost. This marginal cost together with the marginal external cost is the marginal _____ cost.

10 If there are external costs in the production of steel (for example pollution), the output of steel produced by the market will be _____ than the allocatively efficient level.

11 The _____ voter theorem predicts that successful political parties will pursue policies that maximize the net _____ of the _____ voter.

12 A(n) _____ tax is a tax on the sale of a particular commodity.

TRUE OR FALSE

____ **1** Restriction of output by monopolies is an example of market failure.

____ **2** According to the public choice theory of government behaviour, not only is there the possibility of market failure, but there is also the possibility of 'government failure'.

____ **3** The existence of public goods gives rise to the free-rider problem.

____ **4** Any good made available by the government is a public good.

____ **5** The economy's marginal benefit curve for a public good is obtained by adding the marginal benefits of each individual at each quantity of provision.

____ **6** The private market will produce much less than the efficient quantity of pure public goods.

____ **7** If the production of a good involves no external cost, then marginal social cost is equal to marginal private cost.

____ **8** If, at the current level of production of good A, marginal social benefit is less than marginal social cost, then output of good A should increase to achieve allocative efficiency.

____ **9** The government can enhance allocative efficiency by subsidizing the production of goods that generate external benefits and taxing the production of goods that generate external costs.

____ **10** The public choice theory of government behaviour assumes that politicians and bureaucrats are motivated primarily by concern for the public interest.

____ **11** In order to be elected, a politician will tend to choose policies that appeal to the median voter.

____ **12** It is irrational for voters to be uninformed about an issue as important as defence.

MULTIPLE CHOICE

1 Which of the following is *not* a source of market failure?
a the existence of public goods
b external costs
c external benefits
d an unequal distribution of income
e the existence of monopolies

2 A good that exhibits both rivalry and excludability is a(n)
a private good.
b public good.
c government good.
d mixed good.
e external good.

3 Governments provide pure public goods like national defence because
a governments are more efficient than private firms at producing such goods.
b of the free-rider problems, which result in underproduction by private markets.
c people do not value highly national defence.

d of the potential that private firms will make excess profits.

e of external costs.

4 Which of the following goods has the non-excludability feature?

a a city bus

b a toll-bridge

c a lighthouse

d a museum

e all of the above

5 The economy's total demand curve for a public good is obtained by

a summing the individual marginal cost curves horizontally.

b summing the individual marginal cost curves vertically.

c summing the individual marginal benefit curves horizontally.

d summing the individual marginal benefit curves vertically.

e none of the above methods.

6 The total benefit of a given level of provision of a public good can be obtained by

a adding the marginal benefit of each level of provision up to the given level.

b adding the marginal benefit of each level of provision and then subtracting the marginal cost of each level of provision.

c adding the net benefit of each level of provision up to the given level.

d multiplying net benefit by the quantity of the public good provided.

e none of the above methods.

7 Figure 18.1 depicts the demand for good *A* as well as the marginal private cost *(MPC)* and marginal social cost *(MSC)* associated with the production of good *A*. Production of the sixth unit of output generates an external

a cost of £1.50.

b cost of £3.

c cost of £6.

d benefit of £3.

e benefit of £6.

8 In Fig. 18.1, how many units of good *A* will be produced in an unregulated market?

a 0 units

b 5 units

Figure 18.1

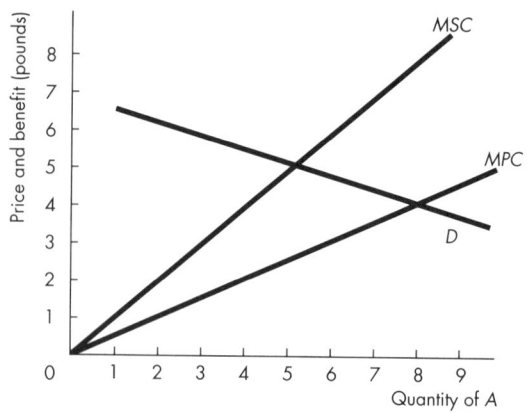

c 6 units

d 8 units

e impossible to calculate without additional information

9 In Fig. 18.1, what is the allocatively efficient quantity of good *A*?

a 0 units

b 5 units

c 6 units

d 8 units

e impossible to calculate without additional information

10 Figure 18.2 depicts the demand curve for good *B* as well as the marginal social benefit *(MSB)* and marginal cost *(MC)* curves. How many units of good *B* will be produced and consumed in an unregulated market?

a 0 units

b 3 units

c 5 units

d 6 units

e 9 units

11 In Fig. 18.2, what is the allocatively efficient quantity of good *B*?

a 0 units

b 3 units

c 5 units

d 6 units

e 9 units

Figure 18.2

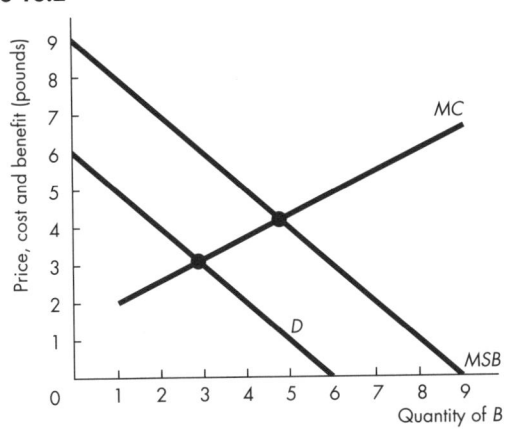

12 In Fig. 18.2, which of the following government policies would induce the market to achieve allocative efficiency?
  a Tax the production of B in the amount of £3 per unit.
  b Tax the production of B in the amount of £4 per unit.
  c Subsidize the consumption of B in the amount of £1 per unit.
  d Subsidize the consumption of B in the amount of £3 per unit.
  e Subsidize the consumption of B in the amount of £4 per unit.

13 Public choice theory
  a argues that government has a tendency to conduct policies that help the economy towards allocative efficiency.
  b argues that politicians and bureaucrats tend to be more concerned about the public interest than individuals in the private sector.
  c argues that the public choices of government maximize net benefits.
  d applies economic tools used to analyse markets to the analysis of government behaviour.
  e applies the tools of political analysis to the analysis of economic markets.

14 Public choice theory assumes that those involved in the political process are generally motivated by
  a self-interest.
  b the desire to achieve allocative efficiency.
  c dishonesty.
  d public spirit.
  e the desire for maximum profit.

15 Competition between two political parties will cause those parties to propose policies
  a that are quite different.
  b that are quite similar.
  c of rational ignorance.
  d that reduce the well-being of middle-income families and benefit the rich and the poor.
  e that equate total benefits and total costs.

SHORT ANSWER

1 Explain the *non-rivalry* and *non-excludability* features of a pure public good.

2 What is the free-rider problem?

3 Explain how a tax can be used to achieve efficiency in the face of external costs.

4 Briefly compare an equilibrium in a political market with an equilibrium in the market for goods and services.

5 The *Reading Between the Lines* article points out that so far no penalties have been spelt out for failure to reach targets. Why?

PROBLEMS

1 The first two columns of Table 18.1 give the demand schedule for education while the third column gives the marginal private cost. Since education generates external benefits, marginal social benefit, given in the last column, is greater than marginal private benefit.

Table 18.1

Quantity (number of students)	Marginal private benefit (pounds)	Marginal private cost (pounds)	Marginal social benefit (pounds)
100	500	200	800
200	400	250	700
300	300	300	600
400	200	350	500
500	100	400	400
600	0	450	350

  a Represent the data in Table 18.1 graphically.
  b What equilibrium price and quantity would result if the market for education is unregulated?

c What is the allocatively efficient number of students?

2 In an attempt to address the inefficient level of education the government has decided to subsidize schooling.

a The government offers £200 to each student who buys a year of education.

  i Draw the new marginal private benefit curve, which includes the subsidy, on your graph and label it MPB_2.

  ii What are the approximate new equilibrium price and number of students?

b The government increases the subsidy to £400.

  i Draw another marginal private benefit curve, which includes the subsidy, on your graph and label it MPB_2.

  ii What are the approximate corresponding equilibrium price and number of students?

c What level of subsidy will achieve the efficient number of students in education?

3 Two candidates are competing in an election for president of the Economics Club. The only issue dividing them is how much will be spent on the annual club party. The seven members of the club (*A* to *G*) have preferences as shown in Table 18.2 regarding how much should be spent on the party.

a How much will each candidate propose to spend?

b To demonstrate that your answer to **a** is correct, consider the outcome of the following two contests.

  i Candidate 1 proposes the amount you gave in **a** and candidate 2 proposes £1 less. Which candidate will win? Why?

  ii Candidate 1 proposes the amount you gave in **a** and candidate 2 proposes £1 more. Which candidate will win? Why?

Table 18.2

Voting member	Proposed amount (pounds)
A	10
B	20
C	30
D	40
E	50
F	60
G	70

DISCUSSION QUESTION

1 How might governments take action that would create inefficiency?

DATA QUESTIONS

In recent years there has been growing opposition to the building of new motorways and other roads. For example, the decision to build a bypass round Newbury provoked widespread opposition from conservationists.

Rather than leaving it to the market, the government decides the quantity of motorways to be built, largely because motorways can be regarded as a semi-public good.

1 Explain what is meant by a 'public good' and show why motorways might be regarded as a semi-public good.

2 Why do conservationists oppose the building of motorways?

ANSWERS

CONCEPT REVIEW

1 market failure

2 interest; choice

3 private; rivalry; excludability

4 pure public

5 free rider; less

6 marginal benefit

7 externality; cost; benefit

8 private property right

9 private; social

10 greater

11 median; benefit; marginal

12 excise

TRUE OR FALSE

1 T Allocatively inefficient output.

2 T Believe government agents act in their own interest, not necessarily public interest.

3 T Non-excludability means no incentive to pay.

4 F 'Public good' has precise meaning.

5 T Definition.

6 T Because it ignores external benefits.

7 T $MSC = MPC$ + externality.

8 F Output should be cut.

9 T This will equalize MSC and MSB.

10 F The theory assumes that they are concerned for their own self-interest.

11 T Because this will maximize votes.

12 F There are costs involved in acquiring information, so it may be rational to stay ignorant.

MULTIPLE CHOICE

1 d Any income distribution can be associated with allocative efficiency.

2 a Definition.

3 b Providing public goods would not be profitable for private firms.

4 c Cannot exclude ships from seeing the light.

5 d See Figure 18.5, text page 437.

6 a b–d involve irrelevant costs.

7 b Vertical distance between MSC and MPC at $Q = 6$.

8 d Where MPC intersects demand.

9 b Where MSC intersects demand.

10 b Where MC intersects demand.

11 c Where MC intersects MSB.

12 d Shift MC down by vertical distance between MSB and demand.

13 d Political marketplace.

14 a It assumes that people are motivated by self-interest.

15 b They will maximize their vote according to the principle of minimum differentiation.

SHORT ANSWER

1 A good has the non-rivalry feature if its consumption by one person does not reduce the amount available for others. The non-excludability feature means that if the good is produced and consumed by one person, others cannot be excluded from consuming it as well.

2 The free-rider problem is the problem of unregulated markets producing too little of a pure public good because there is little incentive for individuals to pay for the good. The reason is that the person's payment is likely to have no perceptible effect on the amount the person will be able to consume.

3 The existence of external costs means that producers do not take into account all costs when deciding how much to produce. If a tax is levied that is exactly the amount of the external cost, the cost will no longer be external. As a result, the producer will take it into account and thus be induced to produce the efficient quantity.

4 In both cases the equilibrium is a state of rest in the sense that no group has an incentive to change its choices. When a political market is in equilibrium neither demanders (voters) nor suppliers (politicians and bureaucrats) are able to make an alternative choice that will make them better off.

5 One reason that no penalties have been proposed is that they are difficult to devise. For example, if the penalties are financial, who should pay? If it is the government department, then a financial penalty would mean that less would be spent on services provided by the department.

PROBLEMS

1 a Figure 18.3 is a graphical representation of the data in Table 18.1. The demand for education is given by the marginal private benefit curve (labelled MPB); the marginal private cost curve is labelled MPC and the marginal social benefit curve is labelled MSB.

Figure 18.3

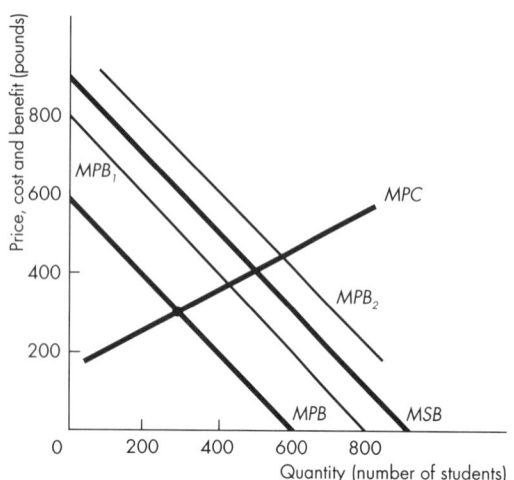

b In an unregulated market, equilibrium price and quantity are determined by the intersection of the *MPB* and *MPC* curves. Thus the equilibrium price would be £300 and the equilibrium quantity is 300 students.

c Since there are no external costs, the efficient quantity is determined by the intersection of the *MPC* and *MSB* curves. This implies that allocative efficiency is attained at a quantity of 500 students.

2 a i The subsidy increases the marginal private benefit to each student by the amount of the subsidy, £200. The new *MPB* curve, labelled *MPB₁*, is included in Fig. 18.3.

  ii The new equilibrium after the £200 subsidy is at the intersection of the *MPC* and *MPB₁* curves. The price of a unit of education will be approximately £370 (£366.67) and there will be approximately 430 (433.33) students.

b i With a subsidy of £400 per student, the *MPB* curve will shift to *MPB₂* in Fig. 18.3.

  ii With this subsidy the equilibrium will be at the intersection of the *MPC* and *MPB₂* curves. The corresponding price of a unit of education will be approximately £430 (£433.33) and the number of students will be approximately 570 (566.67).

c In order to achieve an efficient outcome, the subsidy must make the *MPB* curve coincide with the *MSB* curve. This requires a subsidy of £300 per student.

3 a Each candidate will propose spending £40 since that is the preference of the median voter (voter *D*)

  b i Candidate 1 will win because *D*, *E*, *F* and *G* will vote for that candidate since £40 comes closer to matching their preferences than the £39 proposed by candidate 2. Only *A*, *B* and *C* will vote for candidate 2.

    ii Candidate 1 will win with the votes of *A*, *B*, *C* and *D*; only *E*, *F* and *G* will vote for candidate 2.

DISCUSSION QUESTION

1 The idea that governments won't create inefficiency is called the 'public interest' theory of government. It is based on the assumption that government actions lead to allocative efficiency.

On the other hand, public choice theories assert that well-informed interest groups are able to persuade government to undertake programmes that do not maximize net benefits because most voters are rationally ignorant. For most voters, the costs of gaining information may exceed the benefits obtained. Hence interest groups will have an influence on government that exceeds their size.

DATA QUESTIONS

1 A public good is one that can be consumed simultaneously by everyone and from which no one can be excluded. A lighthouse is a good example; one ship looking at the light does not stop others from seeing it, and the owner of the lighthouse cannot stop ships from seeing the light.

Roads can be used simultaneously by many people, and while it is possible to exclude cars it is often 'pure' public goods.

2 New roads are opposed by conservationists largely because of their undesirable side effects on the environment. Economists call these 'externalities' and they are discussed in detail in Chapter 20.

Chapter 19 Regulation and Privatization

Chapter in Perspective, Text Pages 452–477

This chapter examines government industrial policy. It focuses in particular on the economic aspects of public corporations and natural monopolies and examines how governments attempt to control such firms. This chapter also describes the competition policies adopted by the United Kingdom and the European Union and the reasons for regional policy.

Helpful Hints

1 According to the public interest theory, regulations and anti-monopoly laws should be designed to make markets behave more competitively.

2 The defining characteristic of a natural monopoly in a diagram is that its *ATC* curve slopes down till it crosses the demand curve. This implies that one firm can serve the market with lower costs than could two firms. This creates problems for society. Natural monopoly means that having one firm means lower costs, but it also means higher prices and lower output unless the industry is regulated.

SELF-TEST

CONCEPT REVIEW

1 There are two principal ways in which the government intervenes in monopolistic and oligopolistic markets. The first of these is _____ , which consists of rules administered by a government agency and intended to restrict the behaviour of firms.

The second is _____ _____ _____ , which legally prohibit certain kinds of monopoly practice.

2 The factors that affect the demand for regulation are consumer _____ per buyer, number of _____ , _____ surplus per firm and the _____ of firms.

3 According to the _____ theory, regulations benefit interest groups by large amounts but impose small costs on everyone else.

4 _____ monopoly occurs when one firm can supply the entire market at a lower price than can two or more firms.

5 The _____ _____ theory of intervention claims that intervention is supplied in order to attain allocative efficiency. The _____ theory of intervention states that intervention is intended to maximize producer surplus.

6 The process of selling a publicly owned corporation to private shareholders is called _____ .

7 The pricing rule that maximizes total surplus and achieves allocative efficiency is the _____ _____ pricing rule.

8 When a regulatory agency sets the price of a regulated natural monopolist so that the regulated firm is able to earn a specified target percentage return on its capital, it is using_____ _____ _____ regulation. If the target rate of return is a normal rate of return, this form of regulation gives the same result as the _____ _____ pricing rule.

9 British regulatory bodies such as OFTEL have adopted _____ cap regulation using the RPI _____ formula.

TRUE OR FALSE

___ **1** Regulation and privatization are the two main ways that the government intervenes in the operation of monopolistic and oligopolistic markets.

___ **2** Intervention is supplied by politicians and bureaucrats.

___ **3** Evidence of higher-than-normal rates of return for regulated natural monopolies would match the predictions of the capture theory.

___ **4** According to the public interest theory of intervention, all government intervention will move the economy closer to allocative efficiency.

___ **5** A natural monopoly will always produce on the downward sloping portion of its average total cost curve.

___ **6** For a natural monopoly, marginal cost will always be less than average total cost.

___ **7** An average cost pricing rule will achieve allocative efficiency.

___ **8** Under rate of return regulation, firms can get closer to maximizing producer surplus if they inflate their costs.

___ **9** According to the public interest theory, regulators will regulate a cartel to make sure that firms do not cheat on the collusive cartel agreement to restrict output.

MULTIPLE CHOICE

1 A large demand for regulation by consumers will result when there is a
  a small consumer surplus per buyer.
  b large consumer surplus per buyer.
  c small number of buyers.
  d large producer surplus per firm.

2 The capture theory of intervention predicts that government intervention will maximize
  a producer surplus.
  b consumer surplus.
  c deadweight loss.
  d total surplus.

3 A large demand for intervention by _producers_ will result when there is a
  a small consumer surplus per buyer.
  b large consumer surplus per buyer.
  c large number of buyers.
  d small producer surplus per firm.
  e large producer surplus per firm.

4 Which of the following is consistent with the public interest theory of intervention?
  a regulation of a natural monopolist by setting price equal to marginal cost
  b regulation of a competitive industry in order to increase output
  c regulation of the airline industry by establishing minimum airfares
  d regulation of agriculture by establishing barriers to exit from the industry
  e none of the above

5 Which of the following is consistent with the capture theory of intervention?
  a regulation of a natural monopolist by setting price equal to marginal cost
  b regulation of a competitive industry in order to increase output
  c regulation of the airline industry by establishing minimum airfares
  d regulation of agriculture by establishing barriers to exit from the industry
  e none of the above

6 Figure 19.1 gives the revenue and cost curves for an industry. This industry will become a natural monopoly because
  a one firm can supply the entire market at a lower price than can two or more firms.
  b there are decreasing returns to scale over the entire range of demand.
  c there are diseconomies of scale over the entire range of demand.
  d even a single firm will be unable to earn a positive profit in this industry.
  e all of the above are true.

Figure 19.1

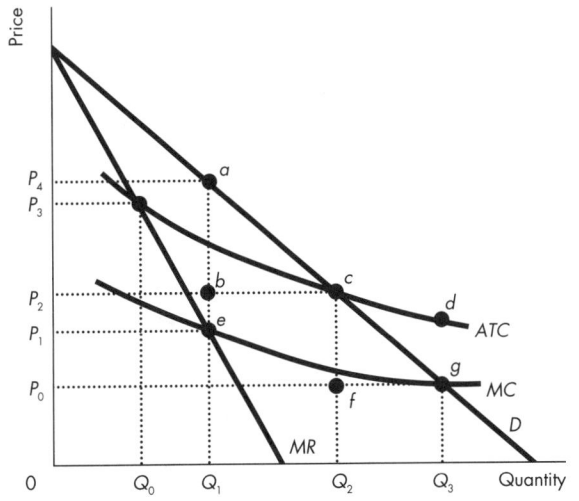

7 Consider the natural monopoly depicted in Fig. 19.1. If the firm is unregulated and operates as a private profit-maximizer, what output will it produce?

  a 0, because the firm suffers economic losses when $P = MC$.
  b Q_0
  c Q_1
  d Q_2
  e Q_3

8 Consider the natural monopoly depicted in Fig. 19.1. If a regulatory agency sets a price just sufficient for the firm to earn normal profits, what output will it produce?
  a 0, because the firm suffers economic losses when $P = MC$
  b Q_0
  c Q_1
  d Q_2
  e Q_3

9 Consider the natural monopoly depicted in Fig. 19.1. Total surplus is a maximum when quantity is
  a Q_0 and price is P_3.
  b Q_1 and price is P_1.
  c Q_1 and price is P_4.
  d Q_2 and price is P_2.
  e Q_3 and price is P_0.

10 Consider the natural monopoly depicted in Fig. 19.1. Producer surplus is a maximum when quantity is
  a Q_0 and price is P_3.
  b Q_1 and price is P_1.
  c Q_1 and price is P_4.
  d Q_2 and price is P_2.
  e Q_3 and price is P_0.

11 A monopolist under rate of return regulation has an incentive to
  a pad costs.
  b produce more than the efficient quantity of output.
  c charge a price equal to marginal cost.
  d maximize consumer surplus.
  e do both **a** and **b**.

12 The demand for intervention depends on
  a consumer surplus per buyer.
  b number of buyers.
  c producer surplus per firm.
  d number of firms.
  e all of the above.

SHORT ANSWER

1 Regulation of monopoly is necessary because of the tension between the public interest and the producer's interest. Explain.

2 In the regulation of a natural monopoly, when would an average cost pricing rule be better than a marginal cost pricing rule?

3 Why is rate of return regulation equivalent to average cost pricing?

4 Explain the problem that the recent deregulation process poses for the capture theory of intervention.

5 With reference to the *Reading Between the Lines* article, why do you think BT can make such large profits?

PROBLEMS

1 a It has been suggested that government should eliminate monopoly profit by taxing each unit of monopoly output. What effect would such a policy have on the quantity a monopolist produces and the price it charges?
b What is the effect on economic efficiency?

2 The demand for Aerodiscs, a disc made from a unique material that flies a considerable distance when thrown, is given by this equation:

$$P = 10 - 0.01\, Q_D.$$

The corresponding marginal revenue (*MR*) equation is:

$$MR = 10 - 0.02\, Q.$$

The Aerodisc Company is a natural monopoly. The firm's total fixed cost is £700 and the marginal cost is constant at £2 per disc. (*Note*: This implies that average variable cost is also constant at £2 per disc.) Suppose that the Aerodisc Company is not regulated.
a What will be the quantity sold and the price of an Aerodisc?
b How much is total profit or loss?
c How much is producer surplus?
d How much is consumer surplus?
e How much is total surplus?

3 Now suppose that the Aerodisc Company becomes regulated and that the regulator uses a marginal cost pricing rule.
a What will be the quantity sold and the price of an Aerodisc?
b How much is total profit or loss?
c How much is producer surplus?
d How much is consumer surplus?
e How much is total surplus?

4 Suppose that the regulator of the Aerodisc Company uses an average cost pricing rule.
a What will be the price of an Aerodisc and how many will be sold?
b How much is total profit or loss?
c How much is producer surplus?
d How much is consumer surplus?
e How much is total surplus?

5 Figure 19.2 illustrates the industry demand, marginal revenue (*MR*) and marginal cost (*MC*) curves in an oligopoly industry. The industry is regulated.
a What price and quantity will be predicted by the public interest theory of regulation? Why?
b What price and quantity will be predicted by the capture theory of regulation? Why?
c Can you explain why the firms in this industry might be demanders of regulation?

Figure 19.2

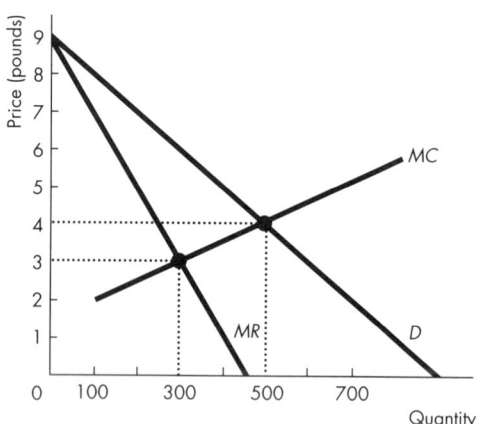

DISCUSSION QUESTION

1 How do natural monopolies originate?

DATA QUESTIONS

The Green Paper

The 1998 consultation paper suggested that four aspects were crucial in giving expression to the concept of fair regulation:

- a strenghthened framework relating to the roles of Ministers and regulators;

- setting out social and environmental objectives;

- safeguarding the interests of consumers through the creation of independent statutory bodies for each utility sector;

- more open and accountable regulation.

Within these four themes there seemed considerable emphasis on a 'fair deal for consumer'.

Source: Adapted from P. Maunder 'The regulation of Privatised Utilities' in *Developments in Economics*, G.B.J. Atkinson (ed.) **15**, 1999, Ormskirk, Causeway Press.

1 What is a 'Green Paper'?

2 What is a 'utility sector'?

3 What do you think is meant by 'fair regulation'?

ANSWERS

CONCEPT REVIEW

1 regulation; monopoly control laws

2 surplus; buyers; producer; number

3 capture

4 Natural

5 public interest; capture

6 privatization

7 marginal cost

8 rate of return; average cost

9 price; –X

TRUE OR FALSE

1 F Regulation but not privatization.

2 T Definition.

3 T Regulators are captured and act in the interests of the monopoly.

4 T In this theory governments act in the public interest.

5 T To maximize profits.

6 T This is why ATC is always downward sloping.

7 F Marginal cost pricing will do this.

8 T Increased costs will allow them to increase profits.

9 F Regulators will prohibit collusive cartels.

MULTIPLE CHOICE

1 b A large consumer surplus increases the potential pay-off if regulations are introduced.

2 a By capturing the regulators, producers will promote their own interests.

3 e **b**, **c** lead to increased demand by buyers.

4 a This is the only option which will lead to increased efficiency.

5 c Helps airline firms, not consumers.

6 a Definition of natural monopoly.

7 c Where $MC = MR$.

8 d Where $P = ATC$.

9 e Where $P = MC$.

10 c Private monopoly outcome.

11 a Higher costs will allow higher profits.

12 e Definition.

SHORT ANSWER

1 It is in the public interest to achieve allocative efficiency; to expand output to the level that maximizes total surplus. On the other hand, it is in the interest of the monopoly producer to restrict output in order to maximize producer surplus and thus monopoly profit.

Since these interests are not the same, monopoly must be regulated in order to achieve allocative efficiency. The public interest theory of regulation suggests that this is the principle that guides regulation of monopoly industries.

2 An average cost pricing rule will create a deadweight loss, but so will a marginal cost pricing rule, through the need to impose a tax.

Since for a natural monopoly marginal cost is less than average total cost, regulation by use of a marginal cost pricing rule requires the government to pay a subsidy in order for the firm to be willing to produce at all.

To pay that subsidy the government must levy a tax, which will impose a deadweight loss on the economy. If the deadweight loss associated with the tax (for example, the deadweight loss of the marginal cost pricing rule with its attendant subsidy) is greater than the deadweight loss of an average cost pricing rule, the average cost pricing rule is superior.

3 The key here is to recall that economic cost includes a normal rate of return. Thus because rate of return regulation sets a price that allows the firm to achieve a normal rate of return; it is setting the price equal to average total cost.

4 The capture theory predicts that producers will capture the regulatory process and use it to maximize producer surplus. But if the producer lobby was strong enough to achieve regulation, why have producers been unable to stop deregulation? A further question is why do many producers *favour* deregulation? The capture theory has no good answers to these questions.

5 One reason for BT's huge profits is that only a few years ago it was the monopoly supplier. Customer inertia has allowed it to keep many customers (there are costs, such as time, in switching). This is combined with other factors such as economies of scale, good marketing and efficiency.

PROBLEMS

1 a Imposing a tax on each unit sold by a monopolist will increase marginal cost. As a consequence the profit-maximizing monopolist will raise the price and reduce the quantity produced.

b The tax will certainly reduce the profit of the monopolist and may even eliminate it, but the consequence will be to make the inefficiency owing to monopoly even worse. This is illustrated in Fig. 19.3. The curve *MC* is the marginal cost curve before the tax. An unregulated monopolist will produce amount Q_2, while the economically efficient output is Q_3. The tax, however, causes the monopolist to reduce output from Q_1 to Q_2, which moves the market outcome further away from efficiency.

2 Figure 19.4 will be helpful in answering questions about the Aerodisc market. It gives the relevant revenue and cost curves for the Aerodisc Company.

Figure 19.3

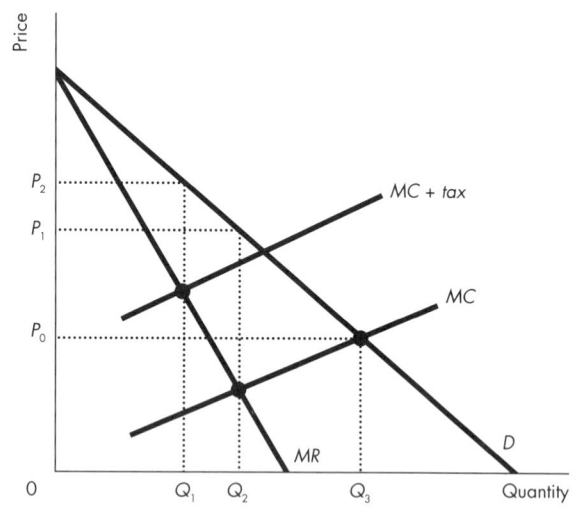

Figure 19.4

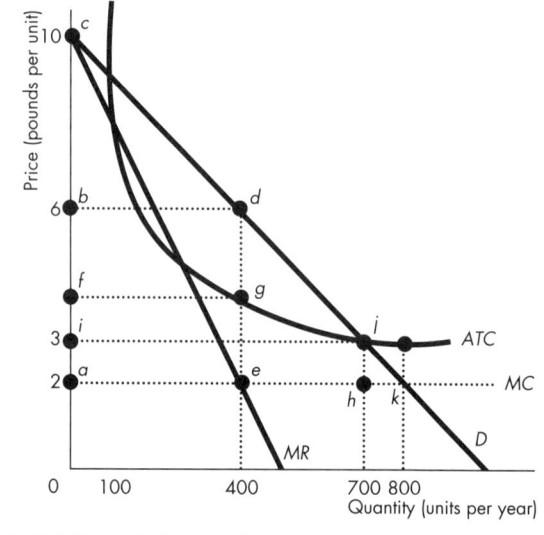

a In an unregulated market, the Aerodisc Company will choose output so as to maximize profit, where $MR = MC$. To calculate this output, set $MR = MC = 2$ and solve for Q:

$$10 - 0.02Q = 2$$
$$8 = 0.02Q$$
$$400 = Q$$

To calculate price, substitute $Q = 400$ into the demand equation:

$$P = 10 - 0.01Q_D$$
$$= 10 - 0.01 (400)$$
$$= 10 - 4$$
$$= 6$$

So 400 Aerodiscs will be produced and sold at a price of $6 each.

b To determine total profit we first determine average total cost (ATC) when output (Q) is 400 units.

$$ATC = AFC + AVC$$
$$= (TFC/Q) + AVC$$
$$= (700/400) + 2$$
$$= 3.75.$$

Therefore, total profit is the difference between price (average revenue) and ATC times the quantity sold. This is equal to $90 and is represented in Fig. 19.4 by the region $fbdg$.

c Producer surplus is the difference between the producer's revenue and the opportunity cost of production. Total revenue is $2,400 ($6 × 400 units) and total opportunity cost is $800 ($2 × 400 units). Thus producer surplus is $1,600. Graphically, producer surplus is the area of the rectangle $abde$ in Fig. 19.4.

d Consumer surplus is readily obtained graphically as the area in the triangle denoted bcd in Fig. 19.4. The area of that triangle is $800.

e Total surplus is $2,400, the sum of producer and consumer surplus.

3 a Under a marginal cost pricing rule, the price of an Aerodisc will be equal to marginal cost or $2. To calculate the quantity sold, substitute the price into the demand equation:

$$P = 10 - 0.01Q_D$$
$$2 = 10 - 0.01Q_D$$
$$0.01Q_D = 8$$
$$Q_D = 800.$$

b To determine the amount of profit or loss, we must first determine ATC when output is 800. Using the procedure in the previous problem we find that at $Q = 800$, ATC is $2.875 which is greater than price by $0.875 (87.5 pence). Therefore, the Aerodisc Company will make a loss of $700 ($0.875 × 800). Alternatively, since MC is constant, if the price is set equal to MC, which is equal to AVC, the total loss will be just TFC or $700.

c Producer surplus is zero.

d Consumer surplus is given by the area of the triangle ach in Fig. 19.4, which is $3,200.

e Total surplus is $3,200 (a maximum).

4 a Computation of ATC at various levels of output allows us to determine that the ATC curve crosses the demand curve when $Q = 700$ and $ATC = $3. Thus under an average cost pricing rule, the price of an Aerodisc will be $3 and 700 units will be sold.

b Since price is equal to average total cost, profit is zero.

c Producer surplus is $700, the area of the rectangle $aijh$ in Fig. 19.4.

d Consumer surplus is $2,450, the area of the triangle ijc in Fig. 19.4.

e Total surplus is $3,150.

5 a The public interest theory predicts that regulators will set price and quantity so as to maximize total surplus. This means that they will choose quantity (and price) where MC is equal to demand. This corresponds to a quantity of 500 units and a price of $4 per unit.

b The capture theory predicts that the regulator will choose quantity and price so as to maximize the profit of the industry. This is the quantity that would be chosen by a profit-maximizing monopolist, 300 units, where $MC = MR$. The highest price that could be charged and still sell that quantity can be read from the demand curve: $6 per unit.

c Firms in the industry would be demanders of regulation if the regulation had the effect of increasing profit to the industry. As we discovered in Chapter 14, cartels are unstable because there is always an incentive to cheat on output restriction agreements and it is very difficult to enforce the agreements. If, however, the firms in an industry can get the government, through regulation, to enforce a cartel agreement, they will want to do it.

DISCUSSION QUESTION

1 Natural monopolies occur when the technology within an industry allows one firm to serve the market at a lower cost than more than one firm. For example, the technology of supplying water to a street is such that the fixed costs of laying pipes are extremely high, so that it would be inefficient for a second firm to lay pipes in the same street.

DATA QUESTIONS

1 A 'Green Paper' is a consultative document issued by government. After the consultation process is concluded it is often followed by a 'White Paper' setting out proposed legislation.

2 'Utility' in economics usually refers to the satisfaction obtained by a consumer, but here it relates to industries such as water, gas and electricity.

3 'Fair regulation' is difficult to define. The Green Paper linked it to fair deals for consumers, but this is inadequate since it does not clarify what is 'fair'. Most economists would suggest that fair regulation is one that minimizes deadweight losess, maximizes consumer surplus and gives consumers the benefits of competition.

Chapter 20

Externalities, the Environment and Knowledge

Chapter in Perspective, Text Pages 478–501

This chapter focuses on the economist's approach to the environment and knowledge. It discusses important concepts such as externalities and property rights and shows how they can be used to analyse the environment and can lead to better policies.

The chapter also discusses intellectual property rights.

Helpful Hints

1 The equilibrium quantity in a competitive market is the amount at which the marginal private cost equals the marginal private benefit. The efficient quantity is the amount at which the marginal social cost and the marginal social benefit are equal.

   If the marginal private cost equals the marginal social cost and the marginal private benefit equals the marginal social benefit, the equilibrium amount that is produced equals the efficient amount. This outcome reflects Adam Smith's idea of the invisible hand – that people, seeking to do only what is best for themselves, will be led to do what is best for society 'as if by an invisible hand'.

   In most transactions, there are no affected third parties and so there are no external costs or benefits. In other words, private and social costs

along with private and social benefits coincide and competitive markets are efficient.

   But when third parties are affected, external costs or benefits arise and competitive markets will not be efficient. With external benefits, the marginal private benefit curve lies to the left of the marginal social benefit curve. With external costs, the marginal private cost curve lies to the right of the marginal social cost curve. In both instances, the amount produced in an unregulated market – the level at which the marginal private benefit and private cost curves intersect – is not the efficient amount.

2 If the production of a good or service produces external costs, a competitive market results in a quantity that exceeds the allocatively efficient level. This conclusion makes sense in terms of marginal analysis. People continue an action as

long as the marginal benefit from it exceeds the marginal cost. If they ignore some of the marginal costs of the action, they will do 'too much' of it; that is, more than the efficient amount of the product is produced. Similarly, with external benefits, some of the marginal benefits from the action are ignored. As a result, too little of the action is undertaken, and less than the efficient amount is produced. If you keep this explanation in mind, you will not go wrong when thinking about the impact of externalities on a private market.

3 Competitive markets with externalities are not efficient because some of the costs or benefits are external. If those costs or benefits could be internalized somehow, the market would be efficient. The chapter discusses two general approaches to internalizing externalities.

The first is to define property rights clearly and enforce them strictly. Then costs (or benefits)

imposed on (enjoyed by) non-participants in a transaction will no longer be external. The affected individual will have a voice in the transaction because some of his or her property is affected and the costs (or benefits) become internal through this voice.

The second is to tax or otherwise charge activities that generate external costs and subsidize or otherwise reward activities that generate external benefits. Charging a tax equal to the external cost makes the entire cost internal. Similarly, paying a subsidy in the amount of the external benefit makes the entire benefit internal.

Both of these general methods strive to ensure that the private marginal cost and private marginal benefit accurately reflect the social marginal cost and social marginal benefit. If the private marginal cost and benefit curves correctly mirror the social marginal cost and benefit curves, the level of the good that will be produced is the efficient amount.

SELF-TEST

CONCEPT REVIEW

1 An _____ is a cost or benefit arising from a transaction that affects someone who is not part of the original transaction. Externalities create market _____ .

2 The _____ theorem holds that if property rights exist and _____ costs are low, there are no externalities.

3 To maximize society's well-being, the government should aim at producing the level of output at which _____ social cost equals marginal _____ .

4 One way to tackle externalities is to issue _____ permits which give polluters tradable permits. Alternatively, the government can levy a tax equal to the marginal_____ cost.

5 Three policies the government can use to achieve an efficient allocation of resources in the presence of external benefits from education and

development are subsidies, _____ - _____ _____ and patents.

6 A subsidy is a payment to producers that depends on the level of _____ .

7 Patents increase the incentive to _____ .

TRUE OR FALSE

— **1** If negative externalities exist, marginal social cost and marginal external cost are equivalent.

— **2** Externalities arise from the absence of private property rights.

— **3** Knowledge is an example of a product with external benefits.

— **4** Assigning a property right will cure the problem of an externality.

— **5** The efficient amount of pollution is always no pollution.

— **6** The private market produces more than the efficient amount of a good having a positive externality.

— **7** One reason that there is not a high tax on carbon fuels is that the cost of the tax is incurred now but any benefits from the tax would be obtained in the future.

— **8** If the production of a good involves no external costs, the marginal social cost equals the marginal private cost.

— **9** The inefficiency created by an external cost in the production of a good can be overcome if the government subsidizes production of the good.

— **10** The Coase theorem states that externalities do not exist if property rights are defined and transactions costs are low.

— **11** Externalities can create market failure.

MULTIPLE CHOICE

1 An externality is a cost or benefit arising from an economic transaction that falls on
   a consumers but not producers.
   b producers but not consumers.
   c someone not party to the transaction.
   d rivals.

2 The production of too many goods with negative externalities is an example of
   a consumer sovereignty.
   b producer sovereignty.
   c public failure.
   d market failure.

3 A copper ore refiner pollutes the water upstream from a brewery. The transactions costs of reaching an agreement between the two are low. When will the amount of water pollution be at its efficient level?
   a only if the property right to the stream is assigned to the ore refiner
   b only if the property right to the stream is assigned to the brewery
   c whenever the property right to the stream is assigned to either the refiner or the brewer
   d none of the above because the premise of the question is wrong: there is no such thing as the efficient level of pollution

4 Suppose that production of rubber for trainers creates an external cost of £2 per tonne of rubber but no external benefits. Then the efficient amount of rubber will be produced when the government imposes a
   a subsidy of more than £2 per tonne of rubber.
   b subsidy of £2 per tonne of rubber.
   c tax of more than £2 per tonne of rubber.
   d tax of £2 per tonne of rubber.

5 Which of the following illustrates the concept of external cost?
   a Bad weather decreases the size of the wheat crop.
   b A reduction in the size of the wheat crop causes the income of wheat farmers to fall.
   c Smoking harms the health of the smoker.
   d Smoking harms the health of nearby non-smokers.

6 A reason for not enacting a high carbon-fuel tax in the United Kingdom is that
   a both the costs of and benefits from the tax will occur sometime in the future.
   b less developed nations may not decrease their consumption of fuels.
   c the costs of global warming have been accurately estimated to be small.
   d scientific evidence no longer supports the hypothesis that carbon dioxide adds to global warming.

Use Fig. 20.1 for questions 7–11.

Figure 20.1

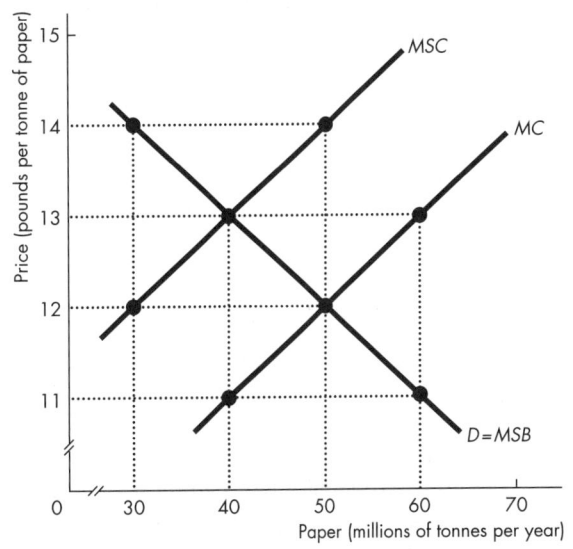

7 As illustrated in Fig. 20.1, the production of paper creates
a only a positive externality.
b only a negative externality.
c both positive and negative externalities.
d no externalities.

8 The amount of the externality illustrated in Fig. 20.1 is
a £14 per tonne.
b £12 per tonne.
c £2 per tonne.
d £0 per tonne because no externality is produced.

9 In the absence of any government intervention, how many tonnes of paper are produced in a year?
a 60 million tonnes
b 50 million tonnes
c 40 million tonnes
d 30 million tonnes

10 The allocatively efficient amount of paper produced in a year is
a 60 million tonnes.
b 50 million tonnes.
c 40 million tonnes.
d 30 million tonnes.

11 What amount of tax is necessary to cause the efficient amount of paper to be produced?
a £14 per tonne
b £12 per tonne
c £2 per tonne
d £0 per tonne because the efficient amount is produced without any government intervention

12 An externality is
a the amount by which price exceeds marginal private cost.
b the amount by which price exceeds marginal social cost.
c the effect of government regulation on market price and output.
d a cost or benefit that arises from a decision but is not borne by the decision maker.

13 Patents are a solution to the
a positive externality from attending college.
b positive externality from discovering new knowledge.
c negative externality from attending college.
d negative externality from discovering new knowledge.

Use Table 20.1 for the next four questions.

Table 20.1

Quantity	Marginal private cost (pounds)	Marginal private benefit (pounds)	Marginal social benefit (pounds)
500	5	9	11
550	6	8	10
600	7	7	9
650	8	6	8
700	9	5	7

14 Table 20.1 represents the market for a good with
a only a negative externality.
b only a positive externality
c both positive and negative externalities.
d no externalities.

15 Left alone, the equilibrium amount produced is
a 550.
b 600.
c 650.
d 700.

16 The allocatively efficient level of output is
a 550.
b 600.
c 650.
d 700.

17 What can the government do to cause the efficient amount to be produced?
a subsidize suppliers £8 per unit
b subsidize suppliers £2 per unit
c tax suppliers £2 per unit
d tax suppliers £8 per unit

18 Which of the following statements about property rights is correct?
a Property rights have nothing to do with externalities.
b The absence of property rights creates negative externalities but has nothing to do with the creation of positive externalities.
c Property rights pertain only to the rights of owners of real estate.
d Copyrights are a method of assigning intellectual property rights.

SHORT ANSWER

1 Governments provide education at a price (tuition fee) less than cost. What economic argument supports this policy?

2 Explain how a tax can be used to achieve efficiency in the face of external costs.

3 What is the marginal social benefit of pollution?

PROBLEMS

1 In a small town two factories – factory A and factory B – each produce 10 units of pollution so that the total pollution is 20 units. Factory A can decrease its pollution at a constant marginal cost of £50 per unit; factory B can reduce its pollution at a constant marginal cost of £100 per unit.

   a If both factory A and factory B decrease their pollution by 5 units, what is the total amount of pollution in the town and what is the total cost of attaining this level of pollution?

   b If factory A decreases its level of pollution by 10 units and factory B does not decrease its pollution, what is the total amount of pollution in the town and what is the total cost of achieving this level of pollution?

   c From a social standpoint, to obtain a total of 10 units of pollution, which is more desirable: both factories cutting back by 5 units each or A cutting back by 10 units and B not cutting back? Why?

2 Vaccination creates a positive externality. Use Fig. 20.2 to illustrate the market for chicken pox vaccination. Label as Q_0 the doses that will be taken in the absence of any government intervention and as Q_1 the efficient number of doses. How might the government move this market towards allocative efficiency?

3 The first two columns of Table 20.2 give the demand schedule for education in Transylvania, and the third column gives the marginal private cost. Because education generates external benefits, the marginal social benefit shown in the last column is greater than marginal private benefit.

   a What equilibrium price and quantity would result if the market for education is unregulated?

   b What is the allocatively efficient quantity of students in Transylvania?

Figure 20.2

Price (pounds per dose)

Vaccine (millions of doses per year)

4 In an attempt to address the inefficient level of education in his country, Igor – the newly appointed minister of education – has decided to provide a low-cost public university, Igor Omphesus (Igor's middle name is Omphesus) University.

   a To attain the efficient level of schooling, what must tuition fees be at the new university, IOU?

   b What is the marginal cost of schooling the last student at this university?

Table 20.2 Education in Transylvania

Quantity (number of students)	Marginal private benefit (Euros)	Marginal private cost (Euros)	Marginal social benefit (Euros)
1	500	200	800
2	400	250	700
3	300	300	600
4	200	350	500
5	100	400	400
6	0	450	300

DISCUSSION QUESTIONS

1 Explain how it can be efficient to allow some pollution.

2 How can we decide what is an efficient level of pollution?

DATA QUESTION

Urban congestion

There are several reasons why the market is unable to supply transport services which would be regarded as 'efficient' in terms of relative quantities and qualities. For instance, road space is not sold in the usual manner, nor is it supplied whenever and wherever it makes a profit. Public transport systems follow price and supply policies which are very different from what would result in the absence of severe regulation of any alternative suppliers. Intervention by several institutions takes place to control, regulate, encourage, and often to discourage, various transport activities.

Because road space is not sold in the usual way, high-demand road space has a 'price' that is similar to low-demand road space. Therefore high-demand road space is rationed not by price, but by congestion and over-crowding. The failure to ration by price has caused the use of private motor vehicles to increase and that of public transport to decrease during off-peak periods.
Source: Adapted from B. Atkinson, P. Baker and B. Milward, *Economic Policy*, Macmillan, 1996.

1 Why are markets not used to determine the quantity of transport services?

2 How would an increase in fuel tax affect this market?

3 Explain what is meant by 'the failure to ration by price'.

ANSWERS

CONCEPT REVIEW

1 externality; failure

2 Coase; transactions

3 marginal; social benefit

4 marketable; external

5 below-cost provision

6 output

7 innovate

TRUE OR FALSE

1 F Marginal social cost equals the marginal private cost plus the marginal externality cost.

2 T The fundamental reason for the existence of externalities is that property rights are not well defined.

3 T Because knowledge has external benefits, the unregulated private market produces less than the efficient amount.

4 F As the Coase theorem points out, assigning property rights will cure the problem of an externality only when transactions costs are low.

5 F The efficient amount of pollution is the amount that equalizes the marginal social benefit and cost from pollution.

6 F The private market produces *less* than the efficient amount of a good that has a positive externality.

7 T Because the benefits are obtained in the future, to take any actions at present to reap these benefits may not be worthwhile.

8 T The marginal social cost equals the marginal private cost plus the marginal externality cost. If there is no marginal externality cost, the marginal social cost equals the marginal private cost.

9 F If a good creates a negative externality, to attain allocative efficiency its production needs to be taxed, not subsidized.

10 T This essentially is the definition of the Coase theorem.

11 T Externalities are a reason for market failure; that is, the private, unregulated market does not produce the allocatively efficient level of a good.

MULTIPLE CHOICE

1 c Definition.

2 d By producing more than the allocatively efficient amount, the private market has failed.

3 c The Coase theorem shows that, when transactions costs are low, to whom a property right is assigned makes no difference. The externality will be internalized, and the efficient level of production will result.

4 d Imposing a tax equal to the marginal external cost will set equal the marginal private cost – which includes the tax – and the marginal social cost, thereby ensuring that the efficient amount of rubber will be produced.

5 d Bystanders are not part of the initial transaction (the smoking), so the harm that befalls them is an external cost.

6 b The equilibrium in this prisoners' dilemma game may be that neither developed nor less-developed nations impose a carbon-fuel tax.

7 b Because the *MSC* curve is leftward of the *MC* curve, the figure indicates that the good is creating a negative externality.

8 c The vertical difference between the *MSC* curve and the *MC* curve is the marginal external cost, which in this case is $2 per tonne.

9 b In the absence of any intervention, the private market produces where the private demand curve (which is the same as the private marginal benefit curve) crosses the private supply curve (which is the same as the private marginal cost curve).

10 c Allocative efficiency requires that production be at the level where marginal social cost, *MSC*, equals marginal social benefit, *MSB*.

11 c The tax must shift the private *MC* curve until it is the same as the *MSC* curve. Imposing a $2 tax will shift the *MC* curve higher by the amount of the tax, $2, which is the amount desired. More generally, by imposing a tax equal to the marginal externality cost, the new marginal private cost, which includes the tax, is the same as the marginal social cost.

12 d Because the cost or benefit is not borne by the decision maker, the cost or benefit is *external* to the decision maker's choice. Being external, the cost or benefit is ignored by the decision maker.

13 b New discoveries often may be used by many people, which is an externality from the point of view of the discoverer.

14 b At any level of output, the marginal social benefit exceeds the marginal private benefit, which indicates that there must be a positive external benefit.

15 b The private market produces the level of output that equalizes the marginal private cost (the private supply curve) and the marginal private benefit (the private demand curve).

16 e Efficiency requires that the amount of the good produced equalize the marginal social cost and the marginal social benefit. In this case, efficiency requires that output be 650.

17 b If suppliers are granted a $2 per unit subsidy, the marginal private cost schedule drops by $2 at every unit of output. Hence to produce 650 units of output the new marginal private cost becomes $6. This equals the marginal private benefit of 650 units, so the (new) equilibrium price is $6 and the quantity produced is the efficient amount, or 650 units.

18 d Definition.

SHORT ANSWER

1 The economic argument is that education generates external benefits. In particular, when individuals are educated, society at large receives benefits beyond the private benefits that accrue to those choosing how much education to obtain. The presence of this positive externality means that in the absence of government intervention, the private sector would provide too little education for allocative efficiency. Hence to attain efficiency in the market for education, the government provides below-cost education at public colleges and universities.

2 The existence of external costs means that producers do not take into account all costs when deciding how much to produce. If a tax is levied that is exactly the amount of the external cost, the cost is no longer external. As a result, the producer takes it into account and thus is induced to produce the efficient quantity.

3 The marginal social benefit of pollution is the benefit firms receive from being able to pollute. For instance, by polluting the air, an electric utility reduces its costs because it does not have to install expensive pollution reduction devices, such as scrubbers, to decrease air pollution. Hence society benefits from pollution because firms are part of society. (More basically, the fact that the firm does not need to install pollution reduction devices means that the resources that might have been used to produce these devices can be used to produce other goods and services.) The fact that society benefits from pollution must be balanced against the fact that pollution imposes a cost on society, expressed as the marginal social cost of pollution.

PROBLEMS

1 a The total amount of pollution is 10 units, 5 (remaining) units from factory *A* and 5 (remaining) units from factory *B*. The total cost of achieving this level of pollution is $750, the cost of $250 incurred by factory *A* plus the cost of $500 incurred by factory *B*.

b The total amount of pollution (again) is 10 units, comprising no pollution from factory *A* and 10 units from factory *B*. The total cost of attaining this level of pollution is £500, all incurred by factory *A*.

c From a social standpoint, having factory *A* decrease its pollution by 10 units and factory *B* do nothing is the most desirable. This solution has the lowest total social cost – £500 compared with £750 for an equal reduction at each factory – which means that eliminating the 10 units of pollution has inflicted the lowest possible total cost on society, which certainly is a desirable outcome.

Figure 20.3

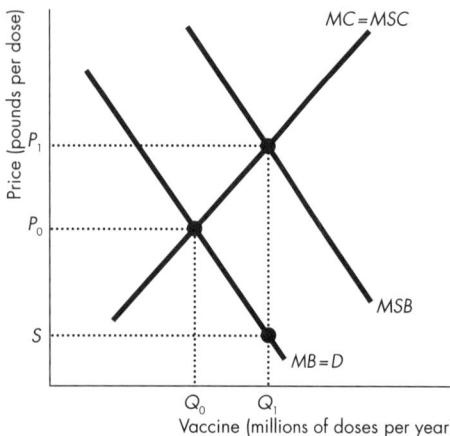

Vaccine (millions of doses per year)

2 Figure 20.3 shows the market for chicken pox vaccine. Because there are no negative externalities, the marginal social cost curve equals the marginal private cost. This curve is labelled $MC = MSC$ in the figure. It is also the private supply curve. However, the presence of the positive externality means that the marginal social benefit *(MSB)* curve lies rightward of the marginal private benefit curve, which is the same as the private demand curve (labelled $MB = D$). The vertical distance between the curves equals the marginal externality; that is, it is the additional (external) benefit to society over and above the benefit to the private individual. In the absence of government intervention, Q_0 is produced, and the efficient amount is Q_1.

To move this market closer to the efficient level of output, the government might subsidize production or use of the vaccine. This policy could take the form of paying producers to produce more vaccine. The aim is to shift the private supply curve rightward so that it intersects the private demand curve at output Q_1, the efficient amount, and price *S*.

Alternatively, the government might buy Q_1 worth of doses and then resell them to consumers below cost at price *S*, the price necessary to induce consumers to buy Q_1 doses.

3 a In an unregulated market, the equilibrium price and quantity are determined by the intersection of the marginal private benefit and cost curves because these are the demand and supply curves, respectively. Thus the equilibrium price is E300, and the equilibrium quantity is 3 students.

b Because there are no external costs, the efficient quantity is determined by the intersection of the marginal private cost and marginal *social* benefit curves. This result implies that allocative efficiency is attained at a quantity of 5 students attending college.

4 a Igor wants 5 students to attend his new university, IOU. Five students will attend only when the tuition fee is E100.5

b When 5 students attend the university, the marginal cost of the fifth student is E400. By charging the student only E100 in tuition, Igor appears to be losing money on this student. However, the loss is only apparent. Five students are the efficient level of education because the *total* marginal social benefit from the fifth student is E400, which equals the marginal cost of educating this student.

DISCUSSION QUESTIONS

1 Pollution is undesirable, but clearly to eliminate it totally isn't optimal. Society could get rid of all air pollution by outlawing all cars, all trains, all planes, shutting down all factories and eliminating all cows. (Cows produce methane.) But we won't do this. The reason is obvious: it's just too expensive. The cost to achieve zero pollution is prohibitive – a whole lot more than the benefit! Moreover, some pollution may be desirable – we get to drive rather than walk, have pizza delivered rather than doing without, and heat our homes rather than freeze.

2 The 'efficient' level of pollution is the level at which the marginal social cost of pollution reduction equals the marginal social benefit. Suppose that we're at the benefit from the reduction point where the marginal social cost of reducing pollution equals the marginal social benefit. If we decreased pollution any more, the marginal social cost would *exceed* the marginal social benefit. In other words, the cost of any further reduction would exceed the benefit from the reduction

DATA QUESTIONS

1 Markets are not used to determine the quantity of road transport services because this industry has several characteristics which would lead to market failure. In particular, roads are semi-public goods – it would be almost impossible to prevent people having access without paying. Moreover, transport has major externalities such as pollution, congestion and the likelihood of road accidents.

2 An increase in fuel tax would reduce the distance travelled by private cars. Some people would walk; others would use public transport. The effect would depend on the price elasticity of demand.

3 By 'the failure to ration by price' the author means that market forces are not used to determine the quantity. Since no system of allocating resources can produce all the goods that people might like, in a market system prices act as a rationing device to limit the quantity of goods.

Part 7 Macroeconomics and Fundamentals

Looking back at Part 6 (Chapters 18–20)

A number of important terms were introduced in Chapter 18. Three in particular can be identified: externalities, market failure and public goods. Can you explain these? If not, go back and check. These are used in many parts of economics and are worth mastering.

There is considerable emphasis in this book on economic theory; that is necessary because this gives us the tools of analysis that we can apply. In Chapter 19, the theories of markets were applied to policy, and you should have a fairly clear idea of how competition policy is operated in the UK and the European Union and also why privatized industries are regulated.

Chapter 20 should have given you several ideas about the economics of the environment and also how government intervention in the form of subsidies and public provision can make education more efficient.

Questions

1 Look back at the *Understanding Externalities* article. What did Ronald Coase 'discover and clarify'?

2 There are quite a lot of websites covering topics discussed in this Part. For material on regulating, try sites such as OFTEL (www.oftel.gov.uk), OFWAT (www.open.gov.uk/ofwat/index.htm) and OFGAS (www.ofgas.gov.uk) as well as sites mentioned earlier. Data on the environment can be found from The Environment Agency in the UK (www.environment-agency.gov.uk), the European EGDGXI (europa.eu.int/comm/environment) and Friends of the Earth (www.foe.co.uk). Which of these are most useful?

3 Why does Carol Propper (in the *Talking with...* article) believe that governments should act to overcome market failure in health care?

Looking forward to Part 7 (Chapters 21–26)

Here we move forward from micro to macroeconomics. The key ideas that you have already met will still be relevant, but the focus is now on the economy as a whole. As always, before reading a chapter look at the *After reading this chapter...* section since this will orientate you. For example, Chapter 21 sets the background by looking at policy issues such as economic growth, inflation and unemployment. Chapter 22 looks at measurement issues; how do we measure economic growth and inflation and what are the shortcomings of these measurements? Chapter 23 is concerned with one of the most important policy issues in economics: unemployment. In Chapter 24 we develop tools to analyse the economy: aggregate demand and aggregate supply. Chapter 25 looks at various multipliers. In essence, these suggest that an increase in one variable, such as government spending, will have a multiplied impact on the economy. The final chapter in this Part, Chapter 26, looks at fiscal policy; that is, taxation and government spending.

Answers

1 Coase was responsible for clarifying the significance of transactions costs. These are the costs of doing business; of buying and selling. For example, before I buy a pair of shoes, I have to travel to town and look around various shops. These are transactions costs. Coase also developed ideas about property rights; fundamental to the working of markets.

2 The answer to this will depend on what you discovered in your search.

3 She suggests that markets fail to provide adequate amounts of health care for two reasons. One is people lack information, and so could be exploited by people selling expensive and inappropriate

remedies. The other argument is concerned with values – a normative argument. Most people believe that health care should be accessible. Markets would fail to achieve this; for example poor people would not be able to afford treatment.

Chapter 21

A First Look at Macroeconomics

Chapter in Perspective, Text Pages 504–527

This chapter sets the scene for the rest of the course. It begins by discussing the origins of macroeconomics and then focuses on economic growth. It analyses recent economic growth in the United Kingdom and other countries and the benefits and costs of growth.

The chapter discusses major macroeconomic issues such as unemployment, inflation and international payments.

Helpful Hints

1 The inflation rate is calculated as the percentage change in prices using the formula:

$$\frac{\text{current price level} - \text{previous price level}}{\text{previous price level}} \times 100$$

Thus if the current price level is, say, 110 and the previous price level was 100, the inflation rate between these two price levels equals

$$\frac{110 - 100}{100} \times 100, \text{ or 10 per cent}$$

Similarly, if the current price level is 121 and the previous price level is 110, then using the formula shows that the inflation rate again equals 10 per cent. Keep in mind that the inflation rate is calculated by using the formula presented above and is *not* just the difference in the two price levels!

2 The relationship between the current account and the capital account for a country can be understood by making an analogy with your budget. Suppose that you spend more than you earn. In this event you must borrow from other people to make up the shortfall of income.

Return now to the relationship between the current account and the capital account. A country's current account is its (foreign) spending and earnings on goods and services. Exports are the earnings abroad and imports the spending abroad. If the spending on imports exceeds the earnings from exports, the country must borrow from other countries to make up the difference. The capital account shows precisely this information: it shows how much the country is borrowing from (or lending to) other countries. Thus if a country is spending £100 billion more on imports than it earns on exports – so that the current account has a £100 billion deficit – it must be borrowing the £100 billion from other countries – so that the capital account has a £100 billion surplus.

3 As Helpful Hint 2 demonstrated, whenever the value of a country's imports exceeds the value of its exports, it must borrow from other countries to make up the difference. In this case, the original country is going into debt. Whether this is 'good' or 'bad' perhaps depends on what the borrowing financed.

A current account deficit, with its associated borrowing from abroad, may be 'good' or 'bad'. For instance, if the country is borrowing to make a lot of investments so that its income will be higher in the future, most observers might suggest that the current account deficit is 'good'. But if it is borrowing to buy a lot of goods and services that it uses immediately, many observers might think that the deficit is 'bad'. Thus the question of whether a current account deficit helps or harms a country is not a question that always has the same answer.

SELF-TEST

CONCEPT REVIEW

1 The origin of macroeconomics was the publication of _____'s *The General Theory of Employment, Interest and* _____ .

2 The long-term trend in economic growth is measured by the growth rate of_____ GDP.

3 The main benefit of economic growth is expanded _____ possibilities. The main costs are less current _____ , resource _____ and environmental pollution.

4 Real GDP growth fluctuates in a _____ cycle.

5 Inflation is a process of rising _____ and _____ of money.

6 Fluctuations in the inflation rate bring fluctuations in _____ rates.

7 To meet macroeconomic policy challenges the government uses _____ policy tools and the Bank of England uses the monetary policy tools of _____ rates and _____ supply.

TRUE OR FALSE

___ **1** Ignoring interest income and gifts, if UK exports exceed UK imports, the United Kingdom has a current account deficit.

___ **2** Discouraged workers are not counted as unemployed.

___ **3** If the average level of prices doubles, the value of money is half of what it was.

___ **4** In the recession phase of a business cycle, the unemployment rate rises.

___ **5** The inflation rate can never be negative.

___ **6** Fiscal policy refers to changes in the interest rate that are designed to influence the economy.

___ **7** The trough is the lower turning point of the business cycle.

___ **8** Real GDP is the amount of goods and services that are produced when resources are fully employed.

MULTIPLE CHOICE

1 If last year the price level was 150 and the current price level is 165, over the year the inflation rate has been
a 10 per cent.
b 15 per cent.
c 150 per cent.
d 165 per cent.

2 Counting discouraged workers as unemployed would
a not change the unemployment rate.

b lower the unemployment rate.

c raise the unemployment rate.

d probably change the unemployment rate, but in an unpredictable direction.

3 During the Great Depression,

a the unemployment rate was nearly 25 per cent and the major focus of macroeconomics switched to economic growth.

b a productivity growth slowdown occurred and macroeconomics changed its focus to business cycles.

c economists switched their focus so that macro-economics began to emphasize business cycles.

d John Maynard Keynes suggested that long-term economic growth was the major problem facing capitalist nations.

4 Real GDP

a measures only the output of real goods, such as machines, not 'unreal' things such as services.

b includes all the goods and services produced in the economy, including those produced in the home.

c is measured by using prices from a single year in order to eliminate the effects of inflation.

d is the amount of goods and services that the country is able to produce when its resources are fully employed.

5 Real GDP rose in all four quarters of 1999; thus 1999 was definitely a year

a of expansion.

b with a business cycle peak.

c of recession.

d with a business cycle trough.

6 Which of the following is *not* a cost of more rapid economic growth?

a current consumption that is lost

b environmental damage may increase

c consumption possibilities expand in the future

d jobs and consumption patterns change more rapidly

7 The unemployment rate generally rises during _____ in the business cycle.

a a peak

b a recession

c a trough

d an expansion

8 Which of the following is *not* a cost of unemployment?

a increased incidence of theft

b increased numbers of unemployed workers entering college

c increased amounts of domestic violence

d decreased future job prospects

9 If the United Kingdom has a current account deficit, the

a value of UK exports must exceed the value of UK imports.

b United Kingdom is lending to other countries.

c United Kingdom has a capital account surplus.

d none of the above.

10 Which of the following is an example of monetary policy?

a changing the interest rate

b changing government spending

c changing tax rates

d changing the government's deficit

11 Potential real GDP

a falls during a recession.

b grows less rapidly because of the slowdown in productivity growth.

c can never be attained.

d equals actual real GDP.

SHORT ANSWER

1 What are the costs of unemployment?

2 What is meant by the value of money? Why does the value of money fall when there is inflation?

3 What happens to real GDP and the unemployment rate during each of the four phases of the business cycle?

4 Re-read the *Reading Between the Lines* article. Why do you think economic recovery takes so long?

PROBLEMS

1 a At the end of 1997 the price level is 120. At the end of 1998 the price level is 135. What is the inflation rate in 1998?

b At the end of 1999 the price level is 150. What is the inflation rate in 1999?

c At the end of 2000 the price level is 160. What is the inflation rate in 2000?

2 Complete Table 21.1.

Table 21.1   Interest Rates and the Inflation Rate

Real interest rate (per cent)	Inflation rate (per cent)	Nominal interest rate (per cent)
3	4	
3	8	
	1	4

DISCUSSION QUESTION

1 Which is more important, stabilizing the business cycle or boosting long-term economic growth?

DATA QUESTIONS

Economic growth is wonderful – or is it? Growth brings undeniable advantages. If an economy produces more goods and services, then it can afford to spend more on desirable services such as education and health. It can also spend more on relieving poverty. Moreover, ordinary citizens will have higher standards of living.

However, it also brings costs. Suppose the government decides to build a new road. This will raise GDP but it will also impose environmental damage. In addition, local people may have to install double glazing to cut out noise. This will also increase GDP. Local children may be hurt in traffic accidents on the road. Their medical costs will also increase GDP.

1 How do we measure economic growth?

2 Summarize the advantages of economic growth.

3 Summarize the disadvantages of economic growth.

4 Do you think economic growth is a desirable objective for government?

ANSWERS

CONCEPT REVIEW

1 Keynes; *Money*

2 potential

3 consumption; consumption; depletion

4 business

5 prices; value

6 interest

7 fiscal; interest; money

TRUE OR FALSE

1 **F** If exports exceed imports, the United Kingdom has a current account *surplus*.

2 **T** Discouraged workers are not looking for a job and so are not counted as unemployed.

3 **T** When the price level doubles, each pound buys half as many goods as before.

4 **T** As real GDP falls during a recession, the unemployment rate rises.

5 **F** The inflation rate can be negative (called deflation), although in recent years inflation has rarely been negative.

6 **F** Interest rate changes are part of monetary policy.

7 **T** After the trough, the economy enters the expansion phase of the business cycle.

8 **F** Potential real GDP is the amount of goods and services produced when all resources are fully employed.

MULTIPLE CHOICE

1 **a** The inflation rate between these years equals $\frac{165 - 150}{150} \times 100$, or 10 per cent.

2 **c** Counting discouraged workers among unemployed people would boost the unemployment rate.

3 **c** During the Great Depression, the extraordinarily high unemployment rates caused economists to stress short-term, business cycle factors, such as reducing the severity of recessions or depressions.

4 c By using prices from a single year, real GDP eliminates the effects of changes in prices, such as inflation.

5 a By definition, an expansion is a period of time during which real GDP increases.

6 c The expansion in future consumption possibilities is a benefit of economic growth.

7 b As real GDP falls in a recession, unemployment rates rise.

8 b Some unemployed workers start college, but this is not a cost of unemployment.

9 c A current account deficit must be matched by an equal capital account surplus.

10 a Monetary policy includes changing the interest rate and/or the country's money supply. The other answers are examples of fiscal policy.

11 b By slowing the growth rate of potential real GDP, the productivity growth slowdown harmed people because it significantly lowered their consumption possibilities in future years.

SHORT ANSWER

1 One important personal cost is that when workers are unemployed for long periods of time, their skills and abilities deteriorate, hurting their future job prospects. In addition, substantial social costs are incurred, such as higher theft rates, greater alcohol and drug abuse, more domestic violence and, in general, a loss of human dignity.

Finally, there is a fall in the output that could be produced if the unemployed were working.

2 The value of money is the quantity of goods and services that can be purchased with one pound of money. Because inflation means that prices are rising on average, one pound of money will buy less. Thus the value of money falls when there is inflation.

3 During the recession phase of the business cycle, real GDP falls. During this phase the unemployment rate rises, although the rise in unemployment lags behind the fall in real GDP somewhat. At the trough, real GDP reaches its lowest point below trend, and soon thereafter the unemployment rate is at its highest point over the business cycle. The trough is the turning point between the recession phase and the expansion phase. During expansion, real GDP grows and the unemployment rate generally falls. At the end of an expansion, the economy reaches the peak of the business cycle. The peak is characterized by real GDP at its highest point above its trend and the rate of unemployment is either then or soon thereafter at its lowest point over the business cycle.

4 The article gives several reasons. In particular, it is difficult for one country to recover when its trading partners are in recession. Moreover, it takes a long time to reorganize institutions such as banks.

PROBLEMS

1 a The inflation rate in 1998 is 12.5 per cent.
b In 1999 the inflation rate is 11.1 per cent, from

$$\frac{150 - 135}{135} \times 100.$$

Note that, even though the price level changed by the same amount in 1999 as in 1998 (15, or 135 − 120 in 1998 and 150 − 135 in 1999), the inflation rate in the two years is different.
c In 2000 the inflation rate is 6.7 per cent.

Table 21.2   Interest Rates and the Inflation Rate

Real interest rate (per cent)	Inflation rate (per cent)	Nominal interest rate (per cent)
3	4	7
3	8	11
3	1	4

2 The answers are in Table 21.2. The real interest rate equals the nominal interest rate minus the inflation rate. Alternatively, the nominal interest rate equals the real interest rate plus the inflation rate. Thus for the first row, the nominal interest rate equals the real interest rate, 3 per cent, plus the inflation rate, 4 per cent, or 7 per cent. The first two rows demonstrate the point that when the inflation rate increases, so too does the (nominal) interest rate. Hence the correlation between the inflation rate and the nominal interest rate should be positive.

DISCUSSION QUESTION

1 Economists don't agree about which of these macroeconomic challenges is more important.

Some economists think that boosting long-term growth is more important. They point out that if we are able to increase the growth rate of potential real GDP by 1 percentage point, after one generation, or two decades, real GDP per person will be over 22 per cent higher than otherwise. This means that our consumption possibilities will expand by 22 per cent so that, on average, we could buy 22 per cent more goods and services than otherwise. These economists also point out that this 22 per cent increase in consumption possibilities dwarfs the fall of real GDP per person in a recession. Thus they argue that increasing the growth rate of potential GDP is significantly more important than eliminating business cycles.

Other economists disagree. Although they agree that boosting the growth rate of potential real GDP is important, they point out that sustaining even a 1 per cent increase in real GDP over 20 years is extremely difficult. Instead, they argue that taming the business cycle should be considered the major goal of macroeconomic policy. They contend that this task is easier than increasing the growth rate of potential real GDP. Indeed, some of these economists suggest that we have tamed the business cycle a bit because there hasn't been a recession nearly as severe as the Great Depression.

DATA QUESTIONS

1 Economists usually measure economic growth by using GDP.

2 The advantages are usually given as higher living standards, so more goods and services are produced, making it possible to devote more resources to such problems as pollution and poverty.

3 The disadvantages are that the environment may be harmed; for example, by the depletion of resources such as oil. Growth may also cause pollution and it is often associated with social and economic change, which may cause problems.

4 There is no correct answer to the question of whether or not growth is desirable. The answer largely depends on the values of the person answering the question.

Chapter 22 Measuring GDP, Inflation and Economic Growth

Chapter in Perspective, Text Pages 528–551

How do we measure aggregate economic activity or the price level? In this chapter we address these questions in some detail.

The most widely used measure of economic activity is gross domestic product, or GDP. Here we discuss what it is and how it is measured. We will also examine the Retail Price Index and the GDP deflator, two measures of the price level. As indicated in Chapter 1, one of the components of any science is careful and systematic measurement. In this chapter, we will see how measurements of the behaviour of the aggregate economy are made and also discuss their limitations. The concepts measured here will lay a foundation for our analysis of macroeconomic theory.

Helpful Hints

1 Be sure to distinguish carefully between intermediate goods and investment goods. Both are typically goods sold by one firm to another, but they differ in terms of their use. Intermediate goods are goods that are processed and then resold, while investment goods are final goods themselves. Also note that the national income accounts include purchases of residential housing as investment because housing, like business capital stock, provides a continuous stream of value over time.

2 Note the difference between government spending on goods and services (G) and government transfer payments. Both involve payments by the government, but transfer payments are not payments for currently produced goods and services. Instead, they are simply a flow of money, just like taxes. Indeed it is often useful to think of transfer payments as negative taxes. Therefore, we define net taxes (NT) as taxes minus transfer payments.

3 Figure 22.2 on text page 532 is particularly important and leads to a fundamental equation:

$$Y = C + I + G + EX - IM$$

This equation reflects the expenditure approach to measuring GDP. It tells us that GDP is equal to the total amount of spending on domestic output in the economy by households, firms, government and foreigners. Spending on imports is subtracted to account for the fact that imports are not domestically produced. You need to ensure that you understand this equation.

4 A price index for the current year is computed as the ratio of the value of a basket of goods in the current year to the value of the *same* basket of goods in a base year, multiplied by 100. It therefore

attempts to calculate the cost of purchasing the same choice of goods in two different years. Note that the basket of goods used to calculate the Retail Price Index (RPI) contains goods that are purchased by a typical household. The basket of goods used to calculate the GDP deflator, on the other hand, contains all goods and services included in GDP. It would, therefore, include capital goods.

SELF-TEST

CONCEPT REVIEW

1 Gross _____ _____ is the value of total production of goods and services in an economy during a given period.

2 Capital and wealth are macroeconomic _____ .

3 The aggregate expenditure by households on consumption goods and services is called _____ _____ . Total spending by firms on new plant, equipment and buildings, and additions to stocks is called _____ .

4 Payments from the government to households which are not payments for currently produced goods and services are called _____ _____ .

5 _____ is equal to disposable income minus consumers' expenditure. Disposable income equals aggregate income minus net _____ .

6 Investment, government spending on goods and services, and exports are examples of _____ into the circular flow of income. Taxes, saving and imports are examples of _____ from the circular flow of income.

7 The method of measuring GDP which adds consumption expenditure, investment, government purchases of goods and services and net exports is called the _____ approach. The _____ _____ approach measures GDP by adding together all incomes paid to households by firms. The _____ approach measures GDP by adding together the value added by each firm in the economy.

8 The amount by which the value of the capital stock is reduced from wear and tear and passage of time is called _____ . When we subtract this amount from gross investment we have _____ investment. Gross domestic product is equal to net domestic product plus _____ .

9 The value of the output of a firm minus the value of its inputs is called _____ _____ . We are double counting if we include expenditures on _____ goods as well as final goods in our calculation of GDP.

10 We refer to economic activity that is legal but not reported to the government as the _____ _____ .

11 The _____ _____ _____ is a measure of the average level of prices of consumption goods and services purchased by a 'typical' urban household. The _____ _____ measures the average level of prices of all final goods and services produced in the economy.

TRUE OR FALSE

___ **1** In the aggregate economy, income is equal to expenditure and to GDP.

___ **2** The government pays High Flyer Aircraft Company for a military jet. This is an example of a transfer payment.

___ **3** Disposable income is equal to consumption expenditure plus saving.

___ **4** Imports is an example of an injection into the circular flow of income.

__ **5** Net domestic product equals gross domestic product minus depreciation.

__ **6** If two economies have the same GDP, then the standard of living is the same in each economy.

__ **7** The GDP deflator is calculated as real GDP divided by nominal GDP, multiplied by 100.

__ **8** If you are interested in knowing whether the economy is producing a greater physical volume of output, you would want to look at real GDP rather than nominal GDP.

__ **9** If the price of good *A* rises much more rapidly than the prices of other goods, then good *A* is responsible for high inflation.

__ **10** Consumers shift their purchases away from goods whose relative prices increase and therefore cause the RPI to overstate the actual inflation rate.

MULTIPLE CHOICE

1 Which of the following is *not* an example of investment in the expenditure approach to measuring GDP? Peugeot
  a buys a new auto stamping machine.
  b adds 500 new cars to stocks.
  c buys French government bonds.
  d builds another assembly plant.
  e replaces some worn-out stamping machines.

2 Which of the following is true for the aggregate economy? Income equals
  a expenditure, but these are not generally equal to GDP.
  b GDP, but expenditure is generally less than these.
  c expenditure equals GDP.
  d expenditure equals GDP only if there are no government or foreign sectors.
  e expenditure equals GDP only if there is no depreciation.

3 Saving can be measured as income minus
  a taxes.
  b transfer payments.
  c taxes minus consumers' expenditure.
  d net taxes minus consumers' expenditure.
  e net taxes plus subsidies.

4 Interest plus miscellaneous investment income is a component of which approach to measuring GDP?

  a factor incomes approach
  b expenditure approach
  c injections approach
  d output approach
  e opportunity cost approach

5 To obtain the factor cost of a good from its market price, one must
  a add indirect taxes and subtract subsidies.
  b subtract indirect taxes and add subsidies.
  c subtract both indirect taxes and subsidies.
  d add both indirect taxes and subsidies.
  e subtract depreciation.

6 Which of the following is an example of a leakage from the circular flow of income?
  a exports
  b investment
  c saving
  d subsidies
  e government purchases

7 The value of a firm's output minus the value of inputs purchased is
  a net exports.
  b value added.
  c net profit.
  d indirect production.
  e capital consumption allowance.

8 The existence of which of the following is *not* a reason for the fact that GDP gives an underestimate of the value of total output in the economy?
  a crime
  b non-market activities
  c the underground economy
  d capital consumption allowance
  e externalities such as pollution

Table 22.1

Item	Price (pounds)		Quantity	
	Base	Current	Base	Current
Deck chairs	1.00	1.25	100	100
Beach towels	9.00	6.00	12	14

9 Table 22.1 gives price and quantity data for an economy with only two consumers' goods: deck chairs and beach towels. What is the RPI for the current year?
  a 100

b 112
c 105.6
d 100.5
e 94.7

10 Refer to the data in Table 22.1. Between the base year and the current year, what happened to the relative price of deck chairs?
a remained unchanged
b fell
c rose
d cannot be determined with the amount of information given
e depends on what happens to the RPI

11 If 1999 is the base year for the GDP deflator, we know that nominal GDP
a equals real GDP in 1998.
b is greater than real GDP in 1998.
c is less than real GDP in 1998.
d in 1999 will be greater than real GDP in 1998.
e in 1999 will be greater than nominal GDP in 1998.

12 Consider the data in Table 22.2. What is the GDP deflator in 1999?
a 160
b 250
c 200
d 88.89
e 125

Table 22.2

Year	Nominal GDP (billions of pounds)	Real GDP (billions of 1990 pounds)	GDP deflator (1990=100)
1998	125	125	100
1999	250	200	
2000	279		122.22

---

13 Use the data in Table 22.2. What is real GDP in 2000?
a 225
b 275
c 220
d 336.22
e 110

SHORT ANSWER

1 In the aggregate economy, why does income equal expenditure?

2 In obtaining GDP we count expenditure only on final goods. Why do we *not* count expenditure on intermediate goods?

3 a What productive activities are not measured and thus are not included in GDP?
b Is this a serious problem?

4 Does a 5 per cent increase in the RPI mean that the cost of living has increased by 5 per cent? Why or why not?

PROBLEMS

1 Use the data for an imaginary economy given in Table 22.3 to compute the following.
a GDP
b net investment
c net exports
d disposable income
e saving
f total leakages from and total injections into the circular flow of income. (Are they equal?)

Table 22.3

Item	Amount (billions of pounds)
Consumers' expenditure (C)	600
Taxes (TX)	400
Transfer payments (TR)	250
Exports (EX)	240
Imports (IM)	220
Government spending on goods and services (G)	200
Gross investment (I)	150
Depreciation (Depr)	60

---

2 Table 22.4 gives data for an economy in which there are three consumers' goods: bananas, coconuts and grapes.

Table 22.4

Good	Base period			Current period	
	Quantity in basket (boxes)	Price (pounds per box)	Expenditure (pounds)	Price (pounds per box)	Value of quantities (pounds)
Bananas	120	6		8	
Coconuts	60	8		10	
Grapes	40	10		9	

a Complete the table by computing expenditures for the base period and the appropriate value of quantities in the current year for computing the RPI.

b What is the value of the basket of consumers' goods in the base period? In the current period?

c What is the RPI for the current period?

3 Table 22.5 gives data for an economy in which there are three final goods included in GDP: pizzas, staplers and shoes.

Table 22.5

Good	Base period			Current period	
	Quantity in basket	Price (pounds)	Expenditure (pounds)	Price (pounds)	Expenditure (pounds)
Pizzas	110		6	8	880
Staplers	50		8	10	500
Shoes	50		10	9	450

a Complete the table by computing expenditure on each good evaluated at base period prices.

b What is the value of nominal GDP in the current period?

c What is the value of real GDP in the current period?

d What is the GDP deflator in the current period?

4 Complete Table 22.6.

Table 22.6

Year	Nominal GDP (pounds)	Real GDP (pounds)	GDP deflator
1997	3,055		94
1998		3,170	100
1999	3,410	3,280	
2000		3,500	108

DISCUSSION QUESTION

1 Why is it important to be able to measure variables such as GDP and inflation?

DATA QUESTIONS

Table 22.7 Prices and GDP in Europe

Country	GDP by volume 1998 (1995 = 100)	Consumer prices 1998 (1995 = 100)
Denmark	110.1	108.8
Finland	117.5	104.4
France	108.0	104.4
Germany	105.3	105.4
Italy	104.1	110.1
Netherlands	113.1	108.3
Spain	112.7	110.1
United Kingdom	109.1	110.8

Source: Main Economic Indicators, OECD, 1998.

1 Explain what is meant by 'GDP by volume, 1995=100'.

2 Which country had (a) the highest, and (b) the lowest rate of economic growth in the period 1995–98?

3 Which country had (a) the largest, and (b) the smallest rise in consumer prices?

4 To what extent are GDP statistics a good measure of living standards?

ANSWERS

CONCEPT REVIEW

1 domestic product

2 stocks

3 consumers' expenditure; investment

4 transfer payments

5 Saving; taxes

6 injections; leakages

7 expenditure; factor incomes; output

8 depreciation; net; depreciation

9 value added; intermediate

10 hidden economy

11 Retail Prices Index; GDP deflator

TRUE OR FALSE

1 **T** From circular flow diagram, production is sold (expenditure) and earnings used to pay out income.

2 **F** It is payment for a good.

3 **T** $Y = C + S + T$ so $Y - T$ (that is, disposable income) $= C + S$.

4 **F** Imports are a withdrawal.

5 **T** Definition.

6 **F** Standard of living depends on level of GDP divided by population.

7 **F** GDP deflator $= [(\text{Nominal GDP})/(\text{Real GDP})] \times 100$.

8 **T** Real GDP measures amount of goods and services while nominal GDP measures current money value and includes impact of inflation.

9 **F** Changes in relative prices do not cause inflation.

10 **T** The RPI is based on a fixed basket of goods and assumes that people continue to buy the same goods (although the RPI basket is periodically changed).

MULTIPLE CHOICE

1 **c** This is purchase of a capital asset, not capital stock.

2 **c** Definition; the three ways of measuring the nation's accounts should be equal.

3 **d** Income after tax must be either spent or saved.

4 **a** Definition.

5 **b** Market price = Factor cost + Indirect taxes – Subsidies.

6 **c** Savings take money out of the circular flow; others are injections.

7 **b** Definition.

8 **d** This is depreciation and is part of GDP.

9 **e** RPI = [(Sum of current prices × Base quantities)/(Sum of base prices × Base quantities)] × 100.

10 **c** Relative price = Change in price (deck chairs) – Inflation rate = 25% – (–5.3%) = 30.3%, where inflation rate = 94.7 – 100.

11 **a** Definition of a base year.

12 **e** GDP deflator = [(Nominal GDP/(Real GDP)] × 100.

13 **a** Real GDP = [(Nominal GDP)/(GDP deflator)] × 100.

SHORT ANSWER

1 When an expenditure is made, firms receive money payments. The amount received by firms in the aggregate is aggregate expenditure. All that firms receive is distributed as income to households who own the factors of production. Remember that profit is income. Since the aggregate amount firms receive is expenditure and firms pay out all they receive as income, in the aggregate economy, income equals expenditure.

2 Counting both final goods and the intermediate goods that were combined to produce them will result in 'double counting'. For example, counting the value of the steel that is sold to a car manufacturer to build a car and then counting it again when the car is sold as a final good will overstate the value of final goods and services since the steel is counted twice.

3 **a** Activities that produce goods and services that are not included in GDP are criminal activities, production in the underground economy and non-market activities. The first are not reported because the activities themselves are illegal. The second refer to goods and services that are legal but are not reported to circumvent taxes or government regulations. The third include those productive activities which households perform for themselves. Because they do not hire someone else to mow the lawn or wash the car, these are not included in GDP.

b The seriousness of the problem depends on the actual size of activity and this is difficult to measure precisely.

4 A 5 per cent increase in the RPI does not mean that the cost of living has increased by 5 per cent if relative prices also change (and they generally will). Changes in relative prices will cause consumers to make substitutions from goods whose relative price has risen to goods whose relative price has fallen. This reduces the effect on the cost of living. The fact that some goods disappear from use and new goods appear also means that changes in the RPI do not precisely reflect changes in the cost of living.

PROBLEMS

1 a GDP = $C + I + G + (EX − IM)$ = £970 billion
b Net $I = I − Depr$ = £90 billion
c $NX = EX − IM$ = £20 billion
d Disposable income = GDP + $TR − TX$ = £820 billion
e Saving = Disposable income − C = £220 billion
f Total leakages = $(TX − TR) + IM + S$ = £590 billion
  Total injections = $I + G + X$ = £590 billion
  So total leakages = total injections.

2 a Table 22.4 is completed here as Table 22.8. Note that the base period quantities are evaluated at current prices to find the value of quantities in the current year.

Table 22.8

| Good | Base period | | | Current period | |
	Quantity in basket (boxes)	Price (pounds per box)	Expenditure (pounds)	Price (pounds per box)	Value of quantities (pounds)
Bananas	120	6	720	8	960
Coconuts	60	8	480	10	600
Grapes	40	10	400	9	360

b The value of the basket of consumers' goods in the base period is the sum of the expenditures in that period: £1,600. The value of the basket of consumers' goods is obtained as the sum of the values of quantities in that period: £1,920.
c The consumer price index is the ratio of the value of quantities in the current period to the base period expenditure, times 100:

RPI = $(1,920/1,600) \times 100$ = 120.

3 a Table 22.5 is completed as Table 22.9. Base period expenditure for each item is obtained by evaluating the current period quantity at the base year price.

Table 22.9

| Good | Base period | | | Current period | |
	Quantity in basket	Price (pounds)	Expenditure (pounds)	Price (pounds)	Expenditure (pounds)
Pizzas	110	660	6	8	880
Staplers	50	400	8	10	500
Shoes	50	500	10	9	450

b The value of nominal GDP in the current period is the sum of expenditures in the current period: £1,830.
c The value of real GDP in the current period is the sum of the current period quantities evaluated at base period prices; in other words, what the expenditures would have been at base year prices: £1,560.
d The GDP deflator for the current period is the ratio of nominal GDP to real GDP, times 100:

GDP deflator = $(1,830/1,560) \times 100$ = 117.3.

4 Table 22.6 is completed as Table 22.10. The following equation is used:

GDP deflator = (Nominal GDP/Real GDP) × 100.

Table 22.10

Year	Nominal GDP (pounds)	Real GDP (pounds)	GDP deflator
1997	3,055	3,250	94
1998	3,170	3,170	100
1999	3,410	3,280	104
2000	3,780	3,500	108

DISCUSSION QUESTION

1 We have to know what GDP is in order to understand growth and business cycles, since we're going to study what makes GDP grow faster and what makes it fluctuate. Similarly, other material in this chapter will lay the foundation for much of what follows. More generally, good economics often depends on knowing the uses and the limitations of statistics.

DATA QUESTIONS

1 'GDP' is an abbreviation for 'Gross Domestic Product', which is a measure of the output produced by a country, usually over one year. 'Volume' implies that the figures are in real terms, that is, excluding the effects of inflation. '1995=100' means that 1995 is the base year so that, for example, in the United Kingdom GDP rose by 9 per cent in the period 1995–98.

2 (a) The highest rate of growth of GDP was in Finland.
(b) The lowest rate of economic growth was in Italy.

3 (a) Inflation was highest in the United Kingdom.
(b) Inflation was lowest in Finland and France.

4 GDP is probably the best measure of living standards, but it has serious inadequacies. First, a number of economic activities are not included in the figures for GDP; for example, non-market activities such as DIY and housework. Second, the underground economy is excluded, and this may amount to 5 per cent of GDP, although there are no precise estimates. Third, the figures contain errors, and it is not possible to estimate these accurately.

Even if all these limitations were overcome, the figures would not be a precise measure of living standards. GDP often rises in times of war because the economy is producing at full capacity, but living standards may be low because the goods produced are weapons of war. Other factors affecting living standards include the amount of leisure time, the quality of the environment, and the amount of crime. These are not included in the statistics of GDP. Lastly, an average figure for GDP per head says nothing about the distribution of that income. In some countries a small minority may take a large share of the national income.

Chapter 23 Employment and Unemployment

Chapter in Perspective, Text Pages 552–577

In this chapter we focus on one of the principal topics of macroeconomics – employment and unemployment. We define some of the main concepts and the labour market is analysed using demand and supply to explain what determines the level of employment.

The chapter also discusses some of the main ideas used to explain unemployment.

Helpful Hints

1 Note that there is no perfect way to measure unemployment. One way is to use a survey of the labour force; alternatively the number of people seeking work and claiming benefit can be used.

2 In a dynamic economy, not all unemployment is inefficient. In fact, frictional unemployment benefits both the individual and society.

Younger workers typically experience periods of unemployment as they try to find jobs that match their skills and interests. The benefit to them of the resulting frictional unemployment is a much more satisfying and productive work life when they succeed. Society benefits because the frictional unemployment that accompanies such a job-search process allows workers to find jobs in which they are most productive. As a result, the total production of goods and services in the economy rises.

Structural unemployment is different from frictional unemployment because structurally unemployed workers will not get a new job without retraining or relocation. Thus the cost to the worker is much greater – for example, structurally unemployed workers typically are unemployed for long time periods. These workers bear the brunt of the cost of restructuring industries in our economy. So although society may ultimately benefit in that goods and services in higher demand are produced, structural unemployment can impose a significant cost on the worker.

3 When economists use the term 'full employment', they do not mean that everyone has a job. Rather, they mean that the only unemployment is frictional and structural in nature. When there is no cyclical unemployment, the rate of unemployment is called the natural rate of unemployment.

The actual rate of unemployment may be less than the natural rate of unemployment. This statement is the same as saying that the level of employment can exceed full employment. In these situations, people are spending too little time searching for jobs, and therefore less productive job matches are being made.

SELF-TEST

CONCEPT REVIEW

1 Two measures of unemployment are published in the United Kingdom. One is based on the _____ _____ _____ , the other makes use of a _____ count.

2 The unemployment rate is the percentage of people in the _____ - _____ who are _____ .

3 Unemployment can be classified into three types, _____ , _____ and _____ .

4 _____ unemployment is the fluctuating unemployment that coincides with the _____ cycle.

5 Economists disagree about the magnitude of the _____ rate of unemployment.

6 Labour _____ and labour _____ interact to determine the level of employment and the _____ real wage rate.

7 Unemployment is always present because of job _____ .

8 The natural rate of unemployment depends on the _____ distribution of the population, _____ benefit and technological _____ .

9 Unemployment arises from job _____ , job _____ and _____ wages.

TRUE OR FALSE

___ **1** The unemployment rate equals the total number of unemployed people divided by the total working-age population.

___ **2** Full-time students not looking for work are unemployed.

___ **3** Mary lost her job and looked for a new job for eight months. Mary stopped looking for work because she believes she cannot find a job. Mary is frictionally unemployed.

___ **4** A rise in the real wage increases the quantity of labour supplied.

___ **5** Sticky wages are a cause of cyclical unemployment.

___ **6** At full employment, there is no unemployment.

___ **7** An increase in the demand for labour raises the real wage rate.

___ **8** The natural rate of unemployment equals the sum of frictional and cyclical unemployment.

___ **9** Bill has just graduated and is looking for his first job. Bill is frictionally unemployed.

MULTIPLE CHOICE

1 Who of the following is cyclically unemployed?
  a Cara, a farmer who lost her farm because of foreign competition and is unemployed until retrained
  b Omar, a fishery worker who is searching for a better job closer to home
  c Eugene, a steelworker who was laid off but has stopped looking for a new job because the economy is in a recession and he thinks he won't be able to find a job
  d Amanda, an office worker who lost her job because of a general slowdown in economic activity

2 Who of the following is frictionally unemployed?
  a Cara, a farmer who lost her farm because of foreign competition and is unemployed until retrained
  b Omar, a fishery worker who is searching for a better job closer to home
  c Eugene, a steelworker who was laid off but has stopped looking for a new job because the economy is in a recession and he thinks he won't be able to find a job
  d Amanda, an office worker who lost her job because of a general slowdown in economic activity

3 If the economy is at full employment, the
  a entire population is employed.
  b entire work-force is employed.

c only unemployment is frictional unemployment plus discouraged workers.

d only unemployment is frictional and structural unemployment.

4 One possible cause of unemployment is that
a flexible wages lead to too many fluctuations in real wages.
b sticky wages lead to too many fluctuations in real wages.
c unemployment compensation payments are too low.
d insiders will not allow firms to hire outsiders if that means lower wages.

5 The demand for labour and the supply of labour are both increasing over time, but the demand for labour is increasing at a faster rate. Over time therefore you would expect to see the
a real wage rate rising and employment falling.
b real wage rate rising and employment rising.
c real wage rate falling and employment rising.
d real wage rate falling and employment falling.

6 In a country with a working-age population of 200 million, 130 million workers are employed and 10 million workers are unemployed. What is the size of the work-force?
a 200 million
b 140 million
c 130 million
d 10 million

7 In a country with a working-age population of 200 million, 130 million workers are employed and 10 million workers are unemployed. What is the work-force participation rate?
a 100 per cent
b 70 per cent
c 65 per cent
d 5 per cent

8 In a country with a working-age population of 200 million, 130 million workers are employed and 10 million workers are unemployed. What is the unemployment rate?
a 5 per cent
b 7.1 per cent
c 7.7 per cent
d 65 per cent

9 The insider–outsider theory
a explains why wages are sticky.

b refers to the idea that unemployed workers (workers 'outside employment') must search for jobs.
c is not related to the presence of unemployment.
d suggests that unions bargain so that their employed members are paid high wages even though other workers remain unemployed.

10 An increase in the demand for labour causes the real wage to _____ and the quantity of employment to _____ .
a rise; increase
b rise; decrease
c fall; increase
d fall; decrease

11 Suppose that the money wage rate is E5 per hour and that the price level is 100. If the money wage rate rises to E10 per hour and the price level rises to 200, what happens to the real wage rate?
a the real wage rate doubles
b the real wage rate rises but does not double
c the real wage rate does not change
d the real wage rate falls

12 In a recession, what is the largest source of unemployment?
a job leavers
b job losers
c new entrants to the work-force
d re-entrants to the work-force

13 At the natural rate of unemployment, there is no
a frictional unemployment.
b structural unemployment.
c cyclical unemployment.
d unemployment.

14 Which of the following best characterizes a recession?
a Real GDP falls, aggregate hours rise and the unemployment rate falls.
b Real GDP rises, aggregate hours fall and the unemployment rate rises.
c Real GDP, aggregate hours and the unemployment rate all fall.
d Real GDP and aggregate hours fall and the unemployment rate rises.

15 The work-force equals the number of
a employed plus unemployed workers.
b employed people.

c people 16 years old and older who are not in jail.

d employed minus unemployed workers.

16 An efficiency wage refers to

a workers being paid wages below the equilibrium wage rate in order to increase the economy's efficiency.

b wages being set to generate the efficient level of unemployment.

c workers being paid wages above the equilibrium wage rate in order to increase their productivity.

d none of the above.

SHORT ANSWER

1 For the following time periods, describe Igor's labour market status. When Igor is unemployed, say whether it is frictional, structural, or cyclical unemployment.

a From January 1 to June 30, 1999, Igor was a full-time student pursuing his bachelor's degree.

b On July 1, Igor graduated with his degree in body building. He spent three months looking for work before Dr Frankenstein hired him on October 1.

c From October 1 to January 1, 2000, Igor worked full-time on the night shift.

d On January 1, because of generally worsening economic conditions, Igor was put on part-time work on the night shift even though he wanted to work full time.

e On February 28, as economic conditions worsened, Dr Frankenstein fired Igor. Igor looked for work until May 1.

f On May 1, Igor became convinced that he couldn't find a job, so until October 31 he looked after the house but did not look for work.

g On October 31, Count Dracula dropped by for a bite and offered Igor a job, which he accepted.

2 Can the unemployment rate increase while the total amount of employment also increases?

3 The *Reading Between the Lines* article describing the Bank of England estimate of the natural rate of unemployment was dated August 1998. Was the Bank's analysis correct?

PROBLEMS

Table 23.1

Employed workers	Unemployed workers	Work-force	Unemployment rate (%)
100	10		
80		100	
		200	5.0
130	8		

1 Complete Table 23.1.

2 Suppose that the initial money wage rate is E5 an hour and that the initial price level is 100. Now assume that both the money wage rate and the price level double.

a What happens to the real wage rate?

b What happens to the quantity of labour supplied; does it increase, decrease, or not change? Why?

c What happens to the quantity of labour demanded; does it increase, decrease, or not change? Why?

3 a In Fig. 23.1 illustrate a real wage rate at which jobs are rationed. Indicate the amount of unemployment.

b What can account for job rationing?

Figure 23.1

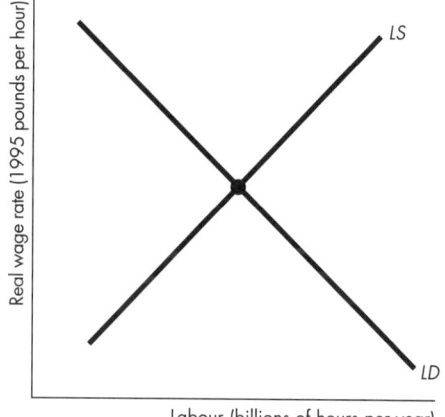

DISCUSSION QUESTIONS

1 Explain why understanding the different types of unemployment is useful.

2 Why is a goal of zero unemployment neither realistic nor desirable?

DATA QUESTIONS

Structural unemployment
We can differentiate different types of structural unemployment:

◆ Regional – some regions have been over-reliant on particular industries such as coal.

◆ Occupational – some industries suffer disproportionately so far as unemployment is concerned. The construction industry is an example.

◆ Technological – this allows more to be produced with fewer workers and it makes some skills obsolete.

◆ Seasonal – in some cases workers are required for only part of the year. The tourism industry is an example.

Source: B. Atkinson, P. Baker and B. Milward, *Economic Policy*, Macmillan, 1996, pp. 239–40.

1 Explain what is meant by structural unemployment.

2 What policy measures can be taken to reduce structural unemployment?

ANSWERS

CONCEPT REVIEW

1 Labour Force Survey; claimant
2 work-force; unemployed
3 structural; cyclical; frictional
4 Cyclical; business
5 natural
6 demand; supply; equilibrium
7 search
8 age; unemployment; change
9 search; rationing; sticky

TRUE OR FALSE

1 F The unemployment rate equals the total number of unemployed workers divided by the work-force, not the total working-age population.

2 F These students are not in the work-force.

3 F Mary is a discouraged worker because she stopped looking for a job.

4 T A rise in the real wage rate boosts the amount of goods and services that can be purchased by working, so the quantity of labour supplied increases.

5 T If wages are sticky, changes in economic activity that affect the price level will cause changes in real wage rates and can create unemployment.

6 F At full employment, the unemployment rate equals the natural rate, comprising frictional and structural unemployment.

7 T An increase in the demand for labour means that the demand curve of labour shifts rightward, thereby raising the real wage rate.

8 T The natural rate of unemployment is *defined* as the sum of frictional and structural unemployment.

9 T Bill is part of the normal turnover in the labour market and thus is frictionally unemployed.

MULTIPLE CHOICE

1 d Amanda's job was lost because of a recession, so Amanda is cyclically unemployed.

2 b Omar is part of the normal turnover in the work-force, so he is frictionally unemployed.

3 d At full employment, the unemployment rate is the natural rate, which equals the sum of frictional and structural unemployment.

4 d Insider–outsider theory states a potential cause of unemployment.

5 b When demand rises faster than supply, then price will rise.

6 b The work-force equals the sum of employed workers (130 million) and unemployed workers (10 million), or 140 million.

7 b The work-force participation rate equals the per centage of the working-age population in the work-force, that is, the total work-force (140 million) divided by the total working-age population (200 million), multiplied by 100.

8 b The unemployment rate equals the number of unemployed workers divided by the work-force, multiplied by 100.

9 d Because unions negotiate on behalf of their employed members, unions do not bargain for lower wage rates even though lower wage rates would reduce the unemployment rate.

10 a As Fig. 23.2 illustrates, the rightward shift in the labour demand curve from LD_0 to LD_1 raises the wage rate to W_1 and increases the level of employment to L_1.

Figure 23.2

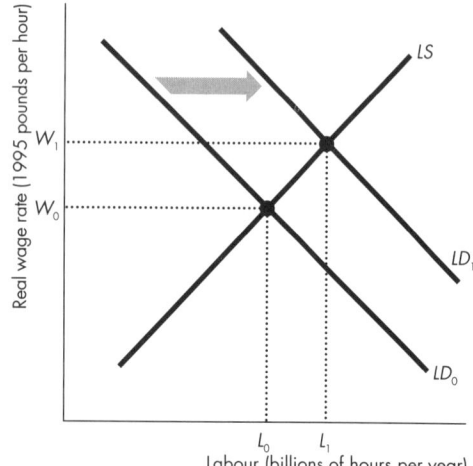

11 c The real wage rate equals the money wage rate divided by the price level. Thus when both the money wage rate and price level double, the real wage rate does not change.

12 b Job losers include workers who have been fired or laid off, and these workers account for the majority of unemployment during a recession.

13 c The natural rate comprises only frictional and structural unemployment.

14 d In a recession, economic activity slows so that real GDP and aggregate hours of work fall and the unemployment rate rises.

15 a The definition of the work-force is the sum of employed and unemployed workers.

16 c Definition.

SHORT ANSWER

1 a As a full-time student, Igor was not in the work-force.
  b While Igor searched for his first job, he was frictionally unemployed.
  c When working full-time for Dr Frankenstein, Igor was an employed worker.
  d Even though Igor wanted full-time work, he nonetheless was still counted as (fully) employed when he was on the part-time night shift.
  e From February 28 to May 1, Igor was cyclically unemployed because his unemployment was the result of a downturn in the economy.
  f From May 1 to October 31, Igor was not in the work-force because he was not looking for work. Igor was a discouraged worker.
  g Igor is employed after October 31.

2 Although it is not common, both the number of employed workers and the unemployment rate can increase at the same time. This situation occurs most often just after the trough of the business cycle when the economy moves into an expansion. In these months, the economy is growing, real GDP is expanding, and so the total amount of employment rises. In addition, previously discouraged workers begin to perceive that they may now be able to find a job. Hence a large number of discouraged workers rejoin the work-force, start searching for jobs, and add significantly to the number of unemployed workers. (Recall that as discouraged workers they were not counted as unemployed; rather they were not in the work-force.) Hence the unemployment rate may increase even though the total number of employed workers increases.

3 To answer the question you need to look at recent statistics on inflation and unemployment and make your own analysis.

PROBLEMS

Table 23.2

Employed workers	Unemployed workers	Work-force	Unemployment rate (per cent)
100	10	110	9.1
80	20	100	20.0
190	10	200	5.0
130	8	138	5.8

1 The answers are in Table 23.2. To calculate them, recall that the work-force equals the sum of employed and unemployed workers. Hence in the first line the total work-force equals 100 + 10 or 110. In the second line, the number of unemployed workers equals the work-force, 100, minus the total number of employed workers, 80. Thus unemployed workers number 20. The unemployment rate equals the total number of unemployed workers divided by the work-force, multiplied by 100. Thus in the first row the unemployment rate equals

$$\frac{10}{100} \times 100 = 9.1 \text{ per cent.}$$

In the third row, rearranging the definition of the unemployment rate shows that the total number of unemployed workers equals the unemployment rate multiplied by the work-force. Hence in the third row the total number of unemployed workers is 5 per cent × 200 so that unemployment is 10. The number of employed workers in that row is therefore 190.

2 a The real wage rate does not change. The real wage rate is defined as the money wage rate divided by the price level. Because both the money wage rate and price level double, the doubling 'cancels' so that the real wage rate is unaffected. Alternatively, if the money wage rate doubles and the price level doubles, people receive twice as much money for each hour's work, but the money buys only half what it did before. Hence the real wage rate – the number of goods and services that can be purchased with an hour's work – does not change.

b Because the real wage rate does not change, neither does the quantity of labour supplied. The quantity of labour supplied depends on the real wage rate, *not* the money wage rate, because the real wage rate indicates how many goods and services can be purchased with an hour's work.

c The quantity of labour demanded does not change. Similar to the supply of labour, the demand for labour depends on the real wage rate, not the money wage rate. Essentially, the real wage rate shows the cost of hiring labour (the money wage) relative to the price of the firm's output (the price level). When both the cost of hiring labour and the price of the firm's output double, the firm has no incentive to hire either more or less labour because the profit from hiring workers has not changed.

3 a In Fig. 23.3, any wage rate higher than the equilibrium wage rate, W, creates some job rationing. For instance, at the wage rate W', the demand for labour is only 40 billion hours of labour, yet at this wage rate 100 billion hours of labour are supplied. At this wage rate unemployment is 60 billion hours of labour. More generally, the extent of unemployment equals the difference between the quantity of labour supplied and the quantity demanded.

Figure 23.3

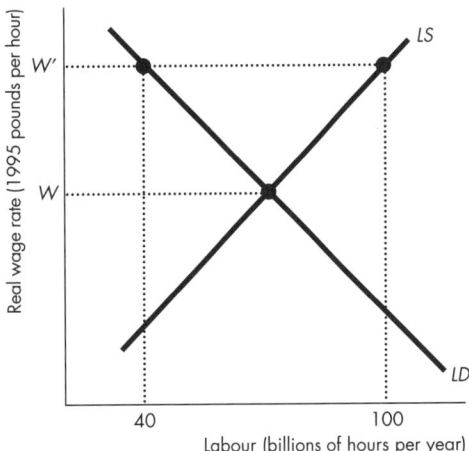

b Three factors can account for job rationing: efficiency wages, insider interest and the minimum wage.

Efficiency wages occur when firms pay above-equilibrium wage rates to increase their workers' productivity. Hence firms might pay a wage rate of W' knowing that, although the higher wage rate increases their costs, this effect is more than offset by the higher productivity of the workers receiving the higher wage rate.

The idea of insider interest indicates that unions may bargain to further *only* the interests of their employed members. Hence unions bargain for a high wage rate because the union does not represent the workers remaining unemployed by an above-equilibrium wage rate.

Lastly, the minimum wage may be at a level that is above the equilibrium wage rate. In this case the quantity of labour demanded is less than that supplied, and jobs are rationed because not everyone who wants to work at the going (minimum) wage rate can find employment.

DISCUSSION QUESTIONS

1 The classification of unemployment can be extremely useful for us, as students, because it makes clear some of the causes of unemployment. Once we know the causes, we can also get a lot of insight into what we should do about them.

For example, take the idea of structural unemployment. Structurally unemployed workers will need a different type of help than those who are cyclically unemployed. A worker who is cyclically unemployed doesn't necessarily need a lot of retraining. But a worker who is structurally unemployed may benefit from this type of training. So by recognizing that structural reasons are one cause of unemployment, we can see that offering retraining may be a good idea if we want to reduce the unemployment rate.

2 Reducing frictional unemployment to zero would be costly, since some people are always looking for work and the economy needs some flexibility. It would probably be equally impossible to reduce structural unemployment to zero. But cyclical unemployment is a different issue. The more we can tame the business cycle, the more we can reduce cyclical unemployment.

DATA QUESTIONS

1 Structural unemployment is caused by changes in the structure of the economy which lead to changes in the demand for and supply of labour in particular industries and occupations.

2 No policies can completely eliminate structural unemployment since the structure of the economy will continue to change. However, retraining workers so that they can change jobs is a useful policy. Some economists would argue that this should be augmented by regional policy to help depressed areas; for example, giving grants to firms moving into the area and using other measures to help particular industries.

Chapter 24 **Aggregate Supply and Aggregate Demand**

Chapter in Perspective, Text Pages 578–601

What determines the amount of goods and services that an economy produces? What causes inflation and how can it be controlled? What are the causes of unemployment, and why does the unemployment rate fluctuate over time? The fundamental purpose of macroeconomic analysis is to address these kinds of issues; issues regarding the behaviour of the national economy as a whole.

In this chapter we begin to build the basic tool of macroeconomic analysis: the aggregate demand and aggregate supply model. This model will prove to be extremely helpful as we attempt to explain the growth of real GDP and inflation as well as business cycle fluctuations in real GDP and unemployment. In subsequent chapters we develop in more detail the underlying principles of aggregate demand and aggregate supply.

Helpful Hints

1 This chapter discusses the fundamental concepts of aggregate demand, aggregate supply and macroeconomic equilibrium. The model developed is the principal means by which we interpret macroeconomic activity. While later chapters will refine our understanding of these concepts, the basic model is introduced here. As a result, this chapter should be reviewed until it is mastered.

2 Two reasons for the negative slope of the aggregate demand curve are discussed: the real money balances effect and the substitution effect.

3 There is one important reason for the positive slope of the short-run aggregate supply curve: input prices are held constant. Given constant input prices, a change in the price level, that is the price of output, will affect the amount of goods and services that producers are willing to supply. For example, if the price of output rises but the price of input remains constant, profit-maximizing firms will increase output.

4 As in our study of microeconomics, in macroeconomics we do not define the short run and long run in terms of a length of calendar time but rather in terms of whether or not key variables can change. Here, in the short run the prices of factors of production do not change, whereas in the long run they do change. The principal implication is that, in the short run, a change in the price level causes the price of output relative to the price of input to change and thus firms will change their rate of output. On the other hand, in the long run, input prices adjust and there is no long-run change in output because the initial price of output relative to input prices is restored.

5 The distinction between the short run and the long run gives rise to the differences among the various factors that affect the short-run and long-run aggregate supply curves. Since input prices are held constant for the short-run aggregate supply curve but not for the long-run aggregate supply curve, a change in input prices will shift the short-run curve but not the long-run curve.

SELF-TEST

CONCEPT REVIEW

1 The quantity of real GDP supplied depends on the quantity of _____ and _____ and on the state of _____ .

2 A firm's _____ output is the output at which its cost per unit produced is minimized. The level of real GDP that results when all firms are producing at this level of output and when there is full employment is _____ - _____ aggregate supply.

3 With input prices held constant and the economy producing below its physical limit, an increase in the price level will cause the quantity of real GDP supplied to _____ . Thus the _____ - _____ aggregate supply curve is _____ sloped. When the economy reaches its physical limit to produce, this curve becomes _____ .

4 If the quantity of real GDP demanded equals the quantity of real GDP supplied, the economy is in _____ _____ . If this occurs when the economy is on its long-run aggregate supply curve, then the economy is said to be in _____ - _____ equilibrium. If this occurs at a level of real GDP below long-run aggregate supply, a(n) _____ equilibrium has occurred.

5 The graphical representation of the relationship between the quantity of real GDP demanded and the price level is called the _____ _____ curve. As the price level increases, the quantity of real GDP demanded _____ .

6 There are three separate effects of the price level on the quantity of real GDP demanded. The first of these is the real money balances effect. As the price level rises, the quantity of real money _____ , which causes the quantity of real GDP demanded to _____ .

7 The second effect involves the substitution of goods now for goods later or vice versa; this is the _____ _____ effect. A lower price level will tend to lead to _____ interest rates, which causes the quantity of real GDP demanded to _____ .

8 The third effect is the _____ substitution effect. If the UK price level rises (holding everything else constant), the quantity of UK-produced goods demanded will _____ and the quantity of foreign-produced goods demanded will _____ .

9 If the quantity of money increases (holding everything else constant), the aggregate demand curve will shift to the _____ . The aggregate demand curve will shift to the right if the government _____ taxes.

10 If the economy is producing below its physical limit, an increase in aggregate demand (other things remaining the same, including input prices) will result in a(n) _____ in the price level and a(n) _____ in the level of real GDP.

11 An increase in the price of raw materials (other things remaining constant) will result in a(n) _____ in the price level and a(n) _____ in the level of real GDP.

TRUE OR FALSE

___ **1** According to the real money balances effect, the lower the quantity of real money, the larger is the quantity of real GDP demanded.

___ **2** As interest rates decline, the aggregate quantity of goods and services demanded rises.

___ **3** An increase in the expected rate of inflation will decrease aggregate demand.

___ **4** If the government decides to increase its expenditures on goods and services, the aggregate demand curve will shift to the right.

___ **5** An increase in income taxes will cause the aggregate demand curve to shift to the right.

___ **6** If the economy is on its long-run aggregate supply curve, there is full employment.

___ **7** If the stock of capital increases, both the long-run and short-run aggregate supply curves will shift to the right.

___ **8** It is possible to have a macroeconomic equilibrium at a level of real GDP above full employment.

___ **9** If there is a significant technological advance (other things remaining the same), the long-run aggregate supply curve will shift to the right but the short-run aggregate supply curve will not shift.

___ **10** If there is significant technological advance (other things remaining the same), the price level will rise.

___ **11** The main force generating the underlying tendency of real GDP to expand over time is increases in long-run aggregate supply.

___ **12** The main force generating a long period of inflation is persistent increases in aggregate demand.

___ **13** A large increase in the price of oil, such as in 1973, will generally result in an inflationary recession.

MULTIPLE CHOICE

1 The aggregate demand curve (*AD*) illustrates that, as the price level falls, the quantity of
  a real GDP demanded increases.
  b real GDP demanded decreases.
  c nominal GDP demanded increases.
  d nominal GDP demanded decreases.
  e real money balances falls.

2 Which of the following is a reason for the downward slope of the aggregate demand curve?
  a the intertemporal substitution effect
  b the international substitution effect
  c the expected inflation effect
  d the nominal balance effect
  e both **a** and **b**

3 As the price level rises, the quantity of real money balances
  a increases, and thus the aggregate quantity of goods and services demanded increases.
  b increases, and thus the aggregate quantity of goods and services demanded decreases.
  c decreases, and thus the aggregate quantity of goods and services demanded increases.
  d decreases, and thus the aggregate quantity of goods and services demanded decreases.
  e decreases, and this has no effect on the aggregate quantity of goods and services demanded.

4 Which of the following will cause the aggregate demand curve to shift to the right?
  a an increase in interest rates (at a given price level)
  b an increase in expected inflation
  c an increase in taxes
  d a decrease in the price level
  e an increase in the price level

5 Long-run aggregate supply is the level of real GDP at which
  a each firm is producing its capacity output.
  b there is full employment.
  c the economy is producing its physical limit.
  d each firm is producing its capacity output and there is full employment.
  e prices are sure to rise.

6 Short-run aggregate supply is the relationship between the price level and the quantity of real GDP supplied, holding constant the
  a wage rate.
  b quantities of factors of production.
  c level of government spending.
  d price level.
  e prices of factors of production.

7 The short-run aggregate supply curve (*SAS*) is positively sloped but becomes vertical at the level of real GDP at which

a each firm is producing its capacity output.
b each firm is producing output at its physical limit.
c there is full employment.
d it intersects the aggregate demand curve.
e hyperinflation starts.

8 A technological improvement will shift
  a both the short-run aggregate supply and the aggregate demand curves to the right.
  b both the short-run aggregate supply and long-run aggregate supply curves to the left.
  c the short-run aggregate supply curve to the right but leave the long-run aggregate supply curve unchanged.
  d the long-run aggregate supply curve to the right but leave the short-run aggregate supply curve unchanged.

  e both the short-run aggregate supply and long-run aggregate supply curves to the right.

9 Macroeconomic equilibrium occurs when the
  a economy is at full employment.
  b economy is producing at its physical limit.
  c aggregate demand curve intersects the short-run aggregate supply curve along its vertical portion.
  d quantity of real GDP demanded equals the quantity of real GDP supplied.
  e aggregate demand curve intersects the long-run aggregate supply curve.

10 Which of the graphs in Fig. 24.1 illustrates an unemployment equilibrium?
  a (a)
  b (b)
  c (c)

Figure 24.1

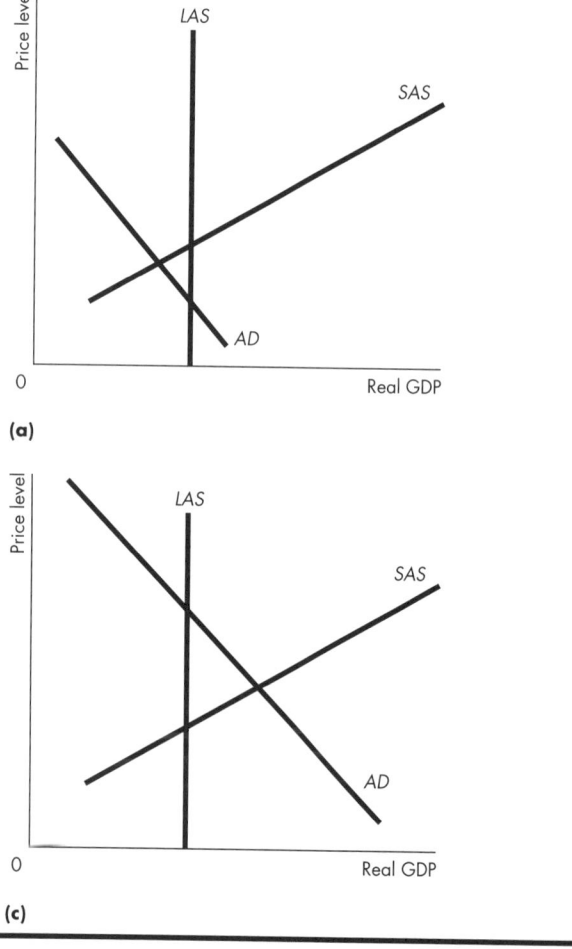

(a)

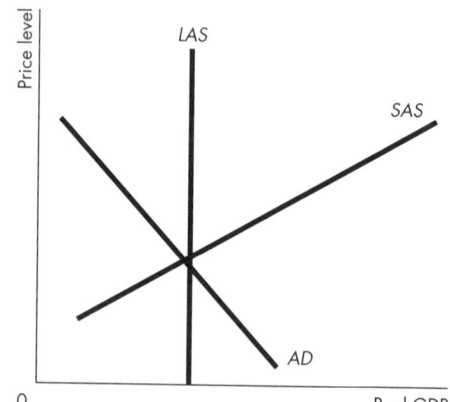

(b)

(c)

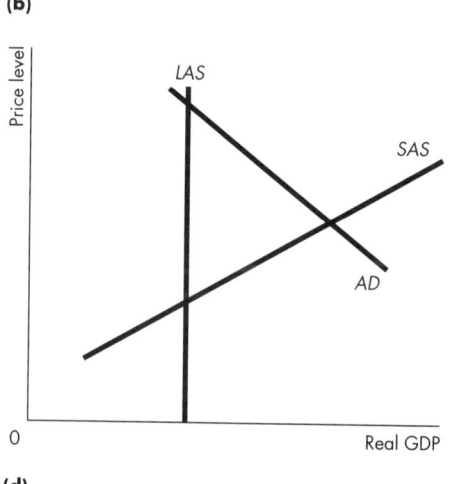

(d)

d (d)

e both (c) and (d)

11 Which of the graphs in Fig. 24.1 illustrates an above full-employment equilibrium?

a (a)

b (b)

c (c)

d (d)

e both (c) and (d)

12 If real GDP is greater than long-run aggregate supply, then the economy is

a not in macroeconomic equilibrium.

b in a full-employment equilibrium.

c in an above full-employment equilibrium.

d in an unemployment equilibrium.

e in long-run equilibrium.

13 If input prices remain constant and firms are producing at levels less than their physical limits, an increase in aggregate demand will cause

a an increase in the price level and an increase in real GDP.

b an increase in the price level and a decrease in real GDP.

c a decrease in the price level and an increase in real GDP.

d a decrease in the price level and a decrease in real GDP.

e an increase in the price level but no change in real GDP.

SHORT ANSWER

1 The intertemporal substitution effect implies that an increase in the price level will lead to a decrease in the aggregate quantity of goods and services demanded. Explain.

2 The international substitution effect implies that an increase in the price level will lead to a decrease in the aggregate quantity of goods and services demanded. Explain.

3 Why is the long-run aggregate supply curve vertical?

4 Why is the short-run aggregate supply curve positively sloped over most of its range?

5 Why does the *Reading Between the Lines* article refer to a 'central forecast'? What reasons are given for the 'short shelf life' of the projections?

PROBLEMS

1 Suppose the economy is initially in full-employment equilibrium. Assuming that input prices remain constant, graphically illustrate the effect of an increase in foreign income. What happens to the price level and the level of real GDP?

2 Suppose the economy is initially in full-employment equilibrium. Assuming that input prices remain constant, graphically illustrate the effect of an increase in the stock of human capital. What happens to the price level and the level of real GDP?

3 Suppose the economy is initially in full-employment equilibrium. Graphically illustrate the effect of an increase in wages. What happens to the price level and the level of real GDP?

4 Consider an economy that is initially at a full-employment equilibrium. In each of four successive years, an economic event occurs:

Year 1: The government increases its expenditures on goods and services.

Year 2: OPEC increases the price of oil.

Year 3: The government increases the money supply.

Year 4: The government decreases the money supply.

a Graphically illustrate the successive consequences of these four events on a diagram similar to that shown in Fig. 24.2(a). Label the initial equilibrium point *a* and label the new equilibrium points after years 1, 2, 3 and 4, *b*, *c*, *d* and *e*, respectively.

b Suppose that each new equilibrium is achieved gradually over one year. In Fig. 24.2(b), point *a* refers to the initial level of real GDP; time is measured on the horizontal axis. Plot the behaviour of real GDP during the succeeding four years. Comment on the pattern of that behaviour.

DISCUSSION QUESTIONS

1 Why does a drop in the price level not shift the *SAS* curve?

2 Draw a diagram to show what happens in the long run after an initial decrease in aggregate demand has occurred.

Figure 24.2

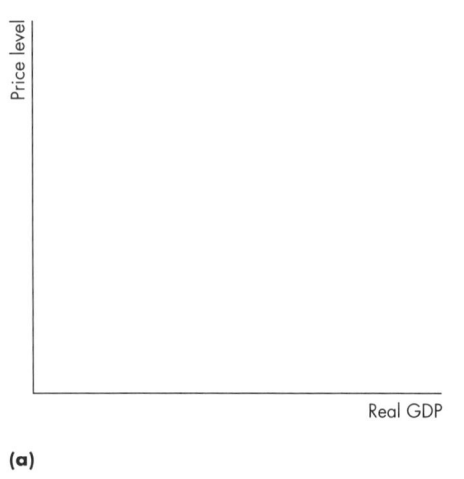

(a)

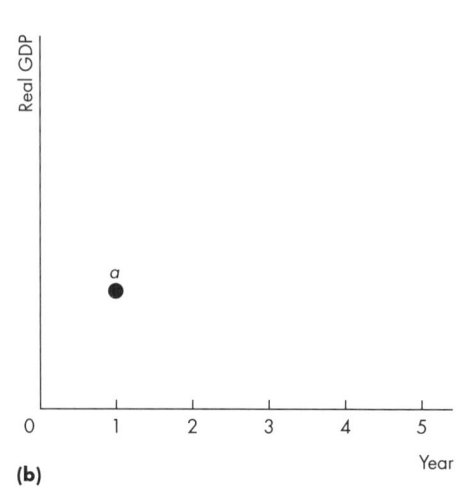

(b)

DATA QUESTION

Draw diagrams to illustrate the effect on UK price levels and real GDP of the following changes (assume that the economy is originally below full-employment equilibrium).

a Quantity of money (£M4)

1992	1999
£507 billion	£791 billion

b In the 1991 budget the VAT rate was increased from 15 per cent to 17.5 per cent.

c Population of OECD countries (the OECD is the organization of the richest countries)

1980	1999
780 million	895 million

d UK average weekly earnings (male)

1992	1997
£333	£409

ANSWERS

CONCEPT REVIEW

1 labour; capital; technology

2 capacity; long-run

3 increase; short-run; positively; vertical

4 macroeconomic equilibrium; full-employment; unemployment

5 aggregate demand; decreases

6 falls; decrease

7 intertemporal substitution; lower; increase

8 international; fall; rise

9 right; decreases

10 increase; increase

11 increase; decrease

TRUE OR FALSE

1 F With a lower quantity of real money, individuals cut spending to increase the level of real money.

2 T People will have more money to spend.

3 F If individuals expect a higher inflation rate they will spend more today to avoid higher prices in the future.

4 T Government spending is an injection into the circular flow.

5 F Curve will shift to left because people will have less money to spend.

6 T Definition.

7 T Increase in capital will lead to rise in productivity so that more output is produced at every price.

8 T Equilibrium may be at, above or below full-employment level.

9 F Anything that shifts the *LAS* curve also shifts the *SAS* curve.

10 F Technological change will increase productivity and lower prices.

11 T Increased population, more capital stock and new technology shift the *LAS* curve rightward over time.

12 T Rises in *AD* not matched by increases in *AS* will pull up prices.

13 T It will shift the *AS* curve to the left.

MULTIPLE CHOICE

1 a *AD* curve is downward sloping owing to three substitution effects. It is real GDP by definition, not nominal. Also real money balances increase here.

2 c **c** shifts *AD* curve, and **d** doesn't exist.

3 d Price rises so money buys fewer goods (real money balances fall), so *AD* falls.

4 b People will buy now before prices rise.

5 b Definition.

6 e Definition.

7 b At vertical portion of *SAS* curve firms cannot produce more output because they are at their physical limits.

8 e Technological improvements mean that labour is more productive leading to increase in supply in both short and long run.

9 d Macroeconomic equilibrium always occurs where *AD* = *SAS*; equilibrium *may* occur at answers **a–c**, but it doesn't always occur there.

10 a Unemployment equilibrium occurs when *AD* = *SAS* to left of *LAS*.

11 e Above full-employment equilibrium occurs when *AD* = *SAS* to right of *LAS*.

12 c Equilibrium is where *AD* = *SAS*; if this is greater than *LAS* then there is above full-employment equilibrium.

13 a Firms will increase output and prices will also rise (*AD* curve shifts to right).

SHORT ANSWER

1 Intertemporal substitution means the substitution of goods now for goods later or vice versa. There are two keys to understanding the intertemporal substitution effect.

The first of these is that changes in interest rates influence households to engage in intertemporal substitution. For example, if interest rates rise, households will tend to borrow and spend less now, thus decreasing the aggregate quantity of goods and services demanded.

The second key is that interest rates are determined by the demand for loans and the supply of loans and that these are affected by changes in the quantity of real money. In particular, a decrease in real money will make households less willing to lend. This means that the supply of loans will decrease, which will cause the interest rate to rise.

Combining these keys, the intertemporal substitution effect is described as follows: an increase in the price level decreases the quantity of real money, which reduces the supply of loans and thus raises interest rates. The rise in interest rates will lead to a decrease in the aggregate quantity of goods and services demanded.

2 International substitution means substituting domestically produced goods for foreign-produced goods or vice versa. If the price of domestic goods rises and foreign prices remain constant, domestic goods become relatively more expensive, and so households will buy fewer domestic goods and more foreign goods.

This means that there will be a decrease in the quantity of real GDP demanded. Thus an increase in the price level (the prices of domestic goods) will lead to a decrease in the aggregate quantity of (domestic) goods and services demanded through the international substitution effect.

3 Long-run aggregate supply is the level of real GDP supplied when each firm in the economy is producing at its capacity output and there is full employment. Since this level of real GDP is independent of the price level, the long-run aggregate supply curve is vertical. It should also be noted that this is the level of real GDP attained when input prices are free to adjust so as to clear factor markets.

4 The short-run aggregate supply curve is positively sloped because it holds input prices constant. Thus when the price level rises, firms see the prices of their output rising, but the prices of their inputs remain unchanged. Each firm is then induced to increase output and so aggregate output increases.

5 The article refers to a 'central forecast' because economic forecasts can never be precise; hence the monetary policy committee gives a range of forecasts. The reasons given for the changed forecast are the American trade deficit, lower domestic demand in the UK and less acute worries about the labour market.

PROBLEMS

1 In Fig. 24.3, the economy is initially at point a on the original AD curve, AD_0. An increase in foreign income will shift the AD curve to the right, from AD_0 to AD_1. At the new equilibrium, point b, the price level has risen and the level of real GDP has increased.

2 The economy in Fig. 24.4 is initially at point a on the LAS_0 and SAS_0 curves. An increase in the stock of human capital will shift both the LAS and SAS curves to the right, to LAS_1 and SAS_1, respectively. At the new equilibrium, point b, the price level has fallen and the level of real GDP has increased.

Figure 24.3

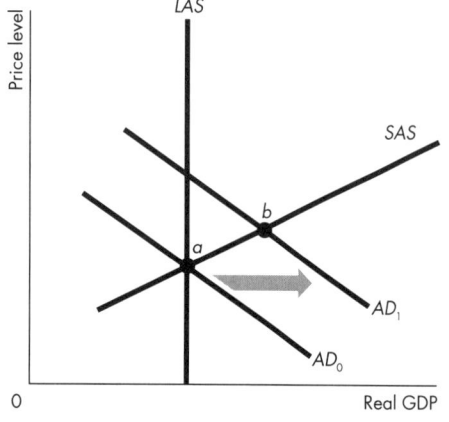

3 In Fig. 24.5, the economy is initially at point a on the SAS_0 curve. An increase in wages will shift the SAS curve upward, to SAS_1. At the new equilibrium, point b, the price level has risen and the level of real GDP has decreased.

Figure 24.4

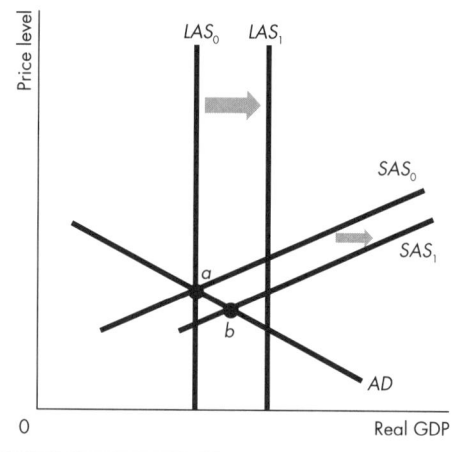

Figure 24.5

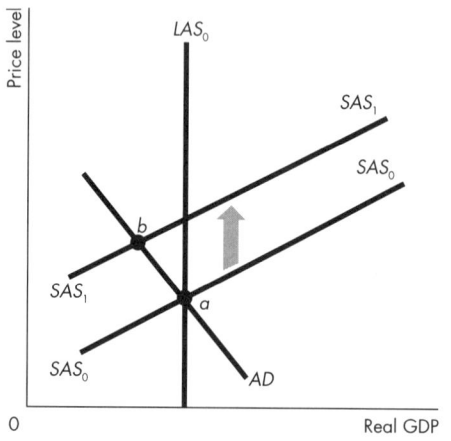

4 a The required diagram is shown in Fig. 24.6(a). The initial equilibrium is at point a with AD_0, SAS_0, and LAS.

At the beginning of year 1, the increase in government spending shifts the AD curve from AD_0 to AD_1 producing a new equilibrium (by the end of the year) at point b. We note that real GDP has increased.

At the beginning of year 2, OPEC increases the price of oil, which shifts the SAS curve from SAS_0 to SAS_2. Real GDP falls, producing a new equilibrium at point c.

At the beginning of year 3, the government increases the money supply (perhaps to combat the fall in output), which causes the AD curve to shift from AD_1 to AD_3. The new equilibrium is at point d and real GDP has risen.

Figure 24.6

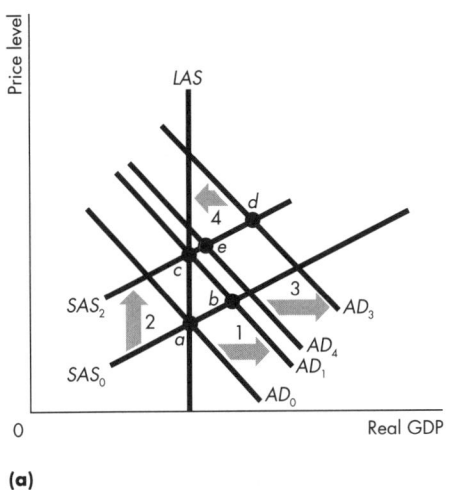

(a)

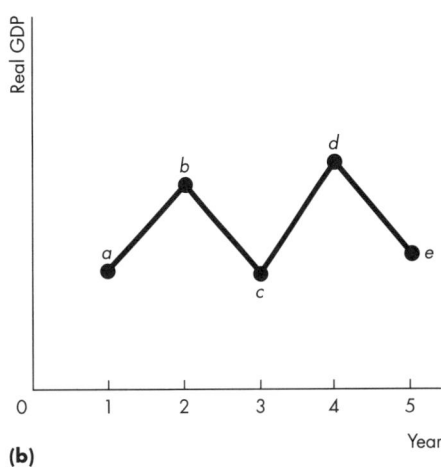

(b)

Lastly, in year 4, the government decreases the money supply (perhaps to combat the continuing increase in the price level) and the AD curve shifts to the left, from AD_3 to AD_4, say. The consequence is a decline in real GDP and a new equilibrium at point e.

b The behaviour of real GDP over time is illustrated in Fig. 24.6(b). At the beginning of year 1, the output level is given by point a but the shift in AD causes output to rise by the beginning of year 2 (point b). Similarly, as indicated in **a**, in years 2, 3 and 4, real GDP falls, rises and falls again (points c, d and e). These real GDP movements are characteristic of the business cycle movements in real GDP.

DISCUSSION QUESTIONS

1 A change in the price level does not shift the AD or AS curves; instead the price level itself changes in response to a shift in the AD or AS curves. For example, if firms lose confidence in future profits they will cut investment. This will shift the AD curve leftward along the SAS curve. The result will be a fall in prices.

2 The fall in price reached in **1** is a short-term effect because unemployment is below the natural rate. The result will be a series of adjustments such as a fall in wages and other input costs. Thus firms are willing to increase their supply of goods even if the price level does not change. This causes the SAS curve to shift rightward as shown in Fig. 24.7. The new equilibrium

Figure 24.7

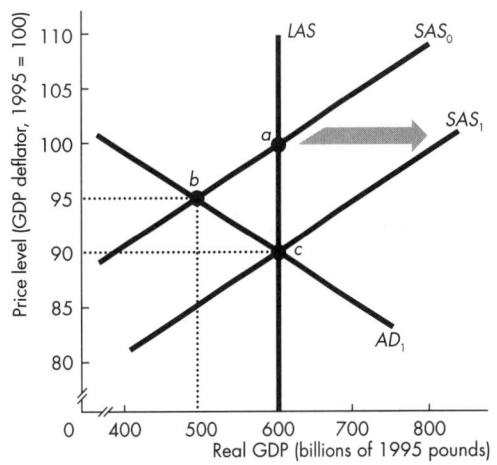

will be where SAS_1 intersects AD_1. The new long-run equilibrium is at point c where the new equilibrium level of GDP equals potential real GDP. Compared with the original equilibrium, the long-term result of the fall in investment is that the price level is lower, but real GDP is the same.

DATA QUESTION

a Other factors remaining the same, an increase in the quantity of money will increase aggregate demand as shown in Fig. 24.8(a). The result will be a move from *a* to *b*, giving rise in prices and in GDP. Note that if the economy had been at full employment there would have been no rise in GDP.

b An increase in VAT will shift the aggregate supply curve upward as shown in Fig. 24.8(b). The result will be a move from equilibrium *a* to *b*, a rise in prices and a fall in GDP.

c An increase in population in OECD countries will increase demand for UK goods and services and the result will be identical to that described in part **a**.

d A rise in weekly earnings that is not accompanied by any change in productivity will increase firms' costs and shift the short-run *AS* curve upward, and the result will be that described in **b**. There may also be an increase in aggregate demand if people expect the inflation rate to increase. This would further push up prices but would also increase GDP.

Figure 24.8

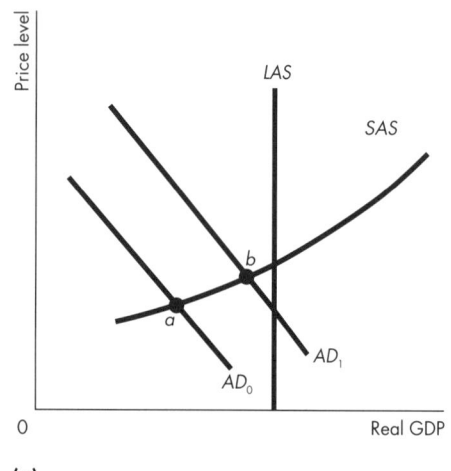

(a)

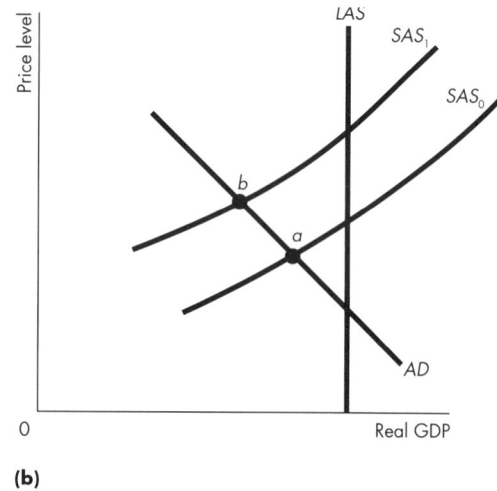

(b)

Chapter 25

Expenditure Multipliers

Chapter in Perspective, Text Pages 602–629

This chapter introduces several important concepts. The marginal propensity to consume and marginal propensity to save are linked to changes in disposable income and their relationship needs to be understood. Another important concept is the aggregate expenditure schedule which shows how aggregate expenditure depends on real GDP.

However, the focus of the chapter is on the multiplier which shows that a change in autonomous expenditure creates an additional change in induced expenditure.

Helpful Hints

1 The basic idea of the multiplier is that an increase in (say) government spending has a multiplied effect. For example, when a new school is built the builders will have a rise in income and most of this will be spent on consumer goods, so increasing the income of those who made and sold those goods. In turn, these people will buy other goods and services. The effect is reduced by leakages; for example, when people save this reduces the multipler effect.

2 This chapter distinguishes between autonomous expenditure and induced expenditure. Autonomous expenditure is independent of changes in real GDP, whereas induced expenditure will vary as real GDP varies. In general, a change in autonomous expenditure creates a change in real GDP, which in turn creates a change in induced expenditure. The induced changes are at the heart of the multiplier effect.

However, even though autonomous expenditure may be independent of changes in real GDP, it will not be independent of changes in other variables (for example, the price level).

3 Note that the AD curve is derived from the AE curve. In other words, the AE curve shows the equilibrium level of expenditure for a particular price level. This price level together with the equilibrium level of expenditure (which equals real GDP) is a point on the AD curve. Hence not only are the AE and AD curves quite different, but we actually use one to derive the other!

4 The concept of the multiplier is extremely important. It is a result of the interaction of the various components of aggregate expenditure. In particular, an initial increase in autonomous expenditure, such as investment, increases real GDP directly, but that is not the end of the story. The initial increase in real GDP generates an increase in induced expenditure, which further increases real GDP and thus induces further increases in (induced) expenditure.

The total effect on real GDP is larger than the initial increase in autonomous expenditure because of the induced expenditure.

Induced expenditure occurs because the initial increase in real GDP (created by the increase in autonomous expenditure) raises people's disposable incomes. For instance, an increase in investment purchases of personal computers raises the incomes of workers who are hired to manufacture the additional personal computers. Then, because the marginal propensity to consume is greater than zero, the increase in disposable income increases these workers' (induced!) consumption expenditures. You should become thoroughly familiar with both the concept of and the mathematics behind the multiplier.

Income taxes have a stabilizing effect. The higher the income tax rate, the less any change in GDP translates into a change in disposable income. In turn, the smaller change in disposable income creates a smaller change in (induced) consumption expenditure and therefore makes the multiplier smaller. This automatic stabilizer effect works by reducing the induced effects in the multiplier process.

5 The multiplier shows the change in equilibrium expenditure. Thus if the multiplier is, say, 5.0 and investment (a component of autonomous expenditure) increases by $10 billion, equilibrium expenditure increases by $50 billion.

However, an increase in equilibrium expenditure of $50 billion does not necessarily mean that equilibrium real GDP also increases by $50 billion. The change in equilibrium real GDP depends on the interaction of aggregate demand and aggregate supply. The $50 billion increase in equilibrium expenditure implies that the *AD* curve shifts rightward by $50 billion, but this shift is only one part of the picture. Depending on the aggregate supply curve, real GDP could increase by an amount close to $50 billion (if the *SAS* curve is relatively flat) or by an amount less than $50 billion (how much less depends on the steepness of the *SAS* curve) or $0 (which is the case in the long run, when the *LAS* curve is vertical).

The multiplier generally overstates the change in GDP because the multiplier ignores the effect of changing prices. But when the *AD* curve shifts rightward, the price level rises. The rise in the price level decreases equilibrium expenditure, an effect ignored by the multiplier. Thus always keep in mind that the multiplier gives the shift in the *AD* curve, that is, the change in equilibrium aggregate expenditure. However, the multiplier does *not* necessarily give the change in equilibrium GDP.

6 Distinguishing between two types of changes in autonomous spending is crucial. One type adds to the instability of the economy; it includes changes in autonomous consumption, investment and exports. The other type of change usually is a planned shock that will (its proponents hope) reduce the instability of the economy; it includes changes in government spending and taxes. As both types of changes work through the same multiplier process, the same process that creates instability also is available to reduce instability.

SELF-TEST

CONCEPT REVIEW

1 The components of aggregate expenditure are _____ expenditure, investment, government purchases and net _____ .

2 Consumption and saving are influenced by several factors including _____ interest rates, disposable _____ , assets minus _____ , and expected _____ _____ .

3 The marginal propensity to consume is a fraction of the _____ in disposable income that is _____ .

4 Imports are determined by _____ GDP, comparative prices and foreign _____ rates.

5 With a steady price level, aggregate _____ determines real GDP.

6 Equilibrium expenditure occurs when aggregate _____ expenditure equals real _____ .

7 A change in autonomous expenditure changes real GDP by an amount determined by the _____ .

8 The greater the marginal propensity to _____ the greater is the multiplier.

9 A change in the price level shifts the *AE* curve and brings a movement along the _____ curve.

TRUE OR FALSE

___ **1** In the short run, an increase in investment expenditure of £1 billion will generate an increase in equilibrium expenditure of more than £1 billion.

___ **2** In the long run, an increase in investment expenditure of £1 billion will generate an increase in equilibrium expenditure of more than £1 billion.

___ **3** When real GDP increases, induced expenditure also increases along the *AE* curve.

___ **4** When aggregate planned expenditure exceeds real GDP, stocks rise more than planned.

___ **5** The multiplier is greater than one because an increase in autonomous expenditure leads to an induced increase in consumption expenditure.

___ **6** An increase in investment shifts the *AE* curve upward and the *AD* curve rightward.

___ **7** The multiplier equals $\dfrac{1}{(1 - MPS)}$.

___ **8** Equilibrium expenditure occurs when aggregate planned expenditure equals real GDP.

___ **9** Planned aggregate expenditure can be different from actual aggregate expenditure.

___ **10** The sum of the marginal propensity to consume and the marginal propensity to save equals 1.

___ **11** If the marginal propensity to consume is 0.8 and there are no income taxes or imports, the multiplier equals 5.0.

MULTIPLE CHOICE

1 An increase in the price level shifts the *AE* curve _____ and _____ equilibrium expenditure.
a upward; increases
b upward; decreases
c downward; increases
d downward; decreases

2 Autonomous expenditure is *not* influenced by
a the interest rate.
b the foreign exchange rate.
c real GDP.
d any variable.

3 The aggregate expenditure curve shows the relationship between aggregate planned expenditure and
a government purchases.
b real GDP.
c the interest rate.
d the price level.

4 If unplanned stocks rise, aggregate planned expenditure is
a greater than real GDP and firms will increase output.
b greater than real GDP and firms will decrease output.
c less than real GDP and firms will increase output.
d less than real GDP and firms will decrease output.

5 Which of the following conditions shifts the consumption function downward?
a an increase in current disposable income
b an increase in future expected income
c an increase in the purchasing power of net assets
d a decrease in the purchasing power of net assets

6 When the marginal propensity to consume is 0.50 and there are no income taxes or imports, the multiplier equals
a 10.0.
b 5.0.
c 2.0.
d 0.5.

7 If the marginal propensity to consume is 0.75 and there are no income taxes nor imports, what is the multiplier?
  a 1.33
  b 1.50
  c 2.00
  d 4.00

8 The fraction of the last pound of disposable income saved is called the
  a marginal propensity to consume.
  b marginal propensity to save.
  c marginal tax rate.
  d none of the above.

9 The multiplier is 2.0 and, owing to an increase in expected future profit, investment increases by £10 billion. The *AD* curve
  a shifts rightward by £20 billion.
  b shifts rightward by more than £20 billion.
  c shifts rightward by less than £20 billion.
  d shifts upward by £20 billion.

10 The multiplier is 2.0 and, owing to an increase in expected future profit, investment increases by £10 billion. In the short run, equilibrium real GDP will
  a increase by £20 billion.
  b increase by more than £20 billion.
  c increase by less than £20 billion.
  d be unaffected.

11 The multiplier is 2.0 and, owing to an increase in expected future profit, investment increases by £10 billion. If potential real GDP is unaffected, in the long run, equilibrium real GDP will
  a increase by £20 billion.
  b increase by more than £20 billion.
  c increase by less than £20 billion.
  d be unaffected.

12 An increase in autonomous expenditure shifts the *AE* curve
  a upward and leaves its slope unchanged.
  b upward and makes it steeper.
  c upward and makes it flatter.
  d downward and makes it steeper.

13 What is the marginal propensity to consume, *MPC*, in Fig. 25.1?
  a 1.00
  b 0.90
  c 0.67
  d £3 billion

Figure 25.1

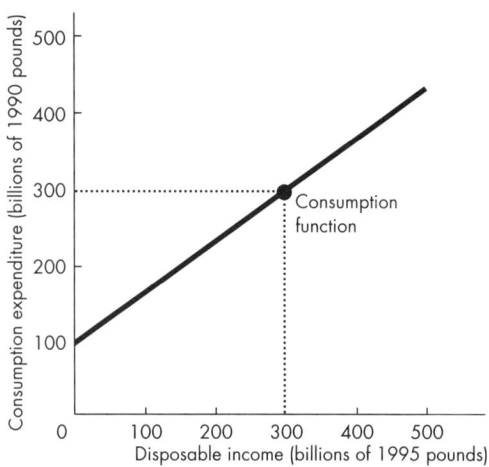

14 The multiplier equals
  a $1/(MPC)$.
  b $MPC/(1 - MPC)$.
  c MPS/MPC.
  d $1/(1 - MPC)$.

15 Firms increase their investment spending. In the short run, which of the following increases the effect of this change on equilibrium real GDP?
  a a smaller value for the marginal property to consume
  b income taxes
  c a steeper short-run aggregate supply curve
  d a flatter short-run aggregate supply curve

SHORT ANSWER

1 What is the difference between autonomous expenditure and induced expenditure?

2 Explain why the *MPC* plus the *MPS* must total 1.

3 Explain why the multiplier is larger if the marginal propensity to consume is larger.

4 Suppose that aggregate planned expenditure is greater than real GDP so that stocks are decreasing. If prices are sticky, explain the process by which equilibrium expenditure is achieved.

5 Briefly explain what the *AE* curve illustrates and how it is related to the *AD* curve.

6 With reference to the *Reading Between the Lines* article, what effects will consumer confidence, the 'Asian drag' and the change in builders' confidence have in the French economy?

PROBLEMS

1 The island country of Wet has no international trade and no income taxes. The marginal propensity to consume in Wet is 0.75.

  a Investment increases by £20 billion. Before prices change, what is the change in equilibrium expenditure?

  b By how much and in what direction does the aggregate demand curve shift?

  c Suppose that, instead of being 0.75, the marginal propensity to consume was 0.90. With this marginal propensity to consume, what is the change in equilibrium expenditure? The shift in the aggregate demand curve?

  d In the short run, prices rise. Without giving a precise numeric answer, what is the effect of the higher price level on the change in equilibrium expenditure? The shift in the aggregate demand curve?

2 a Complete Table 25.1.

  b Based on Table 25.1 how does a decrease in the size of the *MPC* affect the multiplier?

Table 25.1 The *MPC*, *MPS* and Multiplier

MPC	MPS	Multiplier
0.9		
0.8		
0.7		
0.6		
0.5		

Table 25.2 Aggregate Expenditure Components

Real GDP	Consumption expenditure (billions of 1995 pounds)	Investment	Government purchases
0.5	0.2	0.3	0.2
1.0	0.6	0.3	0.2
1.5	1.0	0.3	0.2
2.0	1.4	0.3	0.2
2.5	1.8	0.3	0.2

Figure 25.2

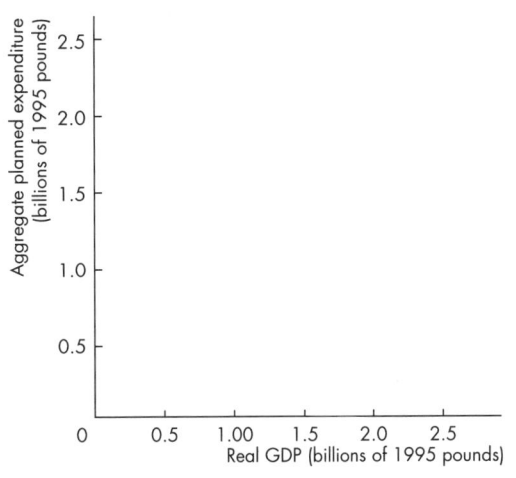

3 Table 25.2 shows the components of aggregate expenditure in the country of Woodstock. Woodstock has no foreign trade and no taxes.

  a Plot these components of aggregate expenditure in Fig. 25.2. Label the consumption line *C*, the investment line *I*, and the government purchases line *G*.

  b Complete Table 25.3 to show aggregate expenditure in Woodstock.

  c Use Table 25.3 and plot the aggregate expenditure line in Fig. 25.2. Label it *AE*.

  d Draw a 45° line in Fig. 25.2. What is equilibrium expenditure in Woodstock?

  e Use either Fig. 25.2 or Table 25.3 to determine the equilibrium amount of consumption expenditure, investment and government purchases.

Table 25.3 Aggregate Expenditure

Real GDP (billions of 1995 pounds)	Aggregate expenditure (billions of 1995 pounds)
0.5	
1.0	
1.5	
2.0	
2.5	

DISCUSSION QUESTION

1 Explain how the shift in the *AD* curve is determined, what the short-run effects are on the price level and real GDP, and what the long-run effects are on the price level and GDP.

DATA QUESTIONS

Investment and GDP

The amount of bread we eat next year will be fairly similar to the amount we ate last year. This is because consumption patterns of staple foods such as bread are fairly stable. The pattern of investment is different. When incomes and expenditures are rising, firms buy more machines and put in orders for new offices and factories. When national income is constant or falling, firms do not need extra machines and so investment falls. Thus gross fixed capital formation at constant prices was £113,042 million in 1994. By 1998 it had risen to £144,184. These changes in investment have a multiplied effect on national income.

1 How do changes in investment affect GDP?

2 What factors affect the size of the effect on GDP?

ANSWERS

CONCEPT REVIEW

1 consumption; exports

2 real; income; debts; future income

3 change; consumed

4 real; exchange

5 demand

6 planned; GDP

7 multiplier

8 consume

9 *AD*

TRUE OR FALSE

1 T An increase in investment creates a larger increase in equilibrium expenditure because of the action of the multiplier.

2 F In the long run, the economy returns to potential GDP, so the long-run multiplier is zero.

3 T The increase in GDP *induces* increases in aggregate expenditure. Indeed, that is why the *AE* curve has a positive slope.

4 F When aggregate planned expenditure exceeds real GDP, stocks fall because more goods and services are being purchased than are being produced.

5 T This is why a multiplier exists.

6 T Any increase in autonomous expenditure *not* caused by a change in the price level shifts the *AE* curve upward and the *AD* curve rightward.

7 F With the *MPC*, the multiplier is $\dfrac{1}{(1-MPC)}$, with the *MPS*, the multiplier is $\dfrac{1}{MPS}$.

8 T Definition.

9 T If the economy is not in equilibrium, actual aggregate expenditure is different from planned aggregate expenditure.

10 T Because *MPC* + *MPS* = 1, the two formulas for the multiplier, $\dfrac{1}{(1-MPC)}$ and $\dfrac{1}{MPS}$, are equivalent.

11 T The multiplier is $\dfrac{1}{(1-MPC)}$, so when the *MPC* is 0.8, the multiplier is 5.0.

MULTIPLE CHOICE

1 d An increase in the price level decreases consumption expenditure, thereby shifting the *AE* line downward and hence decreasing the equilibrium level of expenditure.

2 c The definition of autonomous expenditure is expenditure that is not affected by changes in real GDP.

3 b The aggregate expenditure curve shows that, as real GDP increases, so too does the quantity of planned expenditure.

4 d If unplanned stocks rise, aggregate planned expenditure is less than production, that is, less than GDP.

In response to the unplanned rise in stocks, firms reduce their level of production and real GDP decreases.

5 d A decline in the purchasing power of net assets makes people poorer, so they decrease their consumption expenditure.

6 c The multiplier is $\dfrac{1}{(1-MPC)}$, which means that, here, the multiplier equals 2.0.

7 d Comparing the answer to this question with the answer to **6** shows that as the *MPC* increases in magnitude, so does the multiplier.

8 b Definition.

9 a The rightward shift in the *AD* curve equals the multiplied impact on equilibrium expenditure, which in this case is 2.0 × £10 billion = £20 billion.

10 c Even though the *AD* curve shifts rightward by £20 billion, the *SAS* curve slopes upward. Hence in the short run, the increase in the equilibrium level of real GDP is less than £20 billion. Figure 25.3 illustrates this situation, where the £20 billion rightward shift in the *AD* curve creates only a £10 billion increase in equilibrium GDP.

Figure 25.3

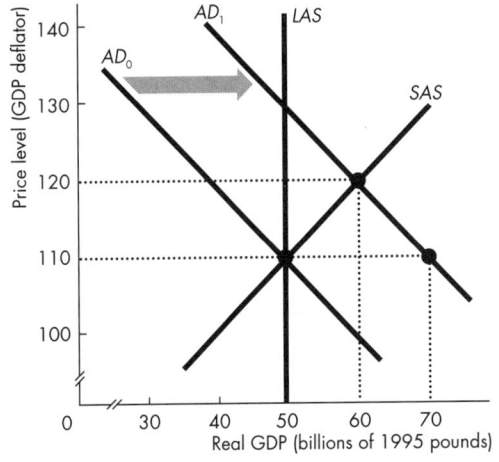

11 d In the long run, GDP returns to potential GDP without any long-run effect on real GDP. In Fig. 25.3, in the long run GDP returns to the potential GDP of £50 billion.

12 a An increase in autonomous expenditure shifts the *AE* curve upward; a decrease shifts it downward.

13 c The *MPC* is $\Delta C/\Delta YD$, which here is £2 billion/£3 billion = 0.67.

14 d Definition.

15 d The flatter the *SAS* curve, the less prices rise and the larger is the increase in equilibrium GDP and aggregate expenditure.

SHORT ANSWER

1 Autonomous expenditure does not change when real GDP changes, whereas induced expenditure does change.

2 Only two things can be done with an additional pound of disposable income: spend all or part of it or save all or part of it. The *MPC*, or marginal propensity to consume, indicates the fraction of the additional pound of disposable income that is spent on consumption, whereas the *MPS*, or marginal propensity to save, indicates the fraction of the additional pound that is saved. Because consumption and saving are the only two uses to which the pound can be put, the two fractions must sum to 1.

3 Any initial increase in autonomous expenditure generates a direct increase in equilibrium expenditure. The basic idea of the multiplier is that this initial increase in aggregate expenditure generates *further* increases in aggregate expenditure as increases in consumption expenditure are induced. In each round of the multiplier process, the increase in spending, and thus the further increase in aggregate expenditure, are determined by the marginal propensity to consume. Because a larger marginal propensity to consume means a larger increase in aggregate expenditure at each round, the total increase in equilibrium expenditure is greater. Thus the multiplier is larger if the marginal propensity to consume is larger.

4 In the discussion of aggregate expenditure and equilibrium expenditure in this chapter, we assume that prices are sticky so that the price level is fixed. This 'thought experiment' allows us to develop the economic model of the components of aggregate expenditure without worrying about the complication of price level changes. As a result of this assumption, when we discuss how firms adjust to unwanted decreases in their stocks, we assume that firms respond by raising production, without prices changing. However, in the *AS/AD* model, we relax this assumption and 'allow' prices to change by reintroducing the aggregate supply curve. In the *AS/AD* model, we get the more realistic result that firms change both prices and production. In other words, in the short run, an increase in aggregate expenditure, which shifts the *AD* curve rightward, raises the price level *and* increases real GDP.

5 The purpose of investigating aggregate expenditure is to deepen our understanding of aggregate demand. The *AE* curve answers the question: for a given price level, how is equilibrium expenditure determined? For instance, when the price level rises, aggregate expenditure decreases (so that the *AE* curve shifts downward) and equilibrium expenditure decreases. Aggregate demand is different. It relates the quantity of real GDP demanded to differing values of the price level. In other words, the *AD* curve uses the results derived using the *AE* curve to show how equilibrium expenditure changes when the price level changes.

6 The rise in consumer confidence will mean a rise in the proportion of income spent, i.e. a rise in the marginal propensity to consume, so increasing the size of the multiplier. The 'Asian drag' will mean a smaller multiplier, but the rise in builders' confidence will lead to a higher multiplier. These varying factors indicate how difficult it is to forecast the economic future.

PROBLEMS

1 a The multiplier in Wet is

$$\frac{1}{(1 - \text{MPC})} \text{, or}$$

$$\frac{1}{(1 - 0.75)} = 40.$$

Thus the change in equilibrium expenditure is $4.0 \times$ £20 billion, or £80 billion.

b The aggregate demand curve shifts by an amount equal to the change in equilibrium expenditure. Hence because equilibrium expenditure increases by £80 billion, the aggregate demand curve shifts rightward by £80 billion.

c If the marginal propensity to consume is 0.90, the multiplier is 10.0. Hence in this case, equilibrium expenditure increases by $10.0 \times$ £20 billion = £200 billion, and the aggregate demand curve shifts rightward by £200 billion.

d When prices start to rise, the aggregate expenditure curve shifts downward. (The higher prices decrease people's consumption expenditure.) The downward shift in the aggregate expenditure curve reduces equilibrium expenditure. However, the aggregate demand curve does *not* shift. Instead, a movement occurs along the aggregate demand curve to a lower level of equilibrium real GDP.

2 a Table 25.1 is completed here as Table 25.4. Because $MPC + MPS = 1.0$, $MPS = 1.0 - MPC$. Thus for the first row, $MPS = 1.0 - 0.9 = 0.1$. The multipliers can be calculated using either of two equivalent formulas, namely,

$$\text{multiplier} = \frac{1}{(1 - MPC)} = \frac{1}{MPS}.$$

b As Table 25.4 shows, when the *MPC* falls in size, so too does the multiplier.

Table 25.4 The *MPC*, *MPS* and Multiplier

MPC	MPS	Multiplier
0.9	0.1	10.0
0.8	0.2	5.0
0.7	0.3	3.3
0.6	0.4	2.5
0.5	0.5	2.0

Figure 25.4

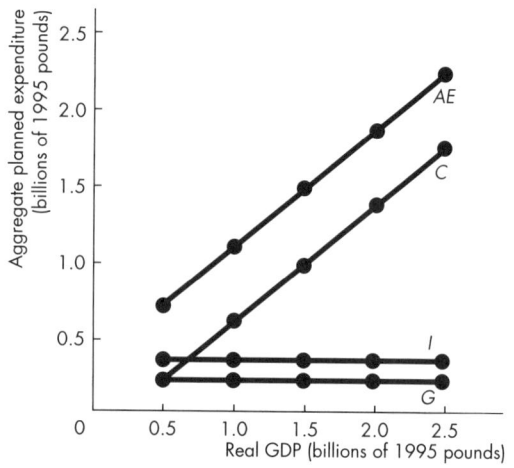

3 a Figure 25.4 shows the consumption line, *C*, the investment line, *I*, and the government purchases line, *G*.

b Table 25.5 shows the schedule of aggregate expenditure. Aggregate expenditure equals the sum of consumption expenditure, investment, and government purchases. Thus when GDP is, say, £1.0 billion, aggregate expenditure equals £0.6 billion + £0.3 billion + £0.2 billion, or £1.1 billion.

Table 25.5 Aggregate Expenditure

Real GDP (billions of 1995 pounds)	Aggregate expenditure (billions of 1995 pounds)
0.5	0.7
1.0	1.1
1.5	1.5
2.0	1.9
2.5	2.3

Figure 25.5

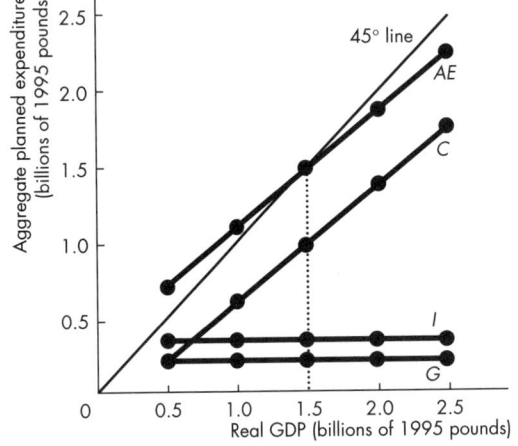

c The aggregate expenditure curve, *AE*, is plotted in Fig. 25.4. It is the vertical sum of the $C + I + G$ curves in the figure.

d Figure 25.5 shows the 45° line. The equilibrium level of expenditure equals £1.5 billion because the *AE* line crosses the 45° line at that point.

e In Fig. 25.5 the dotted line indicating the equilibrium level of expenditure shows that the equilibrium level of consumption is £1.0 billion, the equilibrium level of investment is £0.3 billion, and the equilibrium level of government purchases is £0.2 billion. Alternatively, in Table 25.2, the data in row 3 – the row for which GDP is £1.5 billion – give the same answers for consumption, investment and government purchases.

DISCUSSION QUESTION

1 Assume that investment increases by £10 billion. Let's also assume that the *MPC* equals 0.67.

First, we calculate the multiplier. We know that the multiplier equals

Figure 25.6

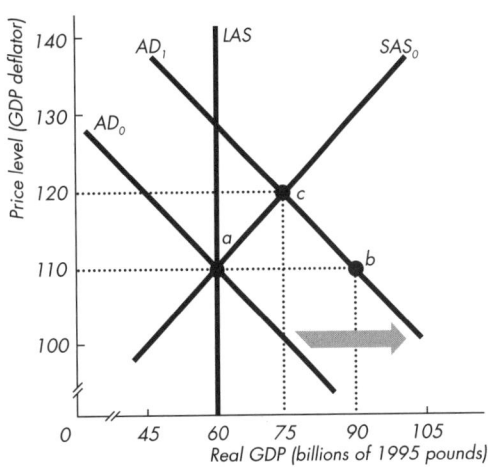

$$\frac{1}{(1 - MPC)}$$

so in this case we get

$$\frac{1}{(1 - 0.67)} = 3.0.$$

In other words, we know that the multiplier is 3.0 and that the £10 billion increase in investment leads to a 3.0 × £10.0 billion = £30.0 billion increase in equilibrium expenditure.

In Figure 25.6, before investment increased, the economy was in equilibrium at point *a*. The initial aggregate demand curve, AD_0, crossed the short-run aggregate supply curve, SAS_0, and the long-run aggregate supply curve, *LAS*. The equilibrium price level was 110 and real GDP was £60 billion.

The increase in investment shifts the *AD* curve rightward, and the size of the shift equals the change in equilibrium expenditure. In other words, the *AD* curve shifts rightward to AD_1, and the size of the shift equals £30 billion. The shift is the difference between point *b* and point *a* along the double headed arrow; this difference is £30 billion. So the *AD* curve shifts rightward by the multiplied impact on equilibrium expenditure.

A key point is that, in the short run, real GDP doesn't increase by the whole £30 billion. It would increase by the whole £30 billion only if prices didn't change. But, in the short run, prices will start to change. As they rise, people reduce their consumption expenditure, and the equilibrium amount of expenditure doesn't change by the whole £30 billion; it changes by something less. Figure 25.6 shows that the short-run equilibrium – where AD_1 crosses SAS_0 – is at point *c*. At point *c*, real GDP increases by (only) £15 billion, to £75 billion. Why don't we go to point *b*? Because, in the short run, the price level has increased, from 110 to 120.

But, point *c* is not the end of the story. At point *c*, the price level has increased but money wages haven't changed. As more time passes, workers negotiate higher wages, which take into account the higher prices. And, as money wage rates rise, the short-run aggregate supply curve shifts leftward.

The last part of the story is illustrated in Fig. 25.7. Here the *SAS* curve has shifted leftward and the new, long-run equilibrium point is *d*, where the *AD* curve crosses the *LAS* curve and the *SAS* curve, *SAS₁*. Thus at point *d*, we've returned to the long-run equilibrium because prices *and* money wages have both adjusted: real GDP has returned to its potential level ($60 billion) and the price level has increased to 130.

Table 25.6 shows some results that can help you tie all these changes together. It lists the four points shown in Figs 25.6 and 25.7. We begin at point *a*. Then the increase in investment starts to move us to point *b*. If prices are sticky long enough, the multiplier process will have time to complete itself and we'll get to point *b*. But in the short run prices rise, so if we do reach *b* we move pretty quickly to point *c*, where prices – but not money wages – have changed. Then, from point *c*, money wages start to adjust and we eventually move from point *c* to point *d*, where both prices and money wages have risen. Point *d* is the final, long-run equilibrium.

Table 25.6 Different Points

Point	Situation
a	Initial equilibrium
b	Price level constant, money wage constant
c	Price level increased, money wage constant
d	Price level increased, money wage increased

DATA QUESTIONS

1 Changes in the level of investment affect GDP through the multiplier process. This process occurs because when investment rises the people who benefit from the investment will in turn increase their spending, and the process will be repeated. The process also occurs when there is a fall in investment.

2 The size of the multiplier effect depends on the amount of leakages from the system. If marginal propensities to save, tax and import are high, then the multiplier effect will be small. If these propensities are small, there will be few leakages, and the multiplier effect will be large.

Figure 25.7

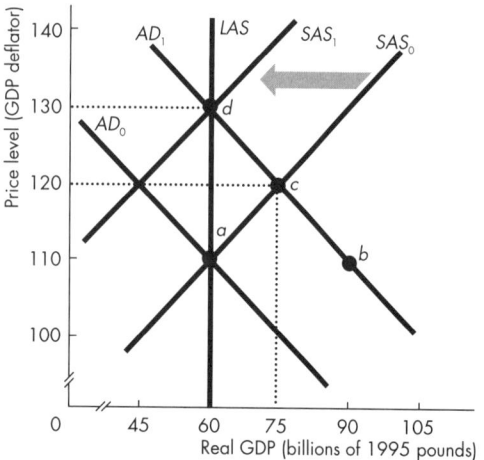

Chapter 26   **Fiscal Policy**

Chapter in Perspective, Text Pages 630–653

Fiscal policy – government policy concerning taxes and public spending – is the subject of this chapter. The background to fiscal policy is described and the effects in both the short run and the long run are discussed.

Helpful Hints

1 In Chapter 25 the idea behind the multiplier was discussed. This chapter continues the discussion by introducing additional multipliers, including the government purchases multiplier and the lump-sum tax multiplier. These multipliers exist for the same reason that the multiplier existed in the preceding chapter. An initial autonomous change that affects people's disposable income leads them to change their consumption expenditure, which further affects disposable income and thereby induces further changes.

2 That the multipliers in this chapter exist for the same reasons as those in Chapter 25 is reinforced by the fact that the investment multiplier (derived in Chapter 25) is identical to the government spending multiplier. In the simplest case without income taxes or imports, both multipliers are

$$\frac{1}{(1 - MPC)}.$$

The reason is that, for example, a £1 billion increase in either investment or government purchases initially adds £1 billion to the stream of aggregate expenditure. In other words, the effect on aggregate expenditure from a change in invest-ment spending is identical to the effect of a similar change in government purchases.

3 The fact that the investment multiplier equals the government purchases multiplier occasionally leads to confusion among students, who realize that an increase in investment spending will increase the country's capital stock but that an increase in government purchases may not affect the country's capital stock. These students argue that the capital stock changes must therefore cause the effect of an increase in investment to differ from the effect of an increase in government spending.

Although this analysis has some long-run merit, it is incorrect in its application to aggregate demand and is incorrect in the short run.

First, remember that multipliers calculate the amount by which the *aggregate demand* curve shifts when autonomous spending changes. The total demand for goods and services changes by the same amount regardless of whether the initial change in expenditure was by firms (for their investment) or by the government (for its purchases of goods and services). Hence the multiplier – which measures the size of this shift – is identical for investment and government spending.

Second, remember that the aggregate demand curve does not depend on the amount of the country's capital. The aggregate supply curve(s) shifts when the country's capital stock changes. An increase in investment spending will change the capital stock, whereas an increase in government purchases does not necessarily change the capital stock. Thus the response of the aggregate supply curve(s) may be different for the two increases in spending.

Even though the aggregate supply curve(s) might respond differently, ignoring any differences is convenient for two reasons. First, for the short run, time is needed for the capital to be installed and come online. Thus in the short run, the country's capital stock does not change when investment increases and so, in the short run, the aggregate supply curve(s) does not shift. Second, even in the long run the change in investment spending creates only a minuscule fraction of a change in the country's total capital stock. In the analysis of business cycle fluctuations in economic activity, that amount of change generally is ignored as too small to matter. Thus although it is important for the topic of long-term economic growth, for multiplier analysis a change in investment spending is treated the same as a change in government purchases.

SELF-TEST

CONCEPT REVIEW

1 The United Kingdom, like almost all other countries, usually runs a budget_____ .

2 Like changes in investment, changes in government spending have a(n) _____ effect.

3 Automatic _____ are mechanisms that operate without the need for action by government. For example, if real GDP begins to fall, government _____ increases and _____ revenues fall.

4 In the short run, when prices are sticky, a change in government spending will have a(n) _____ effect on GDP.

5 Public expenditures are classified in three categories: expenditure on _____ and services, _____ payment and _____ interest.

6 The presence of income taxes and international trade _____ the fiscal policy multipliers.

7 Income taxes and unemployment benefits work as automatic _____ to dampen the business cycle.

8 A tax cut increases real _____ but it can either raise or lower the _____ level.

TRUE OR FALSE

1 Raising government spending and lump-sum taxes at the same time and by the same amount will increase aggregate demand.

2 Changes in lump-sum taxes are an example of an automatic stabilizer.

3 The government purchases multiplier is greater than 1 because an increase in government purchases leads to an induced increase in consumption expenditure.

4 If the marginal propensity to consume is 0.8 and there are no income taxes or imports, the government purchases multiplier is 5.0.

5 If the marginal propensity to consume is 0.8 and there are no income taxes or imports, the lump-sum tax multiplier is –4.0.

6 If the marginal propensity to consume is 0.8 and there are no income taxes or imports, the balanced budget multiplier is 1.0.

7 In the short run, an increase in government purchases increases real GDP.

8 In the long run, expansionary fiscal policy increases real GDP.

9 Taxes and transfer payments that vary as income varies act as automatic stabilizers in the economy.

___ **10** An increase in lump-sum taxes shifts the *AE* curve upward and the *AD* curve leftward.

___ **11** The larger the marginal propensity to consume, the larger the government purchases multiplier becomes.

MULTIPLE CHOICE

1 Which of the following happens automatically if the economy goes into a recession?
  a government purchases of goods and services increase
  b net taxes rise
  c the deficit rises
  d lump-sum taxes fall

2 Suppose that the government purchases multiplier is 2. If government purchases increase by £10 billion but prices do not change, equilibrium expenditure
  a increases by £20 billion.
  b increases by more than £20 billion.
  c increases by less than £20 billion.
  d is unaffected.

3 Suppose that the government purchases multiplier is 2. If government purchases increase by £10 billion, in the short run, equilibrium GDP
  a increases by £20 billion.
  b increases by more than £20 billion.
  c increases by less than £20 billion.
  d is unaffected.

4 Suppose that the government purchases multiplier is 2. If government purchases increase by £10 billion and potential real GDP does not change, in the long run, equilibrium GDP
  a increases by £20 billion.
  b increases by more than £20 billion.
  c increases by less than £20 billion.
  d is unaffected.

5 Which of the following increases the multiplier?
  a an increase in the marginal propensity to import
  b an increase in the marginal tax rate
  c a decrease in the marginal propensity to consume
  d an increase in the marginal propensity to consume

Table 26.1 shows consumption, investment and government purchases in a country that has no taxes and no foreign trade (both imports and exports equal zero). Use Table 26.1 for the next five questions.

Table 26.1 Aggregate Expenditure

Real GDP	Consumption expenditure (billions of 1995 pounds)	Investment	Government purchases
4	2.0	1	1
5	2.5	1	1
6	3.0	1	1
7	3.5	1	1
8	4.0	1	1

6 What is the aggregate expenditure when GDP equals £7 billion?
  a £7 billion
  b £5.5 billion
  c £3.5 billion
  d £1 billion

7 What is the equilibrium level of expenditure?
  a £7 billion
  b £6 billion
  c £5 billion
  d £4 billion

8 What is the *MPC*?
  a 1.00
  b 0.90
  c 0.50
  d £4 billion

9 What is the government purchases multiplier?
  a 0.5
  b 2.0
  c 5.0
  d 10.0

10 If government purchases increase by £1 billion, before the price level changes, what is the new equilibrium level of expenditure?
  a £7 billion
  b £6 billion
  c £5 billion
  d £4 billion

For the next three questions, there are no income taxes and no foreign trade.

11 If the *MPC* is 0.9, what is the lump-sum multiplier?
 a 10.0
 b 9.0
 c –9.0
 d –10.0

12 If the *MPC* is 0.9, what is the government purchases multiplier?
 a 10.0
 b 9.0
 c –9.0
 d –10.0

13 If the *MPC* is 0.8, what is the government purchases multiplier?
 a 10.0
 b 8.0
 c 5.0
 d –9.0

14 Which of the following is largest?
 a government spending
 b government tax revenues
 c the budget deficit or surplus
 d the government's debt

SHORT ANSWER

1 Explain why the multiplier effect on real GDP from an expansionary fiscal policy is smaller when the aggregate supply curve is considered. If the expansionary policy has no incentive effects on aggregate supply, what is the long-run multiplier for real GDP?

2 Suppose that an expansionary fiscal policy has incentive effects that increase aggregate supply. How does the effect on the price level and real GDP of this policy compare with that of a policy that has no supply side effects? What is the long-run multiplier when the policy has incentive effects?

3 Briefly explain whether the following events will shift the *AE* curve and/or the *AD* curve. (For each case, assume that other variables remain constant.)
 a a rise in the price level
 b a rise in expected future profits for businesses
 c a tax cut
 d an increase in government purchases
 e an increase in government purchases combined with an equal increase in lump-sum taxes

PROBLEMS

1 Igor has been elected finance minister of Transylvania. Igor's first action is to hire a crack team of economists and to tell them that he wants a prediction of Transylvania's equilibrium expenditure for next year.
 a The economists compile their estimates of next year's real GDP, consumption expenditure, investment and government purchases. These data are shown in Table 26.2. (The stake is the unit of currency in Transylvania.) Transylvania has no foreign trade. Unfortunately, the economists lost their calculator and need your help to complete Table 26.3, which lists real GDP and aggregate expenditure.
 b Based on Table 26.3, what is equilibrium expenditure in Transylvania predicted to be?

Table 26.2 Expenditure in Transylvania

Real GDP	Consumption expenditure (billions of 1995 stakes)	Investment	Government purchases
1.0	0.8	0.3	0.1
1.5	1.2	0.3	0.1
2.0	1.6	0.3	0.1
2.5	2.0	0.3	0.1
3.0	2.4	0.3	0.1
3.5	2.8	0.3	0.1

Table 26.3 Aggregate Expenditure in Transylvania

Real GDP (billions of 1995 stakes)	Aggregate expenditure (billions of 1995 stakes)
1.0	
1.5	
2.0	
2.5	
3.0	
3.5	

2 The economy is in long-run equilibrium. The aggregate supply curve is AE_0, as shown in Fig. 26.1, and the aggregate demand curve is AD_0, as shown in Fig. 26.2. The *MPC* is 0.75, and the government then lowers its lump-sum taxes by $2 billion. There are no income taxes and no imports.

Figure 26.1

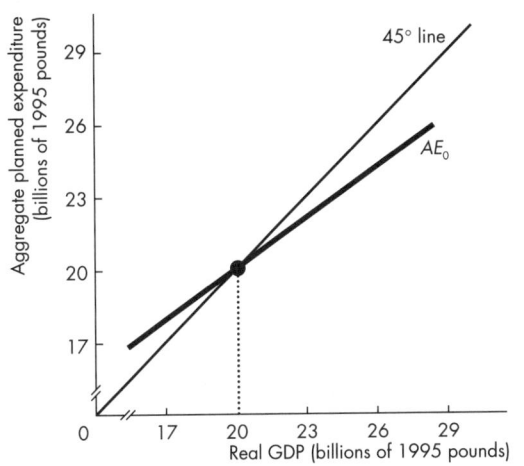

c In the long run, ignoring any incentive effects on the supply side, what is the effect on the price level? On real GDP? Without drawing it, what happens to the *AE* curve in Fig. 26.1? Does the *AD* curve in Fig. 26.2 shift as a result of the change in the price level?

DISCUSSION QUESTION

1 Explain why the interest payments on the government debt are not necessarily harmful to the economy as a whole.

DATA QUESTIONS

Figure 26.2

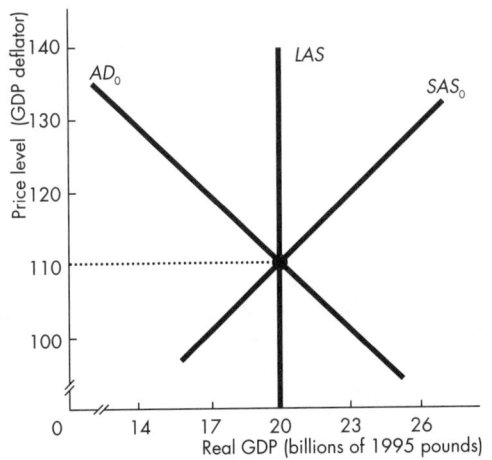

Do Tax Cuts Promote Economic Growth?
Economic theory suggests that lower tax rates could boost growth in several ways. For example, they might encourage people to work harder, and they might stimulate savings and investment.

So much for theory. Is there empirical evidence to support it? Cross-country comparisons do not provide much evidence that tax cuts boost growth. Comparing average growth rates and average tax burdens of OECD countries does appear to give some support to the idea. Unfortunately, this simple correlation does not mean much because so many factors influence a country's growth rate, notably initial income levels. Poorer countries are more likely to grow faster than rich ones.

Such intercountry studies also have a big drawback: they typically measure a country's average tax burden when it is the marginal ones which matter. So even if spending is cut, the economic evidence still suggests that, on their own, tax cuts will make little difference to long-term growth.

Source: Adapted from *The Economist*, 24 August 1996, p. 74. © *The Economist*, London, (24 August 1996).

a In Figs 26.1 and 26.2, show the initial effect of the decrease in lump-sum taxes on the aggregate expenditure curve and aggregate demand curve. Draw your answers for the period of time over which the price level does not change.

b From Fig. 26.2, what is the short-run effect on the price level and real GDP? Label the short-run equilibrium *a*. Without drawing it, explain the effect of the change in the price level on the *AE* curve in Fig. 26.1.

1 Summarize the theory which suggests that lower taxes might encourage growth.

2 Why do marginal tax rates matter more than average rates?

ANSWERS

CONCEPT REVIEW

1 deficit

2 multiplier

3 stabilizers; spending; tax

4 multiplier

5 goods; transfer; debt

6 reduces

7 stabilizers

8 GDP; price

TRUE OR FALSE

1 T Simultaneously increasing government spending and lump-sum taxes is an example of a balanced budget change; equilibrium aggregate expenditure – and hence aggregate demand – increases by an amount equal to the change in spending (and taxes).

2 F *Income* taxes are automatic stabilizers, falling when income decreases and rising when income increases.

3 T Definition.

4 T The government purchases multiplier is
$\dfrac{1}{(1 - MPC)}$ or, in this case, $\dfrac{1}{(1 - 0.8)} = 5.0$.

5 T The lump-sum tax multiplier is
$-\dfrac{MPC}{(1 - MPC)}$, or $-\dfrac{0.8}{(1 - 0.8)} = -4.0$.

6 T The balanced budget multiplier always equals 1.0.

7 T An increase in government purchases shifts the *AD* curve rightward and, in the short run, increases real GDP.

8 T If incentive effects increase potential GDP and thereby shift the *LAS* curve rightward, real GDP increases in the long run. But with no incentive effects, potential GDP does not change and real GDP does not increase in the long run.

9 T By changing with real GDP, both taxes and transfer payments help limit the fluctuations in disposable income and thereby reduce business cycle fluctuations.

10 F An increase in taxes shifts the *AD* curve leftward but shifts the *AE* curve downward.

11 T The larger the *MPC*, the more people change their consumption expenditure when their disposable income changes, increasing the government purchases multiplier.

MULTIPLE CHOICE

1 c During a recession, tax revenues fall and transfer expenditures rise, thereby increasing the budget deficit.

2 a When the price level is constant, equilibrium expenditure (or, equivalently, the shift in the *AD* curve) equals the government purchases multiplier times the change in government purchases, or 2 × $10 billion = $20 billion.

3 c The *AD* curve shifts rightward by $20 billion and, in the short run, the equilibrium point moves along the upward-sloping *SAS* curve so that the equilibrium level of real GDP increases by less than $20 billion.

4 d In the long run, the equilibrium returns to potential GDP, so if potential GDP does not change, neither does real GDP.

5 d When the marginal propensity to consume increases, each change in disposable income induces a larger change in consumption expenditure, so the multiplier is larger.

6 b Aggregate expenditure equals the sum of consumption expenditure, investment and government purchases, so when real GDP equals $7 billion, aggregate expenditure equals $3.5 billion + $1 billion + $1 billion, or $5.5 billion.

7 d Equilibrium expenditure is the level of aggregate expenditure that equals real GDP. In Table 26.1, when real GDP is $4 billion, aggregate expenditure also equals $4 billion, the level of equilibrium expenditure.

8 c The *MPC* equals $(\Delta C)/(\Delta YD)$. With no taxes, real GDP equals disposable income. Hence when real GDP changes by $1 billion, consumption expenditure changes by $0.5 billion, so the *MPC* equals $0.5 billion/$1 billion, or 0.50.

9 b The government purchases multiplier is
$$\frac{1}{(1 - MPC)}.$$
Hence, with an *MPC* of 0.50, the government purchases multiplier is 2.0.

10 b The equilibrium level of expenditure has increased by an amount equal to the government purchases multiplier times the change in government purchases, or $2 \times \pounds 1$ billion, so the new equilibrium is $\pounds 6$ billion. Alternatively, $\pounds 1$ billion can be added to the schedule of government purchases in Table 26.1. Then the equilibrium expenditure becomes $\pounds 6$ billion, the level of real GDP that creates a (new) level of aggregate expenditure equal to real GDP.

11 c The lump-sum tax multiplier is

$$-\frac{MPC}{(1-MPC)} \text{, which equals } -\frac{9.0}{(1-0.9)} = -9.0.$$

12 a The government purchases multiplier is

$$\frac{1}{(1-MPC)}.$$

When $MPC = 0.9$, this multiplier is

$$\frac{1}{(1-0.9)} = 10.0.$$

13 c The answer to **12** shows how to calculate the government spending multiplier. Comparing the answers to **12** and **13** shows that the smaller the MPC is, the smaller the government purchases multiplier becomes.

14 d Government (national) debt is far larger. Government budget deficit (or surplus) is the smallest of these items.

SHORT ANSWER

1 The multiplier indicates the size of the change in real GDP relative to the size of an initial change in autonomous expenditure, as long as the price level does not change. More generally, the multiplier indicates the size of the shift in the AD curve. The AS curve shows that the price level rises as aggregate demand increases. The rise in the price level lowers aggregate expenditure, leading to a smaller increase in real GDP than if the price level had remained constant. Indeed, in the long run, the economy returns to potential GDP. In the absence of effects on aggregate supply, the long-run multiplier is zero.

2 If the expansionary fiscal policy has incentive effects that increase aggregate supply, not only does the AD curve shift rightward, but so too do the aggregate supply curves. As a result, the rise in the price level is less and the increase in real GDP is greater when the aggregate supply curves shift. Indeed, if potential real GDP increases as a result of the incentive effects, the long-run multiplier exceeds zero because real GDP increases in the long run.

3 In general, any change that changes autonomous spending shifts the AE curve. Therefore all the changes shift the AE curve. Any change in autonomous expenditure not caused by a change in the price level shifts the AD curve. Therefore **a** involves a movement along the AD curve, and **b–e** create shifts in the AD curve.

  a The rise in the price level shifts the AE curve downward and creates a movement upward along the AD curve.

  b The rise in future expected profits increases investment, thereby shifting the AE curve upward and the AD curve rightward.

  c The decrease in taxes increases consumption expenditure, and shifts the AE curve upward and the AD curve rightward.

  d An increase in government purchases shifts the AE curve upward and the AD curve rightward.

  e A simultaneous increase in government purchases and lump-sum taxes shifts the AE curve upward and the AD curve rightward.

PROBLEMS

Table 26.4 Aggregate Expenditure in Transylvania

Real GDP (billions of 1995 stakes)	Aggregate expenditure (billions of 1995 stakes)
1.0	1.2
1.5	1.6
2.0	2.0
2.5	2.4
3.0	2.8
3.5	3.2

1 a Table 26.4 shows the aggregate expenditure schedule in Transylvania. The schedule is computed by adding consumption expenditure, investment and government purchases. For example, when real GDP is 3.5 billion stakes, aggregate expenditure equals the sum of consumption expenditure, 2.8 billion stakes, investment, 0.3 billion stakes, and government purchases, 0.1 billion stakes, or 3.2 billion stakes.

  b Equilibrium expenditure is 2 billion stakes, because that level of real GDP equals aggregate expenditure.

2 a Figures 26.3 and 26.4 show the effect of the tax reduction on the AE and AD curves.

  In Fig. 26.3, the $\pounds 2$ billion reduction in taxes raises disposable income by $\pounds 2$ billion. From the $\pounds 2$ billion increase, with the MPC equal to 0.75, $0.75 \times \pounds 2$ billion, or $\pounds 1.5$ billion goes to increased consumption expenditure. Hence, as shown in Fig. 26.3, the AE curve shifts upward (by $\pounds 1.5$ billion, the length of the small arrow) to AE_1. Figure 26.3 also shows that the increase in equilibrium expenditure is £6 billion, from £20 billion to £26 billion. Alternatively, the £6 billion increase in equilibrium expenditure equals the reduction in taxes, –£2 billion, multiplied by the lump-sum tax multiplier,

$$-\frac{MPC}{(1-MPC)}, \text{ which is } -3.0.$$

In Fig. 26.4, the aggregate demand curve shifts rightward, from AD_0 to AD_1. As shown by the length of the double-headed arrow, the extent of the rightward shift is £6 billion, the increase in equilibrium expenditure.

Figure 26.3

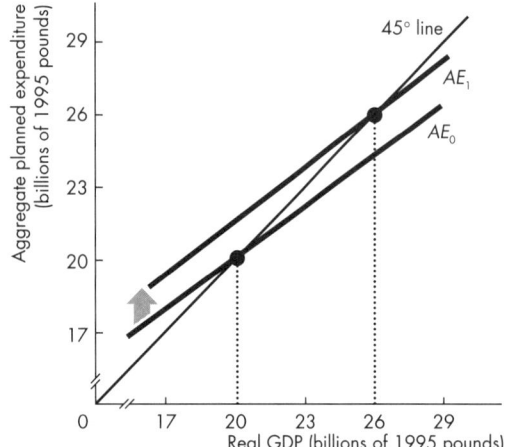

Figure 26.4

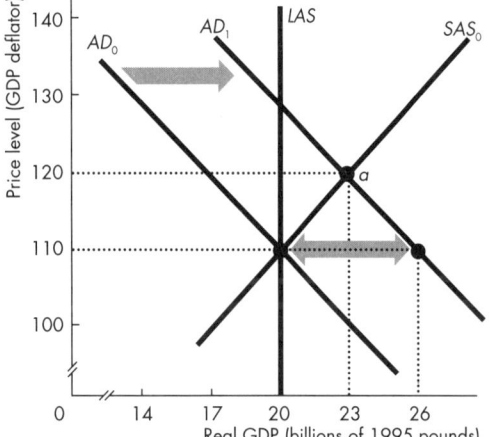

b In Fig. 26.4, the short-run equilibrium point is at a. The price level rises to 120, and real GDP increases to £23 billion. The increase in the price level from 110 to 120 decreases aggregate expenditure; that is, in Fig. 26.3, the AE curve shifts downward from AE_1. Indeed, the AE curve shifts downward enough so that the equilibrium level of expenditure is £23 billion, the same level as real GDP in Fig. 26.4.

Figure 26.5

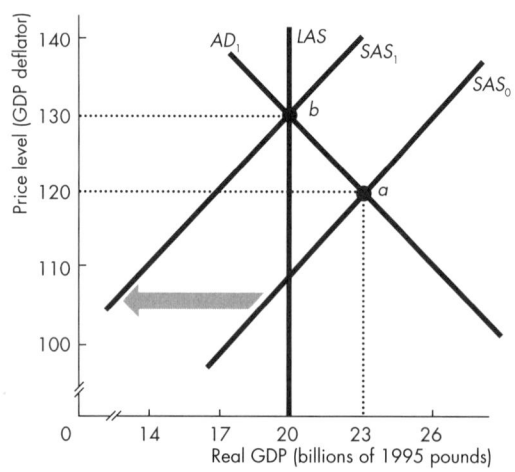

c In the long run, the economy returns to potential GDP. Hence in the absence of any supply side effects, as money wages rise and the SAS curve shifts leftward, the equilibrium eventually returns to the point where the AD curve crosses the LAS curve (point b in Fig. 26.5). In the long run, the price level equals 130 and real GDP equals £20 billion. The rise in the price level decreases aggregate expenditure, so the AE curve in Fig. 26.3 continues to shift downward. Eventually, when the long-run equilibrium is reached, the AE curve has shifted all the way back to AE_0. At this point, equilibrium expenditure is the same as initially, £20 billion, which also equals the level of potential GDP. The AD curve does *not* shift as a result of the higher price level.

DISCUSSION QUESTION

1 Who exactly receives the interest that is paid on government debt? It's the people who own the debt, who are mainly nationals of the country concerned. Look at the issue like this. UK citizens pay taxes that go towards paying the interest on the government's debt. However,

UK citizens also receive most of these interest payments. So some people pay the interest (through taxes) and other people receive the interest payments.

DATA QUESTIONS

1 The theory that tax cuts lead to economic growth depends in large part on how the labour market reacts. A tax cut will cause some people, particularly women, to join the labour market, and also cause others to work more since they will receive more money. On the other hand, this higher income will cause some people to choose more leisure. There will also be effects on savings and investment. The main text, page 782–785 deals with the determinants of investment in some detail.

2 Marginal matters more than average because decisions are taken at the margin. Whatever the average rate of tax, a person will ask the question: 'If I work extra hours, how will this affect my income?' In other words, the crucial factor will be the marginal effect

Part 8 The Central Bank and Monetary Policy

Looking back to Part 7 (Chapters 21–26)

These chapters form an introduction to macroeconomics. The first of these, Chapter 21, introduced the main policy areas and you should now be familiar with the two policy areas, fiscal and monetary policy.

Chapter 22 was rather technical, since it was concerned with measuring variables such as GDP and inflation. This is important since precision is characteristic of science, so you should know how these statistics are compiled and also their limitations.

Chapter 23 brought a discussion of two very important policy areas: inflation and unemployment. If you have read this carefully, you should now know about such things as efficiency wages, frictional unemployment and the natural rate of unemployment.

Chapter 24 develops two very useful theoretical tools: aggregate demand and aggregate supply. These will be used frequently in the rest of the book, so you should know their determinants and be able to explain macroeconomic equilibrium.

After reading Chapter 25 you should understand terms such as the marginal propensity to consume and how this affects the size of various multipliers.

Chapter 26 looks in detail at fiscal policy, so can you explain the effects of fiscal policy in the short and the long run?

Questions

1 Re-read the interview with Professor Walters. What is the Walters critique?

2 Re-read the article on *Macroeconomic Revolutions* and contrast the ideas of Say and Keynes.

The Office for National Statistics (www.ons.gov.uk) is a good starting point for material on macroeconomics, as is the Treasury site (www.hm-treasury.gov.uk). The Institute of Fiscal Studies (www.ifs.org.uk/press/index.shtml) is an independent source. For European material try Eurostat (europa.eu.int/comm/eurostat). The DfEE site (www.dfee.gov.uk) also provides material on employment issues.

Looking forward to Part 8 (Chapters 27–34)

This is a long part. Chapters 27 and 28 give us our first extended look at money and banking. Perhaps the most important idea here is that banks create money. (If you close your eyes and think of 'money' you will probably picture piles of bank notes; but this would be inaccurate. This chapter will explain why.) Chapter 29 examines the interaction of fiscal and monetary policy and this analysis is then used in Chapter 30 to look at the causes of inflation

The final chapters in this part are concerned with saving and investment, with the determinants of long-term economic growth and with fluctuations in economic activity – that is, with the business cycle.

Answers

1 The Walters critique suggests that if you have a pegged exchange rate (i.e. the value of the pound is fixed, at least in the short run), then monetary policy will not work. One reason is that it will lead to massive flows of capital into and out of countries because there will be very large differences in interest rates between countries.

2 Say's law was that supply creates its own demand. His argument was that production creates incomes that are sufficient to buy everything that is produced. Keynes argued that this was not correct – some incomes will be spent on imports, saved or taken in taxes so that supply would exceed demand. Instead, production depends on effective demand. The implication of this is that governments should intervene in the economy to stimulate demand when there is a recession.

Chapter 27 **Money**

Chapter in Perspective, Text Pages 656–685

What exactly is money and what are its functions? How does a particular monetary system arise? What role do banks play in the creation of money? These are a few of the important issues addressed in this chapter.

Our major reason for pursuing a deeper understanding of money and banks, however, is to help us understand the connection between money and macroeconomic activity, especially the behaviour of the price level. This is done using one of the most famous and influential theories in economics: the quantity theory of money.

Helpful Hints

1 What is money? You should be able to answer this question on several levels. First, at the level of general definition: money is a medium of exchange, and so on. Second, at the level of classification: currency notes are money but cheques are not. Third, at the level of specific definitions such as M4.

2 One of the most important concepts presented in this chapter is the money multiplier process by which banks create money. There are two fundamental facts that allow banks to create money.

First, one of the liabilities of banks is money: chequeable deposits. Banks create money by creating new chequeable deposits. Second, banks hold fractional reserves. This means that when a bank receives a deposit, it will hold only part of it as reserves and can loan out the rest. Note that the bank is not indulging in a scam – it is still maintaining assets (reserves plus loans) to match its liabilities (the deposits). When that loan is spent, at least part of the proceeds are likely to be deposited in another bank, creating a new deposit (money).

The money multiplier process follows from this last fact: banks make loans when they receive new deposits and these loans are spent and will return to another bank, creating another new deposit. The process then repeats itself, adding more money (but in progressively smaller amounts) in each round. Practise going through examples until the process becomes second nature.

3 Why does the aggregate demand curve shift to the right when there is an increase in the quantity of money?

For the answer, we return to the discussion of aggregate demand in Chapter 24. There we discovered that an increase in the quantity of *real* money caused aggregate demand to increase for two reasons. The first was the real money balances effect and the second was the intertemporal substitution effect, which is a result of the fact that interest rates will fall when real money increases.

At a given price level, an increase in the quantity of money is an increase in the quantity of real money. Thus aggregate demand increases through these two effects and, since the price level is given, the aggregate demand curve shifts to the right.

4 Analysts often use the quantity theory to help shape their thinking about future inflation. In particular, they look at the rate of growth of money supply to help predict whether the inflation rate is likely to rise or fall, although you should note that the relationship is not always precise or constant.

SELF-TEST

CONCEPT REVIEW

1 Money is defined by its main function: money is a(n) _____ _____ _____ . This means that money is anything that is generally acceptable in exchange for goods and services.

2 Money has four functions, the first of which gives the definition of money. It also serves as a medium of _____ , a(n) _____ of account and a(n) _____ _____ _____ .

3 Money takes four different forms. A physical commodity that is valued in its own right and also serves as a medium of exchange is called _____ money. A paper claim to a commodity that circulates as money is called _____ _____ money. An intrinsically worthless (or almost worthless) commodity that serves the functions of money is called _____ money. Lastly, a loan that the borrower promises to pay on demand which is used by the lender in exchange for goods and services is called _____ money.

4 A firm that takes deposits from households and firms and makes loans to other households and firms is called a(n)_____ _____ .

5 Assets that can be quickly converted into a medium of exchange at a reasonably certain price are known as _____ assets. The degree to which an asset has this property is known as _____ .

6 The fraction of a bank's total deposits that are actually held in reserves is called the _____ _____ . The ratio of reserves to deposits that a bank regards as necessary to conduct business is called the _____ _____ _____ . Actual reserves minus desired reserves equal _____ _____ .

7 The proposition that an increase in money leads to an equal percentage increase in the price level is the _____ theory of _____ . Its original basis follows from certain propositions about the equation of _____ . This equation is true by definition since one of its components is defined by it. This component, the _____ of circulation, is the average number of times a pound is used annually to buy the goods and services that make up GDP.

TRUE OR FALSE

1 Barter can take place only if there is a double coincidence of wants.

2 Money is anything that is generally acceptable as a medium of exchange.

3 Unpredictable changes in the rate of inflation enhance the function of money as a standard of deferred payment.

4 Only money serves as a store of value.

5 Gresham's law implies that money that has *not* been debased (good money) will tend to drive debased money (bad money) out of circulation.

6 If a depositor withdraws currency from a bank, that bank's reserve ratio declines.

7 The simple money multiplier is equal to 1 divided by the desired reserve ratio.

8 Other things remaining the same, the currency drain makes the real-world money multiplier larger than the simple money multiplier.

___ **9** An increase in the quantity of money shifts the aggregate demand curve rightward.

___ **10** According to the quantity theory of money, in the long run, an increase in the quantity of money will cause the price level to rise but will leave real GDP unchanged.

___ **11** The quantity theory of money implies that a 10 per cent increase in the quantity of money will cause a 10 per cent increase in the price level.

___ **12** If the quantity of money is £50 billion and nominal GDP is £200 billion, the velocity of circulation is $1/4$.

___ **13** On average, the money supply growth rate is exceeded by the inflation rate.

MULTIPLE CHOICE

1 Which of the following is *not* one of the four functions of money?
 a medium of exchange
 b measure of liquidity
 c standard of deferred payment
 d store of value
 e unit of account

2 When a contract specifies that a certain number of pounds are to be paid in the future for services rendered, money is functioning as a
 a medium of exchange.
 b measure of liquidity.
 c unit of account.
 d store of value.
 e standard of deferred payment.

3 If the prices of goods and services were stated in terms of pounds of salt, then salt is a
 a unit of account.
 b standard of deferred payment.
 c store of value.
 d quasi-money.
 e medium of exchange.

4 UK currency today is an example of
 a fiat money.
 b commodity money.
 c convertible paper money.
 d private debt money.
 e fractionally backed gold-convertible money.

5 A chequeable deposit in a financial institution is an example of
 a commodity money.
 b fiat money.
 c convertible paper money.
 d private debt money.
 e public debt money.

6 Which of the following is an example of quasi-money or 'almost' money?
 a credit cards
 b demand deposits
 c term deposits
 d other chequeable deposits
 e savings deposits

7 A bank can create money by
 a selling some of its investment securities.
 b increasing its reserves.
 c lending its excess reserves.
 d printing more cheques.
 e converting reserves into securities.

8 If all banks hold 100 per cent reserves, what is the simple money multiplier?
 a 0
 b 1
 c 10
 d 100
 e infinite

9 Which of the following equations is correct?
 a $V = PY/M$
 b $V = MP/Y$
 c $V = YM/P$
 d none of the above

SHORT ANSWER

1 What is meant by a double coincidence of wants?

2 What are the four principal functions of money?

3 Explain why credit cards are not money.

4 How do banks create money?

5 According to the quantity theory of money, what is the effect of an increase in the quantity of money?

6 Which of the functions of money does the inflation discussed in the *Reading Between the Lines* article prevent from functioning?

PROBLEMS

1 Suppose an individual sells £1,000 worth of government securities to the Bank of England and deposits the proceeds (£1,000) in Bank 1. Note that this new deposit initially increases the quantity of money by £1,000. Assume that the desired reserve ratio for all banks is 20 per cent (0.2). Also assume that there is no currency drain. As it stands, Table 27.1 gives information for the first round of the money expansion process that will be generated by this new deposit.

   a Follow the first six rounds of the money creation process by completing the six rows of Table 27.1.

Table 27.1 Money Creation Process – No Currency Drain

Bank number	New deposits (pounds)	New loans (pounds)	New reserves (pounds)	Cumulative Increase in money (pounds)	Increase (pounds)
1	1,000	800	200	1,000	1,000
2					
3					
4					
5					
6					

   b What is the total increase in the quantity of money after six rounds?

   c What is the money multiplier?

   d After all rounds have been completed, what will the total increase in money be?

2 Suppose there is a decrease in the quantity of money. Using an aggregate demand–aggregate supply model, show what happens to the price level and the level of real GDP in the short run and in the long run.

3 We observe an economy in which the price level is 1.5, real GDP is £240 billion and the money supply is £60 billion.

   a What is the velocity of circulation?

   b According to the quantity theory of money, what will be the result of an increase in the quantity of money to £80 billion?

DISCUSSION QUESTION

1 Why have many banks gone bankrupt in the past? Is this likely to reoccur?

DATA QUESTIONS

Money and prices

Table 27.2

Year	Quantity of money (M4 £000 million)	Index of Retail Prices (1985 = 100)
1981	129	79.1
1982	155	85.8
1983	175	89.8
1984	199	94.3
1985	226	100
1986	262	103.4
1987	304	107.7
1988	358	113.0
1989	422	121.8
1990	473	133.3
1991	501	141.1
1992	519	146.4
1993	545	149.2
1994	568	152.8
1995	623	145.8
1996	683	147.4
1997	722	153.3
1998	782	157.1

Source: Economic Trends, HMSO, 1999.

1 Explain what is meant by

   a M4.

   b Index of Retail Prices (1985=100).

2 Outline the quantity theory of money. Comment on this theory in the light of the figures in Table 27.2.

ANSWERS

CONCEPT REVIEW

1 means of payment

2 exchange; unit; store of value

3 commodity; convertible paper; fiat; deposit

4 financial intermediary

5 liquid; liquidity

6 reserve ratio; desired reserve ratio; excess reserves

7 quantity; money; exchange; velocity

TRUE OR FALSE

1 **T** Buyer must be selling what seller wants to buy and vice versa.

2 **T** Basic function of money.

3 **F** Unpredictable inflation makes it difficult to sign long-term contracts eroding value of money as a standard of deferred payments.

4 **F** Other assets (such as land) can act as store of value.

5 **F** Agents keep more valuable good money and circulate less valuable bad money.

6 **T** Currency is part of reserve ratio.

7 **T** Definition – see text for explanation.

8 **F** Currency drain makes money multiplier smaller.

9 **T** Increase in money supply causes *MD* to shift to rightward for real money balances effect and intertemporal substitution effect.

10 **T** True in the very long run.

11 **T** Theory assumes that V and Y are independent of money supply so that change in money leads to proportionate change in prices.

12 **F** $V = PT/M = 200/50 = 4$.

13 **F** See Data Questions for evidence.

MULTIPLE CHOICE

1 **b** Definition of a function.

2 **e** Payment is deferred.

3 **a** Definition.

4 **a** Definition.

5 **d** Definition.

6 **a** Most readily changed into currency.

7 **c** Lending its reserves is done by crediting borrower's deposits, creating more deposits = more money.

8 **b** Multiplier = 1/(desired reserve ratio) = 1/1 = 1.

9 **a** Definition.

SHORT ANSWER

1 A double coincidence of wants occurs in barter when an individual who has good A and wants to trade for good B finds an individual who has good B and wants to trade for good A.

2 The four principal functions of money are: medium of exchange; unit of account; standard of deferred payment; store of value.

3 A credit card is not money, but rather a mechanism for borrowing money, which must later be repaid. The repayment of money takes place when the credit card bill is paid by cheque.

4 Banks create money by making new loans. When the proceeds of these loans are spent, the person receiving the money will deposit much of it in a bank deposit which is new money.

5 According to the quantity theory of money, an increase in the quantity of money will cause the price level to increase by an equal percentage amount.

6 Rampant inflation such as that which occurred in Brazil is harmful largely because it prevents money fulfilling its functions. In this case, money cannot be used as a store of value or as a standard for deferred payment because it loses its value. It can be used as a unit of account, but with difficulty; for example, account holders have to be compensated for inflation. Money can still be used as a medium of exchange, but again with difficulty since no one wants to hold money.

PROBLEMS

1 **a** Table 27.1 is completed as Table 27.3. Note that 80 per cent of each new deposit will be loaned out and 20 per cent will be held as reserves. When a new loan is deposited in a bank, it becomes a new deposit and thus money.

Table 27.3 Money Creation Process – No Currency Drain

				Cumulative	
Bank number	New deposits (pounds)	New loans (pounds)	New reserves (pounds)	Increase in money (pounds)	Increase (pounds)
1	1,000.00	800.00	200.00	1,000.00	1,000.00
2	800.00	640.00	160.00	800.00	1,800.00
3	640.00	512.00	128.00	640.00	2,440.00
4	512.00	409.60	102.40	512.00	2,952.00
5	409.60	327.68	81.92	409.60	3,361.60
6	327.68	262.14	65.54	327.68	3,689.28

   b After six rounds the total (cumulative) increase in the quantity of money is £3,689.28. This is obtained from the last column of Table 27.3.

   c The money multiplier in this case is the simple money multiplier given by:

$$\text{Simple money multiplier} = \frac{1}{\text{Desired reserve ratio}}$$

Since the desired reserve ratio is 0.2, the simple money multiplier is 5.

   d The total increase in money will be £5,000 after all rounds are completed. This is obtained by multiplying the initial increase in deposits (£1,000) by the simple money multiplier (5).

2 The consequences of a decrease in the quantity of money are illustrated in Fig. 27.1. The economy is initially in long-run equilibrium at point a, the intersection of AD_0 and SAS_0 (and LAS). The price level is P_0 and GDP is at its full-employment level, Y.

   A decrease in the quantity of money will shift the AD curve to the left, from AD_0 to AD_1. The new short-run equilibrium is at point b. The price level falls to P_1 and real GDP falls to Y_1. In the long run, however, input prices will also fall, which will shift the SAS curve down, from SAS_0 to SAS_1. A new long-run equilibrium is achieved at point c. Thus in the long run, the price level falls further to P_2, while real GDP returns to its initial level, Y.

3 **a** From the equation of exchange, we know that the velocity of circulation is defined by:

$$\text{Velocity of circulation} = \frac{\text{Price level} \times \text{Real GDP}}{\text{Quantity of money}}$$

With the values for the price level, real GDP and the quantity of money given in this problem, we have:

$$\text{Velocity of circulation} = \frac{1.5 \times 240}{60} = \frac{360}{60} - 6$$

   b The quantity theory of money predicts that an increase in the quantity of money will cause an equal percentage increase in the price level. An increase in

money from £60 billion to £80 billion is a one-third (33 per cent) increase. Thus the quantity theory of money predicts that the price level will rise by one-third (33 per cent). Since the initial price level is 1.5, the predicted price level will be 2.0.

Figure 27.1

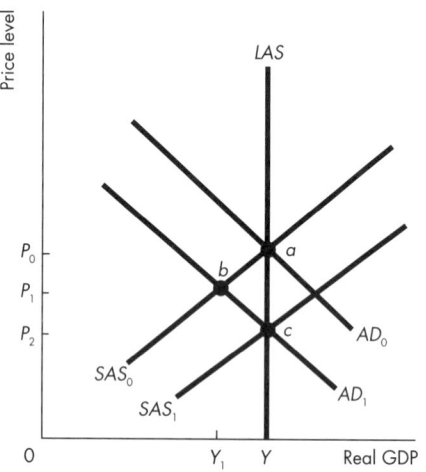

DISCUSSION QUESTION

1 In the past, many banks have gone bust because they have not kept sufficient reserves and there has been a crisis of confidence so that savers have wanted their money back. Since this had been lent out, the banks were unable to repay depositors and so became bankrupt.

   This does not happen now; bank supervision is better and the government guarantees deposits.

DATA QUESTIONS

1 **a** 'M4' is a measure of the money supply in the United Kingdom, which includes cash held outside the Bank of England by the public as well as all sterling deposits at banks and building societies.

   b The Index of Retail Prices is a measure of the change in consumer prices paid by a typical household in the United Kingdom. '1985=100' means that 1985 has been chosen as the base year.

2 The quantity theory of money suggests that an increase in the quantity of money leads to an equal increase in the price level. The theory is discussed in detail in the main text, pages 674–678.

Figure 27.2 takes the data in Table 27.2 and converts the figures into percentage changes in order to make comparisons.

At first sight, the diagram does not give any support to the quantity theory. The increases in the quantity of money are always larger than the changes in the retail price index. However, supporters of the quantity theory would point out that the pattern of the curves is similar; for example, M4 began rising in 1985 and the rate of inflation rose in the years after 1986. Moreover, the theory suggests that price rises will be equal to changes in the money supply *in the long run*, and this may not be apparent in a fairly short set of figures. Also, M4 may not be the most appropriate measure of money, and the Retail Price Index may not be an accurate measure of price changes.

Figure 27.2

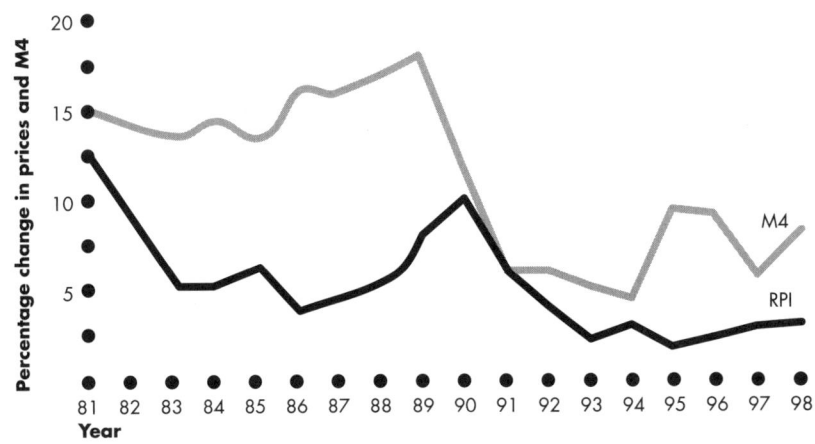

Chapter 28 The Central Bank and Monetary Policy

Chapter in Perspective, Text Pages 686–719

In Chapter 27 we discovered that a new bank deposit will, as it works its way through the banking system, cause a total increase in the quantity of money that is a multiple of the initial new deposit. But how might that new money-creating deposit arise? In this chapter, we find that a central bank, through its use of monetary policy tools, can create such new deposits and thus influence the quantity of money.

The reason we are so interested in the quantity of money, of course, is that changes in the quantity of money can have important effects on real GDP and the price level. For example, an increase in the quantity of money will increase aggregate demand, thus causing the price level to increase and the level of real GDP to increase, at least in the short run.

How does an increase in the quantity of money affect aggregate demand? We will learn that an increase in the quantity of money will cause an increase in aggregate expenditure primarily through its ability to lower interest rates. Then the question becomes: how does a change in the quantity of money cause interest rates to change? A major purpose of this chapter is to present a model that will allow us to explain the determination of interest rates and how these affect the economy.

Helpful Hints

1 One restriction on UK monetary policy is created by the international nature of the UK economy – this will be discussed in later chapters. The fact that UK citizens and foreigners can easily switch between UK and foreign assets is a crucial constraint on policy choices, as we shall see.

2 One of a central bank's most important tasks is to control the money supply. It uses four methods: credit ceilings, changing asset requirements, changing interest rates and open market operations. Since no method is perfect, the actual methods adopted vary over the years, and you should understand all four.

To remember whether an open market purchase will lead to a decrease or an increase in money, it may be helpful to think of open market operations as an exchange of government securities for cash. For example, think of an open market purchase as the Bank of England acquiring government securities by giving cash to the public. Thus the money supply will increase.

3 Ordinary use of the term *money* does not make some of the important distinctions that are made in economics. To avoid confusion regarding the concept of the demand for money, it is important that these distinctions are clear.

For example, we often talk about our income as the amount of *money* we make over a certain period of time. When we use the term in this context, we are speaking of money as a flow – a quantity received over some period of time.

On the other hand, we may talk about how much money we have in our bank account or in our wallet at a certain point in time. In this context we are speaking of money as a stock – a quantity at a point in time. The distinction between these two concepts can be important.

To avoid potential confusion, economists rarely use the term money when referring to a flow. Instead, they will use less ambiguous alternative terms like income or wage. In this chapter, money always refers to a stock. When we talk about the demand for money we are talking about the desire to hold a stock of money and not spend it. (However, it *is* being held for future spending purposes.)

SELF-TEST

CONCEPT REVIEW

1 The attempt by the Bank of England to control inflation and reduce business cycle fluctuations by changing the quantity of money and adjusting interest rates is called _____ _____ .

2 The functions of the Bank of England include acting as _____ to the government and managing _____ policy.

3 The Bank of England uses three main policy tools. It can change required reserve _____ and also the _____ _____ on lending of last resort. The third tool involves the purchase and sale of government securities by the Bank of England. It is called _____ _____ _____ .

4 The four factors that influence the quantity of money people choose to hold are the _____ level, the _____ rate, real _____ and financial innovation.

5 The relationship between the quantity of real money demanded and the interest rate, holding other things constant, is called the _____ for _____ _____ .

6 An increase in real income will shift the demand curve for real money to the _____ ,

and, if the supply of real money is constant, will cause the equilibrium interest rate to _____ .

7 The amount by which an initial increase in bank reserves is multiplied to calculate the effect on total bank deposits is called the _____ _____ multiplier. This multiplier will be larger, the _____ is the desired reserve ratio.

8 A change in the real interest rate changes the opportunity cost of the following two components of aggregate expenditure: _____ expenditure and _____ .

9 When the UK interrerst rate rises, if other factors remain unchanged, then the pound sterling exchange rate _____ .

TRUE OR FALSE

1 An increase in reserve requirements is intended to increase lending by banks.

2 Bank of England notes are non-convertible.

3 The money multiplier is given as the ratio of the quantity of money to the monetary base.

___ **4** If there is an increase in the fraction of deposits that households and firms hold as currency, the money multiplier will decrease.

___ **5** The higher the banks' desired reserve ratio, the larger is the money multiplier.

___ **6** If the price level increases, there will be an increase in the nominal quantity of money people will want to hold.

___ **7** If the price level increases, there will be an increase in the real quantity of money people will want to hold.

___ **8** The velocity of circulation is given by the ratio of real GDP to real money supply.

___ **9** If interest rates rise, the velocity of circulation is likely to increase.

___ **10** If interest rates rise, the quantity of money demanded is likely to decrease.

___ **11** The development of near-money deposits and growth in the use of credit cards in recent years have caused the demand curve for real money to shift to the right.

___ **12** If the price of a bond rises, the interest rate earned on the bond falls.

___ **13** An increase in the demand for real money will cause the interest rate to fall.

___ **14** If households or firms find that they have more money than they want to hold, they will buy financial assets. This will cause the prices of financial assets to rise and the interest rates earned on those assets to fall.

___ **15** If the Bank of England wants to lower interest rates, it should sell government securities in the open market.

MULTIPLE CHOICE

1 The international nature of the UK economy
  a means the Bank of England has an expanded range of actions to choose from.
  b means the Bank of England must ignore exchange rate determination.
  c is due to the many restrictions on capital mobility set by the government.

  d means the Bank of England has no independence.
  e means the Bank of England cannot ignore interest rate pressures from EU countries.

2 A flexible exchange rate regime is one in which the
  a supply of pounds remains flexible.
  b demand for pounds remains flexible.
  c value of the exchange rate is determined by market forces.
  d value of the exchange rate is influenced by the central bank.
  e central bank defines and maintains a flexible exchange rate value.

3 A managed exchange rate regime is one in which the
  a supply of the pound is managed.
  b demand for the pound is managed.
  c value of the exchange rate is determined by market forces.
  d value of the exchange rate is influenced by the central bank.
  e central bank defines and maintains a fixed exchange rate value.

4 Which of the following would *not* affect the size of the monetary base?
  a A bank exchanges government securities for a deposit at the Bank of England.
  b A bank exchanges vault cash for a deposit at the Bank of England.
  c The Bank of England buys government securities from a bank.
  d The Bank of England buys government securities from someone other than a bank.
  e The Bank of England sells government securities to a bank.

5 An open market purchase of government securities by the Bank of England will
  a increase bank reserves and thus increase the monetary base.
  b decrease bank reserves and thus decrease the monetary base.
  c increase bank reserves and thus decrease the monetary base.
  d decrease bank reserves and thus increase the monetary base.
  e decrease bank reserves but increase the money supply if banks have excess reserves.

6 If banks want to hold 3 per cent of deposits as reserves and households and firms want to hold 10 per cent of deposits as currency, what is the money multiplier?

a 8.5

b 11.0

c 36.7

d 10.0

e 33.3

7 The money multiplier will increase if either the fraction of deposits that households and firms want to hold as currency

a increases or the desired reserve ratio increases.

b decreases or the desired reserve ratio decreases.

c decreases or the desired reserve ratio increases.

d increases or the desired reserve ratio decreases.

e none of the above.

8 The quantity of real money demanded will increase if either real income increases or the

a price level increases.

b price level decreases.

c interest rate increases.

d interest rate decreases.

e price of bonds falls.

9 Real money is equal to nominal money

a divided by real GDP.

b minus real GDP.

c divided by the price level.

d minus the price level.

e divided by velocity.

10 The higher the interest rate, the

a lower the quantity of money demanded, and the higher is the velocity of circulation.

b lower the quantity of money demanded, and the lower is the velocity of circulation.

c higher the quantity of money demanded, and the higher is the velocity of circulation.

d higher the quantity of money demanded, and the lower is the velocity of circulation.

e higher the quantity of money demanded, but the money supply remains unaffected.

11 Which of the following will cause the demand curve for real money to shift leftward?

a an increase in real GDP

b a decrease in interest rates

c the expanded use of credit cards

d an increase in the quantity of money supplied

e an increase in the price level

12 If the Bank of England buys government securities in the open market, the supply curve of real money will shift

a leftward, and the interest rate will rise.

b leftward, and the interest rate will fall.

c rightward, and the interest rate will rise.

d rightward, and the interest rate will remain constant as money demand will shift to the right as well.

e none of the above.

13 If real GDP increases, the demand curve for real money will shift

a leftward, and the interest rate will rise.

b leftward, and the interest rate will fall.

c rightward, and the interest rate will rise.

d rightward, and the interest rate will fall.

e rightward, and the interest rate will remain constant.

14 Money market equilibrium occurs

a when interest rates are constant.

b when the level of real GDP is constant.

c when money supply equals money demand.

d only under a fixed exchange rate.

e when both **a** and **b** are true.

SHORT ANSWER

1 Why do international considerations constrain the Bank of England's actions?

2 How does an open market purchase of government securities lead to an increase in the monetary base?

3 Why do people care about the quantity of real money they hold rather than the quantity of nominal money they hold?

4 Why will the quantity of real money demanded fall when the interest rate rises?

5 The market for money is initially in equilibrium when the Bank of England increases the supply of money. Explain the adjustment to a new equilibrium interest rate.

6 With regard to the *Reading Between the Lines* article, do you think that the British government should follow the Japanese example?

PROBLEMS

1 The economy is in recession. The government decides to buy securities from the public. What effect will this have?

2 Figure 28.1 illustrates the current equilibrium in the money market where *MD* is the demand curve for real money and *MS* is the supply curve for real money. Suppose that the Bank of England wants to stimulate aggregate expenditure by lowering the interest rate to 6 per cent. By how much must the Bank of England increase the nominal money supply if the price level is 2?

Figure 28.1

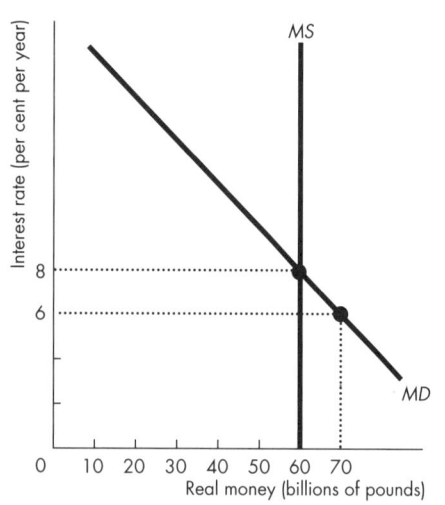

3 Having determined the amount by which the Bank of England must increase the nominal supply of money, we now want to determine the open market operation that will be necessary if the currency to deposits ratio is 0.2 and the desired reserve ratio is 0.1. Will the Bank of England need to buy or sell government securities in the open market and in what amount?

4 Given the values for the currency to deposits and desired reserve ratios assumed in Problem **3**, the round-by-round money multiplier process is examined here.

  a For the open market operation in Problem **3**, complete Table 28.1 by following the first six rounds of the process, then specify the effects in all other rounds, and finally give the total effects.

  b What is the total change in money after six rounds?

  c What is the total change in the money supply? Does this number agree with the desired change from Problem **2**?

DISCUSSION QUESTION

1 'Whenever the government runs a deficit and has to sell government securities it automatically increases the money supply.' Is this true?

Table 28.1 Money Multiplier Effects (billions of pounds)

Round	Excess reserves at start of round	New loans	Change in deposits	Change in currency	Excess reserves at end of round	Change in quantity of money
1						
2						
3						
4						
5						
6						
All others	–				–	
Totals	–				–	

DATA QUESTIONS

Problems for the European Central Bank

Economies grow at different rates. In the last few years the Irish economy has been expanding rapidly whilst Germany's has been in the doldrums.

There is also evidence to suggest that there are longer time lags between changing interest rates and the effect on output in some countries than in others. Moreover, the same change in interest rates will have greater effects in some countries than in others. For example, countries will lower levels of private sector debt will be less hurt by a rise in interest rates which countries with high private sector debt.

All this creates problems for the European Central Bank.

1 Why do time lags differ between countries?

2 What problem do these differences cause for the European Central bank?

ANSWERS

CONCEPT REVIEW

1 monetary policy

2 banker; monetary

3 ratios; interest rate; open market operations

4 price; interest; GDP

5 demand; real money

6 right; rise

7 simple money; smaller

8 consumption; investment

9 rises

TRUE OR FALSE

1 F It will decrease lending.

2 T They are not backed by gold.

3 T Definition.

4 T $mm = (1 + \Delta C/\Delta D)/(\Delta C/\Delta D + \Delta R/\Delta D)$ causes increase in CD and fall in mm.

5 F High reserve ratio means banks can lend less and so create less money.

6 T People will want to hold more money to pay higher prices.

7 F They will want to hold more money in nominal terms.

8 F $V =$ Nominal GDP$/M$.

9 T People will spend money more quickly.

10 T Because the opportunity cost of holding money will rise.

11 F Demand for money is determined by factors such as level of incomes.

12 T Inverse ratio between bond price and interest rate.

13 F Increases in demand push up prices.

14 T If demand for money exceeds supply, people will use excess to buy assets, so pushing up their price.

15 F Selling government bonds leads to fall in banks' reserves and so to fall in banks' ability to create money.

MULTIPLE CHOICE

1 e Financial markets are interdependent; hence so are interest rates.

2 c Definition.

3 d Definition.

4 b Others are all examples of open market operations.

5 a Bank of England pays for securities by crediting banks' reserves, which are part of monetary base.

6 a $mm = (1 + 0.1)/(0.1 + 0.03) = 8.5$.

7 b Both decreases mean there are more reserves to create new loans at each stage of the multiplier process.

8 d Opportunity cost of holding money will fall, so people will hold more.

9 c Definition.

10 a Rise in interest rate means rise in opportunity cost of holding money, leading to fall in demand for money and increase in velocity since velocity $= Y/MD$.

11 c Credit cards will facilitate transactions.

12 e Buying bonds leads to rise in deposits, reserves and money supply; excess supply of money leads to fall in interest rates.

13 c Rise in GDP means people want more money to finance transactions. Increase in demand for money pushes up its price.

14 c Definition.

SHORT ANSWER

1 The Bank of England is constrained by international considerations because UK citizens and foreigners can each hold deposits in the other's country. As a result, interest rates are related across borders, a factor that constrains the Bank of England's ability to manipulate domestic interest rates through monetary policy. It is also constrained by membership of the European Union.

2 An open market purchase of government securities by the Bank of England increases the monetary base by increasing one of its components: banks' deposits at the Bank of England. The process by which this takes place depends on whether the securities are purchased from banks or from the non-bank public.

If the purchase is from banks, the process is direct: the Bank of England pays for the securities by crediting the bank's deposit at the Bank of England, which directly increases the monetary base.

If the purchase is from the non-bank public, the Bank of England pays by writing cheques on itself which the sellers of the securities deposit in their banks. The banks in turn present the cheques to the Bank of England, which credits the banks' deposits at the Bank of England. Thus in either case, the monetary base increases by the amount of the open market purchase.

3 Nominal money is simply the number of pounds. Real money is a measure of what money will buy because it will fall as the price level rises and the number of pounds is constant.

What matters to people is the quantity of goods and services that money will buy, not the number of pounds. If the price level rises by 10 per cent, people will want to hold 10 per cent more pounds (given real income and interest rates) in order to retain the same purchasing power.

4 Much of what constitutes money pays no interest; for example, currency and demand deposits. The interest rate is the opportunity cost of holding money, which pays no interest since interest income on alternative financial assets that could have been held is forgone. When interest rates rise, it becomes more costly to hold money, and so people will reduce their money holdings in order to buy other financial assets and take advantage of the higher interest rates.

5 An increase in the supply of real money means that, at the current interest rate, the quantity of money supplied will be greater than the quantity of money demanded. Money holders will want to reduce their money holdings and will attempt to do so by buying bonds. The increase in the demand for bonds will cause the price of bonds to rise and thus interest rates on bonds to fall. As interest rates fall, the quantity of money demanded increases, which reduces the excess supply of money. This process continues until the interest rate has fallen sufficiently that the quantity of money demanded is the same as the quantity of money supplied.

6 Issuing gift vouchers, as the Japanese have done, might be a useful technique if the economy was expected to go into a recession. If other factors remained unchanged, the effect in the short run would be to raise prices but also to increase real GDP.

PROBLEMS

1 When the government buys securities for the public, the money will go into the bank account of people who sell the securities. The banks can now use this to make more loans, which increases the quantity of money. In turn, this will lower the rate of interest leading to more consumer spending and also more investment by firms.

2 The current equilibrium interest rate is 8 per cent and the Bank of England would like to increase the money supply sufficiently to lower the interest rate to 6 per cent. Since the quantity of real money demanded at an interest rate of 6 per cent is £70 billion, the Bank of England will want to increase the supply of real money by £10 billion: from £60 billion to £70 billion.

Real money is nominal money divided by the price level and the Bank of England controls only the supply of nominal money. Since the price level is 2, the supply of nominal money must rise by £20 billion in order to increase the supply of real money by £10 billion. Therefore, the Bank of England will need to increase the nominal money supply by £20 billion.

3 In order to increase the supply of money, the Bank of England will need to buy government securities in the open market because buying government securities will increase bank reserves and the monetary base. The amount of the open market purchase will depend on the money multiplier. Since $a = 0.2$ and $b = 0.1$, we can calculate the money multiplier as follows:

$$mm = \frac{1+a}{a+b} = \frac{1+0.2}{0.2+0.1} = 4$$

This means that any initial increase in the monetary base will generate a total increase in money equal to 4 times its size. Thus if we want a total increase in money of £20 billion, we need a £5 billion increase in the monetary base. This requires an open market purchase of £5 billion in government securities.

4 a The completed table is shown as Table 28.2. The £5 billion open market purchase will create excess reserves of £5 billion which will be loaned out; 20 per cent of the loan or £1 billion will be held as currency, the remainder will be added to deposits (£4 billion). Of this increase in deposits, 10 per cent or £0.4 billion will be held as desired reserves, and the rest (£3.6 billion) will be excess reserves at the end of round 1. This then becomes the excess reserves at the beginning of round 2 and the process continues.

In subsequent rounds we compute the various entries in the table as follows:

– Excess reserves at start of round = excess reserves at end of previous round
– New loans = excess reserves at start of round
– Change in deposits = 0.8 times new loans
– Change in currency = 0.2 times new loans
– Excess reserves at end of round = 0.9 times change in deposits
– Change in quantity of money = change in deposits + change in currency

The total effects for each relevant column are obtained by using the fact that the money multiplier is 4 (from Problem **3**) and the effect of all other rounds is the difference between the final total and the total after six rounds.

b The total change in money after six rounds is £15.25 billion, the sum of the changes in the quantity of money for rounds 1 to 6.

c The total change in the money supply is £20 billion, which can be obtained by using a money multiplier of 4. This is exactly the desired increase in the money supply from Problem **2**.

DISCUSSION QUESTION

1 The effect depends on how the deficit is funded. If the government funds a deficit by selling securities such as bonds to the commercial banks, then this will also decrease the banks' ability to create money (unless they have excess reserves). This is because they will be able to buy government bonds only at the expense of other securities or making fewer loans and in this case the money supply is not increased. However, if the banks have excess reserves, they will be able to buy bonds without reducing their holdings of other assets, so the money supply would increase. If the government sells bonds to the general public then the public gives money to the government which then spends it, that is, gives it back to the public, so there is no effect on the money supply.

However, if the government funds the deficit by selling bonds to the Bank of England, the result will be a rise in the money supply since the Bank uses newly created money to buy the bonds.

DATA QUESTIONS

1 Time lags cause problems for economic policy makers because actions taken now may not have an effect for some time – sometimes years. Lags vary between countries because financial institutions and money markets vary in their ability to respond to changing circumstances. For example, in some countries firms which cannot pay their debts to the bank will be made bankrupt very quickly. In others the process may be very slow.

2 The basic problem these difficulties cause for the European Central Bank is that actions, such as a rise in interest rates, may be required in some countries, such as those with inflationary pressures, but unsuitable for those in recession. Moreover, the fact that the effects may be stronger or quicker in some countries makes it difficult for the Bank to make decisions that are right for all countries.

Of course, this does not mean that a single currency is undesirable. The benefits may exceed these technical problems.

Table 28.2 Money Multiplier Effects (billions of pounds)

Round	Excess reserves at start of round	New loans	Change in deposits	Change in currency	Excess reserves at end of round	Change in quantity of money
1	5.00	5.00	4.00	1.00	3.60	5.00
2	3.60	3.60	2.88	0.72	2.59	3.60
3	2.59	2.59	2.07	0.52	1.86	2.59
4	1.86	1.86	1.49	0.37	1.34	1.86
5	1.34	1.34	1.07	0.27	0.96	1.34
6	0.96	0.96	0.77	0.19	0.69	0.96
All others	–	4.65	3.72	0.93	–	4.65
Totals	–	20	16	4	–	20

Chapter 29 Fiscal and Monetary Interaction

Chapter in Perspective, text pages 720–751

This chapter brings together many of the concepts introduced in earlier macro chapters. It focuses on the interaction of fiscal and monetary policy and their relative effectiveness. The chapter also discusses the Keynesian–monetarist controversy. The chapter includes an Appendix on the IS-LM model of aggregate demand. This is very useful, if you are intending to study Economics at higher levels.

Helpful Hints

1 Time is very important in economics. Some policies may be very effective in the short run, but have undesirable consequences in the longer term. On the other hand some policies may be unpleasant at first (like some medicines) but have admirable consequences later on.

2 However, remember that the short run may take a (relatively) long time – Keynes once said, 'In the long run we are all dead.' So, in judging policy prescriptions you need to consider how long it will take to be effective.

3 The figures showing how the economy adjusts to expansionary fiscal and monetary policies are very useful summaries and worth studying carefully.

4 Note that a policy that is desirable when the economy is in recession may have adverse effects at full employment.

SELF-TEST

CONCEPT REVIEW

1 In the first round following an expansionary fiscal policy, aggregate demand _____ , real GDP starts to _____ and prices start to _____ .

2 In the second round, increasing real GDP increases the _____ for money and so _____ rates rise.

3 Second-round effects include a fall in interest sensitive _____ and the quantity of real _____ demanded.

4 Rising interest rates makes sterling _____ and which _____ net exports.

5 Following an expansionary monetary policy, interest rates _____ whilst real GDP and prices start to _____ .

6 In the second round, this leads to increased demand for _____ and higher interest _____ .

7 Also in the second round, there will be a fall in interest-sensitive _____ and in real _____ demanded.

8 Other things being equal, the _____ expenditure and the _____ money demand responds to changes in interest rates, the more effective is fiscal policy and the less effective is _____ policy.

9 In the long run, at full employment, an expansionary fiscal policy _____ prices, leaves real GDP _____ and brings a net _____ deficit.

10 At full employment, an expansionary monetary policy will _____ the price level and leave real _____ unchanged.

11 Governments usually take a _____ term view than central _____ .

12 Complete the equation $Y = C + I + G +$ _____ .

TRUE OR FALSE

___ **1** Other things remaining the same, a higher level of aggregate demand means higher GDP.

___ **2** Aggregate demand depends in part on the interest rate.

___ **3** First-round effects of an expansionary fiscal policy include shifting the *AD* curve to the left.

___ **4** A change in transfer payments is an example of fiscal policy.

___ **5** Crowding out leads to a rise in investment.

___ **6** First-round effects of an expansionary monetary policy shift the *AD* curve to the right.

___ **7** The strength of the crowding-out effect depends on the responsiveness of expenditure to the interest rate.

___ **8** The demand curve for real money slopes downward.

___ **9** In the long run, an expansionary monetary policy increases real GDP.

___ **10** Many economists favour an independent central bank.

MULTIPLE CHOICE

1 Which of the following would *not* be regarded as an expansionary fiscal policy?
   a increased public spending
   b cutting direct taxes
   c cutting interest rates
   d more pay for nurses

2 Aggregate demand and short-run aggregate supply determine
   a real GDP.
   b nominal GDP.
   c nominal interest rates.
   d real interest rates.

3 Second-round effects of an expansionary fiscal policy include
   a increased demand for money.
   b higher interest rates.
   c falls in expenditure.
   d all of the above.

4 Which of the following might cause crowding in?
   a entrepreneurs' improved expectations
   b more profitable business opportunities
   c tax cuts on profits
   d all of the above

5 First-round effects of an expansionary monetary policy include
   a higher interest rates.
   b falling interest rates.
   c falling aggregate demand.
   d lower prices.

6 The strength of the crowding-out effect depends in part on
   a the number of firms in the economy.
   b the supply of money.

c changes in real GDP.

d the responsiveness of expenditure to the interest rate.

7 Which of the following is *not* associated with either extreme Keynesianism or extreme monetarism?

   a Expenditure demand is completely insensitive to the interest rate.

   b Demand for real money is highly sensitive to the interest rate.

   c Expenditure is highly sensitive to the interest rate.

   d The demand curve for real money slopes down.

8 Which of the following could cause the *AD* curve to shift as shown in Figure 29.1?

Figure 29.1

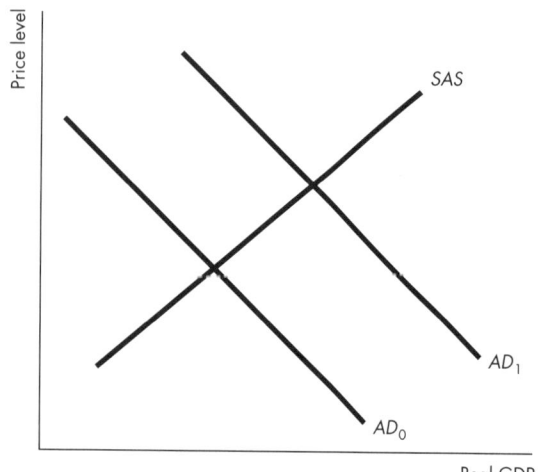

   a Increases in the supply of money.

   b Entrepreneurs invest less.

   c The government raises taxes.

   d Net exports fall.

9 If the economy is at full employment, in the long run an expansionary fiscal policy will cause

   a a deflationary gap.

   b an inflationary gap.

   c the GDP deflator to fall.

   d equilibrium real GDP to rise.

10 Which of the following equations is true?

   a Real GDP = Money GDP + Government spending

   b Real GDP = Consumption + Investment + Government spending = Net expoprts

   c Real GDP = Domestic production + Exports

   d Real GDP = Domestic production – Inflation rate + Exports

11 Long-run neutrality suggests that in the long run, a change in the quantity of money

   a can cause a rise in real GDP.

   b can cause unemployment to rise.

   c can cause a fall in real GDP.

   d changes only the price level.

SHORT ANSWER

1 Summarize the basic idea identified at the beginning of the chapter.

2 What are the first- and second-round effects of an expansionary fiscal policy?

3 What are the first- and second-round effects of an expansionary monetary policy?

4 What is the intermediate position in the Keynesian–Monetarist controversy?

5 Why do policy conflicts arise?

6 Re-read the *Reading Between The Lines* article. What effects do you think strong consumer spending and 'struggling' exporters would have on the economy? What does the author think is the 'trouble'?

PROBLEMS

1 Twenty years hence you are the Economic Advisor to the Chancellor of the Exchequer. Draw a diagram to explain to your boss why an expansionary fiscal policy might help his re-election.

2 A sympathetic researcher for a television company tells you that an interviewer is planning to confuse your boss by asking awkward questions about 'crowding in' and 'crowding out'. Give her a quick briefing.

The following questions relate to the Appendix.

Use Figure 29.2 to answer Question 3.

Figure 29.2

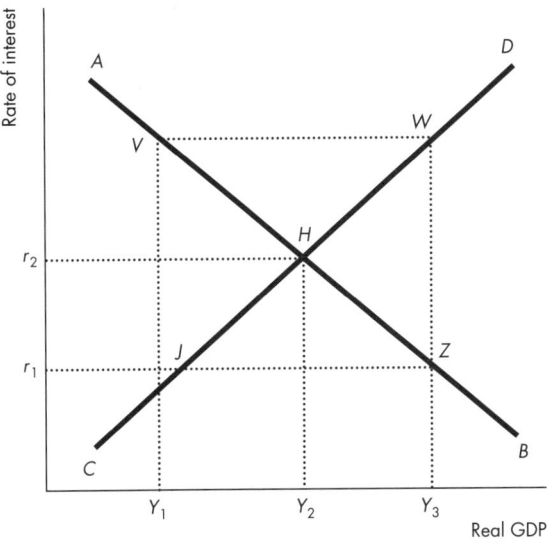

3 a *AB* and *CD* are the *IS* and *LM* schedules. But which is which?

b Comment on the equilibrium/disequilibrium states of the money and goods markets at points *V, W, X, Y, Z.*

c What do you expect to happen to the economy if it is at point *Y*?

4 Assuming no change in other variables, for each of the following, say whether the *IS* or *LM* schedule is likely to shift, and in which direction.

a a rise in business confidence

b a rise in the nominal money supply

c a a cut in government spending

d a fall in business confidence

DISCUSSION QUESTION

1 Explain how fiscal and monetary policy influence real GDP and the price level.

DATA QUESTIONS

Monetary stability: rhyme or reason?
Mervyn King

Inflation in Britain is currently 2.9%. Twenty years ago it was 15% and earlier in the 1970s it had been as high as 27%. Is inflation dead or merely dormant? If dead, was it killed by a wave of creative destruction resulting from intense competition in world markets, was it murdered by contract killers chosen by an electorate disillusioned by the inflationary excesses of the 1970s, or did it simply commit suicide as inflation itself undermined the factors that had led to a sharp acceleration of prices? If dormant, is inflation likely to return to haunt a future government?

Source: *Bank of England Quarterly Bulletin*, **37** (1), February 1997, p. 88.

1 What do you think is meant by 'creative destruction'?

2 What policies would the 'contract killers' have to adopt to end high inflation?

3 Is inflation likely to return?

ANSWERS

CONCEPT REVIEW

1 increases; increase; rise

2 demand; interest

3 expenditure; GDP

4 rise; decreases

5 fall; rise

6 money; rates

7 expenditure; GDP

8 less; more; money

9 raises; unchanged; exports

10 raise; GDP

11 shorter; banks

12 *NX*

TRUE OR FALSE

1 T Higher demand shifts the *AD* curve to the right.

2 T Consumption expenditure and investment are affected by interest rate changes.

3 F This is a second-round effect.

4 T Definition

5 F It leads to a fall, since it results from higher interest rates.

6 T Expansionary monetary policy causes an increase in interest-sensitive expenditure.

7 T If expenditure is highly responsive to interest rate changes then investment will be crowded out.

8 T Verified by empirical evidence.

9 F In the long run, real GDP will be unchanged.

10 T One reason for supporting an independent central bank is that it can take longer-term views.

MULTIPLE CHOICE

1 c Interest rates are an aspect of monetary policy.

2 a See text Figure 29.1a. Interest rates are determined by the demand and supply of money

3 d See text Figure 29.4 on page 726.

4 d All the factors listed might cause firms to invest more.

5 b An expansionary monetary policy increases the money supply and so brings down interest rates. Text figure 29.6 illustrates this.

6 d In addition to this, the other factor determining crowding out is the responsiveness of the demand for money to the interest rate

7 d The first three items are all associated with extreme positions whilst empirical investigation suggests that the intermediate position is correct, i.e. that the demand curve for real money slopes down.

8 a The other factors would cause the *AD* curve to shift to the left.

9 b An expansionary fiscal policy at full employment and above full-employment equilibrium which leads to inflation.

10 b The other equations are false. The components of real GDP are *C+I+G+NX*.

11 d The neutrality argument is illustrated in the text, Figure 29.8. It suggests that in the long run, changes in money supply do not affect real GDP since that is determined by real, not monetary factors.

SHORT ANSWER

1 The basic idea is that aggregate demand and short-run aggregate supply determine real GDP and the price level. Similarly, the interest rate is determined by the demand and supply of money. For example, *ceteris paribus*, an increase in aggregate demand in the short run will lead to rises in real GDP and prices.

2 In the first round, an increase in aggregate demand shifts the *AD* curve to the right causing rises in both prices and real GDP.

In the second round, this leads to increases in money demand and rises in interest rates. In turn, this causes falls in interest-sensitive types of spending (such as some consumption and investment). Hence the demand curve shifts back to the left. There are also second-round effects on prices.

There will be a rise in interest rates (because the real money supply has fallen), and eventually this will lead to a move along the *AD* curve and to higher prices.

3 The first round of an expansionary monetary policy will cause a fall in interest rates (because the supply of money has risen). This will stimulate the economy, shifting the aggregate demand curve to the right, so that there is an increase in real GDP and in prices.

However, in the second round the expansion of the economy will lead to a rise in the demand for money, pushing up the interest rate. In turn, this will cause a fall in aggregate demand and a movement along the aggregate demand curve.

4 The intermediate position in the Keynesian–monetarist controversy is that both fiscal and monetary policy affect aggregate demand. Fiscal policy has an effect because crowding out is not complete. Monetary policy is also effective because interest rates do affect expenditure.

5 Policy conflicts arise for several reasons. For example, as election time looms, governments may want to expand the economy even though the Bank of England believes that this will cause inflation. Another conflict may arise because a government deficit can be financed either by borrowing from the general public or from the Bank of England. In both cases, the government pays interest, but when it borrows from the Bank, the interest comes back to the government. So, this is tempting for the government, but the consequence is that this leads to an increase in the monetary base, a rise in money supply and hence in inflation.

6 Strong consumer spending is an example of rising aggregate demand whilst 'struggling exporters' suggests a fall in net exporters. The overall effect on the economy will depend on which of these two forces is stronger. The 'trouble' pointed out by the author concerns the size of the effects. It is relatively easy to predict rises or falls, but very difficult to predict the exact extent. This is important because large rises in aggregate demand, for example, may cause inflation.

PROBLEMS

1 Figure 29.3 shows the results of an expansionary fiscal policy.

Figure 29.3

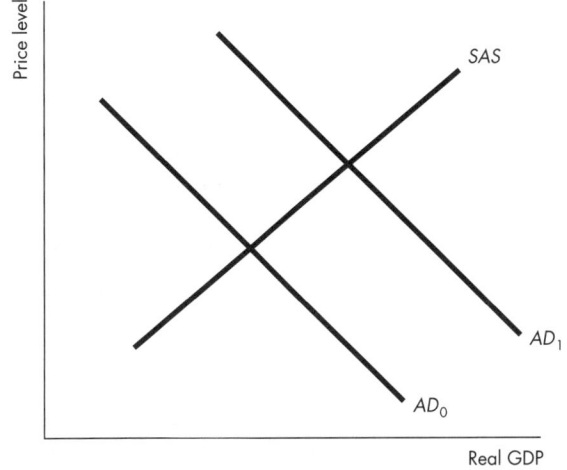

If the government increases its spending, this will have a multiplier effect because it will stimulate consumers to spend more. (For example, if the government raises nurses' salaries, nurses will then spend more on consumer goods.) The result will be a rise in GNP that the Chancellor can claim to be the result of her magnificent policies. Of course, prices will also rise, but she can blame this on trade unions/bosses/foreigners. After the election, second-round effects will start to take hold of the economy, but the political goal will have been achieved.

2 Crowding out occurs when an expansionary fiscal policy causes a fall in interest-sensitive spending such as some items of consumption and investment. If these effects are greater than the original rise in government spending, then we say that crowding out occurs.

On the other hand, there may be 'crowding in'. This can happen when the fiscal policy encourages business optimism, so stimulating investment. Additionally, the government spending might lead to greater efficiency,

or if the expansionary policy is in the form of tax cuts, then business might be encouraged to increase investment.

3 **a** *AB* is the downward sloping *IS* curve, *CD* is the upward sloping *LM* curve.
   b

Point	Money market	Goods market
V	Excess supply	Equilibrium
W	Equilibrium	Excess supply
X	Equilibrium	Equilibrium
Y	Equilibrium	Excess demand
Z	Excess demand	Equilibrium

Only at point X is there equilibrium in both markets.

   c At point J, there is equilibrium in the money market but excess demand for goods. This will lead to rises in output and interest rates.

4 **a** Shifts *IS* to the right
   b Shifts *LM* to the right
   c Shifts *LM* to the left
   d Shifts *IS* to left

DISCUSSION QUESTION

Virtually the whole chapter is an answer to this question. However, a brief summary can cover the essentials. First, we need to distinguish between the short and long run. In the short run expansionary fiscal and monetary policies can stimulate output, but there is a disadvantage – prices will rise, the extent depending on the shape of the *SAS* curve – a flattish *SAS* curve will only lead to small price rises. However, in the long run, the aggregate supply curve is vertical. This means that eventually these price rises will lead to a fall in output so that the long-term result is only a price rise.

Of course, this does not mean that governments should never use expansionary policies. They may be very desirable when unemployment is high and can encourage crowding in.

DATA QUESTIONS

1 The phrase 'creative destruction' is one that is sometimes used to describe the process whereby firms destroy existing machinery and production methods and replace them with ones that are more productive. This may cut costs and bring down inflation.

2 The chapter focuses on expansionary fiscal and monetary policies. In order to end high rates of inflation, governments would have to reverse these policies, to shift the factors affecting the *AD* and *AS* curves in order to lower inflation.

3 The answer to this depends on your own assessment.

Chapter 30 Inflation

Chapter in Perspective, Text Pages 752–777

In previous chapters we have discussed equilibrium real GDP, equilibrium aggregate expenditure, the equilibrium interest rate and the equilibrium real wage rate. In this chapter we bring these things together to examine inflation.

We find that level of inflation depends critically on expectations, especially price level (or inflation) expectations. It thus becomes important to consider how expectations are formed and how expectations affect macroeconomic behaviour. The model developed in this chapter is a powerful tool in explaining the wide variety of macroeconomic events such as the effects of inflation and the relationship between inflation and unemployment.

Helpful Hints

1 An important implication of the rational expectations idea is that the effects of a change in the money supply depend on expectations. The position of the short-run *AS* curve depends on the expected price level. In turn, this depends on the expected change in the money supply. Hence, the effect of an increase in money supply will depend on what was expected.

2 Note that if the expected price level turns out to be correct, employment will turn out to be at the full-employment level and thus real GDP supplied will be equal to full-employment (capacity) real GDP. This is why a short-run aggregate supply curve intersects the long-run aggregate supply curve at the expected price level. If the price level is actually equal to the expected price level, the economy must be at full employment; that is, the economy must be on its long-run aggregate supply curve.

3 Note that the rational expectation of the price level will be at the intersection of the expected aggregate demand curve and the expected long-run aggregate supply curve. (This will yield the best possible forecast, the one most likely to be correct on average.) The rational expectations equilibrium, which determines the actual price level, is at the intersection of the actual aggregate demand curve and the actual short-run aggregate supply curve.

4 Be sure you know why each of the following is true.

– If the actual price level is greater than the expected price level, real GDP is above capacity.
– If the actual price level is less than the expected price level, real GDP is below capacity.
– If the actual price level is equal to the expected price level, real GDP is at capacity.

The wise student will understand all nine possible cases that lead to these three outcomes.

5 An important implication of the rational expectations hypothesis is that the consequences of any macroeconomic event (such as a monetary or fiscal policy) depends on expectations. The effect on the price level and real GDP of a given increase in the money supply will be different for different price level expectations. Its effect on the position of the aggregate demand curve does not depend on the expected price level, but the position of the short-run aggregate supply curve does depend on the expected price level and thus so does the macroeconomic equilibrium. The crucial point is whether the actual level of aggregate demand is anticipated or unanticipated.

6 The Phillips curve and the *AS–AD* model are closely connected. For example, an unexpected rise in aggregate demand will cause a movement along the *SAS* curve, leading to a price rise and also a rise in real GDP (in the short run). This means a fall in inflation. Hence the unexpected rise in aggregate demand has caused a movement along the short-run Phillips curve.

SELF-TEST

CONCEPT REVIEW

1 To measure the inflation rate, we calculate the annual percentage change in the _____ level.

2 We can distinguish two kinds of impulse that can start inflation: _____ pull and _____ push.

3 The two main sources of increases in costs are increases in money _____ and in the money price of raw _____ .

4 Unanticipated inflation has two consequences for the capital market: _____ of income and scarcity or abundance of _____ .

5 The short-run aggregate supply curve intersects the long-run aggregate supply curve at a price level equal to the _____ _____ _____ . If the price level is higher than expected, then real GDP is _____ than capacity output.

6 If inflation turns out to be higher than expected, borrowers _____ and lenders _____ .

7 A forecast that is based on all the available information, is correct on average and minimizes the range of the forecast error is called a(n) _____ expectation. The proposition that the forecasts people make are the same as the forecasts made by an economist using the relevant economic theory as well as all information available is called the _____ _____ hypothesis.

8 The rational expectation of the price level is given by the intersection of the expected aggregate demand curve and the expected _____ - _____ _____ _____ curve.

9 A macroeconomic equilibrium based on expectations that are the best available forecasts is called a(n) _____ _____ equilibrium.

10 The definition of inflation is: the percentage rise in the _____ _____ from one year to another. When aggregate demand is expected to increase and it doesn't, actual inflation is _____ its expected level and actual GDP is _____ capacity output.

11 An unanticipated increase in the money supply will cause the price level to _____ and real GDP to _____ .

12 During periods when the rate of inflation is high, nominal interest rates tend to be _____ . If the Bank of England unexpectedly increases the money supply, the immediate effect is to _____ interest rates. If the Bank of England conducts an anticipated and continuous increase in the money supply, interest rates will _____ .

13 The Phillips curve shows the relationship between _____ and _____ .

TRUE AND FALSE

___ **1** The short-run aggregate supply curve intersects the long-run aggregate supply curve at the expected price level.

___ **2** If the expected price level falls, the short-run aggregate supply curve will shift downward by the amount of the fall.

___ **3** Expectations of inflation are partially self-fulfilling.

___ **4** If people expect aggregate demand to increase but it doesn't, the price level will fall and real GDP will increase.

___ **5** A rational expectation is a forecast that is always correct.

___ **6** The rational expectations hypothesis states that people make forecasts in the same way economists do.

___ **7** In a rational expectations equilibrium the economy will exhibit full employment.

___ **8** If the price level at the beginning of 1999 is 120 and the price level at the beginning of 2000 is 130, the rate of inflation is 8.3 per cent.

___ **9** If the inflation rate rises but nominal interest rates remain unchanged, then real interest rates have fallen.

___ **10** If the inflation rate rises but real interest rates remain unchanged, then nominal interest rates have fallen.

___ **11** If an increase in the money supply is unanticipated, its immediate effect will be to raise interest rates.

MULTIPLE CHOICE

1 Figure 30.1 illustrates an economy initially in equilibrium at point a. What would cause the short-run aggregate supply curve to shift from SAS_0 to SAS_1?
  a an expected increase in the money supply
  b an increase in the price level
  c an increase in the marginal product of labour
  d an increase in the demand for money
  e a decrease in wages

2 Figure 30.1 illustrates an economy initially in equilibrium at point a. If the AD curve is correctly expected to shift from AD_0 to AD_1, the new macroeconomic equilibrium will be real GDP =
  a £380 billion and price level = 125.
  b £500 billion and price level = 150.
  c £500 billion and price level = 100.
  d £620 billion and price level = 125.
  e £500 billion and price level = 125.

Figure 30.1

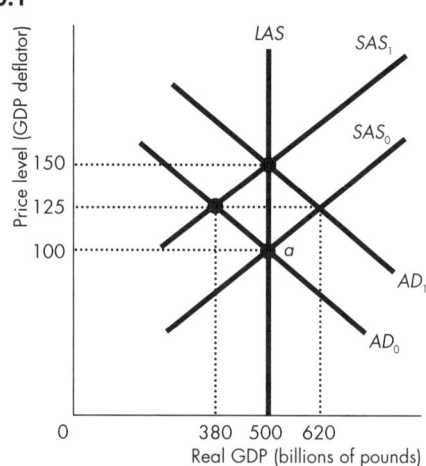

3 Figure 30.1 illustrates an economy initially in equilibrium at point a. If the AD curve is expected to shift from AD_0 to AD_1 but it actually remains at AD_0, the new macroeconomic equilibrium will be real GDP =
  a £380 billion and price level = 100.
  b £500 billion and price level = 150.
  c £500 billion and price level = 100.
  d £620 billion and price level = 125.
  e £380 billion and price level = 125.

4 Figure 30.1 illustrates an economy initially in equilibrium at point a. If the AD curve is expected to remain at AD_0, but in fact, shifts to AD_1, the new macroeconomic equilibrium will be real GDP =
  a £380 billion and price level = 125.
  b £500 billion and price level = 150.
  c £500 billion and price level = 100.
  d £620 billion and price level = 125.
  e £500 billion and price level = 125.

5 If the rate of inflation turns out to be lower than expected, borrowers
  a and lenders both lose.
  b and lenders both gain.
  c gain but lenders lose.
  d lose but lenders gain.
  e lose but lenders are just as well off.

6 If the rate of inflation turns out to be lower than expected, then
  a expectations could not be rational expectations.

b real GDP will be less than full-employment (capacity) real GDP.

c the real interest rate will be lower than expected.

d the real wage rate will be lower than expected.

e the money wage rate will be higher than expected.

7 A rational expectations equilibrium is the price level and real GDP given by the intersection of the

a actual aggregate demand curve and the actual long-run aggregate supply curve.

b actual aggregate demand curve and the expected short-run aggregate supply curve.

c expected aggregate demand curve and the expected short-run aggregate supply curve.

d expected aggregate demand curve and the expected long-run aggregate supply curve.

e aggregate demand curve and the actual short-run aggregate supply curve.

8 According to the rational expectations hypothesis, a correctly anticipated increase in the money supply in an economy with a given long-run aggregate supply will result in

a an increase in the price level and an increase in real GDP.

b an increase in the price level and a decrease in real GDP.

c a proportional increase in the price level and no change in real GDP.

d no change in the price level and an increase in real GDP.

e no change in the price level and no change in real GDP.

9 Suppose OPEC unexpectedly increases the price of oil. This is a negative aggregate supply shock. As a result, the price level will

a rise and real GDP will increase.

b rise and real GDP will decrease.

c fall and real GDP will increase.

d fall and real GDP will decrease.

e rise and real GDP will stay the same.

10 The current year's price level is 180 and the rate of inflation over the past year has been 20 per cent. What was last year's price level?

a 144

b 150

c 160

d 216

e 100

11 Which of the following would cause the aggregate demand curve to keep shifting upward year after year?

a a tax cut

b an increase in government purchases of goods and services

c inflation

d excess wage demands

e a positive rate of growth in the quantity of money

12 Suppose aggregate demand increases by less than anticipated. This will result in an unanticipated

a rise in inflation and real GDP falls below capacity.

b rise in inflation and real GDP rises above capacity.

c fall in inflation and real GDP falls below capacity.

d fall in inflation and real GDP rises above capacity.

e fall in inflation and real GDP stays at capacity.

13 If the actual price level is higher than the expected price level, then real GDP

a must be above capacity.

b must be below capacity.

c must be equal to capacity.

d can be above, below, or equal to capacity depending on the position of the aggregate demand curve.

e can be above or equal to capacity depending on the position of the aggregate demand curve.

14 A rise in the expected inflation rate causes _____ in the long-run Phillips curve and _____ in the short-run Phillips curve.

a an upward shift; no shift

b a leftward shift; no shift

c no shift; no shift

d no shift, an upward shift

SHORT ANSWER

1 What will happen to the price level and real GDP if the government increases its purchases of goods and services and that increase is not anticipated (that is, the price level is not expected to change)?

2 What will happen to the price level and real GDP if the government increases its purchases of goods and services and that increase is anticipated?

3 How is a rational expectation of the price level calculated?

4 What is the relationship between the expected rate of inflation and interest rates?

5 It is frequently argued that high wage demands by workers (based on high price expectations) cause inflation. According to the rational expectations model developed in this chapter, is this true or not? Explain briefly.

PROBLEMS

1 Table 30.1 gives the initial aggregate demand and short-run aggregate supply schedules for an economy in which the expected price level is 80.
   a What is capacity real GDP?
   b What is actual real GDP and the actual price level?

Table 30.1 Aggregate Demand and Supply

Price level (GDP deflator)	Real GDP demanded	Real GDP supplied
60	600	400
80	500	500
100	400	600
120	300	700
140	200	700

2 In year 1 the economy is in the macroeconomic equilibrium characterized in Problem **1**. It is expected that in year 2, aggregate demand will be as given in Table 30.2.
   a What is the vertical amount of the expected shift in the aggregate demand curve when real GDP is $500 billion?
   b What is the rational expectation of the price level for year 2?
   c The expected shift in aggregate demand will cause the short-run aggregate supply (SAS) curve to shift. What will the new SAS curve be? For each price level, give the new values of real GDP supplied in the last column of Table 30.2.

Table 30.2 Aggregate Demand and Supply

Price level (GDP deflator)	Real GDP demanded	Real GDP supplied
60	800	
80	700	
100	600	
120	500	
140	400	

   d Suppose that, in fact, aggregate demand does not change but remains as given in Table 30.1. What will real GDP and the price level be in year 2?
   e Compare the actual change in the price level with the expected change.

3 In year 1 the economy is in the macroeconomic equilibrium characterized by Problem **1**. It is expected that in year 2, aggregate demand will be as given in Table 30.2. It turns out that expectations are correct: the actual aggregate demand in year 2 is as given in Table 30.2.
   a What is the rational expectation of the price level for year 2?
   b What will real GDP and the price level turn out to be in year 2?
   c Compare the actual change in the price level with the expected change.

4 Graphically illustrate the rational expectations equilibrium in an economy for which aggregate demand is higher than expected. Compare the actual equilibrium with the expected equilibrium.

5 Graphically illustrate the rational expectations equilibrium in an economy for which aggregate demand is higher than expected and long-run aggregate supply is lower than expected. Compare the actual equilibrium with the expected equilibrium.

DISCUSSION QUESTION

1 Why does an increase in the monetary growth rate sometimes lower the rate of interest and sometimes raise it?

DATA QUESTIONS

Breaking the cycle

Leading retailers – including such venerable names as Marks & Spencer and Sainsbury – are having a torrid time of it. The invasion of overseas retailers, together with the government's focus on creating a competitive Britain, is contributing to the downward draft on sales and profits.

Inflation modelling has suggested a particular rate of price increase when the economy is operating at various levels. Instead there are hints of a new paradigm for the UK. This rests on microeconomic changes in the economy which might now make it possible to hold inflation low without resorting to escalating interest rate rises.

Source: *The Guardian*, 29 October 1999, p. 21.

1 Can you relate the idea of expectations to this passage?

2 Can you relate the idea of the Phillips curve to this passage?

3 Do you think that the developments discussed here make interest rate changes unncessary?

ANSWERS

CONCEPT REVIEW

1 price

2 demand; cost

3 wages; materials

4 redistributon; finance

5 expected price level; greater

6 gain; lose

7 rational; rational expectations

8 long-run aggregate supply

9 rational expectations

10 price level; below; below

11 increase; increase

12 high; lower; rise

13 inflation, unemployment

TRUE OR FALSE

1 T When expectations are correct, actual real GDP = natural rate.

2 T Changes in expected prices cause changes in supply.

3 T If people expect higher inflation, firms will put up prices and workers will seek higher wages.

4 F See Helpful Hint 4.

5 F Rational expectations are correct *on average*.

6 F Make forecasts in a different way.

7 F Equilibrium may not be at full-employment level – depends on expectations.

8 T Inflation rate = $[(P_1 - P_0)/P_0] \times 100 = [(130 - 120)/120] \times 100 = 8.3$.

9 T Actual real interest rate = Nominal interest rate – Inflation rate.

10 F Nominal rates would have to rise to keep real rate the same.

11 F Immediate effect is rise in real money supply leading to fall in nominal interest rates.

MULTIPLE CHOICE

1 a A rise in the price of a crucial input would lead to leftward shift in SAS curve.

2 b Expected P found from intersection of EAD = AD_1, and actual SAS is set here leading to new equilibrium where actual AD and SAS curves cross.

3 e Expected P found from intersection of EAD = AD_1 and actual SAS is set here leading to equilibrium where actual AD and SAS curves cross.

4 d Expected P found from intersection of EAD = AD_1 and actual SAS is set here, so new equilibrium where actual AS and SAS curves cross.

5 d Borrowers will lose because they will have expected to pay back less.

6 b Economy will be in equilibrium at less than full-employment level.

7 e Definition.

8 c Increase in money supply leads to rise in aggregate demand. Since this is anticipated it causes leftward shift in SAS curve of equivalent amount so rise in price level and no change in real GDP.

9 b SAS curve will shift leftward.

10 b Invert formula. Inflation rate = $[(P_1 - P_0)/P_0] \times 100$.

11 e Others would have only a one-off effect.

12 c Because actual price level = expected when SAS curve crosses *LAS* curve, and equilibrium occurs when *AS* = *SAS* – try drawing a graph.

13 a Because actual price level = expected when *SAS* curve crosses *LAS* curve, and equilibrium occurs when *LAS* = *AD*.

14 d The long-run Phillips curve shifts only when the natural rate of unemployment changes. The short-run curve can also shift when the expected inflation rate changes.

SHORT ANSWER

1 An increase in government purchases of goods and services will shift the aggregate demand curve to the right. If the price level is not expected to change, the short-run aggregate supply curve remains unchanged and the increase in aggregate demand will cause the price level to rise and real GDP to increase.

2 If the shift in the aggregate demand curve is anticipated, the expected price level will rise by the amount of the vertical shift in the aggregate demand curve and thus the short-run aggregate supply curve will shift up by that amount. So when an increase in aggregate demand is fully anticipated, the aggregate demand curve and the short-run aggregate supply curve will shift upward by the same amount. As a result, the price level will rise and real GDP will remain unchanged.

3 A rational expectation of the price level is obtained by using the aggregate demand–aggregate supply model to predict the price level. The actual price level will be given by the intersection of the aggregate demand curve and the short-run aggregate supply curve. Therefore we want to determine where we expect these curves to be and then see where they intersect. The problem is that the short-run aggregate supply curve depends on the expected price level and that is what we are trying to find. We resolve this problem by recognizing that if the price level turns out to be equal to the expected price level, the short-run aggregate supply curve intersects the aggregate demand curve at the point where the latter curve intersects the long-run aggregate supply curve. Since the long-run aggregate supply curve does not depend on the expected price level, the rational expectation of the price level is obtained at the intersection of the aggregate demand curve and the long-run aggregate supply curve.

4 When the rate of inflation is expected to rise, the interest rate will also rise to compensate for the increased rate at which the purchasing power of money is eroding. The essential point is that lenders and borrowers are interested in the quantity of goods and services that a unit of money will buy. Lenders will insist on the higher interest rate (to compensate for the loss of purchasing power of money) and borrowers will be willing to pay it because they realize that the pounds they pay back will buy fewer goods and services.

5 In the short run, a rise in wages will shift the short-run aggregate supply curve to the left, raising the price level. However, a continuing rise in the price level (that is, an inflation), requires a continuing rise in both the *AD* and the *SAS* curves. This therefore requires a positive growth rate of the money supply to sustain or validate the inflation.

PROBLEMS

1 a Capacity real GDP is the quantity of real GDP supplied when the expected price level is equal to the actual price level. The last column of Table 30.1 gives the quantity of real GDP supplied at various price levels assuming that the expected price level is constant at 80. When the actual price level is also 80 the quantity of real GDP supplied is $500 billion, so that is the value of capacity real GDP.

b Actual real GDP and the actual price level are determined by the intersection of the aggregate demand curve and the short-run aggregate supply curve. Real GDP is $500 billion and the price level is 80, since at a price level of 80, the quantity of real GDP demanded equals the quantity of real GDP supplied ($500 billion).

2 a The price level associated with $500 billion of real GDP demanded for the original aggregate curve (Table 30.1) is 80. The price level associated with $500 billion of real GDP demanded for the new expected aggregate demand curve (Table 30.2) is 120. Therefore the aggregate demand curve is expected to shift upward by 40.

b The rational expectation of the price level is given by the intersection of the expected aggregate demand curve (Table 30.2) and the expected long-run aggregate supply curve. Long-run aggregate supply is equal to $500 billion and is not expected to change. Since the price level associated with $500 billion of real GDP demanded is 120, the rational expectation of the price level is 120.

c The quantities of real GDP supplied for the new *SAS* curve are given in Table 30.3. The original expected price level is 80. From **b** we know that the new expected price level is 120, which implies that the *SAS* curve shifts upward by 40. Thus at each quantity of real GDP supplied, the price level on the new *SAS* curve is 40 points higher than on the original *SAS* curve (Table 30.1). For example, real GDP supplied of $500 billion now requires a price level of 120 rather than 80. Similarly, real GDP supplied of $400 billion now requires a price level of 100 rather than 60. (Note that the values in parentheses in the table are inferred by extrapolation rather than calculated from Table 30.1.)

Table 30.3 Aggregate Demand and Supply

Price level (GDP deflator)	Real GDP demanded	Real GDP supplied
60	800	(200)
80	700	(300)
100	600	400
120	500	500
140	400	600

   d The new macroeconomic equilibrium in year 2 will occur at the intersection of the actual *AD* curve and the relevant *SAS* curve. Since the *AD* curve was expected to shift, the relevant SAS curve is the one associated with the expected price level of 120 (the *SAS* curve is completed in Table 30.3). But the *AD* curve did not actually shift, so the *AD* curve is given in Table 30.1. The intersection of these curves is at real GDP equals $400 billion and price level equals 100 (that is, when the price level is 100, the quantity of real GDP demanded is equal to the quantity of real GDP supplied at $400 billion).

   e The price level was expected to rise from 80 to 120, but in fact it only rises from 80 to 100.

3 a Since aggregate demand is expected to increase, the rational expectation of the price level for year 2 is the same as in Problem **2** above: 120.

   b The rational expectations equilibrium will occur at the intersection of the actual *AD* curve and the relevant *SAS* curve. Since the expected price level is 120, the relevant *SAS* curve is the one given in completed Table 30.3. The actual *AD* curve is also given in Table 30.2. Thus real GDP will be $500 billion and the price level will be 120.

   c The price level was expected to rise from 80 to 120, which is exactly what happens.

4 Figure 30.2 illustrates the rational expectations equilibrium. The expected aggregate demand curve is given by *EAD* which intersects the expected long-run aggregate supply curve, *ELAS*, at point a. Thus the rational expec-

tation of the price level is P_0, which implies that the relevant short-run aggregate supply curve is *ESAS*. The actual aggregate demand curve, *AD*, is higher than expected and the actual short-run aggregate supply curve is the same as *ESAS*. The rational expectations equilibrium occurs at point b, the intersection of *AD* and *ESAS*. The equilibrium price level, P_1, is higher than expected and thus real GDP is above capacity (that is, above Y_0).

5 Figure 30.3 illustrates the rational expectations equilibrium in this case. The expected aggregate demand curve, *EAD*, intersects the expected long-run aggregate supply curve, *ELAS*, at point a. Thus the rational expectation of the price level is P_0, which implies that the expected short-run aggregate supply curve is *ESAS*. The actual aggregate demand curve, *AD*, is higher than expected. Also, the actual long-run aggregate supply curve, *LAS*, is lower than expected, which means that the actual short-run aggregate supply curve corresponding to an expected price level of P_0 is given by *SAS*. The rational expectations equilibrium occurs at point b, the intersection of the *AD* and *SAS* curves. The equilibrium price level is P_1, which is much higher than expected. Real GDP can be above, below, or at the expected capacity real GDP, Y_0, depending on the relative magnitudes of the unanticipated shifts (Fig. 30.3 shows real GDP above expected capacity GDP), but real GDP will be above the new actual capacity real GDP, Y_1.

Figure 30.2

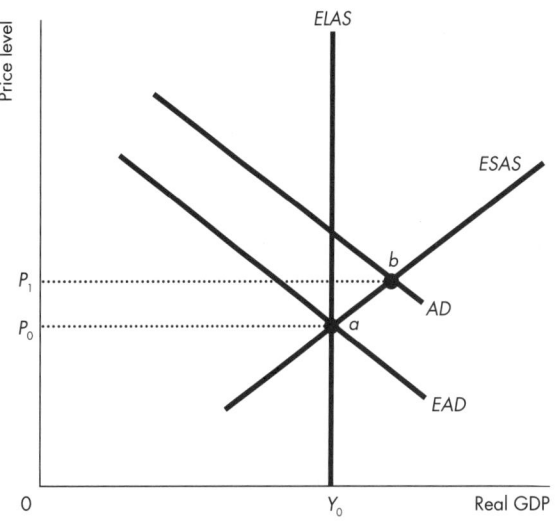

Figure 30.3

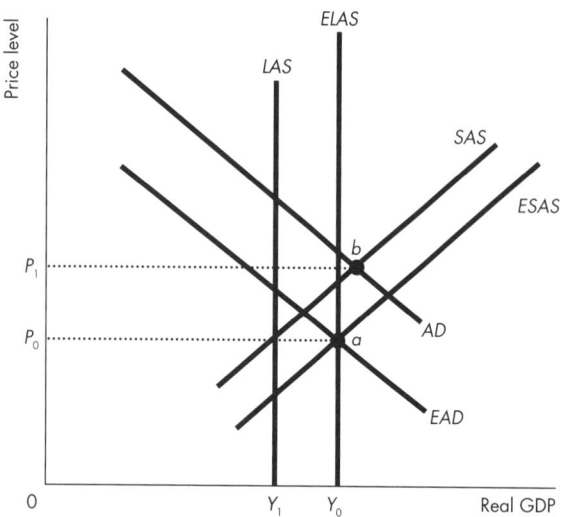

Figure 30.4

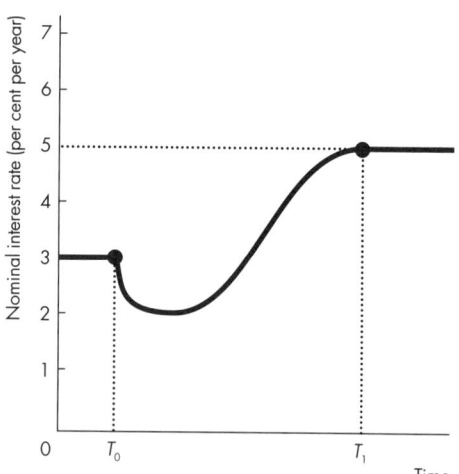

DISCUSSION QUESTION

1 The key to understanding the effect on interest rates of an increase in the rate of monetary growth is to focus on the time frame. In Fig. 30.4, suppose that the nominal rate of interest is 3 per cent. Then at time T_0 there is an unanticipated increase in the money supply which leads to an unexpectedly high level of the real money supply. As we saw in Chapter 28, this will lead to a fall in the interest rate. In Fig. 30.4 this is shown as a fall to 2 per cent.

However, in the long run this will lead to a rise in investment demand and inflation so that at time T_1 people raise their forecasts of inflation and this raises the nominal interest rate to 5 per cent.

Hence assuming that the economy is running at the full employment level, an increase in the money supply will lower and then increase the rate of interest.

DATA QUESTIONS

1 The essential point is that if lower inflation continues, then this will affect expectations and so the wage rate and the *ESAS* curve.

2 The sentence about 'particular price increases when the economy is operating at various levels' is a description of the Phillips curve.

3 You must come to your own conclusion on this.

Chapter 31 Capital, Investment and Saving

Chapter in Perspective, Text Pages 778–801

Our future living standards depend, at least in part, on the level of investment. This chapter analyses the factors that influence investment. It also looks at the factors that influence households' saving and consumption decisions – which also have a large impact on future living standards, as does the effect of net imports.

The chapter integrates these factors to discuss equilibrium in the national economy.

Helpful Hints

1 This chapter is important for at least two reasons.

First, it is a key building block to an understanding of economic growth. Economic growth results from growth in productive inputs and from growth in technology. The two most important inputs are labour, which was discussed in Chapter 23, and capital, which is examined in this chapter. Chapter 32 integrates the topics in this chapter and those in Chapter 30 with some new material (the role of technology and incentives that help foster economic growth) to permit a thorough analysis of economic growth.

Second, it is helpful in understanding business cycles, that is, the recurring fluctuations in economic activity. Investment, and particularly fluctuations in investment, play a crucial role in

business cycles. Thus the discussion of the demand for investment is significant in terms of several key issues concerning the causes of business cycles and potential cures for business cycles.

2 The saving supply and investment demand model is another supply and demand model. The saving supply curve is just another supply curve, and the investment demand curve is simply another demand curve. Thus all the lessons and rules that you have learned about 'ordinary' supply and demand curves directly apply to the saving supply curve and the investment demand curve. For instance, the difference between a movement along a curve and a shift in a curve is exactly the same as before. A change in the variable on the vertical axis (the real interest rate in this case) causes a movement along the (saving) supply

curve and (investment) demand curve. A change in any other relevant variable (such as disposable income) shifts the curve(s).

3 Always remember that the marginal propensity to consume and marginal propensity to save refer to *changes* in consumption expenditure and saving that are caused by *changes* in disposable income. One way to remember these relationships is to think of the question that, say, the marginal propensity to consume answers: if a person's disposable income increases by £100, how much more will the person spend on consumption?

The marginal propensity to consume and marginal propensity to save are important in later chapters because we are often interested in how consumption (and saving) respond to changes in income. For instance, during a recession, income falls and hence we may want to know how that causes consumption to change. For this purpose, the marginal propensity to consume is crucial.

SELF-TEST

CONCEPT REVIEW

1 Net investment (gross investment minus _____) increases the capital stock.

2 The return on capital is the _____ interest rate.

3 Interest depends on the expected _____ rate and the real _____ rate.

4 When the expected profit rate increases, the investment demand curve shifts _____ .

5 Consumption expenditure and saving decisions are influenced by the real interest rate, _____ income, the purchasing power of net _____ and _____ future income.

6 The consumption demand curve is the relationship between consumption expenditure and the _____ _____ rate.

7 The main influences on business investment decisions are the expected _____ rate and the real _____ rate.

8 The saving supply curve is the relationship between saving and the real _____ rate. It slopes _____ .

9 The real interest rate is determined by world _____ supply and world _____ demand.

TRUE OR FALSE

— **1** The real interest rate equals the interest rate on a loan plus the inflation rate.

— **2** An increase in the expected profit rate shifts the saving supply curve rightward.

— **3** An increase in the real interest rate increases the quantity of people's saving.

— **4** On average, the investment rate in developing countries has been higher than that in developed countries.

— **5** If a £100 increase in disposable income causes an increase in saving of £40, the *MPS* is 0.40.

— **6** The amount of net investment is smaller during recessions and larger during expansions.

— **7** When an individual's consumption demand curve shifts rightward, the person's saving supply curve shifts leftward.

— **8** If the world saving supply curve shifts rightward more rapidly than the investment demand curve, the real interest rate falls.

MULTIPLE CHOICE

1 An increase in the expected profit rate shifts the _____ _____ curve rightward and _____ the real interest rate.
 a saving supply; lowers
 b investment demand; raises
 c saving supply; raises
 d investment demand; lowers

2 If the interest rate on a loan is 8 per cent and the inflation rate is 2 per cent, the real interest rate is
 a 16 per cent.
 b 10 per cent.

c 6 per cent.

d 4 per cent.

3 In the long run, the sum of a country's consumption expenditure, investment and government purchases is less than the country's potential GDP. Then in that country

a the real interest rate rises.

b net exports are positive.

c the government raises its spending.

d the investment demand curve will shift rightward.

4 Which of the following does *not* increase consumption expenditure?

a an increase in disposable income

b an increase in the purchasing power of net assets

c an increase in expected future income

d an increase in the expected profit rate

5 Which of the following has the smallest fluctuations?

a gross investment

b net investment

c capital stock

d fluctuations in gross investment and capital are the same and are the smallest

6 An increase in a country's consumption expenditure _____ its real exchange rate and _____ its net exports.

a lowers; decreases

b lowers; increases

c raises; increases

d raises; decreases

7 A household's *MPC* is 0.90. Hence an increase of £100 of disposable income causes

a consumption expenditure to increase by £100.

b consumption expenditure to increase by £90.

c saving to decrease by £90.

d Both **b** and **c** to occur.

8 In Fig. 31.1, the equilibrium real interest rate is

a R_1.

b between R_1 and R_2.

c R_2.

d less than R_2.

9 Which of the following increases both consumption demand and saving supply?

a an increase in the real interest rate

b a decrease in future expected income

Figure 31.1

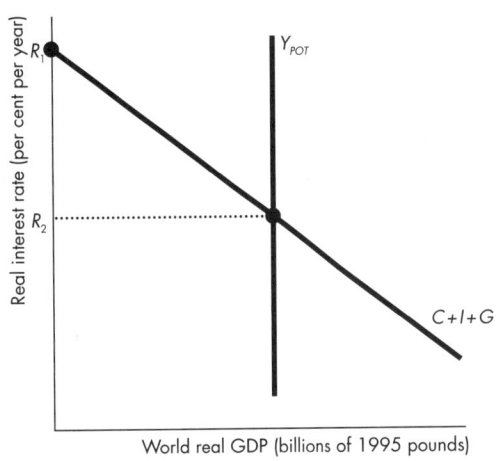

World real GDP (billions of 1995 pounds)

c an increase in net assets

d an increase in disposable income

10 If the real interest rate is less than the equilibrium real interest rate, the quantity of

a saving exceeds the quantity of investment and the real interest rate rises.

b saving exceeds the quantity of investment and the real interest rate falls.

c investment exceeds the quantity of saving and the real interest rate falls.

d investment exceeds the quantity of saving and the real interest rate rises.

11 What could raise the equilibrium real interest rate and increase the equilibrium quantity of investment?

a a rightward shift of the saving supply curve

b a leftward shift of the saving supply curve

c a leftward shift of the investment demand curve

d a rightward shift of the investment demand curve

12 The marginal propensity to save is

a the total amount of saving by a household.

b the fraction of a household's disposable income that is saved.

c the fraction of a change in disposable income that is saved.

d slightly greater than 1.0 for the UK economy.

13 Which of the following raises the equilibrium real interest rate and increases the equilibrium quantity of investment?

a a rightward shift of the saving supply curve with a leftward shift at the investment demand curve.

b a leftward shift of the saving supply curve.

c a leftward shift of the investment demand curve.

d a rightward shift at the investment demand curve.

14 The opportunity cost of consumption expenditure this year versus next year is

a the real interest rate.

b the real exchange rate.

c the expected profit rate.

d none of the above.

SHORT ANSWER

1 The interest rate on a loan in 1977 was 12 per cent; in 1997 the interest rate on a comparable loan was 8 per cent. Based on this information alone, in which year was the real interest rate the highest?

2 Table 31.3 shows how Igor's consumption depends on the real interest rate when his disposable income is £20,000.

a Complete the table.

b In Fig. 31.2 illustrate Igor's consumption demand curve; in Fig. 31.3 show his saving supply curve.

c Suppose that Igor expects his income to increase in the future, which causes his consumption expenditure to increase by £50 at every real interest rate. What happens to his saving at each real interest rate?

d If Igor's current disposable income increases by £100, his consumption expenditure increases by £80 at every interest rate. What is Igor's marginal propensity to consume? His marginal propensity to save?

Table 31.1 Igor's Consumption and Saving

Real interest rate (per cent)	Consumption expenditure (pounds)	Saving (pounds)
3	19,500	
4	19,200	
5	18,900	
6	18,600	
7	18,300	

Figure 31.2

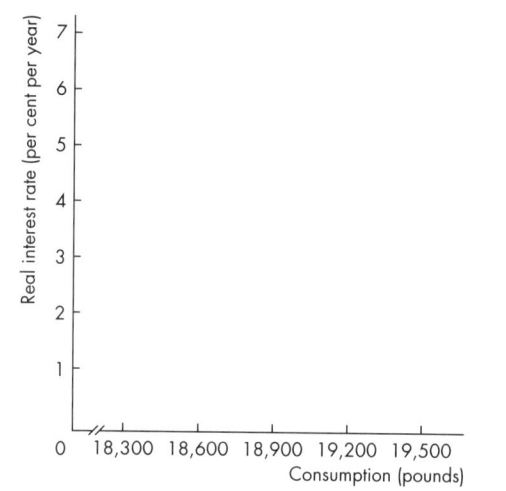

Figure 31.3

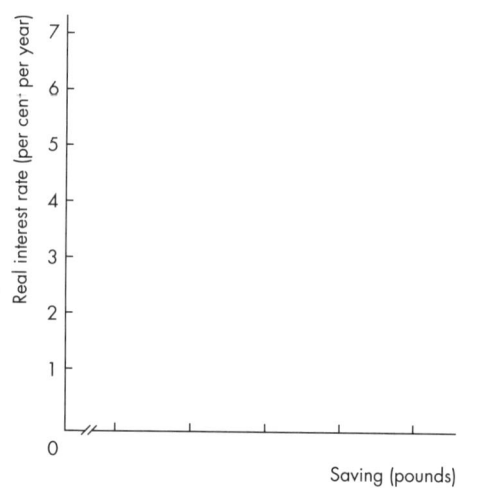

3 In Fig. 31.4, draw a world investment demand and saving supply curve. Show the equilibrium real interest rate and the amount of saving and investment. Use the figure to illustrate what happens when the expected profit rate increases.

Figure 31.4

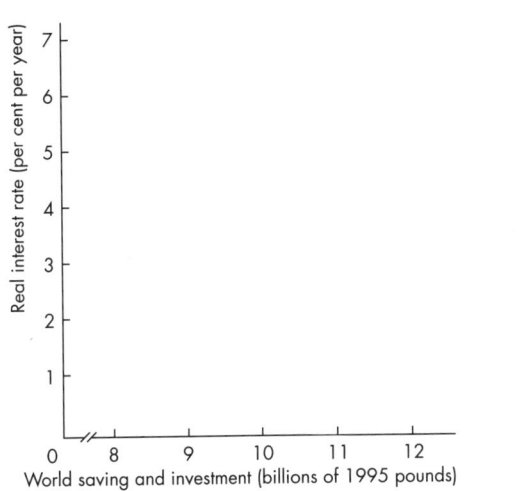

PROBLEMS

Table 31.2 Expenditures in Nirvana

Real interest rate (per cent)	Consumption expenditure (C) (billions of pounds)	Investment (I) (billions of pounds)
3	26	24
4	24	21
5	22	18
6	20	15
7	18	12

1 Table 31.2 gives the consumption demand and the investment demand for the country of Nirvana. At any interest rate, the government of Nirvana buys goods and services worth £10 billion and levies net taxes equal to £10 billion. There is no international trade. Potential real GDP in Nirvana is £45 billion.

  a Complete the investment demand and saving supply schedules in Table 31.3. What is the equilibrium real interest rate?

  b Complete Table 31.4, showing the sum of consumption expenditure plus investment plus government purchases of goods and services, $C + I + G$, and potential real GDP. What is the equilibrium real interest rate?

  c How do your answers for **a** and **b** compare? Why?

Table 31.3 Investment and Saving in Nirvana

Real interest rate (per cent)	Investment demand (I) (billions of pounds)	Saving supply (billions of pounds)
3		
4		
5		
6		
7		

Table 31.4 $C + I + G$ and Potential Real GDP in Nirvana

Real interest rate (per cent)	$C + I + G$ (billions of pounds)	Potential real GDP (billions of pounds)
3		
4		
5		
6		
7		

2 Initially, the small country of Primus is in long-run equilibrium and net exports equal zero. Then the expected profit rate in Primus increases. Because Primus is a small part of the world economy, the world real interest rate does not change. How does this change affect Primus's

  a investment demand curve?

  b $C + I + G$ curve?

  c equilibrium quantity of investment?

Illustrate your answer.

3 In **2**, how does Primus finance the change in its investment?

4 In Figure 31.5, draw a world investment demand and saving supply curve. Show the equilibrium real interest rate and the amount of saving and investment. Use the figure to illustrate what happens when saving increases.

Figure 31.5

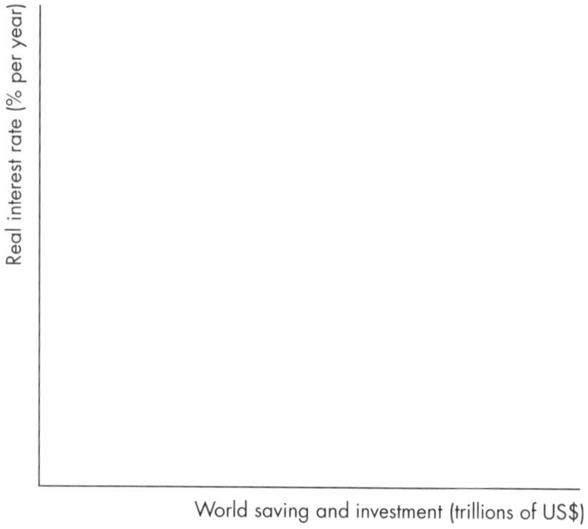

Real interest rate (% per year) / World saving and investment (trillions of US$)

DISCUSSION QUESTION

1 Why does investment decrease when the real interest rate rises?

DATA QUESTIONS

Consumption and income
The data in Table 31.5 refer to the UK economy.

Table 31.5

	Real houeholds' disposable income 1995 = 100	Real consumers' expenditure £ billion, 1995 prices
1995	100	454
1996	102.2	470
1997	105.9	490
1998	106.8	528

Source: *Economic Trends 1999*, National Statistics © Crown Copyright 2000.

1 What is meant by 'real households' disposable income'?

2 What factors might have caused real households' disposable income to change over this period?

3 What is meant by 1995 = 100?

4 What factors other than current disposable income might affect consumption?

ANSWERS

CONCEPT REVIEW

1 depreciation

2 real

3 profit; interest

4 rightward

5 disposable; assets; expected

6 real interest

7 profit; interest

8 interest; upward

9 saving; investment

TRUE OR FALSE

1 F The real interest rate equals the interest rate on a loan *minus* the inflation rate.

2 F An increase in the expected profit rate shifts the investment demand curve rightward; it does not shift the saving supply curve.

3 T As the real interest rate rises, the 'reward' from saving increases, so people increase the quantity they save.

4 T Although not true for all developing countries, on average in developing countries the investment rate exceeds that in developed countries.

5 T The *MPS* is defined as the ratio of the change in saving caused by a change in disposable income or, in this question, $40/$100 = 0.40.

6 T Net investment fluctuates with the business cycle; it is higher during expansions and lower during recessions.

7 F This may be true. The shift in the saving supply depends on the reason for the shift in the consumption demand curve. For instance, if the consumption demand curve shifted rightward because disposable income increased, the increase in disposable income also shifts the saving supply curve rightward. If the shift in the consumption demand curve was caused by an increase in net assets, the increase in net assets shifts the saving supply curve leftward.

8 T The rightward shift in the saving supply curve lowers the equilibrium real interest rate.

MULTIPLE CHOICE

1 b As Fig. 31.6 shows, the shift in the investment demand curve to the right raises the equilibrium real interest rate from R_0 to R_1.

Figure 31.6

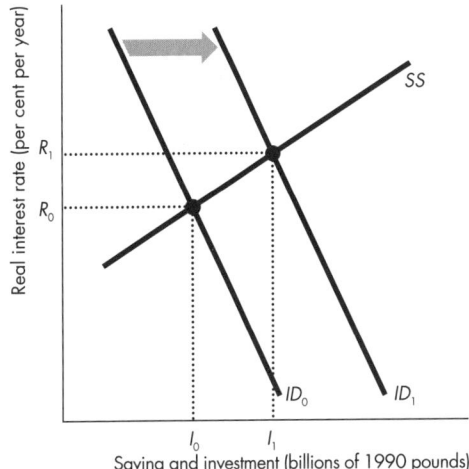

Saving and investment (billions of 1990 pounds)

2 c The real interest rate equals the interest rate on the loan, 8 per cent, minus the inflation rate, 2 per cent.

3 b Net exports are positive as the country exports the excess of its potential GDP over the domestic demand $(C + I + G)$ for it.

4 d An increase in the expected profit rate increases investment, not consumption expenditure.

5 c The capital stock's fluctuations are a much smaller fraction of the total capital stock than fluctuations in either measure of investment.

6 d The increase in consumption expenditure lowers net exports (fewer goods are left to export), and the increase in net exports is associated with a drop in the real exchange rate.

7 b The change in consumption expenditure equals the *MPC* multiplied by the change in disposable income, or $0.90 \times \pounds100$.

8 c The equilibrium real interest rate is the real interest rate that sets the quantity of world real GDP demanded equal to world potential real GDP.

9 d An increase in disposable income shifts both the consumption demand and saving supply curves rightward.

10 d The excess of the quantity demanded of investment over the quantity supplied of saving creates upward pressure on the real interest rate that moves the real interest rate towards its equilibrium.

11 d The rightward shift in the investment demand curve raises both the equilibrium real interest rate and equilibrium quantity of investment.

12 c Definition.

13 d The rightward shift in the investment demand curve raises both the equilibrium real interest rate and equilibrium quantity of investment.

14 a By consuming this year, the household loses the opportunity to save the funds and consume more next year. The amount of increased consumption forgone equals the real interest rate, which essentially is the gain in the purchasing power of savings.

SHORT ANSWER

1 Determining when the real interest rate was the highest is impossible. The real interest rate equals the interest rate on the loan minus the inflation rate. If the inflation rates in the two years were the same, the real interest rate in 1977 was higher. But if the inflation rate was sufficiently higher in 1977 than in 1997, the real interest rate in 1977 would be lower than in 1997. For instance, suppose that the inflation rate in 1977 was 11 per cent and in 1997 was 3 per cent. Then the real interest rate in 1977 was 1 per cent and in 1997 was 5 per cent.

Table 31.6   Igor's Consumption and Saving

Real interest rate (per cent)	Consumption expenditure (pounds)	Saving (pounds)
3	19,500	500
4	19,200	800
5	18,900	1,180
6	18,600	1,400
7	18,300	1,700

2 a Table 31.6 shows Igor's saving. At any real interest rate, Igor's saving equals his disposable income, £20,000, minus his consumption expenditure. Thus at the real interest rate of 3 per cent, Igor's saving equals £20,000 – £19,500, or £500.

b Figure 31.7 illustrates Igor's consumption demand curve, and Fig. 31.8 shows his saving supply curve.

Figure 31.7

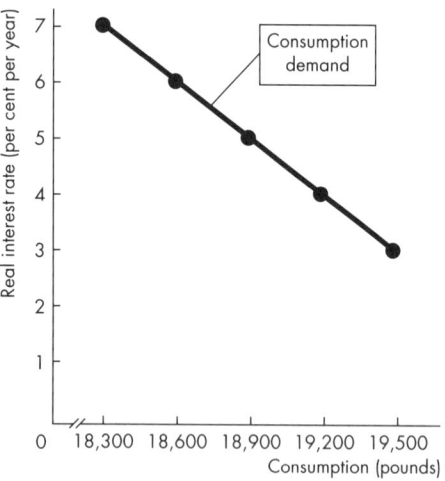

Figure 31.8

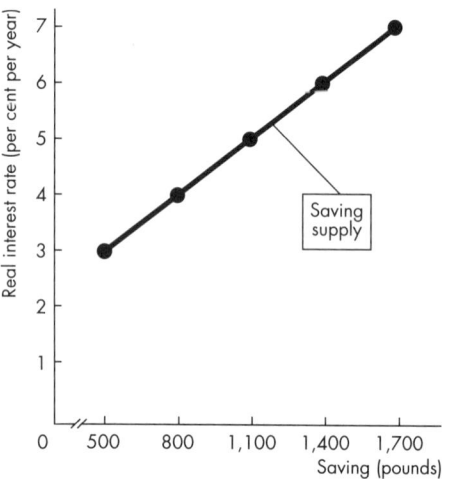

c Igor's saving falls by $50 at every real interest rate. Thus at a real interest rate of 3 per cent, Igor now saves $450 and at a real interest rate of 4 per cent, Igor saves $750.

d The marginal propensity to consume, or *MPC*, is $\Delta C/\Delta YD$ where Δ means 'change in', *C* is consumption expenditure, and *YD* is disposable income. Thus Igor's *MPC* equals $80/$100, or 0.80.

Igor's marginal propensity to save, *MPS*, is defined as $\Delta S/\Delta YD$, where *S* is saving. Because Igor's con-

sumption expenditure increases by $80 when his disposable income increases by $100, Igor's saving must increase by $20. Thus Igor's *MPS* is $20/$100, or 0.20.

Figure 31.9

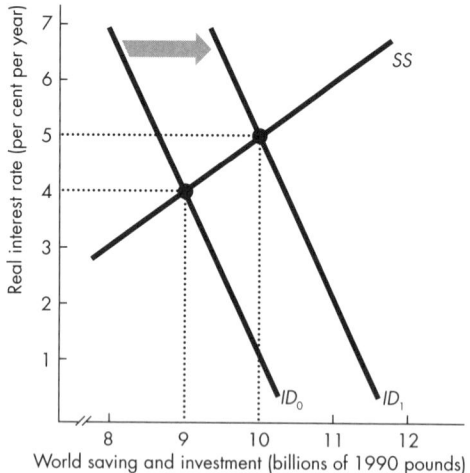

World saving and investment (billions of 1990 pounds)

3 Figure 31.9 shows an investment demand ID_0 and saving supply curve *SS*. The curves do not need to be identical to those shown; however, the investment demand curve must slope downward and the saving supply curve must slope upward. The equilibrium real interest rate is the interest rate at which the two curves cross, or 4 per cent. The equilibrium quantity of saving and investment is $9 billion.

An increase in the expected profit rate shifts the investment demand curve rightward, to ID_1 in the figure. As a result, the equilibrium real interest rate rises, to 5 per cent in the figure, and the equilibrium quantity of saving and investment also increases, to $10 billion in the figure.

PROBLEMS

1 a Table 31.7 shows the investment demand and saving supply schedules for Nirvana. The investment demand schedule was given in the problem question. To get the saving supply schedule, first note that disposable income equals aggregate income of $45 billion (potential real GDP) minus net taxes of $10 billion, or $35 billion. From this amount, at each real interest rate, subtract the consumption expenditure to get saving. Thus at the real interest rate of 3 per cent, households spend $26 billion on consumption, leaving $9 billion for saving. The equilibrium real interest rate is 6 per cent because it is the real interest rate at which the quantity of investment demanded equals the quantity of saving supplied.

Table 31.7

Real interest rate (per cent)	Investment demand (billions of pounds)	Saving supply (billions of pounds)
3	24	9
4	21	11
5	18	13
6	15	15
7	12	17

b Table 31.8 shows the $C + I + G$ and potential real GDP schedules. Potential real GDP was given in the problem question as £45 billion. The $C + I + G$ schedule is obtained at each real interest rate by adding consumption expenditure, investment and government purchases of goods and services. For instance, when the interest rate is 3 per cent, consumption expenditure is £26 billion, investment is £24 billion and government purchases are £10 billion for a total real demand of £60 billion. From Table 31.9, the equilibrium real interest rate is 6 per cent because this real interest rate sets the quantity of consumption expenditure plus investment plus government purchases equal to the potential real GDP.

Table 31.8

Real interest rate (per cent)	$C + I + G$ (billions of pounds)	Potential real GDP (billions of pounds)
3	60	45
4	55	45
5	50	45
6	45	45
7	40	45

c The equilibrium real interest rate in **a** is identical to that in **b**. They are identical because the two approaches (the saving supply/investment demand and the $C + I + G$/potential real GDP) are equivalent. To see the equivalency, take the equality between saving and investment, that is, $S = I$. To both sides, add consumption expenditure, C, which gives $C + S = C + I$. Next, recall that net taxes equal government purchases of goods and services, $NT = G$. Then, to the left side of the formula, $C + S$, add NT and to the right side, $C + I$, add G, giving $C + S + NT = C + I + G$. Now, $C + S$ equals disposable income, and adding taxes to disposable income gives aggregate income. As aggre-

gate income equals potential real GDP, the left side of the equality is potential real GDP. The right side, $C + I + G$, is the demand for real GDP. Thus the equality that initially started as $S = I$, the **a** equality, is equivalent to potential real GDP = consumption demand plus investment plus government purchases, the **b** equality.

2 a The increase in the expected profit rate increases investment demand, shifting the investment demand curve rightward.

b The increase in investment increases the total $C + I + G$ demand for real GDP, and Primus's $C + I + G$ curve shifts rightward.

c The increase in the expected rate of profit combined with no change in the real interest rate means that the quantity of investment increases.

3 Investment can be financed by national saving and borrowing from the rest of the world. In Primus's case, national saving does not change because the real interest rate is constant. Thus the increase in investment is financed by borrowing from the rest of the world, as Primus runs a current account deficit and capital account surplus.

Figure 31.10

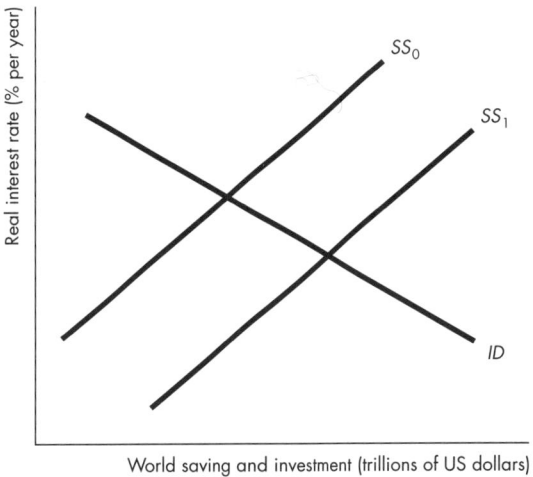

World saving and investment (trillions of US dollars)

4 Figure 31.10 shows investment demand ID and saving supply curve SS_0. (Your curves may have a different slope). The equilibrium quantities of saving and investment are shown by the intersection of these curves. An increase in saving will shift the curve to SS_1, increasing the quantity of saving and investment.

DISCUSSION QUESTION

1 Investment means the purchase of new capital goods; that is, investment refers to buying the actual capital good.

If the real interest rate goes up, people are less likely to borrow to buy a car or anything else. Companies behave in the same way. If the real interest rate goes up, companies will borrow less, cutting back on their investments. So when the real interest rate rises, the quantity of investment that firms demand decreases.

DATA QUESTIONS

1 In 'real households' disposable income', the 'real' refers to data that have been adjusted to remove the effects of inflation. 'Disposable income' is income after income tax has been removed.

2 Any of the factors which cause shifts in aggregate demand or aggregate supply might cause shifts in real income.

3 1995 = 100 means that 1995 has been chosen as a base year. This makes comparisons easy; for example between 1995 and 1997 households' disposable income rose in real terms by 5.9 per cent.

4 Apart from current disposable income, the factors that might affect consumption are such things as expected future income. They are discussed in detail in the main text on pages 785–791.

Chapter 32 | Long-term Economic Growth

Chapter in Perspective, Text Pages 802–827

Why do economies grow? This question is at the heart of this chapter. The sources are varied – markets, property rights and monetary exchange provide a foundation, but technology is also crucial. Various theories of economic growth are discussed here as are the policies needed to achieve growth.

Helpful Hints

1 Economics is sometimes called the 'dismal science'. This nickname came about because of the classical growth theory. The main conclusion from the classical approach is that, in the long run, workers are bound to earn only a subsistence wage. This result is, indeed, dismal! And, from our perspective soon after the start of a new millennium, it also must seem odd. The fact that the classical model of growth was developed at the beginning of the industrial revolution is somewhat ironic. The classical model of growth focuses on population growth and does not allow for continuing technological change and capital growth, two features of the industrial revolution that were to become an increasingly important aspect of the world in which we live. It is these omissions that account for the dismal, subsistence-wage conclusion of the classical model.

One of the advancements made by the neo-classical growth theory was its emphasis on technological growth as an engine of economic development. The new growth theory goes even further by examining the factors that lead to technological change in the form of increasing society's stock of knowledge. In the new growth theory, economic growth can persist indefinitely because the incentive to accumulate more knowledge persists indefinitely. In a real sense, then, the nickname for economics might be changed, perhaps to the 'happy science'!

2 In the neoclassical model, an increase in technology sets off a spurt of economic growth. However, this growth does not continue forever; eventually, unless another technological change occurs, economic growth dies out. The reason that growth eventually stops is important to understand and can be summed up in one phrase: 'the law of diminishing returns'. The law of diminishing returns is a key assumption of the neo-classical theory; it accounts for the downward slope of the capital demand curve.

To understand this law, we need to examine how the 'return' (the additional output that additional capital creates) of 'ordinary' capital changes as more capital is accumulated. A concrete example is industrial robots. When an industrial robot is installed in a factory, only that particular factory can use the robot. The first such robot may be quite valuable as it fits well into the factory's operations, a fairly large number of workers are available to service it, and it can produce a lot of output. Thus its return is quite high and, because it's producing a lot of additional output, economic growth is robust. The second robot in the factory may be almost as valuable, but now consider, say, the twentieth robot installed in the plant. With 20 robots, the factory is starting to get crowded. Workers servicing the robots are starting to be spread thin, with the result that the robots may spend a substantial period waiting to be repaired or reprogrammed. Thus the twentieth robot is likely to produce significantly less additional output than the first robot. Essentially, the amount of economic growth created by the twentieth robot is substantially less than that created by the first robot. As more and more robots are installed, the return continues to fall until eventually it reaches zero and economic growth ceases.

In addition, because the return from additional robots diminishes, the return from installing additional robots falls as more robots are obtained. As a result, more robots are installed only if the opportunity cost of buying them (the real interest rate) falls, which means that the demand curve for industrial robots – or, more generally, ordinary capital – slopes downward.

3 In contrast to the neoclassical theory of growth, discussed in Helpful Hint 2, in the new growth theory, economic growth can persist forever.

The crucial ingredient in the new growth theory is the assumption that the demand for knowledge capital curve is horizontal. What accounts for the assumption? That is, why doesn't this demand curve slope downward like other demand curves, such as the demand curve for (ordinary) capital?

The answers to these questions lie in the behaviour of the return from knowledge capital compared with the return from ordinary capital. Think of knowledge capital as 'a better way to produce output', that is, a new technology. When the first 'better way' is developed, it can be applied to all similar factories in the economy, not just the one that developed it. The new technology will increase output so that economic growth occurs. The second 'better way' also will increase output. Now consider the twentieth new technology. This new technology will continue to increase output. But (unlike the twentieth industrial robot discussed in Helpful Hint 2), nothing diminishes the amount of additional output created. Factories are not getting more crowded, and workers are not being spread more thinly. In other words, *all* similar factories anywhere can use the new technology as can workers in *all* these factories. The twentieth 'new way' may well replace, say, the nineteenth 'new way' so that the gain in output from the twentieth unit of knowledge capital may be as large as the gain in output from the first. Hence, unlike ordinary capital, the return from additional new knowledge capital does not diminish. New knowledge capital will continue to be developed even if the opportunity cost of developing it (the real interest rate) does not fall. Hence the knowledge capital demand curve does not slope downward; it is horizontal, which indicates that, even if the real interest rate does not fall, more knowledge capital will be developed and economic growth will continue.

SELF-TEST

CONCEPT REVIEW

1 Over the 150 years from 1858 to 1998 real GDP per person in the United Kingdom increased at an average of _____ per cent a year.

2 Three institutions are crucial to the creation of incentives. They are markets, _____ _____ and _____ exchange.

3 Growth accounting separates the contribution to economic growth of the growth of aggregate

_____ , of _____ per hour and of _____ change.

4 Economic growth arises from improvements in _____ capital, increases in the _____ stock and improvements in _____ .

5 The three main theories of economic growth are the _____ theory, the neoclassical theory and new _____ theory.

6 New growth theory is that the growth rate depends on the costs and benefits of developing new _____ .

7 To achieve faster growth we must increase the growth of _____ per hour or increase the pace of _____ advance.

TRUE OR FALSE

___ **1** In the new theory of economic growth, economic growth can continue indefinitely.

___ **2** The neoclassical growth theory stressed the role played by people's incentives for discovering new technology.

___ **3** Limiting the extent of international trade increases the rate of economic growth.

___ **4** The lower the real interest rate, the larger is the quantity supplied of capital.

___ **5** Energy price hikes are one of the causes of the productivity growth slowdown.

___ **6** The law of diminishing returns states that, as more capital is used, the total output produced diminishes.

___ **7** An increase in the amount of capital per hour of work shifts the productivity function upward.

___ **8** An assumption of the classical growth theory is that an increase in real wages and incomes increases the population growth rate.

___ **9** In the neoclassical theory of growth, a technological advance that increases the productivity of capital shifts the capital demand curve rightward.

MULTIPLE CHOICE

1 Which of the following is *not* a source of economic growth?
a saving and investment in new capital
b the productivity function
c investment in human capital
d discovery of new technologies

2 The demand curve for knowledge capital
a is vertical.
b slopes downward.
c slopes upward.
d is horizontal.

3 Growth accounting divides changes in productivity into changes resulting from
a markets and property rights.
b saving and investment.
c capital per hour of labour and technology.
d human capital and other capital.

4 With no technological change, a 10 per cent increase in capital per hour of work causes approximately a _____ per cent increase in output per hour of labour.
a 30
b 10
c 3.3
d 1

5 Which theory of economic growth concludes that growth can be a 'perpetual motion machine'?
a the classical theory
b the neoclassical theory
c the new theory
d all of the theories

6 Which theory of economic growth concludes that in the long run people will be paid only a subsistence real wage?
a the classical theory
b the neoclassical theory
c the new theory
d all of the theories

7 An increase in the amount of capital per hour of work causes
a the productivity function to shift upward.
b the productivity function to shift downward.
c a movement along the productivity function to a higher level of output per hour of work.
d a movement along the productivity function to a lower level of output per hour of work.

8 Technological advancement causes
  a the productivity function to shift upward.
  b the productivity function to shift downward.
  c a movement along the productivity function to a higher level of output per hour of work.
  d a movement along the productivity function to a lower level of output per hour of work.

9 A key assumption of new growth theory is that
  a all technological change is exogenous.
  b higher incomes lead to a higher birth rate.
  c a successful innovator has the opportunity to earn a temporary, above-average profit.
  d the rate of time preference is less than the real interest rate.

10 If the real interest rate exceeds the rate of time preference, the capital _____ _____ shifts _____ .
  a demand curve; rightward
  b demand curve; leftward
  c supply curve; rightward
  d supply curve; leftward

11 Suppose that capital per hour of work increases by 30 per cent and that real GDP per hour of work increases by 18 per cent. What is the contribution to the increase in real GDP per hour of work from the change in capital per hour of work?
  a the increase in capital per hour of work increases real GDP per hour of work by 30 per cent
  b the increase in capital per hour of work increases real GDP per hour of work by 18 per cent
  c the increase in capital per hour of work increases real GDP per hour of work by 10 per cent
  d the increase in capital per hour of work increases real GDP per hour of work by 8 per cent

12 Suppose that capital per hour of work increases by 30 per cent while real GDP per hour of work increases by 18 per cent. What is the contribution to the increase in real GDP per hour of work from changing technology?
  a the change in technology increases real GDP per hour of work by 30 per cent
  b the change in technology increases real GDP per hour of work by 18 per cent
  c the change in technology increases real GDP per hour of work by 10 per cent

  d the change in technology increases real GDP per hour of work by 8 per cent

13 Of the following types of capital, which does *not* have diminishing returns?
  a personal computers
  b knowledge
  c new oil discoveries
  d industrial robots

14 A classical growth theory assumption was that
  a the population growth rate increases when real GDP per person increases.
  b saving is more important than investment in determining economic growth.
  c capital plays a major role in determining how rapidly the economy grows.
  d human capital is the ultimate cause of economic growth.

15 In the new theory of economic growth, as long as the real interest rate is greater than the rate of time preference
  a the population growth rate increases.
  b saving is less than investment.
  c international trade is necessary.
  d more knowledge capital is acquired.

16 Dynamic comparative advantage
  a can boost a country's economic growth rate permanently.
  b is temporary and often goes to the supplier who is first in the market.
  c had no role in contributing to the growth of the 'miracle economies'.
  d is a source of permanently higher profits for a firm.

SHORT ANSWER

1 What are the three basic preconditions for economic growth? Explain the role that each plays in promoting economic growth. Are these preconditions sufficient for economic growth to continue for ever? Why or why not?

2 Would the slowdown in productivity growth have been as large if real GDP had included the value of improving the environment?

3 Igor was recently named minister for the economy. His first task is to predict his country's long-term growth prospects. Igor expects that capital per hour of labour will grow at 1 per cent per year. Moreover, he expects technological change of 1 per cent per year. What productivity growth rate will Igor predict?

4 Re-read the *Reading Between the Lines* article. What would be the disadvantages of removing planning regulations?

PROBLEMS

1 **a** In Fig. 32.1, illustrate a productivity function that shows that when capital per hour of work is £30 then £20 of real GDP per hour of work is produced. Label this point *a*.

Figure 32.1

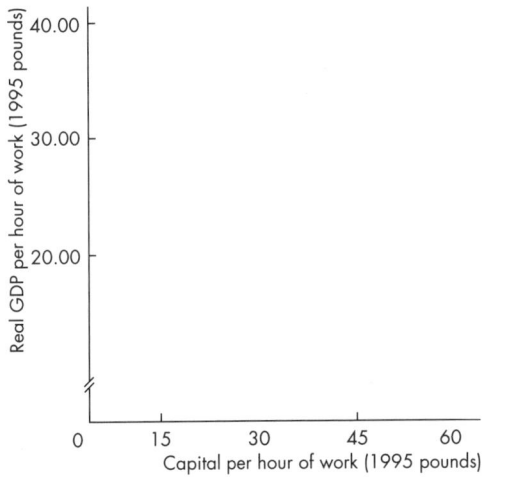

b In Fig. 32.1, show what happens to the amount of real GDP per hour of work when the amount of capital per hour of work increases from £30 to £60. After the increase in capital per hour of work, what is the new amount of real GDP per hour of work? (Use the one-third rule.)

c In Fig. 32.1, show what happens to the productivity function when new technology is developed.

2 **a** In 1999, real GDP per person in the country of Slow is £2,000 and is growing at the rate of 1 per cent per year. After 1 year, what is real GDP per person? After 2 years? After 10 years? After 25 years?

b Real GDP per person in Fast is £2,000 and is growing at the rate of 3 per cent per year. After 1 year, what is real GDP per person? After 2 years? After 10 years? After 25 years?

c Initially the ratio of GDP per person in Fast to GDP per person in Slow is 1.00. What is the ratio after 1 year? After 25 years?

Figure 32.2

3 In Fig. 32.2, draw a demand curve for physical capital, such as machine tools. Label this curve KD_0. Also in Fig. 32.2, draw a demand for knowledge capital curve and label it KD_1. If these curves are similar, explain why; if they are dissimilar, explain why.

DISCUSSION QUESTIONS

1 Explain the relationship between the saving supply curve and capital supply curve.

2 Can you relate shifts in the capital supply curve to the saving supply curve?

DATA QUESTIONS

The advantages of machines

In manufactures the same number of hands, assisted with the best machinery, will work up a much greater quantity of goods than with more imperfect instruments of trade. The expense which is properly laid out upon fixed capital of any kind is always repaid with great profit. [However, this requires that] A certain quantity of materials and the labour of a certain number of workmen, both of which might have been immediately employed to augment the food, clothing and subsistence of society are thus diverted to another employment.

Source: Adam Smith (1776) *The Wealth of Nations*, Penguin, p. 383.

1 Which part of this extract might cause disagreement among modern economists?

2 Can you think of a modern concept which describes the ideas of the last sentence?

ANSWERS

CONCEPT REVIEW

1 1.3

2 property rights; market

3 hours; capital; technological

4 human; capital; technology

5 classical; growth

6 technologies

7 capital; technological

TRUE OR FALSE

1 T Economic growth can persist for ever because the return from new knowledge capital does not diminish.

2 F The neoclassical growth theory stressed the role played by saving and investment; the new growth theory emphasizes people's incentives.

3 F The rapidly growing miracle economies demonstrate that allowing international trade is good economic growth policy.

4 F The lower the real interest rate, the smaller is the quantity of capital supplied.

5 T As a result of massive hikes in the price of energy, technological development was devoted to reducing the amount of energy used in production rather than increasing overall productivity.

6 F The law of diminishing returns states that as more capital is used the *additional* output produced diminishes.

7 F An increase in the quantity of capital per hour of work causes a movement along a productivity function, not a shift in the function.

8 T The data, however, show just the opposite: an increase in real wages and incomes is associated with a decrease in the population growth rate.

9 T By increasing the demand for capital, the equilibrium quantity of capital increases and so, too, does the country's real GDP

MULTIPLE CHOICE

1 b The productivity function can illustrate economic growth, but it is not a source of growth.

2 d The demand curve is horizontal because knowledge capital is not subject to diminishing returns.

3 c Growth accounting is used to divide changes in productivity into different factors so that the factors responsible for growth can be identified.

4 c From the one-third rule, output per hour of labour increases by 10 per cent $\times \frac{1}{3}$, or 3.3 per cent.

5 c Only in the new theory can economic growth continue for ever without some exogenous source of change.

6 a This conclusion of the classical theory for the long run was based on the assumption that population growth rises when income increases.

7 c An increase in capital per hour of work causes a movement along the productivity function.

8 a Technological advances shift the productivity function upward.

9 c The opportunity to earn an above-average profit gives innovators the incentive to develop new technologies.

10 c When the real interest rate exceeds the rate of time preference, people save and the supply of capital increases.

11 c The one-third rule states that the increase in real GDP per hour of work from the increase in capital per hour of work is $\frac{1}{3} \times 30$ per cent, or 10 per cent.

12 d Based on the answer to **11**, the increase in capital per hour of work raised productivity by 10 per cent, leaving technology to account for the remaining 8 per cent.

13 b Knowledge capital does not have diminishing returns, so its demand curve is horizontal.

14 a The data, however, show that this assumption is false. Population growth *decreases* when income increases.

15 d When the real interest rate exceeds the rate of time preference, saving occurs; this saving allows more knowledge capital to be accumulated.

16 b Dynamic comparative advantage refers to the point that the costs of the first supplier in a market often are temporarily lower than those of the latecomers.

SHORT ANSWER

1 The three necessary preconditions for economic growth are markets, property rights and monetary exchange. Markets enable people to buy and sell at low cost. In addition, markets create and convey important information in the form of prices. Monetary exchange also facilities buying and selling. Thus markets and monetary exchange help promote specialization, which can vastly increase the amount of goods and services produced. Property rights are a key to specialization. Without secure property rights, people would be less willing to specialize because the good they produce might be taken from them without their deriving any personal benefit from it.

These preconditions are not sufficient for growth to continue for ever. To have persistent growth, saving, investing in new capital (both physical and human) and developing new technologies must occur. Without the necessary three preconditions, saving, investing and developing new technologies will not occur. But simply having the three preconditions in place is no guarantee that saving, investing and developing new technologies will occur.

2 No, the slowdown in productivity growth would not have been as large. One of the reasons for the slowdown was that the value of an improved environment is not included in real GDP. During the 1970s, investment often was aimed at reducing pollution. If the benefit of the resulting cleaner environment had been included, real GDP would have been larger and, as a result, productivity – which equals real GDP divided by aggregate hours of work – also would have been larger.

3 Use the one-third rule to predict the productivity growth rate. Capital per hour of labour is growing at 1 per cent and will contribute productivity growth of $1/3$ per cent. Technological change contributes another 1 per cent, so Igor will predict that total productivity growth will be $1\frac{1}{3}$ per cent.

4 There is no doubt that planning regulations are a nuisance to many firms. However, they are often needed to prevent market failure. For example, there would be external pollution costs if firms could locate wherever they wished. Similarly, health and safety regulations protect workers and food hygiene regulations protect customers.

PROBLEMS

Figure 32.3

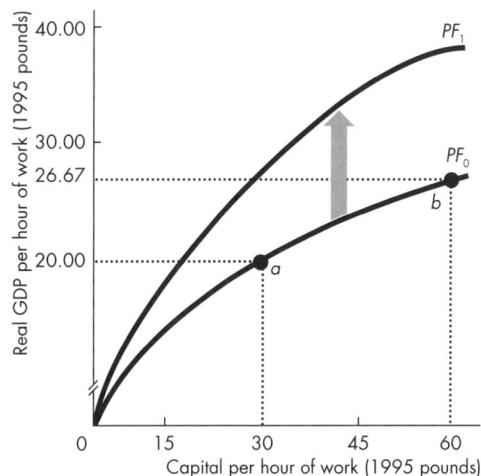

1 a Figure 32.3 shows the initial productivity function PF_0, going through point a.

b An increase in the amount of capital per hour – say, from $30 to $60 – causes a movement along productivity function PF_0 from point a (real GDP of $20 per hour) to point b. The increase in capital per hour is 100 per cent. Thus the one-third rule states that real GDP per hour of work will increase by one-third of 100 per cent, or 33 per cent. The new level of real GDP per hour of work is $26.67.

c An increase in technology shifts the productivity function upward. This shift is from productivity function PF_0 to the new productivity function PF_1.

2 a After 1 year, real GDP per person in Slow is $2,000 × 1.01 = $2,020.00. After 2 years, real GDP per person in Slow is $2,000 × (1.01)^2 = $2,040.20. Similarly, after 10 years real GDP per person is $2,209.24 and after 25 years is $2,564.86.

b Real GDP per person in Fast after 1 year is $2,060.00; after 2 years is $2,121.80; after 10 years is $2,687.83; and after 25 years is $4,187.56.

c After 1 year, the ratio of real GDP per person in Fast to real GDP per person in Slow is £2,060.00/£2,020.00 = 1.02. After 25 years the ratio is £4,187.56/£2,564.86 = 1.63. In other words, after 25 years, real GDP per person in Fast is 63 per cent higher than in Slow. This result demonstrates how a slightly more rapid growth rate compounds over time to create a large difference in real GDP per person.

Figure 32.4

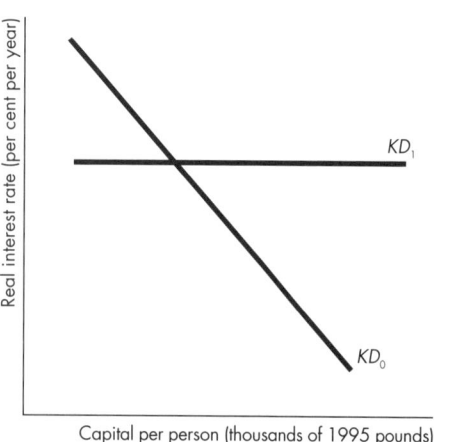

Capital per person (thousands of 1995 pounds)

3 Figure 32.4 illustrates the two types of capital. There is an important difference between the two curves: the demand for physical capital curve slopes downward, whereas the demand for knowledge capital curve is horizontal. The difference in the slopes of the curves reflects the difference in how their returns change when more capital is acquired. As more physical capital is acquired, the return from the capital falls. Thus the quantity demanded of physical capital increases only if the opportunity cost of the new capital decreases, that is, only if the real interest rate falls. However, the return from knowledge capital does not diminish. So if the real interest rate is below the return from knowledge capital, people will demand additional knowledge capital even if the real interest rate does not fall further.

DISCUSSION QUESTION

1 Stocks and flows are the key to the relationship between the saving supply and the capital supply curves.

The capital supply curve shows us the stock of capital, that is, the total amount of capital in the economy. The saving supply curve shows us the flow of saving,

that is, the flow of new capital. So the amount of saving – which we get from the saving supply curve – shows us the addition to the capital stock – which we measure from the capital supply curve.

Figure 32.5

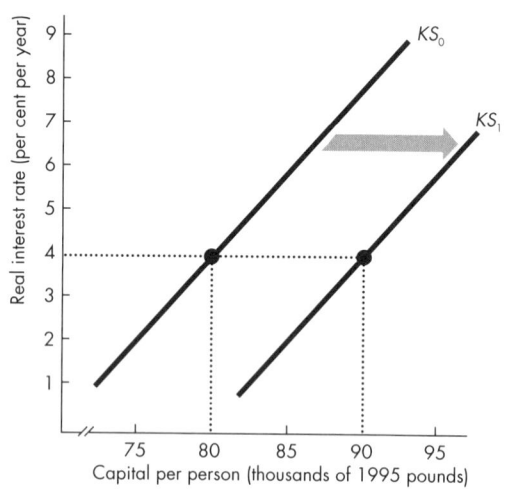

Capital per person (thousands of 1995 pounds)

2 If we assume no depreciation the relationship can be illustrated by Fig. 32.5. Suppose that at the beginning of this year the capital supply curve is KS_0. Also, let's say that the real interest rate is 4 per cent so that the quantity of capital supplied is £80,000 per person. During the year, suppose that the real interest rate remains at 4 per cent and that people save an additional £10,000 of capital per person. Thus at the end of the year, the supply curve of capital will shift rightward to KS_1, which shows that, at a real interest rate of 4 per cent, £90,000 of capital per worker now is supplied. In other words, the deal is that when people save, more total capital is available, so the supply curve of capital shifts rightward and it shifts rightward by the amount of the saving.

DATA QUESTIONS

1 Modern economists might be more cautious in their language. 'Fixed capital of *any* kind will *always* be repaid with great profit' is not necessarily true. Smith is here indulging in a bit of propaganda in favour of capital investment.

2 Smith is describing what modern economists call 'opportunity cost'.

Chapter 33 **The Business Cycle**

Chapter in Perspective, Text Pages 828–857

If economic growth was constant, with, for example, GDP rising by 3 per cent every year, then economic life would be much simpler. Unfortunately, it is characterized by boom and recession. This chapter explores several theories of the business cycle and then uses these theories to analyse recent economic history.

Helpful Hints

1 This chapter should be rewarding for those who have expended the effort required to understand the preceding chapters because it introduces no new analytic methods. Instead, the fully developed aggregate demand and aggregate supply model is applied to the analysis of some interesting macroeconomic episodes, including the Great Depression.

2 As you examine various macroeconomic episodes, focus on a key question: are the primary changes in aggregate demand, in aggregate supply, or possibly in both? Also, as you follow the various changes, be sure that you understand what is going on in the labour market that underlies the goods and services market. The labour market will tell you what is happening to two key variables: employment and unemployment.

3 Competing theories are used to explain real-world events. Facts, such as the level of wages or employment, are not in dispute. The dispute centres on the changes in the economy that caused the facts. It also touches on the government policies that might affect the economy.

Remember, these are theories, not statements of fact, and their explanations could be incorrect. Only proper empirical investigation over time will determine their validity.

4 The real business cycle theory is closely linked to the flexible wage theory of the labour market. In particular, the real business cycle theory is based on the assumption that the economy is always producing on its long-run aggregate supply curve; that is, the economy is always at potential GDP. Because potential GDP is also the full-employment level of GDP, the real business cycle theory asserts that, in the labour market, wages (or other mechanisms) are sufficiently flexible so that the economy is always at full employment. Thus the real business cycle/flexible wage theory view is that fluctuations in employment represent fluctuations in the level of full employment. The level of full employment changes when labour demand and/or labour supply changes. For instance, a decrease in labour demand decreases the level of full-employment equilibrium and actual employment in the economy decreases.

As the text indicates, the real business cycle theory of the economy is highly controversial.

The assumptions underlying this approach seem extreme to many economists. In particular, the views that money wages are so flexible that the economy is always at full employment, that the impulse creating business cycles is fluctuations in technology, and that changes in the money supply do not affect real GDP are rejected by the majority of economists. Nonetheless, real business cycle theory has had a surprising amount of success in explaining various facts about business cycles, and a sizeable minority of economists believe that the real business cycle theory is a good way to analyse the business cycle. Which group of economists is correct? At this time, it is impossible to tell because the evidence on the real business cycle theory is still accumulating. But if this approach ultimately is accepted, it will represent a major change from the more conventional aggregate demand theories.

SELF-TEST

CONCEPT REVIEW

1 Three types of aggregate demand theories are discussed. They are _____ theory, _____ theory and _____ expectations theory.

2 _____ theory says the business cycle is caused by volatile _____ , a multiplier effect and _____ wages.

3 Monetarist theory explains the theory in terms of changes in the growth rate of _____ .

4 Rational expectations theories say the cycle is caused by _____ fluctuations in aggregate _____ .

5 The _____ business cycle theory says economic fluctuations are caused by _____ change that makes productivity growth fluctuate.

6 A 1930s style of depression is unlikely today because of factors such as _____ deposit protection, the Bank of England's role as _____ of last resort and the greater importance of _____ and spending in the economy.

TRUE OR FALSE

— 1 One reason that a recession is likely to be much less severe than during the 1930s is that the government sector is much larger now than it was then.

— 2 The stock market crash of 1929 was the most important cause of the Great Depression.

— 3 The real business cycle theory is based on the assumption that money wages are flexible and adjust quickly.

— 4 The data show that recessions start when investment slows or decreases.

— 5 The new Keynesian theory of the business cycle stresses intertemporal substitution.

— 6 The impulse in the Keynesian theory of business cycles is a change in firms' expectations of future sales and profits.

— 7 Keynesian, monetarist and rational expectations theories of business cycles focus on fluctuations in aggregate demand as the cause of business cycles.

— 8 According to the real business cycle theory, a drop in productivity increases the demand for labour.

— 9 In the Keynesian theory, money wages do not fall in response to a decrease in aggregate demand.

MULTIPLE CHOICE

1 Monetarists and Keynesians assert that the Great Depression reflected a _____ shift of the aggregate _____ curve.
a leftward; supply
b rightward; supply
c rightward; demand
d leftward; demand

2 According to monetarists such as Milton Friedman, the Great Depression was caused by

a the stock market crash of 1929.

b a massive contraction of the money supply, leading to large decreases in aggregate demand.

c an expansion of the money supply, leading to higher inflation.

d loss of business and consumer confidence.

3 Which of the following is the impulse in the Keynesian business cycle theory?

a an unexpected change in aggregate demand

b a change in the growth rate of the money supply

c a change in expectations about future sales and profits

d a change in the growth rate of productivity

4 Which of the following is the impulse in the monetarist business cycle theory?

a an unexpected change in aggregate demand

b a change in the growth rate of the money supply

c a change in expectations about future sales and profits

d a change in the growth rate of productivity

5 Which of the following is the impulse in the rational expectations business cycle theories?

a an unexpected change in aggregate demand

b a change in the growth rate of the money supply

c a change in expectations about future sales and profits

d a change in the growth rate of productivity

6 Which of the following is the impulse in the real business cycle theory?

a an unexpected change in aggregate demand

b a change in the growth rate of the money supply

c a change in expectations about future sales and profits

d a change in the growth rate of productivity

7 An increase in aggregate demand increases GDP by the least amount in the _____ .

a Keynesian theory

b monetarist theory

c new Keynesian theory

d real business cycle theory

8 Multi-income families reduce the probability of another Great Depression by

a reducing the probability of everyone in the family being simultaneously unemployed.

b investing more in the economy.

c paying more taxes.

d increasing fluctuations in consumption.

9 The intertemporal substitution effect refers to the idea that

a a higher real wage rate increases the quantity of labour supplied.

b a higher real wage rate decreases the quantity of labour supplied.

c a higher real interest rate increases the supply of labour.

d the demand for labour depends on the money wage rate, not the real wage rate.

10 According to the _____ theory of business cycles, a change in the monetary growth rate has no effect on real GDP.

a Keynesian

b monetarist

c new Keynesian

d real business cycle

11 An average recession lasts for about _____ ; an average expansion lasts for about _____ .

a 1 year; 1 year

b 4 years; 1 year

c 1 year; 4 years

d 4 years; 4 years

12 In an average recession, real GDP falls by about _____ ; in an average expansion real GDP climbs by about _____ .

a 6 per cent; 6 per cent

b 22 per cent; 6 per cent

c 6 per cent; 22 per cent

d 22 per cent; 22 per cent

13 Which theory of the business cycle has a mechanism that allows the economy to remain in a recession indefinitely?

a Keynesian

b monetarist

c new classical

d new Keynesian

14 Which of the following is *not* a criticism of the real business cycle theory?

a The impulse assumed for the real business cycle theory is implausible.

b The long-run aggregate supply curve is vertical.

c Money wages are sticky.

d The changes in productivity ascribed to technological advances actually are caused by changes in aggregate demand.

SHORT ANSWER

1 What caused the recession that became the Great Depression? What changed the recession into the Great Depression?

2 What is the basic controversy among economists about the behaviour of the labour market during a recession? What is each theory's position in this controversy? Why is the controversy important in terms of designing an appropriate anti-recessionary economic policy?

3 How do government transfer payments help reduce the severity of a recession caused by an unexpected decrease in aggregate demand?

4 List four important features of the economy that make severe depression less likely today. Explain how each factor helps stabilize the economy.

5 The *Reading Between the Lines* article suggests that the UK business cycle has followed the American rather than the European pattern. Do you think that this will continue?

PROBLEMS

Figure 33.1

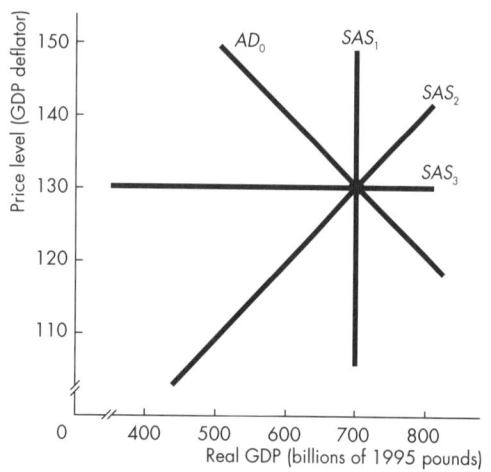

1 Figure 33.1 shows the initial aggregate demand curve, AD_0, and three aggregate supply curves.

a Which aggregate supply curve is consistent with Keynesian theory?

b Which aggregate supply curve is consistent with monetarist theory?

c Which aggregate supply curve is consistent with real business cycle theory?

2 Suppose that the aggregate demand curve in Fig. 33.1 shifts leftward by £200 billion at every price level.

a Draw this shift in Fig. 33.1.

b Along which aggregate supply curve is the decrease in GDP the largest? The least?

c Relate your answers to **b** to your answers to Problem 1. In particular, for a shift in aggregate demand, which theory predicts the largest decrease in GDP? The smallest decrease in GDP? The largest change in the price level? The smallest?

3 Complete Table 33.1 by listing the impulse that each theory stresses as the primary cause of business cycles.

Table 33.1 Theories and Impulses

Theory	Impulse
Keynesian	
Monetarist	
New classical	
New Keynesian	
Real business cycle	

DISCUSSION QUESTION

1 Why are the cause(s) of business cycles not fully understood?

DATA QUESTIONS

Summer surge in company failures
Nearly 1,000 businesses went bust every week over the summer as the commercial failure rate reached its highest third-quarter level since recession in 1992. The surge is blamed on the economic slowdown of last year. Worst hit was Wales where investment cutbacks by Japanese and other companies have sent many businesses over the edge.

Source: *The Guardian*, 4 October 1999, p. 22.

1 Why should 'investment cut-backs' cause bankruptcies?

ANSWERS

CONCEPT REVIEW

1 Keynesian; monetarist; rational

2 Keynesian; expectations; sticky

3 money

4 unanticipated; demand

5 real; technological

6 bank; lender; taxes

TRUE OR FALSE

1 T The government sector tends to stabilize the economy because government purchases do not decline in a recession.

2 F The stock market crash may have increased uncertainty and helped spur the initial recession in 1929, but it was not the cause of the Great Depression.

3 T With rapidly and efficiently adjusting money wages, the real business cycle theory asserts that the economy is always at full employment.

4 T Recessions start when investment slows and expansions begin when investment accelerates.

5 F The real business cycle theory stresses intertemporal substitution.

6 T Because these expectations can change so rapidly, Keynes called them 'animal spirits'.

7 T The sole exception to the focus on aggregate demand is the real business cycle theory, which focuses on fluctuations in aggregate supply.

8 F A decline in productivity *decreases* the demand for labour.

9 T Because money wages do not fall, the economy remains stuck in a recession until aggregate demand increases.

MULTIPLE CHOICE

1 d Although monetarists and Keynesians disagree about what shifted the aggregate demand curve, both agree that the Great Depression reflected massive leftward shifts in the aggregate demand curve.

2 b Monetarists point to the Great Depression as evidence that changes in monetary growth are a major impulse in creating business cycles.

3 c The Keynesian theory emphasizes the 'animal spirits' of future sales and profit expectations.

4 b Monetarists assert that the major impulse in creating business cycles is changes in the growth rate of the money supply.

5 a Rational expectations theories point to unexpected changes in aggregate demand as the impulse that causes business cycles.

6 d The real business cycle theory suggests that the impulse that creates business cycles is changes in the growth rate of productivity.

7 d In the real business cycle theory, changes in aggregate demand have *no* effect on real GDP; instead, they affect only the price level.

8 a Because everyone in the family is not likely to be unemployed simultaneously, the family's income is much less likely to fall to zero. As a result, the family's consumption expenditures are more stable.

9 c Basically, the higher real interest rate boosts the return from saving, so in order to earn more and thus save more, people increase their supply of labour when the real interest rate rises.

10 d Real business cycle theory asserts that only real factors – not monetary factors – can affect real GDP.

11 c Recessions are shorter than expansions.

12 c Generally, after each recession GDP climbs during the next expansion to new heights.

13 a Because money wages are assumed not to respond to decreases in aggregate demand, after a decrease in aggregate demand the economy remains mired in a recession until some other factor causes an increase in aggregate demand.

14 b The long-run aggregate supply *is* vertical because it reflects potential real GDP.

SHORT ANSWER

1 The major cause of the Great Depression was an unanticipated decrease in aggregate demand, which was the consequence of reduced investment and consumer expenditure (especially on durable goods), owing to uncertainty and pessimism. However, these changes created only a 'typical' recession, not the Great Depression. The reason(s) given for the recession's worsening are controversial. Some economists contend that further decreases in aggregate demand caused by uncertainty led to the Great Depression. Other economists assert that governments failed to act in a timely and proper manner. In particular, these economists point to the massive contraction in the money supply and the waves of bank failures in many countries as the factors that converted a recession into the Great Depression.

2 Economists disagree about the speed with which the money (and hence also the real) wage rate adjusts in the labour market.

Some economists (Keynesians and new Keynesians) believe that money wages are sticky and adjust only slowly to price level changes; indeed, Keynesian economists think that money wages do not adjust to decreases in aggregate demand. Monetarists also think that money wages are sticky but not as sticky as Keynesian and new Keynesian economists think. In particular, money wages will adjust to changes in the price level, but not immediately, in the monetarist view. New classical economists also may acknowledge some stickiness in money wages but less so than monetarists do. However, real business cycle economists think that the money wage is flexible and quickly adjusts to changes in the price level. As a result, the labour market always is in equilibrium and any changes in employment reflect changes in full employment.

This issue has a significant implication for the design of an appropriate policy to respond to recession. If the Keynesians and new Keynesians are correct, expansionary monetary or fiscal policies may be useful in counteracting recession because the recessionary decrease in employment is a sign that money wages are failing to adjust rapidly. However, if the real business cycle position is correct (the economy is always at full employment, so the decline in employment during the recession is a sign that the level of full employment has fallen), expansionary monetary or fiscal policy will simply increase the rate of inflation and have no effect on real GDP or unemployment.

3 When a recession arises, unemployment increases and disposable income declines. Less disposable income leads to a reduction in consumption expenditure, which has a further multiplier effect (negatively) on aggregate demand. Transfer payments reduce the secondary effects of a recession by reducing the amount by which disposable income falls. As incomes fall and unemployment increases, government transfer payments increase in the form of higher unemployment benefits or other welfare payments. As a result, the decline in both disposable income and consumption is reduced.

4 The four important features of the economy that make severe depression less likely today are that:

1 bank deposits are insured;

2 national banks are better prepared to be the 'lender of last resort';

3 taxes and government spending are a larger fraction of GDP; and

4 multi-income families are more economically secure.

Reasons (1) and (2) make a collapse of the money supply and the banking system much less likely today. With deposit insurance, bank failures do not feed on each other; that is, if a bank fails today, its depositors are not afraid that they will lose all the deposits that have been entrusted to the bank. Hence bank failures do not feed on each other. The fact that national central banks are more determined to play an active 'lender of last resort' role means that, when banks need emergency funds, the central bank will loan them the funds rather than allow the banks to fail. Hence, for both reasons, a massive wave of bank failures and contraction of the money supply, as occurred during the Great Depression, is unlikely.

The larger size of the government sector helps stabilize aggregate demand. Government purchases do not (automatically) decline during recessions, so aggregate demand may decrease less. In addition, as incomes fall during a recession, so too do income taxes, which helps moderate the drop in disposable incomes and thus stabilizes consumption expenditures.

Finally, the increased number of multi-income families also helps stabilize the economy. In a multi-income family, when one worker becomes unemployed during a recession, the family still has income from its other wage earner(s). Thus this family's consumption expenditures do not decrease as much during a recession and overall consumption expenditure – and hence aggregate demand – becomes more stable.

5 To answer this question you need to decide if the three reasons given for following the US pattern are valid. Then, if they are, you need to decide if they will continue. You may (or may not!) think that in the long run the rise in trade with the rest of the EU will be significant.

PROBLEMS

1 a Aggregate supply curve SAS_3 is consistent with the Keynesian view of a horizontal aggregate supply curve.

b Aggregate supply curve SAS_2 is a monetarist, upward-sloping aggregate supply curve.

c Real business cycle theory asserts that the economy is always on its vertical long-run aggregate supply, so the real business cycle aggregate supply curve is SAS_1.

2 a Figure 33.2 shows the £2 billion decrease in aggregate demand.

b Along aggregate supply SAS_3 the new equilibrium is at point *a*. The price level has stayed constant (at 130), but GDP has declined by £200 billion. The smallest change in GDP occurs with aggregate supply curve SAS_1. Along this aggregate supply curve, the new equilibrium is at point *c*, so the price level falls the most (from 130 to 110) but GDP does not change; it remains at £700 billion.

Figure 33.2

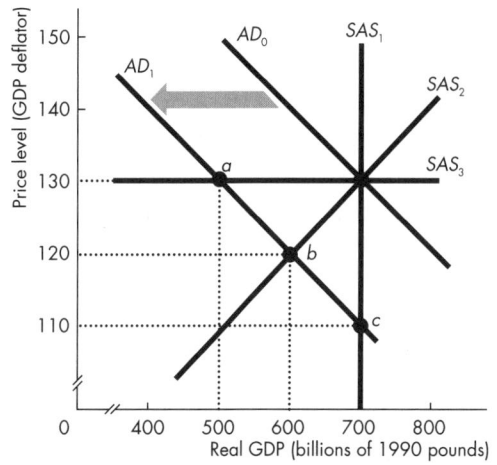

c Figure 33.2 shows that for a change in aggregate demand, the Keynesian theory (with its new equilibrium at point *a*) predicts the largest change in GDP and the smallest change in the price level. The real business cycle theory (with its new equilibrium at point *c*) predicts the largest change in the price level and the smallest change in GDP. Lastly, the monetarist theory (with its new equilibrium at point *b*) is midway between the two extremes.

3 Table 33.2 shows the impulse that each theory stresses as the primary cause of business cycles. You may find this table a helpful summary of the different theories.

Table 33.2 Theories and Impulses

Theory	Impulse
Keynesian	Changes in expectations about future sales and profits
Monetarist	Changes in the monetary growth rate
New classical	Unexpected changes in aggregate demand
New Keynesian	Changes in aggregate demand that were unexpected when labour contracts were signed
Real business cycle	Changes in productivity growth

DISCUSSION QUESTION

1 The real world is incredibly complex. For example, economists would like to know how much a change in the money supply affects real GDP. Think of all the different possibilities. Keynesians and monetarists say that changes in the money supply can have large effects. Rational expectations economists think that only unexpected changes can affect real GDP. The real business cycle theory says that changes in the money supply have no effect.

But think about what we'd have to do to determine which answer is correct. Basically, we'd have to change the money supply and nothing else. That is, government spending couldn't change, the price of oil couldn't change, technology couldn't change – nothing could change. If any of these other things changed, real GDP might change because of that factor, not because of the change in the money supply. If we could conduct this type of 'controlled' experiment, we could figure out exactly how the change in the money supply affected real GDP.

However, this kind of experiment is not possible. So economists have to try to disentangle all the different factors that affect real GDP and unemployment. All these things – taxes, government spending, technology, oil prices, interest rates and the money supply – change every day, and each may have an impact on GDP. Isolating the effect of any one of them is nearly impossible.

DATA QUESTIONS

1 This is an aggregate demand-side explanation of the business cycle. It suggests that a fall in investment has had a multiplied effect on other firms, particularly in Wales where foreign investment has been very substantial.

Chapter 34 **Macroeconomics Policy Challenges**

Chapter in Perspective, Text Pages 858–883

This chapter begins by discussing the *objectives* of economic policy – what the government should try to achieve. It then looks at the policies that can be adopted to achieve these goals, and in particular it distinguishes between fixed and feedback rules.

Helpful Hints

1 As in Chapter 33, only a few new concepts are introduced, and the aggregate demand–aggregate supply model developed in many of the preceding chapters is used to analyse the effects of policy. This use represents a payoff for all the effort required to master that model!

This chapter asks the most important macroeconomic policy question: can the government and the Bank of England carry out successful policies to make individuals' lives better?

The answer to this question makes a great deal of difference to the quality of everyone's life. For instance, if activist policies can be used to avoid business cycles, no college student needs to fear graduating just when a recession hits. However, if activist policies actually worsen the severity of recessions, their use may condemn many students to search for work in the face of a severe recession. So the answer to the question of whether the government can carry out policies to improve our lives is tremendously important – and is currently unknown!

2 Numerous complications arise in real-world use of the aggregate demand–aggregate supply model to make policy decisions. In previous chapters the problems were simplified to maximize learning. Now a more realistic perspective of problems that confront a policy maker is given.

The macroeconomic model that we are using is a good indicator of the *qualitative* effects of changes in factors that affect aggregate demand and aggregate supply. For example, we know that an increase in the money supply shifts the aggregate demand curve rightward. However, in the development and implementation of policy, qualitative knowledge is not sufficient. Policy makers must also have quantitative knowledge. They must know how much an increase in the money supply will increase aggregate demand.

Although economists understand the direction of the effect, knowledge of the magnitude of the effect is much more limited and difficult to obtain. This lack of knowledge reduces the potential for policy to be used to 'fine tune' the economy.

In addition to direction and magnitude, policy makers must also know when to implement a policy. The full effect on aggregate demand of policy changes made today is not immediate. Much, if not most, of that effect occurs only with considerable time lags. Thus policy makers must be able to predict these time lags to ensure that the future effect of a policy change will be appropriate when the effect actually occurs.

Unfortunately, this is extremely difficult. These lags often are long and variable, making them difficult to predict. As a result, policy makers may initiate a policy today that sometime in the future actually shifts aggregate demand in the 'wrong' direction because circumstances have changed. In that case, the policy will be destabilizing and therefore worse than doing nothing.

3 This chapter presents two opposing views of the usefulness of countercyclical policy. Apart from the 'practical' problems discussed so clearly in the text, these differing views come partially from differing assumptions about one crucial factor: the speed with which the private sector reacts to macroeconomic shocks relative to the speed with which government reacts.

The advocates of fixed rules (real business cycle theorists, monetarists and flexible wage theorists) believe that the private sector generally reacts quickly – people have rational expectations and process new information quickly because there are economic incentives to do so, such as signing flexible wage contracts that allow wages to react quickly to changes in the price level. These advocates also believe that government reacts slowly because of lags in recognizing problems, developing policy and implementing policy. Fixed-rule advocates therefore logically arrive at the conclusion that feedback rules at best make no difference and at worst can actually harm the economy.

The advocates of flexible rules (Keynesians and sticky wage theorists) believe that the private sector reacts slowly – people sign long-term contracts that prevent wages from reacting quickly to changes in the price level. They also believe that the government can react more quickly than the private sector and therefore arrive logically at the conclusion that feedback rules can make the economy better off by speeding recovery from a recession.

SELF-TEST

CONCEPT REVIEW

1 The goals of macroeconomic policy are: the highest sustainable rate of _____ _____, smooth out business _____, low _____ and _____.

2 The macroeconomic policy tools are _____ policy and _____ policy.

3 To increase the saving rate, government saving must be increased and _____ for private saving strengthened.

4 A(n) _____ - _____ policy specifies an action to be pursued independently of the state of the economy.

5 A(n) _____ - _____ policy specifies how policy action responds to changes in the state of the economy.

6 _____ policies involve government action to stimulate the economy when it is in recession.

7 When inflation is tamed, a _____ usually results because people form policy _____ based on past policy actions.

TRUE AND FALSE

___ 1 Cost-push inflation is particularly a problem for an economy if it follows monetarist fixed rules.

___ 2 Nominal GDP targeting is an example of a fixed-rule policy.

___ 3 One of the goals (targets) of economic policy is to reduce the unemployment rate below its natural rate.

— **4** Reducing the inflation rate usually leads to a recession.

— **5** Increasing national saving is likely to increase the economic growth rate.

— **6** Discretionary policy can be characterized as a type of sophisticated feedback policy.

— **7** The use of feedback rules cannot make business cycle fluctuations in economic activity more severe.

— **8** The statement 'allow the money supply to grow at the constant rate of 3 per cent per year', is an example of a feedback-rule policy.

MULTIPLE CHOICE

1 Which of the following is an example of a fixed-rule policy?
 a Wear your boots if it snows.
 b Leave your boots at home if it does not snow.
 c Wear your boots every day.
 d Listen to the weather forecast and then decide whether to wear your boots.

2 Monetary policy affects the economy _____ , and fiscal policy affects the economy _____ .
 a immediately; immediately
 b immediately; after a lag
 c after a lag; immediately
 d after a lag; after a lag

3 According to the real business cycle theory, if the government increases the money supply when real GDP declines, real GDP will
 a increase, but only temporarily.
 b increase permanently.
 c not change and neither will the price level.
 d not change but the price level will rise.

4 OPEC once again succeeds in drastically raising the price of oil. This is an aggregate _____ shock, and a _____ policy runs the risk of creating a cost-push inflation.
 a demand; fixed-rule
 b demand; feedback-rule
 c supply; feedback-rule
 d supply; fixed-rule

5 Businesses become convinced that future profits from investment will be less than initially believed. This conviction is an aggregate _____ shock and a _____ policy may be able to keep real GDP from falling below potential GDP.
 a demand; fixed-rule
 b demand; feedback-rule
 c supply; feedback-rule
 d supply; fixed-rule

6 Tax changes that raise the return from private saving can be used to help
 a reduce inflation.
 b eliminate the business cycle.
 c increase the rate of economic growth.
 d increase the natural rate of unemployment.

7 The data show that, in the year before an election, monetary policy generally is _____ , and in the year after an election, monetary policy generally is _____ .
 a expansionary; expansionary
 b expansionary; contractionary
 c contractionary; expansionary
 d contractionary; contractionary

8 A fixed-rule policy that sets the growth rate of the money supply at 4 per cent per year
 a ensures that persisting inflation does not occur.
 b counteracts temporary increases in aggregate demand.
 c counteracts temporary decreases in real output.
 d offsets supply shocks.

9 A fixed-rule monetary policy
 a requires considerable knowledge of how changes in the money supply affect the economy.
 b would be impossible for the government to achieve.
 c would result in constant real GDP.
 d minimizes the threat of cost-push inflation.

10 Expanding the money supply when the economy is in a recession is a policy that may
 a reduce inflation.
 b help smooth the business cycle.
 c increase the rate of economic growth.
 d increase the natural rate of unemployment.

11 Which of the following is one of the two core macroeconomic policy targets?
a unemployment constant at 6 per cent
b steady growth in real GDP
c steady growth in nominal GDP
d inflation at the natural rate

12 According to real business cycle theory,
a any decrease in real GDP is the result of a decrease in long-run aggregate supply.
b fluctuations in aggregate demand change potential real GDP.
c fluctuations in aggregate demand cannot affect the price level.
d feedback-rule policies are best.

13 The rule, 'Reduce taxes in a recession', is an example of a
a Keynesian fixed-rule policy.
b Keynesian feedback-rule policy.
c monetarist fixed-rule policy.
d monetarist feedback-rule policy.

14 Which type of economist believes that fluctuations in aggregate demand combined with sticky money wages are the main source of business cycles and that activist feedback-rule policies should be followed?
a a Keynesian economist
b a monetarist economist
c a real business cycle economist
d all economists

15 Economists who favour fixed-rule policies over feedback-rule policies argue that policy lags are
a shorter than the forecast horizon and that potential GDP is known reasonably well.
b shorter than the forecast horizon and that potential GDP is not known.
c longer than the forecast horizon and that potential GDP is known reasonably well.
d longer than the forecast horizon and that potential GDP is not known.

16 The usual result when inflation is reduced is
a an immediate strong expansion.
b a recession.
c more rapid growth in aggregate demand.
d The premise of the question is wrong because there is no *usual* result when inflation is reduced.

SHORT ANSWER

1 What are the two core macroeconomic policy targets? How are they achieved theoretically with nominal GDP targeting?

2 Distinguish between fixed-rule policy and feedback-rule policy.

3 The purpose of policy is to stabilize. How, then, can feedback rules result in even greater variability in aggregate demand?

4 What is the relationship between policies designed to foster more rapid growth in potential GDP and policies designed to limit business cycle fluctuations in economic activity? Do any of these policies overlap? Explain. Is there a source of potential conflict between the policy goal of more rapid growth and the policy goal of limiting business cycles? If so, what is it?

PROBLEMS

1 Assume that the government knows exactly how much and when the aggregate demand curve will shift, both in the absence of monetary policy and when the government changes the money supply. Moreover, assume that, in 1999, a one-year decrease in aggregate demand occurs because of a drop in government purchases of goods and services but that, in 2000, government purchases return to normal. Between 1999 and 2000, potential GDP does not grow.
a If the government follows the fixed rule, 'Hold the money supply constant', in Fig. 34.1 show how the temporary decrease in aggregate demand affects real GDP and the price level in 1999.
b The government continues to follow the fixed rule in **a**. In Fig. 34.2, show the effect on real GDP and the price level in 2000.
c Assume that the government follows the feedback rule, 'Raise the money supply whenever aggregate demand decreases and lower it whenever aggregate demand increases'. The government's target is to hold real GDP equal to potential GDP. If there are no lags in the effect of monetary policy, in Fig. 34.3 show the effect in 1999 of the temporary decrease in government spending on real GDP and the price level.

Figure 34.1

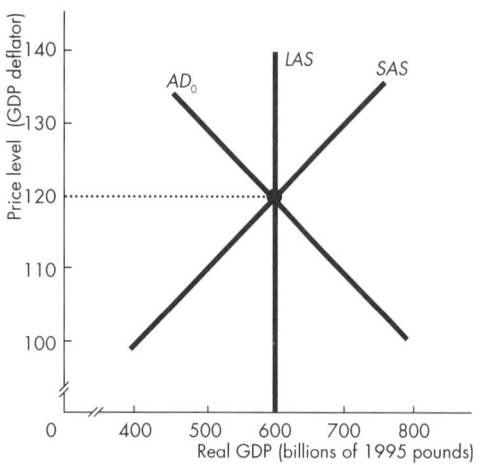

Figure 34.2

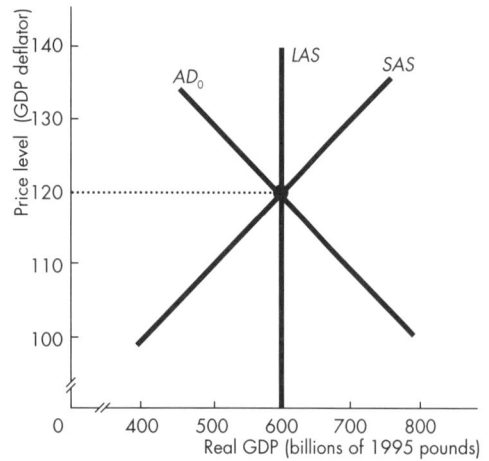

ment purchases return to normal. Between 1999 and 2000, potential GDP does not grow. But now assume that the government does not know when a change in the money supply will shift the aggregate demand curve.

Figure 34.3

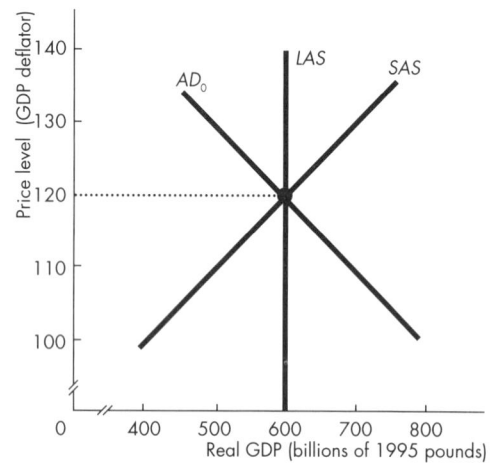

Figure 34.4

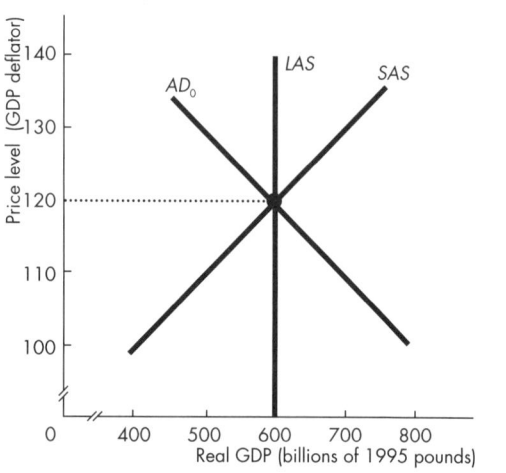

   d The government continues to follow the feed-back rule in **c**. In Fig. 34.4, show the effect in 2000 on real GDP and the price level.
   e Assume that holding GDP as close as possible to potential GDP is a target for policy makers. Which policy – the fixed-rule policy or the feed-back-rule policy – is best?
2 As in Problem **1**, the government knows exactly how much the aggregate demand curve will shift. In 1999, a one-year drop in government purchases of goods and services occurs, but in 2000, govern-

   a Assume that the government follows the feed-back rule, 'Increase the money supply when-ever aggregate demand decreases and decrease it whenever aggregate demand increases', and that the government's target is to hold real GDP equal to potential GDP.

However, the government's policy of increasing the money supply does not have an effect for one year. In Fig. 34.5, show the effect in 1999 of the temporary decrease in aggregate demand on real GDP and the price level.

b The government continues to follow the feedback rule in **a**. In Fig. 34.6, show the effect in 2000 on real GDP and the price level. (Remember the policy that was undertaken in 1999.)

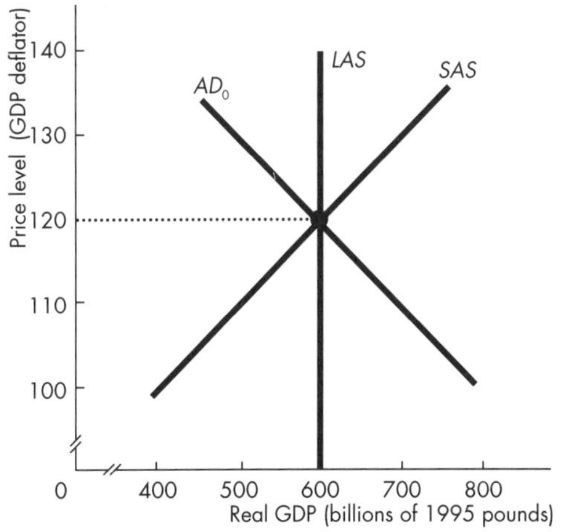

c Has the government helped stabilize or destabilize the economy? Explain.

Figure 34.5

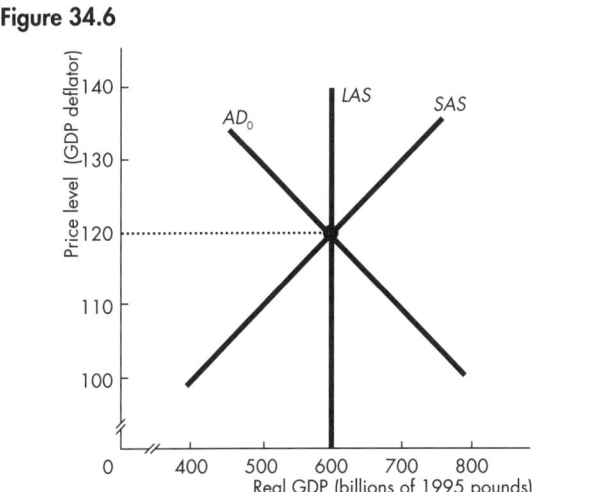

Figure 34.6

DISCUSSION QUESTION

1 Should the government conduct activist, feedback-rule policies or should it stick to non-activist, fixed-rule policies?

DATA QUESTIONS

The aims of economic policy

If we read the speeches of politicians, two policy objectives stand out: bringing down the rate of inflation and increasing the rate of economic growth. Of course, other objectives are sometimes mentioned, but they are given little prominence or seen to be dependent on these two. For example, ministers claim credit when unemployment falls, but even this is often presented as a result of a strong counter-inflation policy.

Many economists would also mention other policy objectives. For example, some would claim that governments should aim to reduce fluctuations in the business cycle. Many other people would emphasize environmental objectives, even though this might mean slower economic growth, or even no economic growth at all.

1 Can governments succeed in achieving all their economic objectives at the same time?

2 Can you think of other economic objectives?

ANSWERS

CONCEPT REVIEW

1 economic growth; fluctuations; unemployment; inflation
2 fiscal; monetary
3 incentives
4 fixed-rule;
5 feedback-rule
6 Feedback
7 recession; expectations

TRUE OR FALSE

1 F Fixed rules do not allow the money supply to react to cost changes, so fixed rules basically eliminate the possibility of cost-push inflation.

2 F Nominal GDP targeting is a feedback rule because policy responds to current changes in nominal GDP.

3 F One of the goals is to hold the unemployment rate equal to the natural rate.

4 T In practice, inflation reduction most often leads to a recession.

5 T By increasing the national saving rate, the country can accumulate more capital, which would increase its rate of economic growth.

6 T Discretionary policy means that policy makers respond to the current state of the economy, which is a form of feedback policy.

7 F Feedback rules can worsen the severity of business cycles if substantial and unpredictable lags occur before the policies can have an effect on the economy.

8 F The statement in the question is a fixed rule because the monetary growth rate is fixed regardless of the current state of the economy.

MULTIPLE CHOICE

1 c This is a fixed rule because it does not depend on the day's weather.

2 d Both monetary and fiscal policies have lags before they affect the economy. These lags offer the possibility that the effect of the policy will be perverse; that is, a policy could have a contractionary effect when the economy is already in a recession.

3 d In the real business cycle view, real GDP is determined solely by long-run aggregate supply, so monetary policy, which affects only aggregate demand, cannot change real GDP. Instead, monetary policy affects only the price level.

4 c By decreasing aggregate supply, the increase in oil prices raises the price level and decreases real GDP. If the government's feedback rule conducts an expansionary monetary policy, the price level will rise still more, leading OPEC, in turn, to again raise the price of oil, which can create a cost-push inflation.

5 b A feedback-rule policy in this case increases aggregate demand. Such a policy offsets the initial decrease in aggregate demand and can keep production at potential real GDP.

6 c By increasing the return from private saving, private saving will increase and the country will accumulate more capital.

7 b The tendency for monetary policy to be expansionary before an election raises the possibility of a 'political business cycle' whereby monetary policy is conducted on the basis of politics rather than economics.

8 a A major benefit of fixed rules that specify low rates of monetary growth is that they eliminate the possibility of high and persisting inflation.

9 d **8** deals with the general result that fixed monetary policy rules limit inflation; **9** covers the specific result that fixed monetary policy rules eliminate the possibility of cost-push inflation.

10 b By increasing aggregate demand, an expansionary monetary policy may reduce the high unemployment rate that results in a recession.

11 b The other core macroeconomic policy target is keeping the inflation rate low.

12 a Real business cycle theory asserts that the economy always produces on its long-run aggregate supply curve.

13 b The rule has taxes that depend on the state of the economy and thus is a feedback rule, the type of rule advocated by Keynesian economists.

14 a The main impulse that causes business cycles in the Keynesian theory is fluctuations in aggregate demand caused by fluctuations in investment. Keynesians also recommend that these fluctuations be countered by activist feedback rules.

15 d Both long lags and uncertainty about potential GDP increase the possibility that fixed rules would be superior to feedback rules.

16 b In theory, a credible, announced policy of reducing inflation might not affect real GDP, but in practice reductions in inflation generally are accompanied by a recession.

SHORT ANSWER

1 The two core macroeconomic policy targets are steady growth in real GDP at the maximum sustainable rate and keeping inflation low and predictable.

Nominal GDP targeting uses feedback rules to try to keep nominal GDP at the target level. Supporters of nominal GDP targeting argue that, if nominal GDP falls below the target, it is the result of falling real GDP, and if nominal GDP rises above the target, it is the result of inflation. Hence conducting expansionary policy when nominal GDP growth is low will increase the growth rate of real GDP so that it moves closer to its maximum sustainable rate. Conducting contractionary policy when nominal GDP growth is high will reduce the inflation rate and keep it low. Hence meeting the target growth rate for nominal GDP will meet both core targets.

2 The difference between a fixed-rule policy and a feedback-rule policy is whether the specified action depends on the state of the economy. A fixed-rule policy specifies an action that will be pursued regardless of the state of the economy. For instance, a fixed-rule policy of increasing the money supply by 3 per cent per year implies that the money supply will be increased by 3 per cent regardless of whether the economy is in an expansion or a recession. In contrast, a feedback-rule policy specifies actions that may change, depending on the state of the economy. For instance, a feedback-rule policy of increasing the growth rate of the money supply if the economy is in a recession and decreasing the growth rate if the economy is in an expansion means that the growth rate of the money supply will change according to the state of the economy.

3 Policy actions affect aggregate demand only after a time lag. This means that a policy action taken today will have its intended effect sometime in the future. Therefore policy makers must forecast the state of the economy a year or two ahead to be confident that the effect of the policy action taken today will be appropriate when the effect occurs. Such forecasting is extremely difficult, both because the lags are long and because they are unpredictable. As a result, policy makers face the likelihood that the policy action taken today will have an inappropriate future effect. For instance, an expansionary monetary policy designed to counter a current recession may actually affect the economy in two years when it is already enjoying a robust expansion. Thus the expansionary policy may lead to accelerating inflation, which could destabilize rather than stabilize aggregate demand.

4 Policies designed to increase the long-term growth of potential GDP generally are quite different from policies designed to combat business cycle fluctuations in economic activity. To increase the growth rate of potential GDP, policies must be designed to increase national saving, to spur investment in human capital, and to increase research and investment in new technologies. Conversely, to reduce business cycle fluctuations, policies must be designed to offset fluctuations in aggregate demand (if, indeed, fluctuations in aggregate demand are the source of the business cycle and if policies can successfully limit the fluctuations). Thus tax policies that increase the return from private saving, policies that increase the quality and access to schooling, and tax poli-

cies that increase the return from investment in new technologies may increase the rate of growth in potential GDP. They are quite different from the fiscal and monetary policies that might be used to limit business cycles.

However, one source of overlap and possible conflict may exist between the two sets of policies. To increase national saving and hence the growth rate of potential GDP, reducing the government's budget deficit is a potential policy. But to combat a recession, a tax cut and an increase in government spending are potential policies, and these policies increase the government's budget deficit. Thus fiscal policy designed to stabilize the business cycle also may have an impact on the growth rate of potential GDP.

PROBLEMS

Figure 34.7

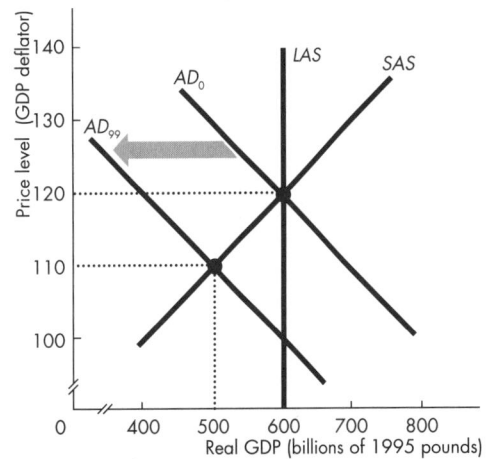

1 a Figure 34.7 shows the effect. With a fixed rule, nothing offsets the decline in government purchases. Hence the decrease in aggregate demand decreases real GDP (from £600 billion to £500 billion) and the price level falls (from 120 to 110).
  b As Fig. 34.8 shows, in 2000 the aggregate demand curve returns to its initial level of AD_0. Hence real GDP returns to its initial, full-employment level of £600 billion, and the price level returns to the initial level of 120.
  c A feedback rule enables the government to offset the initial decrease in aggregate demand. Hence the government's expansionary policy keeps aggregate demand stationary at AD_0. As a result, Fig. 34.9 shows how real GDP remains at its full-employment level (£600 billion), with the price level remaining unchanged.

Figure 34.8

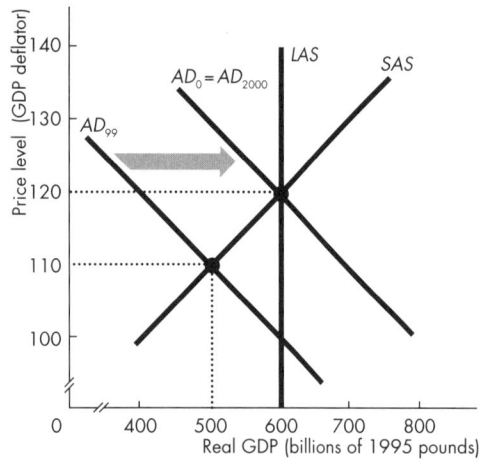

Figure 34.9

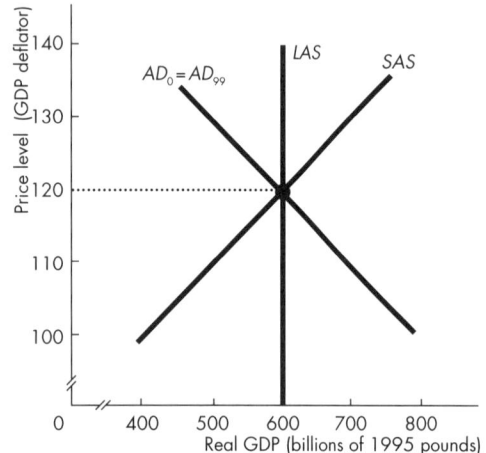

until after a one-year lag, the policy has no effect in 1999. Hence as Fig. 34.11 demonstrates, in 1999, aggregate demand falls to AD_{99}, real GDP decreases to £500 billion, and the price level falls to 110.

Figure 34.10

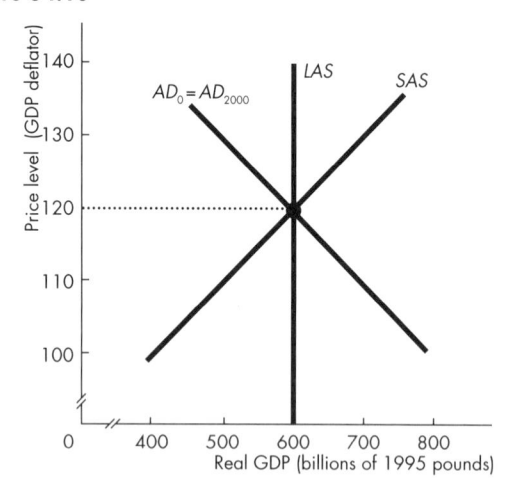

Figure 34.11

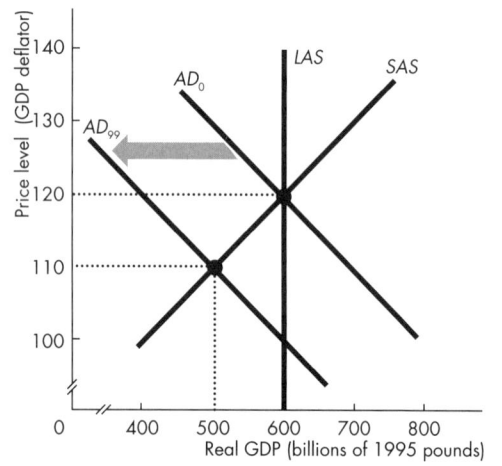

d In 2000, as aggregate demand returns to normal, the feedback rule will lead the government to terminate its expansionary policy. Hence aggregate demand in 2000 remains at AD_0. Thus as Fig. 34.10 shows, real GDP (again) equals potential GDP, £600 billion, and the price level (again) equals 120.

e The feedback-rule policy was best for the economy. With the feedback-rule policy, in neither year did real GDP deviate from potential GDP. With the fixed-rule policy, **a** shows that when aggregate demand decreased in 1996, real GDP fell below potential GDP.

2 a In 1999, the government conducts an expansionary policy, but because the policy does not take effect

b In 2000, with the increase in aggregate demand back to normal, the government's feedback rule causes it to end the expansionary policy. But in 1997, the expansionary policy that was conducted in 1999 affects the economy. Hence aggregate demand increases all the way to AD_{99}, as shown in Fig. 34.12. Thus in 2000, real GDP exceeds potential GDP (£700 billion instead of £600 billion) and the price level is higher (130 instead of 120).

Figure 34.12

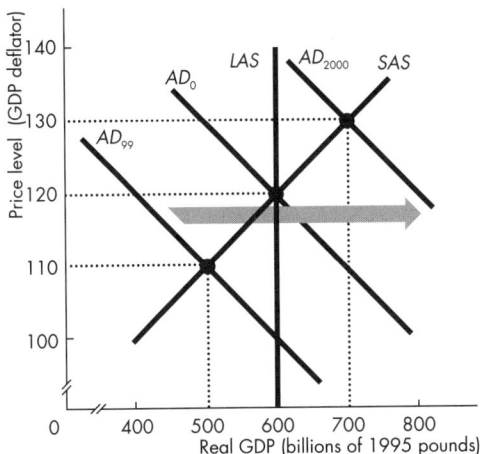

c The government's policy has destabilized the economy. In particular, business cycle fluctuations in economic activity have been made worse, not better. The government did nothing to offset the recession that occurred in 1999 and then, in 2000, the government's actions caused GDP to expand more than it otherwise would have.

DISCUSSION QUESTION

1 Feedback rules require very good knowledge of the economy (for example, the level of full employment), introduce unpredictability into the economy, can generate bigger fluctuations in aggregate demand because of lags and do not work for aggregate supply. Consequently, they can lead to worse results than fixed rules.

However, fixed rules also have disadvantages. What if bad fixed rules are applied over long periods? Moreover, active government intervention can sometimes lead to better results than fixed rules. So the debate continues.

DATA QUESTIONS

1 There are several reasons why the government might be unable to achieve all its objectives at the same time. For example, it may be using inappropriate rules, whether fixed or feedback.

However, even if appropriate rules are followed, objectives may sometimes conflict. For example, the Phillips curve shows a trade-off between inflation and unemployment in the short run. Similarly, rapid economic growth may lead to a worsening of the balance of payments (discussed in later chapters). Rapid growth may also be at the expense of environmental progress.

2 There are several other policy objectives that could be chosen. We have already mentioned environmental considerations. Others might stress the need for a more equal society. This might require higher taxation of rich people and more spending on welfare. In the United States in particular, there is considerable pressure for the government to aim to balance the budget. All these questions are matters of value.

Part 9 The Euro and The Global Economy

Looking back at Part 8 (Chapters 27–34)

As always, a good way to check if you have understood the main ideas in a chapter is to look at the beginning and see if you are able to describe/explain the main ideas listed in the *After studying this chapter you will be able to...* section. For example, after reading Chapter 27 you should be able to explain how banks create money. After Chapter 28 you should know about open market operations. Chapter 29 should have enabled you to discuss the Keynesian–monetarist controversy and Chapter 30 to explain the relationship between inflation and unemployment.

Chapter 31 should have enabled you to explain how interest rates are determined. Chapter 32 should have enabled you to master the factors that determine long-term economic growth and Chapter 33 to explain different theories of the business cycle. The last chapter in this part, Chapter 34, should have made it possible for you to discuss the difference between fixed and feedback rules.

In addition, it is a good idea to look at the key terms listed at the end of each chapter. If you are unsure about any of these, then check back. The sites mentioned earlier have good material on issues covered in this Part. Also look back at the Bank of England (www.bankofengland.co.uk) and Bank of England Monetary and Financial Statistics (www.bankofengland.co.uk/mfsd) sites. The European Central Bank (www.ecb.int) is another good site to take a look at.

Questions

1 Re-read the *Talking with Charles Goodhart* article. What is his view of monetary targeting? What is Goodhart's Law?

Looking forward to Part 9 (Chapters 35 and 36)

These two chapters focus on international aspects. In Chapter 35 you will read about recent trends in international trade. You will also return to a concept you met at the beginning of the course – comparative advantage – and why we have trade restrictions despite the strong arguments in favour of free trade.

The final chapter in the book, Chapter 36, explains how international trade is financed and also examines the foreign exchange market.

Answers

1 Goodhart is sceptical about monetary targeting. His reason is that this depends on a stable relationship between monetary growth and the growth of nominal incomes. In other words, he believes that it depends on being able to predict the velocity of circulation and suggests that we cannot do this. The law named after him – 'Goodhart's Law' – states that any measure of the money supply behaves differently when it becomes an official target. One reason is that there is an incentive for the government to shift accounting practices or techniques to achieve the target.

Chapter 35 **Trading with the World**

Chapter in Perspective, Text Pages 888–915

Why do nations trade? What is the nature of the gains that make trade worthwhile? What determines which goods a country will import and which it will export? In this chapter we also turn to more difficult issues such as: if there are significant gains to free trade, why do countries frequently restrict imports? What are the effects of a tariff or a quota or some other trade restriction?

Helpful Hints

1 It may be useful to recall the discussion in Chapter 3 of opportunity cost, comparative advantage and gains from trade. The current chapter applies the fundamental concepts of opportunity cost and comparative advantage to the problem of trade between countries. The basic principles are the same whether we are talking about trade between individuals in the same country or between individuals in different countries.

2 In addition to the gains from trade, this chapter also discusses the economic effects of trade restrictions. One of the important things we learn is that the economic effects of a tariff and a quota are similar. A voluntary export restraint (VER) is also a quota, but one imposed by the exporting country rather than the importing country. All these trade restrictions raise the domestic price of the imported good, and reduce the volume of and value of imports. They will also reduce the value of exports by the same amount as the reduction in the value of imports. The increase in price that results from each of these trade restrictions produces a gap between the domestic price of the imported good and the foreign supply price of the good. The difference between the alternative trade restrictions lies in which party captures this excess. In the case of a tariff, the government receives the tariff revenue. In the case of a quota imposed by the importing country, domestic importers who have been awarded a licence to import capture this excess through increased profit. When a VER is imposed, the excess is captured by foreign exporters who have been awarded licences to export by their governments.

3 The major point of this chapter is that the gains from free trade can be considerable. Why then do countries have such a strong tendency to impose trade restrictions? The key is that while free trade creates overall benefits to the economy as a whole, there are both winners and losers. The winners gain more in total than the losers lose, but the latter tend to be concentrated in a few industries. We are therefore not surprised that free trade will be resisted by some acting on the basis of rational self-interest. Even though only a small minority benefit from any given trade restriction while the overwhelming majority will be hurt, we are not surprised to see trade restrictions implemented. The reason is that the cost of a given trade restriction to each of the many is indvidually quite small while the benefit to each of the few will be individually large. Thus the few will have a significant incentive to see that restriction takes place while the many will have little incentive to expend time and energy in resisting trade restriction.

4 There is a popular belief that protection saves jobs. This is true for particular workers in particular factories, but overall it is not true. The basic reason is that if we impose taxes or quotas on imports, foreigners will not be able to buy our exports. Hence our export industries suffer. This loss is less visible than the obvious loss of jobs from imports, but it is probably much larger.

SELF-TEST

CONCEPT REVIEW

1 The goods and services purchased from people in foreign countries are called _____ . The goods and services sold to people in foreign countries are called _____ . The value of exports minus the value of imports is called the _____ of _____ .

2 A country is said to have a(n) _____ _____ in the production of a good if it can produce that good at a lower opportunity cost than any other country.

3 The restriction of international trade is called _____ . A tax imposed by the importing country on an imported good is called a(n) _____ . The result of imposing such a tax is to _____ the price that consumers in the importing country pay and _____ the quantity traded. When such a tax is imposed the tax revenue is received by the _____ .

4 A restriction that specifies a limit on the quantity of a particular good that can be imported is called a(n) _____ . The result of such a limit is to _____ the price that consumers in the importing country pay. The extra revenue from such a limit is received by the _____ .

5 An agreement between two governments in which the government of the exporting country agrees to restrict the quantity of its exports to the importing country is called a(n) _____ _____ _____ . Such an agreement will _____ the price that consumers in the importing country pay for the good.

6 When a good is sold in a foreign market at a lower price than in a domestic market or for a price that is lower than the cost of production it is called _____ .

7 International trade is restricted because _____ raise revenue for governments and create economic _____ for some and losses for others.

TRUE OR FALSE

____ **1** When a UK citizen stays in a hotel in France, the United Kingdom is exporting a service.

____ **2** If there are two countries, A and B, and two goods, x and y, and country A has a comparative advantage in the production of x, then country B must have a comparative advantage in the production of y.

___ **3** If country A must give up 3 units of y to produce 1 unit of x and B must give up 4 units of y to produce 1 unit of x, then A has a comparative advantage in the production of x.

___ **4** If countries specialize in goods for which they have a comparative advantage, then some countries will gain and others will lose but the gains will be larger than the losses.

___ **5** Trading according to comparative advantage allows all trading countries to consume outside their production possibility frontier.

___ **6** Countries may exchange similar goods for each other because of economies of scale in the face of diversified tastes.

___ **7** When governments impose tariffs, they are increasing their country's gain from trade.

___ **8** A tariff on a good will raise its price and reduce the quantity traded.

___ **9** A tariff not only reduces the total value of imports but it reduces the total value of exports as well.

___ **10** A quota will cause the price of the imported good to fall.

MULTIPLE CHOICE

1 Suppose there are two countries, A and B, producing two goods, x and y. Country A has a comparative advantage in the production of good x if less
  a of good y must be given up to produce one unit of x than in country B.
  b labour is required to produce one unit of x than in country B.
  c capital is required to produce one unit of x than in country B.
  d labour and capital are required to produce one unit of x than in country B.
  e of good x must be given up to produce one unit of y than in country B.

2 Suppose there are two countries, A and B, producing two goods, x and y, and that country A has a comparative advantage in the production of x. If the countries trade, the price of x in terms of y will be

  a greater than the opportunity cost of x in country A and less than the opportunity cost of x in country B.
  b less than the opportunity cost of x in country A and greater than the opportunity cost of x in country B.
  c greater than the opportunity cost of x in both countries.
  d less than the opportunity cost of x in both countries.
  e dependent on the relative size of each economy.

3 International trade according to comparative advantage allows each country to consume
  a more of the goods it exports but less of the goods it imports than without trade.
  b more of the goods it imports but less of the goods it exports than without trade.
  c more of both goods it exports and goods it imports than without trade.
  d less of both goods it exports and goods it imports than without trade.
  e either **a** or **b**; it depends on the price of the goods.

4 In country A, it requires one unit of capital and one unit of labour to produce a unit of x and it requires two units of capital and two units of labour to produce a unit of y. What is the opportunity cost of good x?
  a the price of a unit of capital plus the price of a unit of labour
  b one unit of capital and one unit of labour
  c two units of capital and two units of labour
  d one half unit of y
  e two units of y

5 Selling a product abroad at a price less than the cost of production is called
  a a reverse tariff.
  b exploitation.
  c dumping.
  d net exporting.

6 The imposition of a tariff on imported goods will increase the price consumers pay for imported goods and
  a reduce the volume of imports and the volume of exports.
  b reduce the volume of imports and increase the volume of exports.
  c reduce the volume of imports and leave the volume of exports unchanged.

d will not affect either the volume of imports or the volume of exports.

e increase the volume of imports but decrease the volume of exports.

7 Who benefits from a tariff on good x?
a domestic consumers of good x
b domestic producers of good x
c foreign consumers of good x
d foreign producers of good x
e no one

8 A tariff on good x which is imported by country A will cause the
a demand curve for x in country A to shift upward.
b demand curve for x in country A to shift downward.
c supply curve of x in country A to shift upward.
d supply curve of x in country A to shift downward.
e demand and the supply curve of x in country A to shift upward.

9 Country A and country B are currently engaging in free trade. Country A imports good x from country B and exports y to B. If country A imposes a tariff on x, country A's x-producing industry will
a expand and its y-producing industry will contract.
b expand and its y-producing industry will expand.
c contract and its y-producing industry will contract.
d contract and its y-producing industry will expand.
e expand and its y-producing industry will be unchanged.

10 Country A and country B are currently engaging in free trade. Country A imports good x from country B and exports y to B. If country A imposes a quota on x, country A's x-producing industry will
a expand and its y-producing industry will contract.
b expand and its y-producing industry will expand.
c contract and its y-producing industry will contract.
d contract and its y-producing industry will expand.

e expand and its y-producing industry will be unchanged.

11 When a tariff is imposed, the gap between the domestic price and the export price is captured by
a consumers in the importing country.
b the person with the right to import the good.
c the domestic producers of the good.
d foreign exporters.
e the government of the importing country.

12 When a quota is imposed, the gap between the domestic price and the export price is captured by
a consumers in the importing country.
b the domestic producers of the good.
c the government of the importing country.
d foreign exporters.
e the person with the right to import the good.

13 When a voluntary export restraint agreement is reached, the gap between the domestic price and the export price is captured by
a consumers in the importing country.
b the person with the right to import the good.
c the government of the importing country.
d foreign exporters.
e the domestic producers of the good.

14 If we import more than we export, then
a we are going to be unable to buy as many foreign goods as we desire.
b we will make loans to foreigners to enable them to buy our goods.
c we will have to finance the difference by borrowing from foreigners.
d our patterns of trade, including the direction of exports and imports, will be different than if exports equal imports.
e both **c** and **d**.

SHORT ANSWER

1 What is meant by comparative advantage?

2 How is it that both parties involved in trade can gain?

3 How does a tariff on a particular imported good affect the domestic price of the good, the export price, the quantity imported and the quantity of the good produced domestically?

4 How does a tariff on imports affect the exports of the country?

5 How does a quota on a particular imported good affect the domestic price of the good, the export price, the quantity imported and the quantity of the good produced domestically?

6 Why might a government prefer a quota to a tariff?

7 The *Reading Between the Lines* article points out that the EU has tried to protect bananas grown in ACP countries. Why?

PROBLEMS

1 Consider a simple world in which there are two countries, Atlantis and Beltran, each producing two goods, food and cloth. The production possibility frontier for each country is given in Table 35.1.

   a Assuming a constant opportunity cost in each country, fill in the rest of the table.

   b What is the opportunity cost of food in Atlantis? of cloth?

   c What is the opportunity cost of food in Beltran? of cloth?

   d Draw the production possibility frontiers on separate graphs.

Table 35.1

Atlantis		Beltran	
Food (units)	Cloth (units)	Food (units)	Cloth (units)
0	500	0	800
200	400	100	600
400		200	
600		300	
800		400	
1,000			

2 Suppose that Atlantis and Beltran engage in trade.

   a In which good will each country specialize?

   b If 1 unit of food trades for 1 unit of cloth, what will happen to the production of each good in each country?

   c If 1 unit of food trades for 1 unit of cloth, draw the consumption possibility frontiers for each country on the corresponding graph from Problem **1d**.

   d Before trade, if Atlantis consumed 600 units of good, the most cloth it could consume was 200 units. After trade, how many units of cloth can be consumed if 600 units of food are consumed?

3 Figure 35.1 gives the import demand curve for shirts for country *A*, labelled *D*, and the export supply curve of shirts for country *B*, labelled *S*.

   a What is the price of a shirt under free trade?

   b How many shirts will be imported by country *A*?

4 Suppose the shirtmakers in country *A* (of Problem 3) are concerned about foreign competition and so the government of country *A* imposes a tariff of £9 per shirt.

Figure 35.1

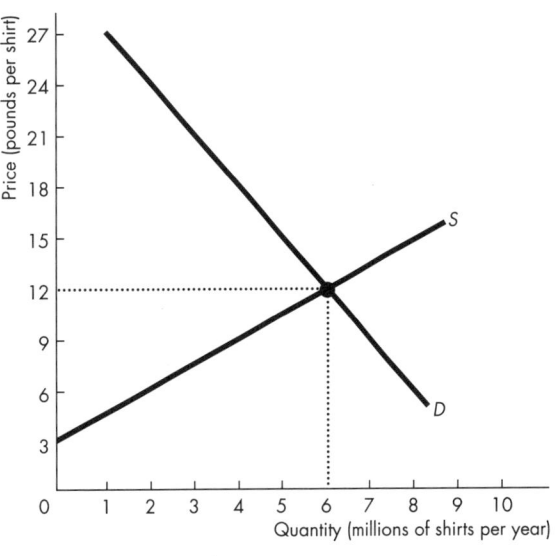

   a What will happen to the price of a shirt in country *A*?

   b What is the price the exporter will actually receive?

   c How many shirts will be imported by country *A*?

   d What is the revenue from the tariff? Who captures it?

5 Suppose that instead of a tariff, country A imposes a quota of 4 million shirts per year.
  a What will be the price of a shirt in country A?
  b What price will the exporter actually receive?
  c How many shirts will be imported by country A?
  d What is the difference between the total amount paid by consumers and the total amount received by exporters – the 'excess profit'? Who captures it?

DISCUSSION QUESTION

1 How can firms in rich countries compete with firms in poorer countries that pay much lower wages?

DATA QUESTIONS

Unfair protection
Protectionism is on the rise – but in a new form. Instead of raising import tariffs or cutting quotas, countries are slapping 'anti-dumping' duties on imports they claim are too cheap. The EU is investigating 13 steel cases from Slovenia to South Korea. It has just extended duties on magnetic discs from Japan, Taiwan and China and on electronic scales from Singapore.

In one sense, 'dumping' is common, since companies often charge less in more competitive markets than they do at home. To prove dumping, it is enough for companies merely to show that sales are being dented by rising imports. Between 1980 and 1997, 71 per cent of anti-dumping claims in the EU did indeed succeed.

Source*: The Economist*, 7 November 1998, p. 129. © *The Economist*, London, (7 November 1989).

1 What is 'dumping'?

2 Why might companies charge less in foreign markets than at home?

3 Who suffers when anti-dumping tariffs are imposed?

ANSWERS

CONCEPT REVIEW

1 imports; exports; balance; trade

2 comparative advantage

3 protectionism; tariff; increase; decrease; government

4 quota; raise; importer

5 voluntary export restraint; raise

6 dumping

7 tariff; rent

TRUE OR FALSE

1 F The United Kingdom is importing (using) a service.

2 T A's comparative advantage means lower units of y lost per unit of x than B, higher units of x lost per unit of y produced than B, hence B has comparative advantage of y.

3 T A has lower opportunity cost $(3y < 4y)$ = lost y per unit of gained y.

4 F All countries gain from specialization and trade, although some groups within countries lose.

5 T Countries will specialize and trade to consume outside *PPF*.

6 T Diversified tastes mean that many products are demanded. These can be provided efficiently only if there is specialization and trade.

7 F Trade restrictions reduce gains from trade.

8 T A tariff leads to shift in export supply curve leading to increase in price and fall in quantity.

9 T Since a tariff reduces imports it will reduce incomes in other countries and so foreigners' ability to import will fall.

10 F Quota means fall in supply and so rise in price.

MULTIPLE CHOICE

1 a Opportunity cost will be less.

2 a Ignoring taxes and so on, prices will be in between differing opportunity costs.

3 c Consumption possibilities frontier is outside *PPF*.

4 d Inputs to make one X could make $^{1}/_{2} Y$.

5 c Definition. However, dumping is difficult to prove because it is not easy to discover the real costs of production. Moreover, for many products marginal cost may be lower than average cost.

6 a It will reduce volume of imports because their price has increased; it will reduce exports since foreigners' incomes will fall and so they will import less.

7 b Domestic producers will benefit from higher price.

8 c Tariff leads to rise in domestic price = export price + tariff, leading to upward shift of supply curve.

9 a Tariff will reduce imports of x so its x-producing industry will expand; but y industry will contract since foreigners will have less money to buy y.

10 a Quota will reduce imports of x so domestic industry will benefit from higher price, but y industry will suffer because foreigners will have less money to buy y.

11 e Government collects tariff revenue = import price – export price.

12 e Under a quota system, domestic government allocates the licence to import.

13 d Because they have the right to export.

14 c Since imports have to be paid for, in long run country has to borrow from foreigners to get foreign exchange to pay for imports.

SHORT ANSWER

1 A country is said to have a comparative advantage in the production of some good if it can produce that good at a lower opportunity cost than any other country.

2 For two potential trading partners to be willing to trade, they must have different comparative advantages; that is, different opportunity costs. If they do, then they will trade and both parties will gain. If the parties do not trade, they will each face their own opportunity costs. A price at which trade takes place must be somewhere between the opportunity costs of the two traders. This means that the party with the lower opportunity cost of the good in question will gain because it will receive a price above its opportunity cost. Similarly, the party with the higher opportunity cost will gain because it will pay a price below its opportunity cost.

3 A tariff on an imported good will raise its price to domestic consumers as the export supply curve shifts upward. The export price is determined by the original export supply curve. As the domestic price of the good rises, the quantity of the good demanded falls and thus the relevant point on the original export supply curve is at a lower quantity and a lower export price. This lower quantity means that the quantity imported falls. The rise in the domestic price will also lead to an increase in the quantity of the good supplied domestically.

4 When country A imposes a tariff on its imports of good x, not only does the volume of imports shrink but the volume of exports of y to country B will shrink by the same amount. Thus a balance of trade is maintained. As indicated in the answer to **3**, the export price of good x falls when a tariff is imposed. This fall in the price received by the exporter means that the price of imports in the foreign country has risen; that is, if the amount of y that country B gets for an x has fallen, the quantity of x that must be given up to obtain a y has increased. This implies that the quantity of y (A's export) demanded by country B will fall and thus A's exports will decline.

5 The effect of a quota on the domestic price of the good, the export price, the quantity imported and the quantity of the good produced domestically are exactly the same as the effects of a tariff discussed in the answer to **3**. The only difference is that the increase in the domestic price resulting from a tariff occurs because foreigners decrease the supply of the good at all prices. A quota, however, forces the export supply curve to become vertical at the quota amount.

6 The effects of tariffs and quotas on prices and quantities have been discussed in the answers to **3** and **5**. The difference is that the excess revenue raised by a tariff is captured by the government whereas the excess revenue raised by a quota is captured by the people who have been given the right to import by the government. In either case the government is in a position to benefit. It may prefer to use quotas to reward political supporters by giving them rights to import and thus allowing them to capture large profits. Quotas give the government more precise control over the quantity of imports. Also, it is politically easier to impose a quota than a tariff.

7 The main reason why EU countries have sought to protect ACP bananas is political. These countries have strong ex-colonial links with France and the UK, and the policy is also seen as helping poor peasant farmers in these countries.

PROBLEMS

1 a Completed Table 35.1 is shown here as Table 35.2. The values in the table are calculated using the opportunity cost of each good in each country (see **b** and **c**).

b In order to increase the output (consumption) of food by 200 units, cloth production (consumption) falls by 100 units in Atlantis. Thus the opportunity cost of a unit of food is $1/2$ unit of cloth. This opportunity cost is constant (as are all others in this problem, for simplicity). Similarly, the opportunity cost of cloth in Atlantis is 2 units of food.

c In Beltran a 100 unit increase in the production (consumption) of food requires a reduction in the output (consumption) of cloth of 200 units. Thus the opportunity cost of food is 2 units of cloth. Similarly the opportunity cost of cloth in Beltran is ½ unit of food.

d Figure 35.2 parts (a) and (b) illustrate the production possibility frontiers for Atlantis and Beltran, respectively (labelled PPF_A and PPF_B). The rest of the diagram is discussed in Problem 2.

Table 35.2

Atlantis		Beltran	
Food (units)	Cloth (units)	Food (units)	Cloth (units)
0	500	0	800
200	400	100	600
400	300	200	400
600	200	300	200
800	100	400	0
1,000	0	–	–

2 a Since (from Problem **1b** and **c**) we see that Atlantis has lower opportunity cost (½ unit of cloth) in the production of food, Atlantis will specialize in the production of food. Beltran, with the lower opportunity cost for cloth (½ unit of food) will specialize in cloth.

b Each country will want to produce every unit of the good in which it specializes as long as the amount it receives in trade exceeds its opportunity cost. For Atlantis, the opportunity cost of a unit of food is ½ unit of cloth but it can obtain 1 unit of cloth in trade. Since the opportunity cost is constant (in this simple example), Atlantis will totally specialize by producing all of the food it can: 1,000 units per year (point *b* in Fig. 35.2a). Similarly, in Beltran, the opportunity cost of 1 unit of cloth is ½ unit of food but 1 unit of cloth will trade for 1 unit of food. Since the opportunity cost is constant, Beltran will totally specialize in the production of cloth and will produce 800 units per year (point *b′* in Fig. 35.2b).

c The consumption possibility frontiers for Atlantis and Beltran (labelled CPF_A and CPF_B) are illustrated in Fig. 35.2, parts (a) and (b), respectively. These frontiers are straight lines that indicate all the combinations of food and cloth that can be consumed with trade. The position and slope of the consumption possibility frontier for an economy depend on the terms of trade between the goods and the production point of the economy. The consumption possibility frontier for Atlantis (CPF_A), for example, is obtained by starting at point *b* on PPF_A, the production point, and examining possible trades. For example, if Atlantis traded 400 units of the food it produces for 400 units of cloth, it would be able to consume 600 units of food (1,000 units produced minus 400 units traded) and 400 units of cloth, which is represented by point *c*.

Figure 35.2

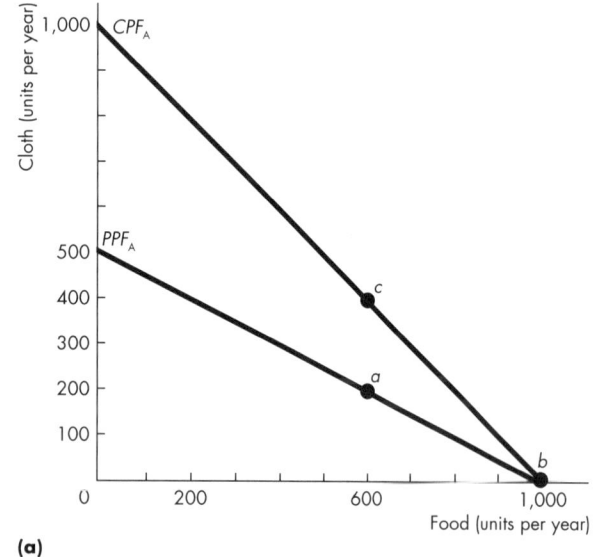

(a)

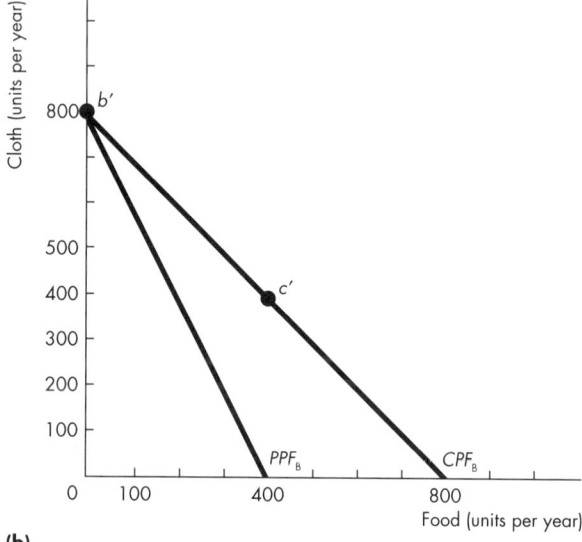

(b)

d If Atlantis consumes 600 units of food, trade allows consumption of cloth to be 400 units, 200 units more than possible without trade. The maximum amount of cloth that can be consumed without trade is given by the production possibility frontier. If food consumption is 600 units, this is indicated by point *a* on PPF_A. The maximum amount of cloth consumption for any level of food consumption with trade is given by the consumption possibility frontier. If food consumption is 600 units, this is indicated by point *c* on CPF_A.

3 a The price of a shirt under free trade will occur at the intersection of country *A*'s import demand curve for shirts and country *B*'s export supply curve of shirts. This occurs at a price of £12 per shirt.

b Country *A* will import 6 million shirts per year.

4 a The effect of the £9 per shirt tariff is to shift the export supply curve (*S*) upward by £9. This is shown as a shift from *S* to *S'* in Fig. 35.3. The price is now determined by the intersection of the *D* curve (which is unaffected by the tariff) and the *S'* curve. The new price of a shirt is £18.

b Of this £18, £9 is the tariff, so the exporter receives only the remaining £9.

c Country *A* will now import only 4 million shirts per year.

d The tariff revenue is £9 (the tariff per shirt) times 4 million (the number of shirts imported), which is £36 million. This money is received by the government of country *A*.

5 a The quota restricts the quantity that can be imported to 4 million shirts per year regardless of the price and is represented by a vertical line in Fig. 35.4 (which corresponds to Fig. 35.1). The market for shirts will thus clear at a price of £18 per shirt.

b This £18 price is received by the people who are given the right to import shirts under the quota. The amount received by the exporter is £9, given by the height of the *S* curve at a quantity of 4 million shirts per year.

c Country *A* will import 4 million shirts per year, the quota limit.

d The 'excess profit' is £9 per shirt (the £18 received by the importer minus the £9 received by the exporter) times 4 million shirts, which is £36 million. This is captured by the importers who have been rewarded by the government of country *A* since they have been given the right to import under the quota. This is essentially a right to make an 'excess profit'.

Figure 35.4

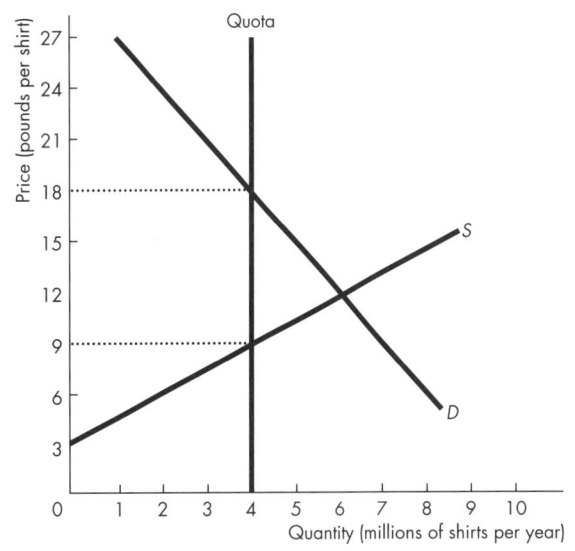

Figure 35.3

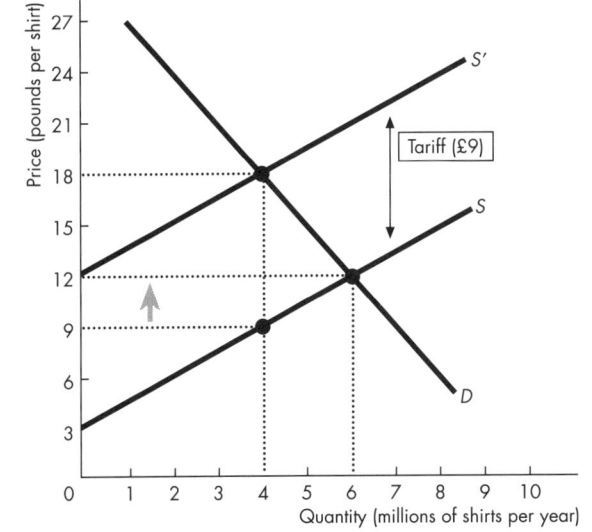

DISCUSSION QUESTION

1 Assume that wages in a rich country, such as the United Kingdom, are 10 times higher than in a poor country, such as India. However, UK workers are also more productive.

Let's take two industries. In the first, industry *A*, UK workers are twice as productive as Indian workers. In the second, industry *B*, they are 20 times as productive. In industry *A*, UK workers won't be able to compete with Indian workers, even though they are more productive. So UK firms will lose out in this industry.

However, in industry *B* UK firms will drive Indian firms out of business even though they are paid 10 times as much. This is because they are so much more productive that unit costs are lower.

This simplified example illustrates comparative advantage.

DATA QUESTIONS

1 'Dumping' occurs when a good is sold in a foreign market for less than the cost of production.

2 Firms might charge less in foreign markets because they respond to demand and supply factors. Markets abroad may be more competitive than domestic markets, so causing prices to be lower. Also, selling abroad may lead to economics of scale and lower costs.

3 Exporters suffer from anti-dumping duties, but so do consumers who are denied the chance to buy the goods.

Chapter 36

The Balance of Payments, the pound and the Euro

Chapter in Perspective, Text Pages 916–943

The world is becoming increasingly interrelated, through both international trade and international finance. In Chapter 35 we examined international trade. In this chapter we continue to explore the international economy by further exploring international finance and its relation to international trade.

What determines the value of the balance of trade and the balance of payments? What is the relation between the balance of trade and international lending or borrowing? Does a government budget deficit have any effect on the balance of trade? What role does the value of the pound have in determining the balance of trade? Or is the relationship in the opposite direction – does the balance of trade determine the value of the pound? What are the implications of the single currency in the European Union? These are some of the basic questions addressed in this chapter.

Helpful Hints

1 The previous chapter demonstrated the gains from trade between countries. Indeed, as noted in Chapter 3, these are the same gains that result from trade within countries as well. However, there is an important difference between trade within a single country and trade between countries. When individuals in the same country engage in trade, they use the same currency and so trade is straightforward. On the other hand, international trade is complicated by the fact that individuals in different countries use different currencies. The person selling the good from Japan will want payment to be in Japanese yen, but the person buying the good in the United Kingdom will probably be holding only UK pounds. This problem complicates trade between individuals in different countries. This chapter addresses this complication by looking at the balance of payments of a country as well as the relation of the balance of payments to the foreign exchange rate.

2 Note that the balance of payments must balance. Individual accounts in the balance of payments can be in deficit or surplus but this will be offset by a surplus or deficit in another account.

3 It is important to understand foreign exchange rates as prices determined by supply and demand. They are prices of currency determined in markets for currency. The demand for UK pounds in the foreign exchange market, for example, is the demand for pound sterling (denominated) assets, including UK money. That demand will arise from the desire on the part of foreigners to purchase UK goods and services (which requires pounds) and the desire on the part of foreigners to purchase UK financial or real assets. The supply of sterling assets is determined by the government and depends on the exchange rate regime.

4 The law of one price is not relevant only in the context of international trade. Any time there is a discrepancy in the price of the same good in two markets, natural economic forces (unless restricted) will eliminate that discrepancy and thus establish a single price.

5 Purchasing power parity is the manifestation of the law of one price in international trade. Purchasing power parity implies that, as long as exchange rates can adjust, they will adjust so that money (of whatever country) will have the same purchasing power in all countries. This means that if one country experiences inflation while others do not, exchange rates will adjust so that the purchasing power of money will be the same in all countries.

6 Note that it is not the edict of a government which fixes the exchange rate of its currency but rather the willingness of its central bank to supply all of the domestic currency denominated assets that are demanded at the fixed exchange rate.

7 With a fixed exchange rate, a country cannot use monetary policy to control inflation. With a flexible exchange rate a country can insulate itself from external shocks by varying the exchange rate. Within the European Union, the exchange rates of the various countries are largely fixed against each other. One reason is that this gives stability and encourages intra-country trade. The introduction of a single currency will strengthen this process.

SELF-TEST

CONCEPT REVIEW

1 The international trading, borrowing and lending activities of a country are recorded in its _____ of _____. The expenditures on imported goods and services and the receipts from the sale of exported goods and services are recorded in the _____ account. The _____ and financial account records lending to and borrowing from the rest of the world. The change in a country's holdings of foreign currency is shown in the _____ _____ account.

2 A country that is borrowing more from the rest of the world than it is lending is called a(n) _____ _____ . A country that is lending more to the rest of the world than it is borrowing is called a(n) _____ .

3 A country that during its entire history has borrowed more from the rest of the world than it has loaned is called a(n) _____ country.

4 The balance of trade deficit is _____ _____ the sum of the government budget deficit and the private sector deficit.

5 Relative prices are determined by_____ and _____ in the _____ market. Money prices are determined by the value of the _____ _____ given the relative prices.

6 The higher the value of the exchange rate, the _____ is the balance of _____. The equilibrium value of the exchange rate is determined by the demand and supply of _____ _____ .

7 If the private sector surplus is constant, a higher government sector deficit means a higher _____ _____ _____ _____ .

8 The market in which the currencies of different countries are exchanged for each other is called the _____ _____ market. The price at which one currency exchanges for another is called the _____ _____ _____ .

9 There are three foreign exchange systems. In the first of these the value of the exchange rate is pegged by a central bank. This is a(n) _____ exchange rate. A(n) _____ exchange rate is a system in which the exchange rate is determined by market forces without government intervention. A(n) _____ exchange rate is a system in which the government does not peg the exchange rate but does intervene in the foreign exchange market in order to influence the price of its currency.

10 In January 1999, some _____ countries formed the European Monetary Union.

TRUE OR FALSE

__ 1 The sale of Scotch whisky to the United States will be recorded in the current account of the balance of payments accounts.

__ 2 If there is a current account deficit then there must also be a deficit in either the capital account or the official settlements account.

__ 3 The official settlements account balance must always be equal to zero.

__ 4 If a country is a net borrower from the rest of the world, it must be a debtor country.

__ 5 If a country is a net borrower for consumption purposes, this is nothing to worry about.

__ 6 If a country has a large government budget deficit and the private sector deficit is small, the balance of trade deficit will be large.

__ 7 If investment is greater than saving, the private sector has a deficit.

__ 8 Net exports is the same as the current account balance.

__ 9 A larger government sector deficit always leads to a higher current account deficit.

__ 10 Money prices are set by the exchange rate, while relative prices are set on the world market.

__ 11 If the Bank of England wishes to prevent the exchange rate from depreciating in value, the best way is to lower the growth rate of the money supply.

__ 12 If the exchange rate between the UK pound and the Japanese yen changes from 130 yen per pound to 140 yen per pound, the UK pound has appreciated.

__ 13 If the foreign exchange value of the pound is expected to rise, the demand for sterling denominated assets increases.

__ 14 Under a fixed exchange rate system, the supply curve of assets valued in the currency is horizontal at the pegged exchange rate.

MULTIPLE CHOICE

1 Which of the following is one of the balance of payments accounts?
a current account
b non-traded goods account
c official reserves account
d net interest account
e public account

2 Suppose the United Kingdom initially has all balance of payments accounts in balance (no surplus or deficit). Then UK firms increase the amount they import from Japan, financing that increase in imports by borrowing from Japan. There will now be a current account
a surplus and a capital account surplus.
b surplus and a capital account deficit.
c deficit and a capital account surplus.
d deficit and a capital account deficit.
e deficit and a capital account balance.

3 The country Plato came into existence at the beginning of year 1. Given the information in Table 36.1, in year 4 Plato is a
  a net lender and a creditor country.
  b net lender and a debtor country.
  c net borrower and a creditor country.
  d net borrower and a debtor country.
  e net lender and neither a creditor nor a debtor country.

Table 36.1

Year	Borrowed from rest of world (billions of pounds)	Loaned to rest of world (billions of pounds)
1	60	20
2	60	40
3	60	60
4	60	80

4 Assuming that Plato is on a floating exchange rate, in which year or years in Table 36.1 did Plato have a current account surplus?
  a year 1
  b year 2
  c years 1, 2 and 3
  d years 1 and 2
  e year 4 only

5 A country is currently a net lender and a debtor country. Which of the following statements applies to that country?
  a It has loaned more capital than it borrowed from abroad this year, but borrowed more than it loaned during its history.
  b It has borrowed more capital from abroad than it loaned this year and also borrowed more than it loaned during its history.
  c It has loaned more capital than it borrowed from abroad this year and has loaned more than it borrowed during its history.
  d Its accounting system must be in error if it shows this country to be a net lender and a debtor country at the same time.
  e Its debts must be currently growing.

6 The distinction between a debtor or creditor country and a net borrower or net lender country depends on
  a the distinction between the level of saving in the economy and the saving rate.

b the distinction between the level of saving in the economy and the rate of borrowing.
  c the distinction between the stock of investments and the flow of interest payments on those investments.
  d the distinction between exports and imports.
  e really nothing; they are the same.

7 Suppose that in a country, government purchases of goods and services are £400 billion, taxes (net of transfer payments) is £300 billion, saving is £300 billion and investment is £250 billion. Net exports are in a
  a surplus of £150 billion.
  b surplus of £50 billion.
  c deficit of £150 billion.
  d deficit of £50 billion.
  e deficit of £250 billion.

8 The country in **7** has a government budget
  a surplus and a private sector surplus.
  b surplus and a private sector deficit.
  c deficit and a private sector surplus.
  d deficit and a private sector deficit.
  e surplus and a private sector balance.

9 The link between the public sector deficit and the private sector surplus can be weak because
  a the interest rate will tend to do the adjusting to a change in public deficits rather than the private sector.
  b real GDP will tend to do the adjusting to a change in public deficits rather than the private sector.
  c the economy may not be operating at close to capacity, and changes in public deficits will not affect the private sector.
  d international capital mobility may cut any strong link between changes in the public sector deficit and changes in interest rates.
  e the government's deficit is partly caused by borrowing abroad.

10 Under a flexible exchange rate regime, if the foreign exchange value of a country's currency starts to rise, that country's central bank will
  a increase the supply of assets denominated in its own currency.
  b decrease the supply of assets denominated in its own currency.
  c decrease the demand for assets denominated in its own currency.

d do nothing.

e do nothing unless there is a government budget deficit, in which case it will increase the supply of assets denominated in its own currency.

11 Which of the following will shift the supply curve of sterling assets rightward under flexible exchange rates?

a an increase in the demand for foreign goods by UK citizens

b a decrease in the demand for UK goods by foreigners

c the pound is expected to appreciate

d the government has a budget deficit

e none of the above

12 Under a managed exchange rate system, a UK government budget deficit will cause the foreign exchange price of the pound to

a fall and the quantity of sterling assets held to fall.

b fall and the quantity of sterling assets held to rise.

c rise and the quantity of sterling assets held to fall.

d rise and the quantity of sterling assets held to rise.

e stay constant, but the quantity of sterling assets held will rise.

13 Which of the following would cause the pound to depreciate against the yen?

a an increase in UK money supply

b an increase in interest rates in the United Kingdom

c a decrease in interest rates in Japan

d an increase in imports from the United Kingdom purchased by Japan

e a government budget surplus

14 Which of the following is an argument in favour of a single European Currency?

a the removal of foreign exchange costs

b the removal of foreign exchange risk

c no exploitation of comparative advantage by artificially lowering currency values

d all of the above

SHORT ANSWER

1 What is the relationship between a country's trade deficit, its government budget deficit and its private sector deficit?

2 What is purchasing power parity?

3 The *Reading Between the Lines* article discusses a fall in the value of the Euro. Why do currencies fluctuate in price?

PROBLEMS

1 The international transactions of a country for a given year are reported in Table 36.2.

Table 36.2

Transaction	Amount (billions of pounds)
Exports of goods and services	100
Imports of goods and services	130
Transfers to the rest of the world	20
Loans to the rest of the world	60
Loans from the rest of the world	
Increase in official reserves	10

a What is the amount of loans from the rest of the world?

b What is the current account balance?

c What is the capital account balance?

d Does this country have a flexible exchange rate?

2 The information in Table 36.3 is for a country during a given year.

Table 36.3

Variable	Amount (billions of pounds)
GDP	800
Taxes (net of transfer payments)	200
Government budget deficit	50
Consumption	500
Investment	150
Imports	150

a What is the level of government expenditure on goods and services?

b What is the private sector surplus or deficit?

c What is the value of exports?

d What is the balance of trade surplus or deficit?

3 Tables 36.4 and 36.5 give the domestic demand and supply for imaginary products called widgets and toffs.

Table 36.4

Price of toffs (£ each)	Supply of toffs	Demand for toffs
2	1,000	7,000
4	3,000	5,000
6	5,000	3,000
8	7,000	1,000
10	9,000	0

Table 36.5

Price of widgets (£ each)	Supply of widgets	Demand for widgets
6	2,000	64,000
8	4,000	12,000
12	6,000	10,000
16	8,000	8,000
20	10,000	6,000
24	12,000	4,000

a Draw a graph of the two markets, clearly identifying the domestic equilibrium if there is no international trade.

b Suppose that the world price for toffs is £4 each and for widgets is £6 each. Calculate what exchange rate would lead to a balance of trade that is neither a deficit nor a surplus. Show this equilibrium on your graph.

4 Suppose that the exchange rate between the UK pound and the Euro is €2 per pound.

a What is the exchange rate in terms of pounds per Euro?

b What is the price in pounds of a camera selling for €250?

c What is the price in Euros of a computer selling for £1,000?

DISCUSSION QUESTION

1 Why is a deficit on the current account often called 'unfavourable'?

DATA QUESTIONS

Influences on the balance of payments

1 Summarize the trends in the three variables.

2 What relationship would you expect to find between the unemployment rate and the exchange rate on the one hand and the balance of payments on the other? Do these statistics confirm your expectations?

Table 36.6

Year	Unemployment (millions)	Sterling exchange rate (1985 = 100)	Current balance (millions of pounds)
1979	1,312	107	−453
1980	1,611	116	2,843
1981	2,482	123	6,748
1982	2,901	113	4,649
1983	3,127	106	3,787
1984	3,158	102	1,832
1985	3,281	100	2,750
1986	3,312	96	−24
1987	2,993	90	−4,182
1988	2,426	97	−15,151
1989	1,784	93	−22,515
1990	1,664	91	−18,268
1991	2,292	92	−8,533
1992	2,279	88	−9,468
1993	2,919	81	−11,042
1994	2,637	84	−1,684
1995	2,308	79	−3,745
1996	2,104	81	−600
1997	1,545	95	−6,142

Source: Economic Trends, 1999. HMSO.

ANSWERS

CONCEPT REVIEW

1 balance; payments; current; capital; reserve assets

2 net borrower; net lender

3 debtor

4 equal to

5 demand; supply; world; exchange rate

6 higher; trade; sterling assets

7 balance of trade deficit

8 foreign exchange; foreign exchange rate

9 fixed; flexible; managed

10 11

TRUE OR FALSE

1 T Whisky is a visible export.

2 F There must be a surplus to offset the current deficit.

3 F Settlements vary according to what happens elsewhere in the accounts.

4 F May be true or untrue. Net borrower means that current account net borrowing > 0. Debtor country means that sum of all net borrowing > 0.

5 F Borrowing will have to be repaid.

6 T Balance of trade (negative) = Government balance (large negative) + Private balance (small negative).

7 T Definition.

8 F See definition.

9 F Perhaps 'uncertain' – it depends on reaction of private sector surplus/deficit.

10 T Exchange rate affects price of goods in international trade.

11 T Lower rate of money supply will increase interest rate and so persuade people to invest in currency to receive higher interest.

12 T Pound is more valuable, so rise in demand for sterling assets.

13 T Rise in foreign exchange value of pound leads to rise in foreign exchange value of sterling assets and so a rise in demand for sterling assets.

14 T Because Bank of England is willing to buy or sell pounds in order to keep exchange rate fixed.

MULTIPLE CHOICE

1 a Definition.

2 c Imports > exports, therefore current account deficit. Borrowing > lending, so capital account surplus (think about which way money is flowing).

3 b Current lending > borrowing, so net lender. Sum of past borrowing > sum of lending, so debtor country.

4 e Flexible exchange rate leads to official settlements balance = 0; hence current account surplus = capital account deficit – occurs only when lending > borrowing.

5 a Definitions of net lender and debtor country. Debts are shrinking.

6 c Net lender – stock of investments rising. Debtor country – negative flow of interest payments on investments.

7 d Net exports = $(T - G) + (S - I) = 300 - 400 + 300 - 250 = -50$.

8 c Government sector deficit = $G - T = 400 - 300 = 100$. Private sector surplus = $S - I = 300 - 250 = +50$.

9 d Link between government sector deficit and private sector surplus is via higher interest rates – international capital mobility restricts changes in interest rates.

10 d Definition of flexible exchange rate regime.

11 d Others all affect demand for pounds.

12 b Rightward shift positively sloped supply curve. Draw a graph to check.

13 a This increases the supply of pounds. **b**, **c** and **d** increase demand, **e** leads to fall in supply.

14 d They are all arguments used to support a single currency.

SHORT ANSWER

1 The national income accounting identities allow us to show that a country's balance of trade deficit is equal to the sum of its government budget deficit and its private sector deficit.

2 Purchasing power parity follows from arbitrage and the law of one price. It means that the value of money is the same in all countries once the differences in risk are taken into account. For example, if the exchange rate between the pound and the yen is 120 yen per pound, purchasing power parity says that a good that sells for 120 yen in Japan will sell for £1 in the United Kingdom. Thus the exchange rate is such that money (pounds or yen) has the same purchasing power in both countries.

3 In a market economy, currencies fluctuate in value for similar reasons as the prices of other goods fluctuate; in other words, because of fluctuations in demand and supply. But there are differences. For most currencies, demand fluctuations can be quite large as speculators buy and sell particular currencies. In these decisions, expectations about the future play a large part.

PROBLEMS

1 a The amount of loans from the rest of the world is £100 billion. This is obtained by recognizing that the overall balance of payments must balance; the sum of the positive entries (exports, loans from the rest of the world and increase in official reserves) must equal the sum of the negative entries (imports, transfers to the rest of the world and loans to the rest of the world).

b The current account balance is a £50 billion deficit: exports minus imports minus transfers to the rest of the world.

c The capital account balance is a surplus of £40 billion: loans from the rest of the world minus loans to the rest of the world.

d This country does not have a flexible exchange rate because official reserves increased. Official reserves would have remained unchanged under flexible exchange rates.

2 a Since we know that the government budget deficit is £50 billion and the taxes (net of transfer payments) are £200 billion, we can infer that government expenditure on goods and services is £250 billion.

b The private sector surplus or deficit is given by saving minus investment. Investment is given as £150 billion but we must compute saving. Saving is equal to GDP minus taxes minus consumption: £100 billion. Thus there is a private sector deficit of £50 billion.

c We know that GDP is consumption plus investment plus government expenditure on goods and services plus net exports (exports minus imports). Since we know all these values except exports, we can obtain that value by solving for exports. The value of exports equals GDP plus imports minus consumption minus investment minus government expenditure on goods and services; the value of exports equals £50 billion.

d There is a balance of trade deficit of £100 billion. This can be obtained in two ways. First, we can recognize that the balance of trade surplus or deficit is given by the value of exports (£50 billion) minus the value of imports (£150 billion). The other method is to recognize that the balance of trade deficit is equal to the sum of the government budget deficit (£50 billion) and the private sector deficit (£50 billion).

3 a Equilibrium in the market for toffs occurs at a price of £5 each, shown in Fig. 36.1(a), with 4,000 units traded (point *a*), while equilibrium in the market for widgets occurs at a price of £16 each, with 8,000 units traded (point *a'*), shown in Fig. 36.1(b).

b A balance of trade will have the amount earned by exports equal to the amount paid out for imports. To start, pick an exchange rate and see what happens to exports and imports. For example, pick £1 equals $1.

Figure 36.1

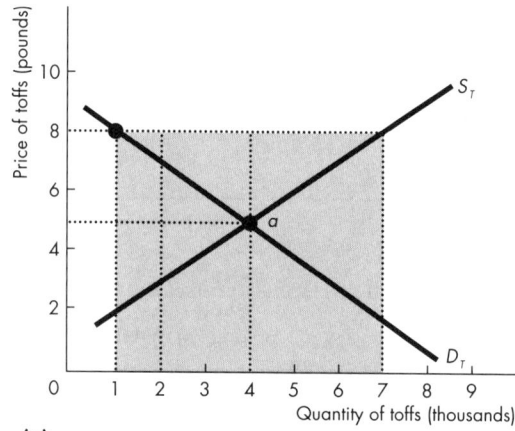

(a)

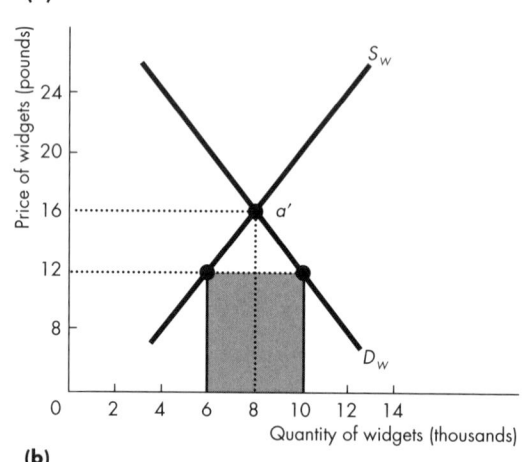

(b)

In this case, the world price of a toff is equivalent to £4, so UK demand is 5,000 units and UK supply is only 3,000 units, leading to imports of 2,000 units at £4 per unit, for a net payment of £8,000. The world price of a widget is £6, so demand is 14,000 units and supply is only 2,000 units, leading to imports of 10,000 units at £6 per unit, for a total payment of £60,000.

Clearly, at this exchange rate we do not have a balance of trade, since the United Kingdom is trying to import both goods. To get rid of a deficit, recall that the exchange rate must fall in value. We would therefore try lower and lower values (for example, £1.50 per $1), until by trial and error we arrive at the correct value of £2 per $1. In this case, the price of a toff is £8, so that demand is 1,000 units and supply is 7,000 units, leading to exports of 6,000 units, earning £48,000. The price of a widget is £12, leading to a demand of 10,000 units and a supply of 6,000 units, and we import 4,000 units, at a total payment of £48,000, for a balance of trade.

We can see this balance demonstrated on the graphs, with the shaded areas showing the export earnings equal to the import payments.

4 a If £1 can be purchased for €2, then the price of a Deutschmark is £½ per Deutschmark.
  b At an exchange rate of DM2 per pound, it takes £125 to obtain the €250 needed to buy the camera.
  c At an exchange rate of €2 per pound, it takes €2000 to obtain the £1,000 needed to buy the computer.

DISCUSSION QUESTION

1 A deficit on the current account is called unfavourable because it almost always means that the value of imports exceeds the value of exports and this can create the impression that a country is living beyond its means. However, note that a deficit on the current account must be balanced by a surplus on the capital account. In turn, this is seen as unfavourable by some people since it means that foreigners are buying UK assets.

DATA QUESTIONS

1 Unemployment rose until 1986, then declined, subsequently rose and fell again after 1993. The exchange rate rose rapidly in the first part of the period, then declined substantially, with a small rise in 1988. It fell rapidly in 1993 then rose again. The balance of payments on current account improved until the mid-1980s, then moved into a substantial deficit until 1997.

2 As unemployment rises consumer spending falls. We should therefore expect to find that as unemployment rises, imports will fall and the balance of payments moves towards a surplus. Figure 36.2(a) shows a clear relationship between unemployment and the balance of payments. In the period 1979–81 unemployment rose sharply and this was reflected in a rise in the current balance. In the middle part of the graph the relationship is less clear. After 1986, unemployment fell and the current deficit rose as we would expect. However, this pattern seems to have changed in the last few years.

As the exchange rate of the pound rises, each pound can buy more foreign goods while UK goods rise in price in foreign markets. We would therefore expect to find that a rise in the exchange rate leads to an increase in imports and a fall in exports, that is, the current account moves towards a deficit. However, there may be time lags while consumers adjust to new prices and producers develop new markets. Thus we can argue that the sharp rise in the exchange rate after 1979 was one reason why the balance of payments moved towards a deficit after 1981. The subsequent fall in the value of the pound could be expected to lead to an improvement in the balance of payments. This does not seem to have happened (unless the effect was delayed until 1997); the exchange rate effect may have been outweighed by the fall in unemployment.

ure 36.2

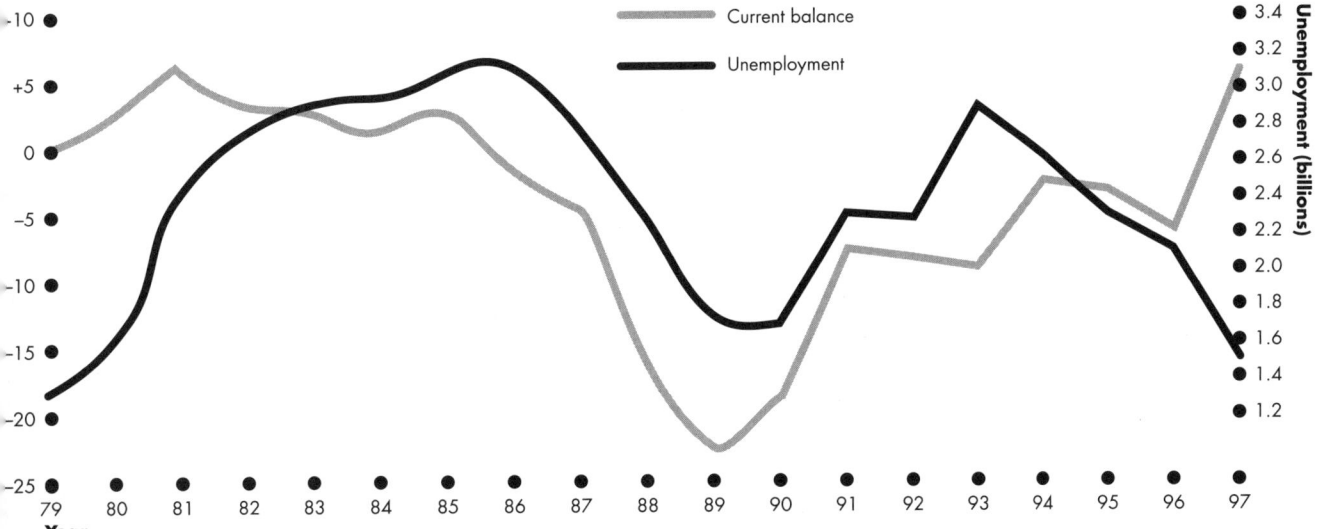

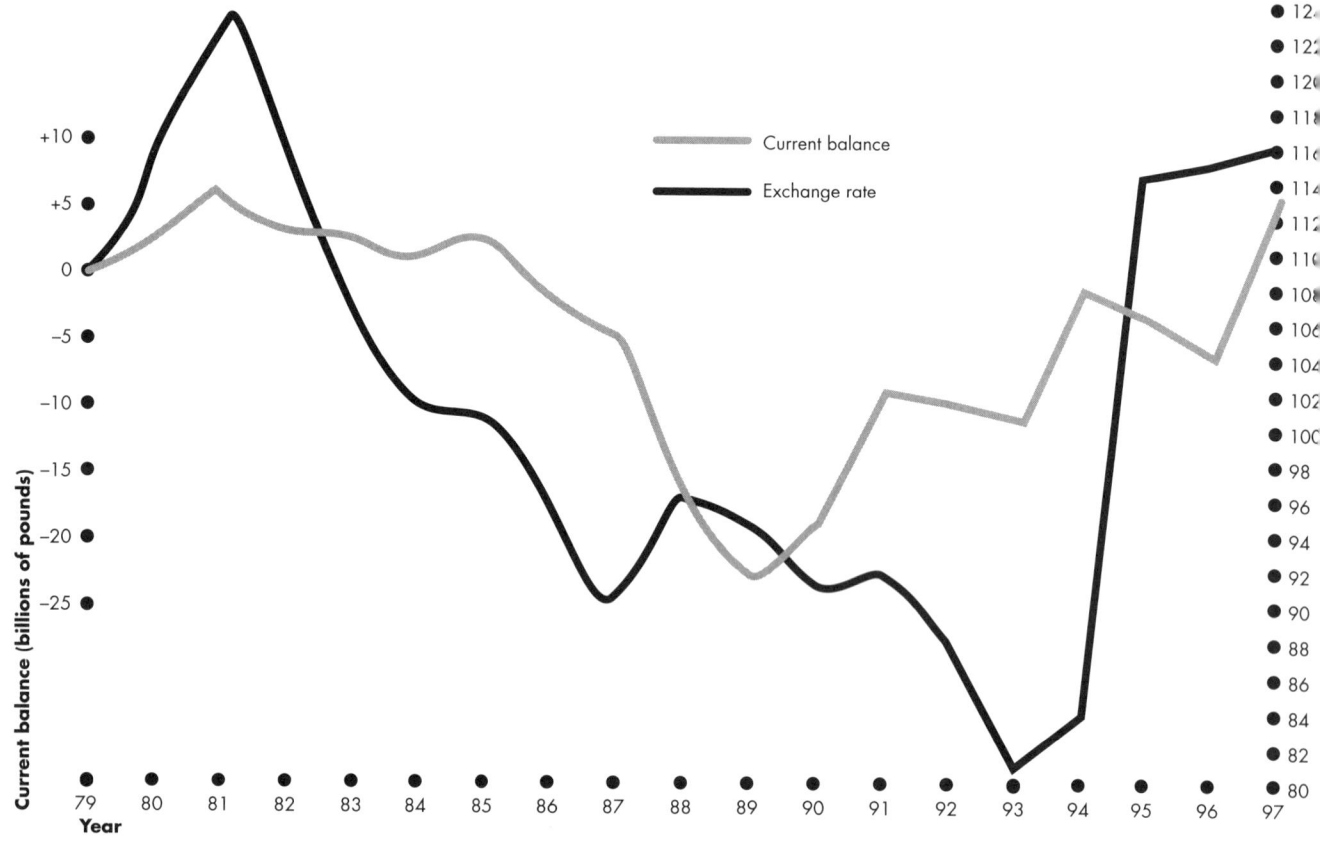

Looking back at Part 9 (Chapters 35 and 36)

These two chapters should have given you a clear view of the international economy. There was relatively little theory in Chapter 35, but you should now be able to explain how the value of the pound is determined. Similarly, after reading Chapter 36 you should be able to articulate the very strong arguments in favour of international trade and also the reason why protectionism persists.

There are no questions here on this part of course, however, if you want web material, look at sites such as the IMF World Financial Outlook database (www.imf.org/external/pubs/ft/weo/2000/01/data/index.htm), the World Bank (www.worldbank.org) and The World Trade Organisation (www.wto.org) sites.

Looking forward

If yours is a typical course, then you must be getting concerned about the end of course exams. One way to revise is to do what we have frequently suggested. That is to use the *After studying this Chapter you will be able to...* introductions to each chapter. If you can describe and explain the points listed in each chapter, you will have a very good knowledge of introductory economics. You can reinforce this by revising the Key Terms at the end of each chapter.